Für Gretta

Vielen Dank
für den ersten
gemeinsamen
tollen Workshop.

Herzliche Grüße
Sabrina

Berlin Mai 2021

Reihe: Controlling · Band 19

Herausgegeben von Prof. Dr. Volker Lingnau, Kaiserslautern, Prof. Dr. Albrecht Becker, Innsbruck, und Prof. Dr. Rolf Brühl, Berlin

Dr. Sabrina Buch

Shared Knowledge

The Comparability of Idiosyncratic Mental Models

With a Foreword by Prof. Dr. Rolf Brühl, ESCP Europe Wirtschaftshochschule Berlin

Bibliografische Information der Deutschen Nationalbibliothek

Die Deutsche Nationalbibliothek verzeichnet diese Publikation in der Deutschen Nationalbibliografie; detaillierte bibliografische Daten sind im Internet über <http://dnb.d-nb.de> abrufbar.

Dissertation, ESCP Europe Wirtschaftshochschule Berlin, 2012, unter dem vollständigen Titel: Shared Knowledge – The Comparability of Idiosyncratic Mental Models. Approaching an Aggregation Method

ISBN 978-3-8441-0186-7
1. Auflage September 2012

© JOSEF EUL VERLAG GmbH, Lohmar – Köln, 2012
Alle Rechte vorbehalten

JOSEF EUL VERLAG GmbH
Brandsberg 6
53797 Lohmar
Tel.: 0 22 05 / 90 10 6-6
Fax: 0 22 05 / 90 10 6-88
E-Mail: info@eul-verlag.de
http://www.eul-verlag.de

Bei der Herstellung unserer Bücher möchten wir die Umwelt schonen. Dieses Buch ist daher auf säurefreiem, 100% chlorfrei gebleichtem, alterungsbeständigem Papier nach DIN 6738 gedruckt.

Foreword

Most management scholars have given up the model of unbounded rationality of social actors. Therefore, managers are modelled as humans with cognitive capacities which are restricted in several ways. At first sight this could lead to the impression of a human being prone to err and somehow defected. On the contrary, a more realistic look on cognitive abilities of managers opens avenues for fruitful research and theories on managerial behavior in organizations. One of these research streams theorizes on cognitive representations of managers and unfolds a variety of concepts in managerial and organizational cognition. This dissertation picks up individual and collective cognitive structures and analyses different approaches to measure them. Sabrina Buch links here research to the knowledge-based approach of mental models which is concerned with domain-specific and knowledge-rich domains.

Research on mental models has been done in the area of managerial and organizational cognition, especially in strategic management but also in other management domains. In the dissertation mental model is defined as a cognitive representation, which is used by humans to describe a system, to explain its function and to predict its future states. Because social actors work in groups/organizations it is important to know how these cognitive representations are shared between them. The so-called team mental models try to capture the notion of sharing knowledge. This research is motivated by the expectation that team mental models are critical to team performance. However, in spite of a long period of research, there is no consensus on the methods to elicit knowledge structures from managers.

Buch investigates those methods to elicit knowledge structures which lend high degrees of freedom to social actors. Therefore, she aims at idiosyncratic mental models which may be of high accuracy but low similarity. Similarity and accuracy are used to compare knowledge structures between mental models and it is posited that similar mental models enhance implicit coordination between team members. It is one of the main objectives of this dissertation to show methods which – despite giving high degrees of freedom to participants – yield similar mental models. Buch restricts her research to the concepts of mental models and omits their structure.

In a series of five studies with a mixed-method-approach Buch explores a card sorting technique in different domains of management (management accounting, strategy and marketing). What do we learn from these studies? Let me sketch two important findings. First and in a nutshell, we know now that we need a tool to compare the meaning of concepts. Based on the theory of prototypes, participants in study IV and V compare meanings of their concepts and, hence, they are able to compare their mental models. As a consequence they decide on the degree of similarity by themselves. Another important finding is a new indicator for team performance. Buch establishes an innovative measure of team performance based on the amount of concepts created on different stages of the studies. With the help of this indicator, she is able to show that teams differ in their performance and in which respect they do. Of course, there are many more results of these studies and readers are encouraged to closely scrutinize the five studies.

Empirical research supports the view that information exchange in a team is enhanced if team work and team discussions are structured. Buch's card sort technique combined with her meaning relation tool seems to fulfil these criteria and thus shows the theoretical as well as the practical relevance of her research. Summing up, Sabrina Buch's innovative and thought-provoking dissertation delivers new insights to the field of managerial and organizational cognition. Her presentation of the state-of-the-art of methods to elicit cognitive structures will be of great help to scholars in this research field.

Prof. Dr. Rolf Brühl

Chair of Management Control

ESCP Europe Business School Berlin

Preface

This thesis was mainly written during my time as a research assistant at the chair of management control at ESCP Europe in Berlin. I would like to thank all persons who accompanied me during that time and who contributed to its development.

Firstly, I would like to thank my supervisor Prof. Dr. Rolf Brühl. He gave me the impetus for this topic. Through critical questions, he inspired many new ideas that influenced this work, and he was open for less conventional directions. My thanks also go to Prof. Dr. Thomas Wrona for his time and efforts in providing the second review of my work. He provided critical, insightful comments. I would also thank Prof. Dr. Markus Bick as the chair of the review commission at ESCP Europe. Thank you all very much!

The empirical studies, the central part of this work, would not have been possible without the generous support of many students from the ESCP Europe in Berlin and the University of Lancaster, UK. A special thanks goes to Dr. Linden J. Ball. He enabled the implementation of the last study at Lancaster University in the first place. I also received input for my work at conferences and seminars, where I presented my results. Special thanks go to the participants of the Colloquium of the ESCP Europe.

Friendly and collegial support was provided by many others, but especially from Anja and Anika Götze, Celina Roeckner, Sophia Oberhuber and Andrea Nägel. Richard Hart-Jones, I would like to thank you for proofreading the work.

Above all, I dedicate this work to my family, especially to my beloved parents, Heinz and Gisela Kunde, and to my husband Robert. In particular, Robert has stood by throughout this time, given me support and encouraged me. This was both the genesis of the work, and of inestimable value. Thank you so much.

Sabrina Buch

Berlin July 2012

Content

FOREWORD VII
PREFACE IX
LIST OF TABLES XVII
LIST OF FIGURES XIX
LIST OF CASES XXI
LIST OF FORMULAS XXI
1.   INTRODUCTION 1

1.1.   RESEARCH SUBJECT 1

1.2.   RESEARCH OBJECTIVE AND THESIS STRUCTURE 7

2.   THEORETICAL UNDERPINNING 13

2.1.   INTRODUCTION 13

2.2.   CONCEPTUAL FRAMEWORK 15
2.2.1.   Fundamentals of the Structure Genesis Approach 16
2.2.2.   Knowledge and Shared Knowledge Based on the Structure Genesis Approach 17
2.2.2.1. Knowledge as Intra-Personal Disposition 17
2.2.2.2. Shared Knowledge as an Inter-Personal Dimension 21
2.2.3.   Mediator Constructs: Mental Models and Team Mental Models 23
2.2.3.1. The Individual Perspective: Mental Models as Internal Representation 23
2.2.3.2. The Team Perspective: Team and Group, Team Mental Model, and Shared Mental Models 26
2.2.3.3. Purpose of Mental Models and Team Mental Models 28

3.   RESEARCH METHODOLOGY 33

3.1.   RESEARCH PARADIGM 33

3.2.   RESEARCH DESIGN STRATEGIES 36

3.3.   STRATEGY OF REASONING 41

3.4.   QUALITY INDICES 43

3.5.   RESEARCH TECHNIQUES IN (SHARED)-KNOWLEDGE RESEARCH 45
3.5.1.   Object of Investigation and its Implications in this Thesis 45
3.5.2.   Nomothetic and Idiographic Mapping Methods 47
3.5.3.   Advantages and Disadvantages of Mapping Methods 51

3.6.   RESEARCH APPROACH FOR ELICITING SHARED KNOWLEDGE 52

3.7.	Research Approach for Aggregating Mental Models	55
3.7.1.	Similarity and Accuracy	55
3.7.2.	Similarity Approaches	56
3.7.2.1.	Consensus and Consistency as Nomothetic-Quantitative Perspectives on Similarity	56
3.7.2.2.	Correspondence Analysis as Nomothetic-Qualitative Approach in Analysing Similarity	58
3.7.2.3.	Complexity and Centrality as a Basis for an Idiographic-Qualitative Approach in Analysing Similarity	62
3.7.3.	Problems of Judging Similarity in Idiosyncratic Mental Models	63
3.8.	Shared Construct from a Methodological Perspective	64
3.9.	Team Performance from a Methodological Perspective	69
4.	**RESEARCH PROJECT 'THE COMPARABILITY OF IDIOSYNCRATIC MENTAL MODELS'**	**75**
4.1.	Empirical Study I: Eliciting Idiosyncratic Knowledge Structures (Approach A)	75
4.1.1.	Outline of the Research Topic of Approach A	75
4.1.2.	Outline of the Research Setting of Approach A	78
4.1.3.	Method	79
4.1.3.1.	Participants	79
4.1.3.2.	Research Design	79
4.1.3.3.	Data Collecting Approach: Structure-Formation-Technique and its Application in this Thesis	79
4.1.3.4.	Stimulus Material for Collecting Data including the Rule System	81
4.1.3.5.	Screening of Data During the Research Process	82
4.1.3.6.	Data Analysis Approaches	83
4.1.3.7.	Equipment	83
4.1.3.8.	Research Process	83
4.1.4.	Results	85
4.1.4.1.	Method Objective 1: Idiosyncratic Mental Models	85
4.1.4.2.	Method Objective 2: Results to the Cause-and-Effect Rule System	86
4.1.4.3.	Content Specific Questions: Description of the Results of the Elicitation of Knowledge	88
4.1.4.3.1.	Central Cause-Concepts and Central Effect-Concepts	88
4.1.4.3.2.	Example of Linked Concepts Using Cause-and-Effect Rules	90
4.1.5.	Interpretation and Discussion	91
4.2.	Empirical Study II: The Delphi-Method for Analysing Idiosyncratic Mental Models in Terms of Similarity (Approach A)	95
4.2.1.	Introduction	95
4.2.2.	Method	98

4.2.2.1.	Adapting the Delphi-Method for Qualitative Expert Aggregation	98
4.2.2.2.	Research Process	101
4.2.2.2.1.	Stage 1 – Process of Free Generation	101
4.2.2.2.2.	Stage 2 – Initial Feedback about the Mental Model of Participant 4	101
4.2.2.2.3.	Stage 3 – Further Feedback about the Mental Model of Participant 4	104
4.2.2.2.4.	Stages 4 and 5 – Feedback about the Mental Model of Participant 3	104
4.2.2.2.5.	Stage 6 – Evaluation of the Experts' Categories by Participant 3	105
4.2.2.2.6.	Summary of the Research Process	105
4.2.3.	Results	106
4.2.3.1.	Results 1: Free Generation Process	108
4.2.3.2.	Results 2: Expert Evaluation for Participant 4	110
4.2.3.3.	Results 3: Expert Evaluation for Participant 3	110
4.2.3.4.	Results 4: Comparison of the Mental Models of Participants 3 and 4 Based on the Experts' Categories (Content Question 1)	112
4.2.3.4.1.	Type and Number of Categories	112
4.2.3.4.2.	Commonalities in Mental Models Considering Relations	113
4.2.3.5.	Results 5: Evaluation of the Experts' Categories by Participant 3	114
4.2.3.6.	Results 6: Comparison between Experts' Results for the Mental Model of Participant 3, and the Evaluation of the Experts' Categories by Participant 3	116
4.2.4.	Discussion	118
4.3.	CONCLUSION OF APPROACH A AND CONSEQUENCES FOR APPROACH B	122
4.4.	EMPIRICAL STUDY III – DEVELOPING A METHOD TO AGGREGATE IDIOSYNCRATIC MENTAL MODELS IN TERMS OF SIMILARITY (APPROACH B)	123
4.4.1.	Introduction to Study III: Preliminary Thoughts	123
4.4.2.	Method	125
4.4.2.1.	Participants	125
4.4.2.2.	Design	126
4.4.2.3.	Procedure	126
4.4.2.3.1.	Collecting Idiosyncratic Mental Models and Team Mental Models: Stimulus Material, Tasks and Data Collection (Stages 1, 2 and 3)	127
4.4.2.3.2.	Aggregation Process: Stimulus Material, Task and the Process of Discovering Similarity in Stage 3	128
4.4.2.3.3.	Data Analysis	129
4.4.3.	Results, Discussion and Conclusion	130
4.4.3.1.	To the Perceived Teamwork	130
4.4.3.2.	To Method Objective 4 and Study Objective: The Similarity Allocation of the Idiosyncratic Concepts to Team Concepts	131
4.5.	EMPIRICAL STUDY IV – IDIOSYNCRATIC MENTAL MODELS AND SEMANTIC RELATIONS	140
4.5.1.	Theoretical Assumptions	140

4.5.1.1.	Introduction	140
4.5.1.2.	Categorization	141
4.5.1.2.1.	Vertical Dimension of Categories: Semantic Constitution	142
4.5.1.2.2.	Horizontal Dimension: Family Resemblances	144
4.5.1.2.3.	Conclusion of Categorization, and Further Consequences for the Thesis Research Process	144
4.5.1.3.	Categorization and Lexical Semantics	148
4.5.1.4.	Meaning Relation Tool based on Semantics	149
4.5.1.5.	Semantic and Propositional Categorization in Mental Models	150
4.5.1.6.	Mental Models and Semantic Constitution	151
4.5.2.	Summary about the Objectives	151
4.5.3.	Method	152
4.5.3.1.	Participants	152
4.5.3.2.	Design	154
4.5.3.3.	Equipment	154
4.5.3.4.	Procedure	155
4.5.3.4.1.	Collection Stage: Stimulus Material, Task and Data Collection of the Elicitation Process in Stage 1 and Stage 2	155
4.5.3.4.2.	Aggregation Stage: Stimulus Material, Task and Conducting of the Similarity Evaluation in Stage 2	156
4.5.3.4.3.	Analysis Process	157
4.5.3.5.	Presumptions about Homogeneous and Heterogeneous Teams and Team Performance	162
4.5.4.	Results	164
4.5.4.1.	Sample	164
4.5.4.2.	Method Objective 6 and Study Objective 2: Meaning Relation Tool	164
4.5.4.3.	Evaluation of the Presumptions: Intra-Individual View – Between-Stage Results	165
4.5.4.4.	Evaluation of the Presumptions: Inter-Individual View – Within-Stage Results	168
4.5.5.	Discussion and Limitations	174
4.6.	EMPIRICAL STUDY V – EVALUATION OF THE MEANING RELATION TOOL	178
4.6.1.	Introduction	178
4.6.2.	Hypotheses	182
4.6.2.1.	Method Objective 7 & Study Objective 1: Group Differences Referring to Concept Numbers	182
4.6.2.2.	Method Objective 8 & Study Objective 2: Group Differences in Performance, Using the 'Meaning Relation Tool' to Adjust Interrelations between Stages	184
4.6.3.	Method	185
4.6.3.1.	Participants	185
4.6.3.2.	Design and Dependent Variables	185

4.6.3.3.	Stimulus Material	186
4.6.3.4.	Procedure	188
4.6.3.4.1.	Pilot Study: Equipment and Task Testing	188
4.6.3.4.2.	Elicitation Process	189
4.6.3.4.3.	Aggregating Process	190
4.6.3.4.4.	Analysis Process	192
4.6.4.	Results	193
4.6.4.1.	Results of the Follow up Questionnaire	193
4.6.4.2.	Main Results	195
4.6.4.2.1.	Method Objective 7 & Study Objective 1: Group Differences Referring to Concept Numbers	195
4.6.4.2.2.	Method Objective 8 & Study Objective 2: Group Differences in Performance based on the Meaning Relation Tool to adjust Interrelations between Stages	200
4.6.5.	Interpretation, Discussion and Conclusion	201
5.	**DISCUSSION AND CONCLUSION**	**213**
5.1.	DISCUSSION OF THE RESEARCH METHODS, INCLUDING THEIR LIMITATIONS	213
5.1.1.	What is the Research Contribution?	213
5.1.2.	Why two Methodological Approaches?	214
5.1.3.	How to Classify the Developed Approach within the Existing Research and How Effective is the Approach?	217
5.1.4.	What Can be Said about the Shared Knowledge Construct, Using the Meaning Relation Tool?	222
5.1.5.	Further Limitations Concerning the Interpretation of the Results	224
5.2.	CONCLUSIONS DRAWN AND POSSIBLE FURTHER RESEARCH	226
6.	**APPENDIX**	**231**
7.	**REFERENCES**	**275**

List of Tables

Table 1:	Outline of Idiographic Mapping Methods, Mixed Form of Mapping Methods, and Nomothetic Mapping Methods	49
Table 2:	Correspondent and Not-Correspondent Concept Pairs in two Mental Models (following A. A. Eckert, 2000, p. 144, table 1)	60
Table 3:	Example Correspondence analysis	61
Table 4:	Outline of Research Question, Method Objectives and Content Specific Questions of Study I	78
Table 5:	Study I – Design	79
Table 6:	Study I – Used Rules a Participant (in Absolute Quantities)	86
Table 7:	Study I – Quantities of Clusters and Concept in a Cluster	87
Table 8:	Study I – Concepts, Which often Influenced by other Concepts and Causes other Concepts	89
Table 9:	Study I – Examples for Human Resources and its Capability Concepts, Named by Participants	90
Table 10:	Study II – Overview about the Relationship between Study I and Study II	96
Table 11:	Study II – Excerpt from the List for Assigning Concepts by Participant 4 to Free Generated Categories by Experts	102
Table 12:	Study II – Summary of the Research Process	106
Table 13:	Study II – Most Frequent Categories per Expert	108
Table 14:	Study II – Common Categories and their Frequency of Nomination	108
Table 15:	Study II – Section about Similar Categories and their Frequency of Nomination between and within the Experts	109
Table 16:	Study II – Overview Expert Categories for Participants 3 and 4	112
Table 17:	Study II – Overview of Connected Categories, Same Direction of the Connections and the Same Value of the Connections	113
Table 18:	Study II – Allocation of the Participant 3's Concepts to the Experts Categories by Participant 3	115
Table 19:	Study II – Identical Assignments of Concepts of Participant 3 to Expert Categories by Participant 3 and Experts	117
Table 20:	Study II – Comparison of Statements by Participant 3 and Participant 4 and Their Fit in Different Meanings	118
Table 21:	Study III – Design	126
Table 22:	Study III – Plan	126
Table 23:	Study III – Results of the Questionnaire about Perceived Teamwork	130
Table 24:	Study III – Number of Concepts Generated in Individual Sessions	131
Table 25:	Study III – Outline of Similarity Allocation Rules	132
Table 26:	Study III – Number of Concepts Generated and Assigned	134
Table 27:	Example 'Motivation' and 'Personal Training'	136
Table 28:	Results for the Process Perspective of the Team (Stage 2)	138
Table 29:	Study IV – Outline of the Sample Size	153
Table 30:	Study IV – Research Design	154
Table 31:	Study IV – Example for the Analysis of the Allocation of the Idiosyncratic Concepts to the Team Concepts	157
Table 32:	Study IV – Analysis of Shared and Distributed Concepts	160

Table 33:	Study IV – Results – Analysis of the Allocation of the Idiosyncratic Concepts to the Team Concepts over All Teams	166
Table 34:	Study IV – Analysis of the Allocation of the Idiosyncratic Concepts to the Team Concepts Related to Group Compositions	167
Table 35:	Study IV – Results – Analysis of Shared and Distributed Concepts over All Teams	171
Table 36:	Study IV – Analysis of Shared and Distributed Concepts Related to Group Composition	172
Table 37:	Study IV – Data Base for Mann-Whitney Test for Distributed Used Concepts in % (see Table 36)	176
Table 38:	Study V – Outline of the Within-Group-Between-Stage Hypotheses	183
Table 39:	Study V – Experimental Design	185
Table 40:	Study V – Outline of the Kind of Measures	186
Table 41:	Study V – Outline of the Dependent Variables	186
Table 42:	Study V – Outline of the Procedure	189
Table 43:	Study V – Overview of the Effects	201
Table 44:	Study V – Range of Concept Numbers and their Difference in Range	203
Table 45:	Study V – Concept Numbers of Team Group	204
Table 46:	Study V – Concept Numbers of Mixed Group	205

List of Figures

Figure 1:	Relation between Theoretical Basis and Methodical Basis	8
Figure 2:	Outline of Approach A	10
Figure 3:	Outline of Approach B	12
Figure 4:	Personal Knowledge	18
Figure 5:	Relationship between Idiosyncratic and Objectified Knowledge	20
Figure 6:	Shared Knowledge	22
Figure 7:	Example of a Hierarchical-Structured Mental Model	30
Figure 8:	Research Design Strategy	40
Figure 9:	Elicitation Methods	47
Figure 10:	Holistic and Collective Approach	53
Figure 11:	Hypothetical Example for Consistency	57
Figure 12:	Hypothetical Example for Consensus	58
Figure 13:	Example for One Type of Model (about Team Work) by two Different Team Types	65
Figure 14:	Example for Four Types of Dependent Models by two Different Team Types	66
Figure 15:	Meanings of Sharedness based on Cannon-Bowers & E. Salas (2001)	68
Figure 16:	Study I – Mental Model by Participant 4	85
Figure 17:	Study II – Example 'Animal' (Example following J. R. Anderson, 2001)	97
Figure 18:	Study II – Example for the Mental Model with the Experts' Categories of Participant 4	103
Figure 19:	Study II – Overview of the Results	107
Figure 20:	Study II – Mental Model of Participant 4 with Replaced Categories (Experts View)	110
Figure 21:	Study II – Mental Model of Participant 3 with Replaced Categories (Experts View)	111
Figure 22:	Study II – Mental Model of Participant 3 with Replaced Categories (Participant View)	115
Figure 23:	Study II – Common Categories Replaced by Experts and Participant 3	117
Figure 24:	Study III – Combination of Collective and Holistic Approach	124
Figure 25:	Study IV – Inner Structure of Taxonomies	143
Figure 26:	Study IV – Example for Inclusiveness of Categories	143
Figure 27:	Study IV – Fictional Example for Horizontal Dimension (Categories are taken from E. Rosch, 1973, p. 133, Table 1)	145
Figure 28:	Study IV – Combination of Vertical and Horizontal Structure based on Fruit Example	148
Figure 29:	Study IV – Schematic Representation of the Projection of idiosyncratic Concepts to Team Concepts	158
Figure 30:	Study IV – Team Concepts used by Both Participants (Shared Concepts)	159
Figure 31:	Study IV – Distributed used Team Concepts	160
Figure 32:	Study IV – Schematic Representation of Shared used and Distributed used Team Concepts	161
Figure 33:	Study IV – Presumption about Similarity, Distribution, and Team Performance	163

Figure 34: Study IV – Relation between Shared and Distributed Concepts along with Team Performance 174
Figure 35: Study V – Within-Group-Between-Stages-View 180
Figure 36: Study V – Between-Group-Within-Stages-View 181
Figure 37: Study V – Aggregation of the Results of Stage 1 and Stage 2 for Participant JE11 191
Figure 38: Study V – Aggregation of the Results of Stage 1 and Stage 2 for Team of Participants ND10 and DN04 193
Figure 39: Study V – Concept Numbers of Control Group 2 (Team Group) 198
Figure 40: Study V – Mean Total Concept Numbers of Different Groups in Stage 1 199
Figure 41: Study V – Mean Total Concept Numbers of Different Groups in Stage 3 200
Figure 42: Study V – Section of the Aggregated Mental Models and the Team Mental Model of Team 3 207
Figure 43: Study V – Section of Team Mental Models of Stages 1, 2 and 3 by Team 3 209
Figure 44: Study V – Original Database of the Similarity Allocation Task by Participant ND10 (Stage 1-2) 210
Figure 45: Study V – Result of the Similarity Allocation Task of Stage 1 Concepts to Stage 2 Concepts by Participant WG22 (Individual group) 212

List of Cases

Case 1: Correspondent and Not-Correspondent Concept Pairs (Hypothetical).....................59
Case 2: Direction of the Connection (Hypothetical) 61
Case 3: Value of the Connections (Hypothetical)...62

List of Formulas

Formula 1: Correspondence Coefficient...60
Formula 2: Formula for Calculation Team Performance in Percentage based on Team
Mental Models using Meaning Relation Tool 162

1. Introduction[1]

1.1. Research Subject

There are many studies of mental models in strategic management, but only a few in management accounting (see for instance studies by B. Vandenbosch & C. A. Higgins, 1995, 1996; B. Vandenbosch & S. L. Huff, 1997; M. A. Abernethy, M. Horne, A. M. Lillis, M. A. Malina, & F. H. Selto, 2005; A. K. Choy & R. R. King, 2005). Strategic management researchers focus on the individual cognitive representation of managers, especially on managers' knowledge about the competitive situation of their companies (C. I. Stubbart, 1989, p. 330). Various researchers found, that managers' mental models are the basis for forming strategy (G. P. Hodgkinson, 1997, p. 626; see J. F. Porac & H. Thomas, 1990). Therefore, the insight into managers' knowledge structures will lead to a better understanding of strategic decision-making (J. P. Walsh, 1995, p. 280 f.; R. P. Wright, 2006, p. 291; see also B. B. Tyler & D. R. Gnyawali, 2009, p. 101).

The main purpose for studying cognitive processes of competition at different levels, such as on an individual, group, or functional level, relates to the notion that differences in environmental contingencies in companies, such as organizational context, function, and responsibility, could have an impact upon the knowledge structures of managers (G. P. Hodgkinson & P. R. Sparrow, 2002, p. 150; G. P. Hodgkinson & G. Johnson, 1994, p. 530; see also B. B. Tyler & D. R. Gnyawali, 2009, pp. 115-117). Such impacts are found in various studies. R. K. Reger (1990, p. 78 f.) shows that strategists of different bank holding companies make different assumptions about the importance of key strategic dimensions. R. Calori, G. Johnson, and P. Sarnin (1992, p. 76) illustrate that managers in various industries and countries have different views about the structure and dynamics of their industry. G. P. Hodgkinson and G. Johnson (1994, pp. 534-541) have observed dissimilarities between the structure and depth of managers' mental models, depending on managers' roles within their organization. R. Calori, G. Johnson, and P. Sarnin (1994, p. 452) found that cognitive maps of managers of companies with an international scope are more complex with regard to the structure of their environment, compared to cognitive maps of managers with a national scope. B. B. Tyler and D. R. Gnyawali (2009, p. 109) found that top-level managers have more complete and integrated cognitive structures than those at the lower levels. Additionally, the competitor dimension was more stressed by higher-level managers than by managers at other levels. G. W. Goodhew, P. A. Commock, and R. T. Hamilton (2005, p. 124) investigated the relationship

---

[1] I should like to thank Richard Hart-Jones for his linguistic help with the English text.

between managers' cognitive maps and their performance. They found cognitive maps of higher performing managers were simpler, using fewer concepts and linkages than the cognitive maps of lower performing managers.

Despite the reported differences, some studies in strategic management detect similarities in the knowledge structures. R. K. Reger and A. S. Huff (1993, p. 110) illustrate that members of large bank holding companies grouped these companies together with regard to their competitive structure. G. P. Hodgkinson and G. Johnson (1994, p. 533, p. 544) have shown similarities in managers' mental models when referring to the fundamental nature of the organisations' major competitors. B. B. Tyler and D. R. Gnyawali (2009, p. 109) found similarities in the evaluation of the customer dimension. This was more important than the competitor dimension for achieving new product success.

The research streams that focus mainly on shared knowledge and similarities in mental models are social cognition (S. Thalemann, 2003, p. 8) and managerial cognition (see chapter 2.1). Social cognition research applies cognitive theories and methodologies to social psychological issues. Managerial cognition research highlights the importance of the construction and change of shared knowledge among company members (see chapter 2.1). Shared knowledge is important for implementing strategies in teams (I. Bamberger & T. Wrona, 2004, p. 368), and it helps to explain differences in team performance (S. Mohammed, R. Klimoski, & J. R. Rentsch, 2000, p. 125; J. C. Ward & P. H. Reingen, 1990, p. 247; S. Mohammed, L. Ferzandi, & K. Hamilton, 2010, p. 877 / p. 879). Team performance is suggested by many researchers as being a critical factor in companies, military and public sector (J. A. Cannon-Bowers, E. Salas, & S. Converse, 1993, p. 223). Consequently, it is important to know which aspects of shared knowledge influence team performance. Some aspects are the characteristics of tasks, teams, or interaction among team members. These are related positively to team performance (M. A. Marks, S. J. Zaccaro, & J. E. Mathieu, 2000; J. E. Mathieu, T. S. Heffner, G. F. Goodwin, E. Salas, & J. A. Cannon-Bowers, 2000; B. K. Griepentrog & P. J. Fleming, 2003; B.-C. Lim & K. J. Klein, 2006; J. R. Rentsch, E. E. Small, & P. J. Hanges, 2008, p. 130; also C. J. Resick, M. W. Dickson, J. K. Mitchelson, L. K. Allison, & M. A. Clark, 2010, pp. 174-175). In particular, shared knowledge influences the ability of team members to handle the needs of the team, to predict correctly the needs of the task and to adapt to changing environmental conditions (P. C. Rasker & W. M. Post, 2000; J. Langan-Fox, J. Anglim, & J. R. Wilson, 2004, p. 336; K. A. Smith-Jentsch, J. E. Mathieu, & K. Kraiger, 2005; S. Mohammed et al., 2010, p. 877 / p. 879)[2].

In summary, shared knowledge and similar mental models are important constructs in managerial cognition research. Especially in the case of a mental model construct, it can be assumed that it is possible to illustrate how strategists represent mentally their knowledge of competition. In addition, there is a strong hint that mental models are similar, but highly individual (see for instance the results by G. P. Hodgkinson & G. Johnson, 1994; B. B. Tyler & D. R. Gnyawali, 2009). Therefore, it is necessary to discuss appropriate methods for researching differences and similarities between individual knowledge structures. The adequacy of the methods depends upon the definition of the constructs. Knowledge is understood as the overarching construct, which includes several specific constructs, such as mental models. Mental models will be defined in this thesis as an internal representation, which includes domain knowledge, and the structure of the domain and which is represented in concepts and their relationships (see chapter 2.2). Moreover, this thesis focuses on highly idiosyncratic mental models, because they form the framework in which decisions take place, according to the perception of the individuals (Langan-Fox et al., 2004, p. 334; see chapter 2.2.3.1).

Generally, there is a range of methods to externalize mental models (see for instance J. Langan-Fox, S. Code, & K. Langfield-Smith, 2000; N. J. Cooke et al., 2000; S. Mohammed et al., 2000; S. Mohammed et al., 2010). Some of these methods, such as interviews, questionnaires, and document analysis are used more often than others (K. E. Weick & M. G. Bougon, 2001, p. 315). In some studies, combinations of different methods are used. Examples are the studies by L. L. Roos and R. I. Hall (1980), R. Calori et al. (1992; 1994), K. Daniels, G. Johnson, and L. d. Chernatony (1994), G. W. Goodhew et al. (2005) and O. C. Iederan, P. L. Curşeu, P. A. M. Vermeulen, and J. L. A. Geurts (2011). For instance, L. L. Roos and R. I. Hall (1980) focussed on document analysis and interviews. R. Calori et al. (1992; 1994) used

---

[2] Especially in risky, time-critical and dynamic situations (J. M. Orasanu, 1990, p. 20) where direct communication is difficult, shared knowledge is an important factor for effective communication and cooperation (J. E. Mathieu et al., 2000, p. 274; see for instance J. A. Espinosa, R. E. Kraut, S. A. Slaughter, J. F. Lerch, J. D. Herbsleb, & A. Mockus, 2002). Hence, research on shared knowledge has been conducted in several man-machine-interaction settings such as flight simulations (R. J. Stout, J. A. Cannon-Bowers, E. Salas, & D. M. Milanovich, 1999; N. J. Cooke, P. A. Kiekel, E. Salas, R. Stout, C. Bowers, & J. A. Cannon-Bowers, 2003; J. E. Mathieu, T. S. Heffner, G. F. Goodwin, J. A. Cannon-Bowers, & E. Salas, 2005; N. J. Cooke, J. C. Gorman, J. L. Duran, & A. R. Taylor, 2007a), military tank simulations (A. P. Banks & L. J. Millward, 2007; M. A. Marks et al., 2000), submarine attack simulations (R. Espevik, B. H. Johnsen, J. Eid, & J. F. Thayer, 2006) and process control environments (M. J. Waller, N. Gupta, & R. C. Giambatista, 2004; J. Sauer, T. Felsing, H. Franke, & B. Rüttinger, 2006; J. Domeinski, R. Wagner, M. Schöbel, & D. Manzey, 2007).

interviews. They examined these with content analysis, and used mapping methods to construct the models (similar the study by O. C. lederan et al., 2011). K. Daniels et al. (1994) used semi-structured interviews, in combination with visual card sorting and repertory grid analysis. G. W. Goodhew et al. (2005) interviewed participants using a survey to identify the content, and they used cause-and-effect questions to establish the structure of the mental models.

The way in which these methods are combined has an impact on the degree of freedom for the participants in constructing their mental models. This degree of freedom influences the idiosyncrasy of the individual mental model (see chapter 3.5). Ultimately, this determines the choice of the aggregation approach and similarity rating (see chapters 3.5 and 3.7). For instance, document analysis is non-reactive; participants do not recognize themselves as being part of a study. The mental models are constructed by a researcher, based on the documents produced by participants. Interviews and questionnaires are reactive methods; participants recognise themselves as part of a study. However, degrees of freedom within interviews and questionnaires are different in the research process. Usually in interviews, participants have a lot of freedom to construct their mental models. In this case, participants are not influenced by predefined answers, and the constructed mental models are highly idiosyncratic. Whereas, when based on questionnaires, participants usually choose from a list of predetermined answers. Hence, the constructed mental model is standardized (see chapter 3.5). An example of a medium degree of freedom for participants is the study by L. Markóczy and J. Goldberg (1995). As a first step, participants had to choose concepts from a predefined list. This represents a lower level of freedom to generate content; concepts are less idiosyncratic. As a second step, participants had to decide for each pair of concepts if and how one influences the other. This procedure involves a higher degree of freedom for the participants in generating the structure between concepts. Hence, the structure is more idiosyncratic when compared to the content. Based on the results, the authors calculated distance ratios between causal maps and assessed similarity by performing statistical tests on distance ratios.

K. Daniels, G. Johnson, and L. d. Chernatony (2002) designed a study in which participants had a higher degree of freedom in generating and constructing mental models. Additionally, they used the participants' view of similarity rating. The study's aim was to compare mental models of participants about competition in the UK personal financial services industry. For that, K. Daniels et al. (2002, pp. 40-41) combined semi-structured interviews, a visual card-sorting technique and a repertory grid. The participants created structure and content of the mental models by themselves, and they evaluated similarities based on comparing the maps of other participants to their own mental model (K. Daniels et al., 2002, p. 41).

Studies by L. Markóczy and J. Goldberg (1995) and K. Daniels et al. (2002) are examples for judging similarities between mental models, given different degrees of freedom for the participants during the research process. Constructed mental models differed in idiosyncrasy. The idiosyncrasy of mental models in the study by L. Markóczy and J. Goldberg (1995) is lower than the idiosyncrasy of mental models in the study by K. Daniels et al. (2002). Consequently, to explore highly idiosyncratic mental models, research should be designed with a high degree of freedom for the participants during the research process, such as in the study by K. Daniels et al. (2002). However, K. Daniels et al. (2002) used a similarity rating by participants to get an indicator for the similarity of the maps. Such ratings are used in most empirical team mental model studies as an approach to aggregate individual mental models (S. Mohammed et al., 2010, p. 885; see chapter 3.7.1). Nevertheless, this procedure of rating the similarity of cognitive maps is criticised by G. P. Hodgkinson (2002) because he said that participants are not able to judge the overall similarity of complex maps. He states that this procedure will introduce bias into the rating (see chapter 3.5.3). Additionally, L. A. DeChurch and J. R. Mesmer-Magnus (2010a, p. 3) state that similarity rating scales "capture levels of knowledge but do not model the structure or organization of that knowledge." Interpretable structures are obscured (S. Mohammed et al., 2000, p. 149; see chapters 3.6 and 3.7.1). Moreover, with such ratings it is assumed indirectly that contributions of the group members are equally important. This is questionable for heterogeneous groups and for teams where the members have different deep knowledge (S. Mohammed et al., 2000, p.149; N. J. Cooke & J. C. Gorman, 2006, p. 271; N. J. Cooke, J. C. Gorman, & J. L. Winner, 2007b, pp. 247-249; S. Mohammed et al., 2010, pp. 885-888; see chapters 1.2, and 3.6). In consequence, other similarity indicators are needed to cope with the problem of comparability of idiosyncratic mental models taking into account content and structure.

C. Eden, F. Ackermann, and S. Cropper (1992, p. 313) sketch some indicators for analysing idiosyncratic mental models, which also emphasise the structure, such as the complexity of the models with a focus on the concept numbers and number of linkages. Another indicator focuses on the domain, by calculating the cause and effect of each concept (see chapter 3.7.2.3). However, these indicators are appropriate for a general similarity index only if the concepts themselves are standardized, when mental models were developed by using nomothetic mapping techniques. Nevertheless, this indicates a lower degree of freedom for the participants during the research procedure, and therefore results in less idiosyncratic mental models. In idiosyncratic mental models, it is likely that these (see chapter 3.7.3 Problems of Judging Similarity in Idiosyncratic Mental Models)

> "... contain a significant number of contradictory beliefs deriving from the different perceptions of the team members as well as concepts that may have virtually identical ver-

bal tags, the meaning of which, however, as elaborated through their conceptual and belief context may be significantly different..." (C. Eden, S. Jones, D. Sims, & T. Smithin, 1981, pp. 41-42).

Moreover, P. E. Jones and P. H. M. P. Roelofsma (2000, p. 1142) state:

"...group members may use particular words or terms (such as 'risk', 'threat' or 'likelihood') under the assumption that the other group members attach the same meaning to such terms, when in actual fact this is not necessarily the case."

Differences in idiosyncratic mental models can cause problems in team working and in implementing strategies:

"While such discrepancies in understanding may appear to be subtle, they may be significant enough to induce unrecognized drift in the group members' mental models, which may ultimately result in unpredictable group decisions." (P. E. Jones & P. H. M. P. Roelofsma, 2000, p. 1142)

They cause different problem perceptions or definitions, or project definitions between, for instance, parent companies and subsidiaries, different business units or in consultant-client situations. Different perceptions or definitions can be the reason for different implementation of company strategies, different approaches to problem solving, differences in decision making as well as the reason for different weighting and scoring of performance indicators (for the differences in problem perception, problem definition, and project definition see C. Kerlen, 2003). For instance, performance indicators are an important tool for control in companies (see, for instance, R. Brühl, 2009, chapter 13). The selection of a particular performance indicator makes assumptions about the cause and effect of certain factors (P. N. Bukh & T. Malmi, 2005, p. 96). There could be two companies setting their growth objectives. One company would target sales, for example, 100,000 Euros per employee in a year. The other company would target stable customer relations. The assumed cause-and-effect relationships, hence the strategies, to achieve the objective of growth may be quite different. The objective of the first company could result in extending the scope of work. The objective of the second company could be to focus on building good working relationships with customers. The intention behind both strategies is that turnover will increase. Nevertheless, the first company could use short-term strategies; the second company could focus on long-term strategies.

However, the modus operandi is a strategic decision, and requires leadership from management. Behind apparently similar objectives, there are different basic assumptions driven by the philosophy and values of the company. Hence, idiosyncratic mental models are also influenced by organisational cultures (see for organisational culture E. H. Schein, 2010). This means that it is useful to compare the idiosyncratic mental models to diagnose the subtle differences and similarities in mental models in situations when processes have stalled, or before cooperation in team work, or to avoid problems appearing during that team work (see for instance the cultural influence on the success or failure of mergers and acquisitions, A. Unterreitmeier, 2004, chapter 1.1.3). Consequently, the comparison of idiosyncratic mental models can help to detect potential conflicts, and create a common knowledge base. However, as C. Eden et al. (1981, pp. 41-42) and P. E. Jones and P. H. M. P. Roelofsma (2000) had stated, concepts in idiosyncratic mental models may have nearly identical verbal tags, the meaning of which may be significantly different (see above). In addition, mental models may include different concepts, which have a similar meaning. Therefore, the following research question encapsulates the entire project (see chapter 3.7.3 Problems of Judging Similarity in Idiosyncratic Mental Models):

How can the similarity (and difference) of idiosyncratic mental models be identified and presented?

1.2. Research Objective and Thesis Structure

"However, the theoretical basis for ... mapping, which allows an interpretation of analysis of those maps, is rarely made explicit, so the link between a theory of cognition and the coding method is usually difficult to detect." (C. Eden et al., 1992, p. 309)

The main objective of this thesis is the development and exploration of a method, which investigates the comparison of highly idiosyncratic mental models using similarities and differences. By making this comparison, the aggregation of similar idiosyncratic concepts of different idiosyncratic mental models permits the identification of shared knowledge whilst taking into account its structure. The process of comparing with the ability to aggregate similar concepts will be referred to as 'aggregation'. A variety of methods for describing idiosyncratic mental models is used in different contextual conditions, and their practice is discussed.

The thesis starts with a theoretical underpinning of the mental model and team mental model construct, which is placed in a context of knowledge and shared knowledge constructs (chapter 2). Knowledge and shared knowledge constructs are theoretically underpinned within Structure Genesis Approach. Therefore, these constructs are basic constructs. Mental models and team mental models are constructs, which are more specific. They are derived from the basic constructs; and they will be used for the operation and the methodological basis for the aggregation process. Therefore, they are mediator constructs (see Figure 1, p. 8, overlapping of the boxes 'theoretical basis' and 'methodical basis'). For the development and exploration of a method, which permits comparison between idiosyncratic mental models, additional theoretical work is needed, and this will be described in the respective studies in chapter 4.

Chapter 3 reflects the research methodology in this thesis. To elicit idiosyncratic mental models, participants should not be influenced by researchers. If participants have free choice in generating the content of concepts and constructing the linkage between concepts, they are able to illustrate how they represent their knowledge mentally. Hence, methods to elicit content and structure of mental models are needed where the participants have a high degree of freedom during the research process. This will be discussed in chapter 3.5, following a consideration of the underlying research paradigm (chapter 3.1), research design strategies (chapter 3.2), strategy of reasoning (chapter 3.3), and quality indices (chapter 3.4) which also underline the methodological development in chapter 4.

Figure 1: Relation between Theoretical Basis and Methodical Basis

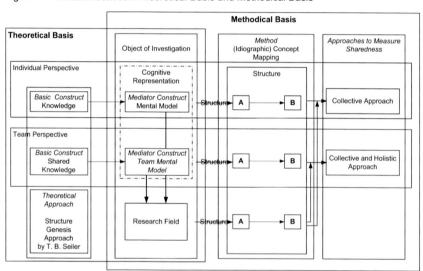

Nevertheless, the focus on idiosyncratic mental models creates difficulties in the construction of team mental models, and hence in the determination of similarity. The construction of a team mental model is based upon idiosyncratic mental models (see chapter 2.2.3.2), and may yield changes in the individual models, as well as changes in the team mental model. This results from discussion within the team (C. Eden et al., 1981, pp. 41-42; C. Eden & F. Ackermann, 1998, p. 193). This correlation is also linked to the individual versus team collection of mental models, hence both a collective and holistic approach to measurement. Both approaches and their relevance for this thesis will be discussed in chapter 3.6. Additionally, most similarity indicators are quantitative. They are appropriate for standardized concepts (see chapter 3.7). Because mental models are concepts as well as links between concepts, and idiosyncrasies as well as similarity of these mental models are of interest, it is appropriate to develop a methodological approach to aggregate idiosyncratic mental models when referring to the similarity between them (see chapters 3.6 and 3.7 as well as chapter 4).

A valid method must be applicable to substantive issues from different research areas, and should always comply with standards that supply information about the quality of the method and the results (for the quality indices see chapter 3.4). Moreover, if there are differences in groups (e.g. management versus work groups), this method should be able to reveal these differences (see chapter 3.8). For this reason, different groups (homogeneous versus heterogeneous; teams versus individuals) were investigated, and substantive issues from the fields of accounting, strategy and marketing have been selected (see chapter 4).

In total, I conducted five studies with two distinct methodological approaches. Approach A includes study I and study II (chapters 4.1 and 4.2); Approach B includes studies III, IV, and V (chapters 4.4, 4.5 and 4.6). The methodical objective of Approach A was the elicitation and comparison of idiosyncratic mental models in terms of content and structure (see Figure 2, p. 10). The methodical objective of Approach B was to explore a method to compare idiosyncratic concepts in terms of similarity.

Study I (Approach A) served two purposes (see Figure 2): firstly, to elicit idiosyncratic concepts of the individual mental models, based on the two-stage approach of Structure-Formation-Technique; and secondly, to create a rule-system to build up cause-and-effect relationships among idiosyncratic concepts. Study II had the objective of comparing the idiosyncratic mental models by aggregation of idiosyncratic concepts to more abstract categories using the Delphi-Method of expert evaluation (see Figure 2).

Approach A produced the desired results. Idiosyncratic mental models of study I were comparable in terms of similarity. However, this comparability is limited. The evaluation of the categories generated by the experts, and assessed by participant 3 (study I) revealed ambiguous results (see chapter 4.2.4); hence, the content validity is low (see chapter 3.4). I suspect that the experts' lack of knowledge about the context could be the cause. Using mapping techniques, the participants' focus is placed on the important things. Context information, such as the reasons for the choice of concepts, and reasons for their connections to other concepts, is hidden. Hence, these reasons are not available to the experts. When I adopted the Delphi-Method in study II as a technique to compare the mental models of study I, I assumed that the knowledge and skills of the experts in study II, as well as the fact that they came from the same company, hence from the same group (C. Eden & F. Ackermann, 1998, p. 196) as the participants in study I, might be sufficient to achieve the desired results. However, the results were not of the requisite quality (see chapter 4.2).

Figure 2: Outline of Approach A

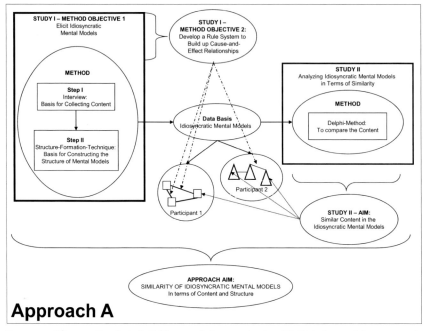

Because of the results of study II (Approach A, see chapter 4.2.3), I changed the approach for comparing and aggregating idiosyncratic concepts (see chapter 4.3). In Approach B, I started focusing primarily on the content of the idiosyncratic mental models (see Figure 3, p. 12). The aim of Approach B was therefore to elicit and compare concepts in terms of similarities. This was done because the compatibility of concepts is the basic requirement for the comparability of idiosyncratic mental models in content and structure. I postponed the methodical examination of the structure in terms of similarity.

Based on an explorative view, and focussing on the perspective of the participants, study III (Approach B) developed a general approach to compare idiosyncratic mental models (chapter 4.4). In study IV (chapter 4.5), a rule-system to compare concepts of the idiosyncratic mental models was developed. The result is the 'meaning relation tool' for making similarity judgements (see chapter 4.5.1.4), which is used by the participants. They use it to judge the meaning of their own concepts, based on the meaning of team concepts.

The meaning relation tool can be used to explore team performance (see study IV, chapter 4.5.3.5, and study V, chapter 4.6). There are researchers who have viewed team performance as a function of each team member's individual input in relation to the process losses when working with others (E. Salas, D. E. Sims, & C. S. Burke, 2005, pp. 556-557). In this thesis, team performance is seen as the output of the team taking into account learning and repetition effects based on individual outputs. This is done using the meaning relation tool and in combination with the holistic and collective approach. With this concept, the proposition of "the whole is more than the sum of its parts" can be tested (see S. C. Schneider & R. Angelmar, 1993, p. 360). Additionally, based on this concept of team performance, the influence can be shown of social interaction and communication processes, which are ignored in most empirical team mental model studies which use similarity ratings (S. Mohammed et al., 2010, p. 885). The team performance construct developed in this thesis, its advantages and disadvantages, will be discussed in chapter 3.9. However, both the meaning relation tool and the team performance approach, were evaluated in an experimental design in study V (see chapter 4.6).

Approaches A and B differ in the way similarities between idiosyncratic concepts are judged (aggregative approach). Hence, the methods for collecting mental models also differ (see chapter 3.6). Approach A focussed on a collective process: study I referred to the elicitation of idiosyncratic mental models, study II referred to the aggregation of idiosyncratic mental models. Approach B focussed on a combination of both processes, collective and holistic. The collective process was used to elicit idiosyncratic mental models; the holistic one was used to elicit team mental models. The meaning relation tool was used to compare the meaning of concepts of idiosyncratic mental models with the meaning of concepts of the team mental models. This is the aggregation part of the collective approach. Figure 3, p. 12, outlines Approach B.

Cause-and-effect relationship issues from the fields of accounting and strategy were used in both approaches to understand shared knowledge about content and structure (see chapter 4.1.1). Tasks led to interesting results, especially the processing of management tasks by participants from academic backgrounds other than business administration (see for instance the results of study III, chapter 4.4.3). For the validation of the method and the team performance approach in the last study (chapter 4.6), I decided to change the issues. In the validation phase of this method, each participant could answer the substantive questions regardless of educational background. For this reason, I chose a marketing topic, using personal preferences and opinions.

Each stage of the development of the aggregation method is discussed in studies I-V. Chapter 5 discusses the results of the approaches, explains the conclusions drawn, their practical applications, as well as the limitations of the research. It also introduces opportunities for further research.

Figure 3: Outline of Approach B

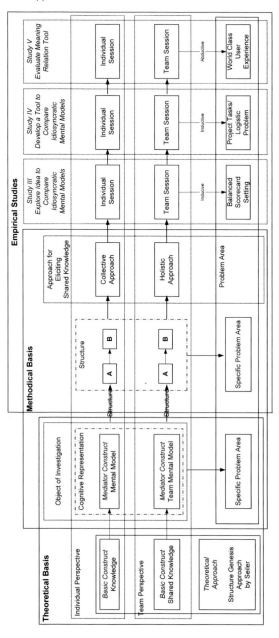

2. Theoretical Underpinning

2.1. Introduction

Knowledge is a broad subject, researched in many sciences, especially in psychology, in many areas of business development, and in computer science. There is no agreed definition for knowledge, hence, several exists (G. Reinmann-Rothmeier, 2003, p. 508; see also Al-Laham, 2003). The theory of knowledge relies upon its context, its specific scientific interests, and goals (G. Reinmann-Rothmeier, 2003, p. 508; G. Müller-Stewens & C. Lechner, 2005, p. 362).

In the context of educational psychology, for instance, J. G. Greeno, A. M. Collins, and L. B. Resnick (1996, pp. 17-21) describe three aspects of knowledge. The first regards knowledge as having associations. Associations result from the link between different mental and/or behavioural entities, which result in concepts or networks. The structures of these associations depend upon existing associations. Hence, knowledge reflects experience. Examples of this are Stimulus-Response-Association-Theories, which describe learning situations (J. G. Greeno et al., 1996, p. 17). The second regards knowledge as having cognitive abilities and concepts, which result from the effect of the environment (R. H. Kluwe, 2002). Supporters of this position discuss processes and structures, which are based upon knowledge (R. H. Kluwe, 2002) such as language abilities, problem solving, and logical thinking, as well as cognitive processes and mental representations (J. G. Greeno et al., 1996, pp. 18-20). The third considers how knowledge is distributed between individuals and their communities. Supporters of this view study the social environment of individuals, their attitudes to the opportunities and limitations presented by their environment and the community, as well as the knowledge which individuals have about these two (J. G. Greeno et al., 1996, p. 20 f.).

Different theoretical approaches about knowledge also exist in the context of strategic management. Each approach seeks to answer the question about the importance of knowledge for creating competitive advantage (G. Müller-Stewens & C. Lechner, 2005, pp. 359-364). The resource-based-view sees enterprises as bundles of different resources, and knowledge as one of these resources (K. M. Eisenhardt & J. A. Martin, 2000, p. 1105). Other resources are information, organizational processes, and structure. These resources, including knowledge, are controlled by enterprises. Enterprises can therefore develop and implement strategies for the improvement of efficiency and effectiveness (J. Barney, 1991, p. 101). With the capability-based-view, knowledge is embodied in the coordinated use of resources. Therefore, the focus here is on the development of management abilities, as well as the combined use of organizational (for example human resources), functional and technical resources which are difficult to replicate (D. J. Teece, G. Pisano, & A. Shuen, 1997, p. 510, p. 516; R.

Amit & P. J. H. Schoemaker, 1993, p. 35). With the knowledge-based-view, knowledge is the fundamental resource, the crucial factor. Enterprises are made up of values, standards, actions, and thought patterns (G. Müller-Stewens & C. Lechner, 2005, p. 362 f.). Typically, these include the importance of knowledge, and the process of gaining further knowledge, as the basis for increasing competitive advantage (I. Bamberger & T. Wrona, 2004, p. 49).

The literature about shared knowledge shows similar patterns. For instance, shared knowledge has gained attention in the field of managerial cognition research (see J. P. Walsh, 1995). Originating in management research, managerial cognition research includes aspects of cognitive sciences and strategic management (C. I. Stubbart, 1989, p. 325). Managerial cognition arose from insights about the divergence from the 'rational manager' and the 'cognitive bounded rational manager' (J.-C. Spender & C. Eden, 1998; G. P. Hodgkinson, 1997; R. Selten, 2002). The mental models, which managers have, differ from the abstract models of business administration theories (J.-C. Spender & C. Eden, 1998, p. 2; G. P. Hodgkinson, 1997). Whereas, business administration theories often assume that all managers think in the same way, and "notice the same threats and opportunities" (C. I. Stubbart, 1989, p. 326), strategic management researchers tend to focus on the cognitive bounded rationality of managers (R. Selten, 2002, p. 15; J.-C. Spender & C. Eden, 1998, p. 2; C. I. Stubbart, 1989, p. 326). In particular, they focus on the knowledge about aspects of their company, such as competition (C. I. Stubbart, 1989, p. 330; see for an overview e.g. G. P. Hodgkinson, 1997). Managerial research cognition concentrates on two levels of analysis (G. P. Hodgkinson & P. R. Sparrow, 2002, p. 123): on a macro level, and a micro level. The macro level compares the competitive structures between different companies. The focus is on company members' mental representations of competition in order to understand the interaction between strategic thinking and environmental conditions. The micro level concentrates on differences in managers' thinking within an organisation. The focus here is on the strategy of a company. The objective is to understand the influences, which cause individual differences in the formulation of strategy, and its implementation within the company. This research recognises that company members in different positions face different environmental contingencies, which lead to different knowledge structures (G. P. Hodgkinson & P. R. Sparrow, 2002, p. 150). There is a special interest in the construction and change of common knowledge between company members, which is important for implementing strategies (I. Bamberger & T. Wrona, 2004, p. 368).

In psychology, shared knowledge is mainly studied in the research of social cognition (S. Thalemann, 2003, p. 8). Social cognition studies the individual mental process in the social environment, such as social perception or the forming of opinions (S. Abele, 2002). L. Thompson, E. Peterson, and L. Kray (1995, p. 6 f.) distinguish three different research positions: social cognition, contextualized social cognition, and socially shared cognition. Social cognition focuses on cognition within the social context. The main issue here is "...how the individual perceiver *processes* social information..." (L. Thompson et al., 1995, pp. 7-8). Contextualized social cognition concentrates on how the context itself inspires cognition. Socially shared cognition focuses on cognitions, which are produced through interaction with other individuals. The first two, social cognition and contextualized social cognition, look at the individual level, whereas socially shared cognition focuses on the group level.

2.2. Conceptual Framework

One reason for the different views of knowledge and shared knowledge, described above, is that knowledge and shared knowledge are constructs. Constructs are dispositions, which are assumed hypothetically. They are not observable directly (J. Bortz & N. Döring, 2006). Therefore, it is necessary to monitor relevant theories and empirical results (see, for instance, H.-J. Fisseni, 1997; see also R. Schnell, P. B. Hill, & E. Esser, 2008). The focus of research in this thesis is idiosyncratic mental models, and their similarities between different individuals. Therefore, knowledge concepts on the individual and group level form a basis for further theoretical underpinning. Common concept pairs are individual versus collective knowledge (see, for instance, G. Probst, S. Raub, & K. Romhardt, 2006) and implicit versus explicit knowledge (see, for instance, I. Nonaka, 1991; I. Nonaka & N. Konno, 1998, p. 42; I. Nonaka, G. von Krogh, & S. Voelpel, 2006, p. 1182; A. Büssing, B. Herbig, & A. Latzel, 2002, pp. 8-12).

Individual knowledge belongs to the person (G. Probst et al., 2006, chapter 2, for instance, p. 22). Collective knowledge is the combination of different knowledge components and the knowledge of different individuals (G. Probst et al., 2006, chapter 2, for instance, p. 20). Implicit knowledge and explicit knowledge are part of individual knowledge. However, they are different depending upon the degree to which they can be articulated (A. Cabrera & E. F. Cabrera, 2002, p. 690). Explicit knowledge is conscious. It can be communicated to another person by using signs, and can therefore be shared with others (I. Nonaka & N. Konno, 1998, p. 42; V. Ambrosini & C. Bowman, 2001, p. 812; D. C. Berry & D. E. Broadbent, 1988, p. 251). Implicit knowledge is not conscious and therefore hard to communicate (D. C. Berry & D. E. Broadbent, 1988, p. 251; A Cabrera & E. F. Cabrera, 2002, p. 690).

Both concept pairs are related. To transform individual knowledge into collective knowledge, it is necessary to transform individual implicit knowledge into individual explicit knowledge (M. Bick, 2004, p. 16). The relationship between individual implicit and explicit knowledge as a basis for sharing knowledge is sketched out by the Structure Genesis Approach. This approach integrates aspects of implicit and explicit knowledge as part of individual knowledge.

At the same time, Structure Genesis Approach makes an assumption about the emergence and development of knowledge. It is a basis for the shared knowledge construct.

Chapter 2.2.1 describes the parts of the approach, which are needed to understand how shared knowledge will be defined in this thesis (see chapter 2.2.2). Chapter 2.2.2 is subdivided into knowledge as an intra-personal disposition (chapter 2.2.2.1) and shared knowledge as an inter-personal dimension (chapter 2.2.2.2). The same structure is in chapter 2.2.3, and refers to the mediator constructs 'mental model' and 'team mental models'. Chapter 2.2.3.1 describes the individual perspective of mental models. Chapter 2.2.3.2 describes the team perspective, the 'team mental models' and 'shared mental model'. Chapter 2.2.3.3 outlines the purpose of mental models and team mental models.

2.2.1. Fundamentals of the Structure Genesis Approach

The Structure Genesis Approach focuses on individuals, and explains the emergence of knowledge and its development, based on theses by Piaget (G. Reinmann, 2005, p. 7; for the approach see T. B. Seiler, 2001b, pp. 15-122). The main concern of Structure Genesis Approach is to explain the cooperation between both the genetic predisposition of the human being and environmental circumstances on the development of individuals' cognitive structures (T. B. Seiler, 2001b, p. 20, p. 27).

The development of individuals' cognitive structures is influenced by the interaction between the individual and the environment (T. B. Seiler & G. Reinmann, 2004, p. 18; T. B. Seiler, 2003, p. 42). Based on environmental conditions, such as problem solving tasks, knowledge development starts from pre-existing cognitive structures. These are used as instruments for the development process, which result in cognitive structures (see T. B. Seiler, 2001b, p. 41 ff.). Therefore, cognitive structures are changeable and dynamic (T. B. Seiler, 2001b, p. 36 f.). Hence (T. B. Seiler, 2001b, pp. 27-40; see also G. Reinmann, 2005):

- Cognitive structures are associated with individuals.
- Cognitive structures are based on experience.
- Cognitive structures are essential for the further development of individuals.

Cognitive structures of **individuals** refer to idiosyncratic activities and abilities as well as aspects, which are responsible for changing processes (T. B. Seiler, 2001b, p. 33).

Experience is the common ground between the ability to act and the ability to realize. The ability to act (action) is to sense the properties of objects. The ability to realize (in the mind) is to understand the properties of objects. Recognition (experience) takes place on both levels. This recognition is fundamental for individuals to adjust properly, and to respond to the environment (T. B. Seiler, 2001b, pp. 27-33; T. B. Seiler, 2004, p. 308 f.). The ability to act, and the ability to realize, affect each other, and are necessary in the development and training of cognitive structures (T. B. Seiler, 2004, p. 314; T. B. Seiler, 2001b, p. 99). Hence, cognitive structures are the basis for recognition, understanding, and knowledge (G. Reinmann, 2005, p. 7). The ability to act includes action-readiness and action-execution (T. B. Seiler, 2001b, p. 28). Action-readiness is a stored, draft cognitive action, which Seiler calls a disposition (T. B. Seiler, 2001b, p. 35). It is dynamic and can be adapted, and updated to changes in the environment. The ability to realize includes mental abilities and procedures such as perceptions, conceptions, mental pictures, memory processes, linguistic meanings, and logical derivatives (T. B. Seiler, 2001b, p. 26 ff.). Additionally, the interaction process between the ability to act and the ability to realize is related to different degrees of consciousness (see in addition T. B. Seiler, 2001b, p. 32).

Cognitive structures have two characteristics, which are necessary for further **development of individuals**. Firstly, they are robust in the processes of realization. At different times, the individual is able to implement similar actions in similar situations. Secondly, structures possess systematic characteristics. Structures are elements and characteristics, which are linked by the relationships between them, and affect one another mutually (T. B. Seiler, 2001b, p. 37). These characteristics, as well as processes of accommodation and assimilation (see below), are important for the further development of cognitive structures, and therefore for the sustainment and change of cognitive structures (G. Reinmann, 2005, p. 7). Assimilation describes the transformation of experienced mental-realizations and action-realizations to new environmental situations; the existing cognitive structures are activated and transferred to new situations. Accommodation describes the transformation of experiences made, because of the new situations, into cognitive structures (J. Piaget 1968, cit. after G. Reinmann, 2005; T. B. Seiler, 2001b, pp. 45-52).

2.2.2. Knowledge and Shared Knowledge Based on the Structure Genesis Approach

2.2.2.1. Knowledge as Intra-Personal Disposition

The fundamentals described above are essential for understanding knowledge and shared knowledge from the Structure Genesis perspective. According to Structure Genesis Approach, individual knowledge includes systems of different cognitive structures (G. Reinmann, 2005, p. 8). These systems are called

- idiosyncratic knowledge and

- objectified knowledge

(T. B. Seiler & G. Reinmann, 2004, p. 18 f.; G. Reinmann, 2005, p. 8, see Figure 4).

Figure 4:   Personal Knowledge

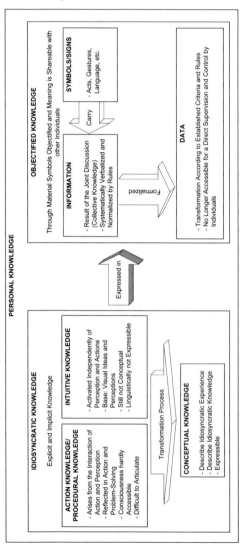

Idiosyncratic knowledge belongs to the individual uniquely, regardless of how this knowledge was obtained (see Figure 4). It is only accessible to and available for that individual (G. Reinmann, 2005, p. 8) in an explicit or implicit manner. It includes action knowledge as well as procedural knowledge, intuitive knowledge, and conceptual knowledge (T. B. Seiler & G. Reinmann, 2004, p. 19).

Action knowledge is original knowledge (T. B. Seiler & G. Reinmann, 2004, p. 19). It emanates from sensorimotor (elementary) structures of actions and perceptions (T. B. Seiler, 2001b, p. 83), which affect each other mutually. Action knowledge is considered as "implicitly contained in action structure" (["implizit in der Handlungsstruktur enthalten"] T. B. Seiler & G. Reinmann, 2004, p. 19) and can be understood as action-readiness or disposition (T. B. Seiler, 2001b). Action knowledge is embodied in acting and problem solving (T. B. Seiler & G. Reinmann, 2004, p. 19; action-execution, T. B. Seiler, 2001b) and is equated to competence (T. B. Seiler, 2001b, p. 81). Action knowledge is only accessible to consciousness with difficulty, and is difficult to explain (G. Reinmann, 2005, p. 8; T. B. Seiler, 2001b, p. 83).

Intuitive knowledge is part of the mental realization ability (see chapter 2.2.1). It relies on internalized perceptions or mental imagination (T. B. Seiler, 2001b, p. 83 f.; G. Reinmann, 2005, p. 9). According to the Structure Genesis Approach, this mental imagery belongs to the early mental structures. Mental imagery is intuitive or instinctive, and is not conceptual and therefore is not expressible (T. B. Seiler & G. Reinmann, 2004, p. 19). These early mental or cognitive structures are linked to local experiences (T. B. Seiler, 2001b, p. 84). However, they can be activated independently of perception, and thus independently of external sensory stimuli, and actions (G. Reinmann, 2005, p. 9).

Conceptual knowledge emanates from transforming action knowledge and intuitive knowledge (T. B. Seiler & G. Reinmann, 2004, p. 1). It represents knowledge, which remains unchanged because of different experiences of constant characteristics, together with changeable qualities (T. B. Seiler, 2001b, p. 84). Therefore, concepts describe idiosyncratic experiences and illustrate idiosyncratic knowledge (T. B. Seiler, 2001b, p. 84).

Objectified knowledge is a precondition for communication between individuals (T. B. Seiler, 2003, p. 46). It is perceived by individuals in a culture or society through "material symbols" (T. B. Seiler, 2004, p. 303) and shared, if the meaning of the material symbols is familiar to the individuals. Therefore, the main characteristics of objectified knowledge can be described as shared and meaningful. According to the Structure Genesis Approach, objectified knowledge includes information, symbols, and data. Information is collective, objectified knowledge. It emanates from a common discourse. Information is standardized by rules and is verbalized systematically (T. B. Seiler & G. Reinmann, 2004, p. 19). Symbols carry the information (T. B. Seiler, 2004, p. 303). Examples are actions, gestures, language, and texts (T. B. Seiler, 2004, p. 304). Data are information, which are transformed by further processes of standardisation, in the form of fixed criteria and allocation rules. Information in the form of data can be processed electronically. Thus, they are no longer accessible through direct supervision and control by individuals (G. Reinmann, 2005, p. 9). It becomes obvious that information carried in symbols is only potential knowledge. This represents knowledge, if the meaning of the material signs is familiar to the individuals (T. B. Seiler, 2004; T. B. Seiler & G. Reinmann, 2004, p. 19). Hence, objectified knowledge represents knowledge, which has the potential to be externalised.

Based on the Structure Genesis view, the following definition of knowledge will be used in this thesis:

Knowledge is a person-dependent variable, which depends on personal experiences and previous understandings. Knowledge results in cognitive representation in the form of procedural structures and mental structures.

For that reason, knowledge can be called 'personal knowledge'. Personal knowledge includes idiosyncratic knowledge and objectified knowledge. Idiosyncratic knowledge is explicit and implicit knowledge. It is only accessible to the individual. Objectified knowledge is *idiosyncratic* knowledge. It is objectified for other individuals through material signs such as actions, gestures, articles, language, and texts. Therefore, personal knowledge can be internal (idiosyncratic knowledge) and external (objectified knowledge), but both are still personal (intra-individual, see Figure 5).

Figure 5: Relationship between Idiosyncratic and Objectified Knowledge

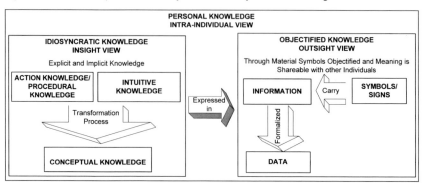

The distinction between objectified knowledge, which is accessible to other individuals, and idiosyncratic knowledge, which is not accessible to other individuals, has important methodological implications. For instance, it was stated that action knowledge is only accessible to consciousness with difficulty, and is therefore hard to explain. However, even if a person is not able to talk about action knowledge, a third person could observe the person's action, such as someone driving a car. This does not imply that the observed person, the car driver, has no longer any driving knowledge, if he or she is not driving the car. The knowledge to drive the car still exists. Therefore, action knowledge is not accessible to a third person if the observed person is not acting. In this case, action knowledge is 'objectifiable' idiosyncratic knowledge. If a person is acting, the person objectifies the knowledge. Thus, the definition of knowledge is expanded to include issues, which can be perceived by others:

> *Knowledge is measurable through material indications such as actions, gestures, articles, language, and texts.*

2.2.2.2. Shared Knowledge as an Inter-Personal Dimension

> *"We need more research that seeks to understand what shared knowledge means and what sharing knowledge means" (D. Shaw, F. Ackermann, & C. Eden, 2003, p. 947)*
> *"Thus, understanding shared knowledge and differences in shared knowledge is essential to understanding group decision making." (J. C. Ward & P. H. Reingen, 1990, p. 247)*

The definition of knowledge is associated with an intra-individual dimension, because knowledge is defined as a person-dependent variable. This dimension is also part of the characteristics of shared knowledge. Shareable knowledge is based on personal knowledge. T. B. Seiler (2004) stated that knowledge could only be shared through objectified information such as actions, language, or gestures. Additionally, it also includes cultural knowledge. Therefore, shared knowledge is linked with a second, Inter-personal dimension. Objectified information is shared knowledge, if the meaning of this objectified information is familiar to a number of individuals. For instance, two people see each other on the street. One person is on one side of the street, while the other person is on the opposite side. One of them starts to raise his or her right hand, and opens and closes the fingers. He or she waves to the other one. In European countries, this gesture is a greeting. In Kenya, especially at the Luos, this gesture means 'come to me'. Therefore, if both persons share the meaning of this gesture, they share knowledge, and they know what to do. If they do not share the same meaning of the objectified information, they do not have shared knowledge. Consequently, shared knowledge is based on individual knowledge.

However, the team mental model literature discusses different understandings of sharedness. To share can mean to divide something up (R. Klimoski & S. Mohammed, 1994, p. 421). This understanding is discussed in terms of sharing as distribution (see N. J. Cooke, E.

Salas, J. A. Cannon-Bowers, & R. E. Stout, 2000, p. 156; S. Mohammed & B. C. Dumville, 2001, p. 103; R. Klimoski & S. Mohammed, 1994, p. 421). Examples are to divide food (N. J. Cooke et al., 2000, p. 156) and to divide workload (R. Klimoski & S. Mohammed, 1994, p. 421). To share can also mean to have something in common (R. Klimoski & S. Mohammed, 1994, p. 421). This kind of sharing can take different degrees of overlapping: from no overlapping, hence, having nothing in common, to the point of identical overlapping, or having everything in common (R. Klimoski & S. Mohammed, 1994, p. 421; see also chapter 3.8).

In this thesis, shared knowledge is understood to be overlapping knowledge when referring to an area of common knowledge. This overlapping knowledge can take different degrees on a continuum with the poles 'identical' and 'no overlapping'. Consequently, based on all the above, shared knowledge will be defined as the following (see Figure 6):

Shared knowledge is defined as overlapping cognitive representation in terms of overlapped procedural and mental structures. Overlapping cognitive representations result in the same understanding of the objectified information among individuals. Shared knowledge is measurable by using material indications in the same way, based on the same understanding.

Figure 6: Shared Knowledge

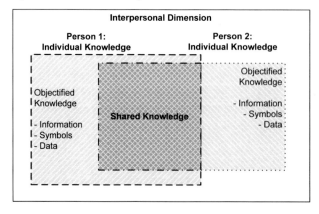

2.2.3. Mediator Constructs: Mental Models and Team Mental Models

2.2.3.1. The Individual Perspective: Mental Models as Internal Representation[3]

Mental models are a mental representation[4]. They are used in this thesis for operating a knowledge construct and a shared knowledge construct. The mental model concept is widely used in different contexts, and various scientists stress "...confusion over the use of the term "mental model"..." (S. J. Payne, 2003, p. 137; see also P. N. Johnson-Laird, 1989; J. R. Wilson & A. Rutherford, 1989). Different domain examples given by N. Moray (1999, p. 224) are, for instance, deductive (logical) reasoning (P. N. Johnson-Laird, 1983), naturalistic human knowledge in physical causal systems such as electricity (for instance, D. Gentner & D. R. Gentner, 1983; D. Gentner & A. L. Stevens, 1983), and human-computer interaction (J. C. Green, 1990, cit. by N. Moray, 1999; M.-A. Sasse, 1992).

Mental models are types of knowledge structures, which have to serve special purposes (W. B. Rouse & N. M. Morris, 1986). According to D. Gentner (2002, p. 9683) there are two main approaches to examine mental models:

- The knowledge-based approach,
- The logical-reasoning approach.

The **knowledge-based approach** is based on domain-specific and knowledge-rich domains. This approach describes knowledge, which bolsters thinking and understanding. In this context, A. B. Markman and D. Gentner (2001, p. 228) define mental models as representations of domains or situations that support understanding, reasoning, and prediction. Stressing that the knowledge-based approach uses the long-term view of knowledge representation, A. B. Markman and D. Gentner characterize these representations as "causal mental models" (2001, p. 229). J. R. Wilson and A. Rutherford (1989, p. 619) summarise this from the 'human factor' point of view as:

---

[3] Mental representation and internal representation are equivalent (M. Richardson & L. Ball, 2009). Therefore, they will be used interchangeably.

[4] Mental representation is a broad term, which includes different kinds of more specific concepts such as mental images, mental models, and propositions (M. Richardson & L. Ball, 2009). Misunderstandings occur if these concepts become interchangeable (T. B. Seiler, 2001a). As M. Richardson und L. Ball (2009) state, the term 'internal representation' is occasionally used as a synonym for mental representation, as well as for mental models. R. Klimoski and S. Mohammed (1994, p. 405) give a similar example for mental models and knowledge in general. One reason for their interchangeable use is their commonality when dealing with knowledge structures; these concepts describe different ways to manage knowledge and human thinking (M. De Vega, M. Marschark, M. J. Intons-Peterson, P. N. Johnson-Laird, & M. Denis, 1996, p. 221; R. Klimoski & S. Mohammed, 1994, p. 405).

> "... a mental model is a representation formed by a user of a system and/or task, based on previous experience as well as current observation, which provides most (if not all) of their subsequent system understanding and consequently dictates the level of task performance."

Various research examples for the domain-specific and knowledge-rich domain approach are given in the edited collection by Gentner and Stevens (1983), such as mechanistic mental models (J. de Kleer & J. Seely Brown, 1983) or mental models of electricity (D. Gentner & D. R. Gentner, 1983).

The **logical-reasoning approach** considers mental models as "an analog representation of a state of affairs that might be derived directly from perception, or indirectly from discourse" (S. J. Payne, 2003, p. 137). Here mental models are constructs from working-memory (D. Gentner, 2002; see also M. Richardson & L. Ball, 2009). According to A. B. Markman and D. Gentner (2001, p. 228) this approach is linked with the research of P. N. Johnson-Laird, which can be described as a logical-reasoning approach, which analyses the rational thinking of humans. In typical experiments, humans use syllogism to test their abilities to perform appropriate deductive reasoning. P. N. Johnson-Laird (1989, p. 488) defines a working definition of a mental model…

> "... as a representation of a body of knowledge----either long-term or short-term that meets the following conditions:
>
> 1. Its structure corresponds to the structure of the situation that it represents.
>
> 2. It can consist of elements corresponding only to perceptible entities, in which case it may be realized as an image, perceptual or imaginary. Alternatively it can contain elements corresponding to abstract notions; their significance depends crucially on the procedures for manipulating models."

Another definition, which focuses on the structure of mental models, is given by S. Mohammad, R. Klimoski and J. R. Rentsch (2000, p. 125). These authors define mental models as networks consisting of concepts and the relationships between them.

The difference between definitions given by P. N. Johnson-Laird (1989) and S. Mohammad et al. (2000, p. 125) on the one hand, and A. B. Markman and D. Gentner (2001, p. 228) and J. R. Wilson and A. Rutherford (1989, p. 619) on the other, is that the first research group stress a more structural-functional side, whereas the second research group stress the content. However, mental models contain both parts: They hold knowledge content such as domain-specific knowledge or logical-reasoning, and they organize knowledge in relation to content (S. S. Webber, G. Chen, S. C. Payne, S. M. Marsh, & S. J. Zaccaro, 2000, p. 308; S. Mohammed et al., 2010, p. 884). Because of both parts – structure and content – mental models are simplifications of understanding, explaining and predicting. Mental models can vary from simple mental ideas or images to complex abstract ideas or images (D. P. Spicer, 1998, p. 126). They form the framework in which decisions take place, according to the perception of individuals (J. Langan-Fox et al., 2004, p. 334).

In this thesis, mental models are defined in the tradition of the knowledge-based approach. The focus is on a person's mental models in specific-domains, such as strategic management, management accounting, and marketing. Simultaneously, the structure of a domain within mental models is important, especially when pertaining to shared knowledge. Shared knowledge has an important impact on communication and coordination processes (R. J. Stout et al., 1999, p. 61; see chapter 1.1). Therefore, even if the content knowledge of a domain, hence concepts, are the same among different people, the structure within the content, hence relationship between concepts, could be different. This would lead to different mental models, and consequently to less overlapping knowledge structures. J. Langan-Fox et al. (2004, p. 334) stated that mental models form the framework in which decisions take place. Hence, different mental models could lead to different decisions. However, this thesis takes another stance, which is the similarity of mental models, which includes the similarity of concepts, and the similarity of a structure between concepts. Therefore, attention is paid to the shared knowledge structures from different people.

Thus, the following definition of a mental model, based on these theories will be used here (R. Brühl & S. Buch, 2005, p.4):

> A mental model is an internal representation of a dynamic system, which is used by humans, to describe the system, to explain the function of the system and to predict future states of the system derived from experience and previous knowledge structures. Mental models include two parts of knowledge: one part is the domain of knowledge; the other part is the structure of the domain. The domain of knowledge and the structure of the domain are expressed in concepts and their relations.

Hence, mental models are explanations, which mediate between knowledge structures and reality (N. M. Seel, 1991). Therefore, considering the degree of freedom given to participants when eliciting mental models (see chapters 1.1 and 3.5.2), these will be called 'idiosyncratic mental models' in this thesis.

2.2.3.2. The Team Perspective: Team and Group, Team Mental Model, and Shared Mental Models

The nature of the subject matter in this thesis is inter-individual similarities in the form of shared knowledge. Therefore, the individual perspective must encompass team and group perspectives. Much research has been done about teams and groups (see e.g. J. E. McGrath, H. Arrow, & J. L. Berdahl, 2000; S. G. Cohen & D. E. Bailey, 1997; D. R. Forsyth, 2009; the reviews by S. W. J. Kozlowski & D. R. Ilgen, 2006; G. M. Wittenbaum & R. L. Moreland, 2008; G. Randsley de Moura, T. Leader, J. Pelletier, & D. Abrams, 2008). Teams contribute significantly to performance in organizations (M. Higgs, 2006a, pp. 79-80). Because of increased autonomy, participation, and taking responsibility for their work, teams produce and share knowledge, maximise organisational innovation, and their earnings (S. I. Tannenbaum, E. Salas, & J. A. Cannon-Bowers, 1996, p. 504; S. Harvey, B. Millett, & D. Smith, 1998, p. 3; J. A. Cannon-Bowers & E. Salas, 1997; E. Salas, D. E. Sims, & C. S. Burke, 2005, pp. 555-556).

However, both terms **'teams' and 'groups'** are discussed in the literature, and they are often used interchangeably (see for instance S. G. Cohen & D. E. Bailey, 1997, p. 241). Sometimes, definitions of teams and groups are similar (see for instance Gibson's definition of groups when referring to McGrath and the definition of teams given by S. Harvey et al., 1998, p. 2; C. B. Gibson, 2001, p. 122; J. E. McGrath, 1984). Instead, explicit distinctions, based on general or specific characteristics, or different applications to social and organisational forms, are made to distinguish both terms. Examples are roles, responsibility, task-relevant knowledge, task interdependencies, common and valued goals, and communication (see J. A. Cannon-Bowers et al., 1993, p. 222; C. R. Paris, E. Salas, & J. A. Cannon-Bowers, 2000, p. 1052 f.; M. T. Brannick & C. Prince, 1997, p. 4). J. R. Katzenbach and D. K. Smith (1993, p. 113) state, for instance, that a team's performance is directly measurable by assessing collective work products, whereas in groups the work is delegated and therefore only measurable indirectly because of the influence of other features, such as financial performance. However, the term 'team' is often used in the context of team mental models or shared mental models. A team is defined as "...a group of two or more individuals who must interact cooperatively and adaptively in pursuit of shared valued objectives" (J. A. Cannon-Bowers et al., 1993, p. 222; similar E. Salas et al., 2005, pp. 559 / 562). Therefore, teams interact and change themselves in an organizational context across a specific period (D. R. Ilgen, J. R. Hollenbeck, M. Johnson, & D. Jundt, 2005, p. 519). Although there is a long history of research about small groups (see especially the article by J. E. McGrath, 1984; J. E. McGrath et al., 2000; J. E. McGrath, 1991), in this thesis, the term 'team' is preferred. A team is defined in a manner consistent with Cannon-Bowers et al. (1993) and Ilgen et al. (2005):

> A team is a group of at least two individuals who interact cooperatively across a specific period to reach a common goal.

Additionally, it should be noticed that the term 'group' is used in this thesis

> on a methodical basis to describe several teams with common qualities. Hence, a group includes several teams, who do not interact, but have the same homogeneous or heterogeneous attributes for example.

Several authors discuss the concepts **'team mental models', and 'shared mental models'** (see for instance J. Langan-Fox, A. Wirth, S. Code, K. Langfield-Smith, & A. Wirth, 2001; R. Klimoski & S. Mohammed, 1994). Both are based on individual mental models. For instance, Langan-Fox et al. (2004, p. 335) define a team mental model as "...the extent of overlap in the mental models of individual team members...". S. Mohammed et al. (2000, p. 125) describe team mental models as a shared mental representation, as well as an understanding of key elements of the team's surroundings (S. Mohammed et al., 2010, p. 877). It is important to realise that different degrees of sharing and overlapping exist between individual mental models (S. Mohammed et al., 2000, p. 125; see chapter 3.8). Additionally, team mental models have a special purpose in the same way as mental models. Team mental models are used to describe and to explain the function of systems. In addition, team mental models have a social aspect. They enable team members to predict expectations, and to adapt to the team task and to other team members. Therefore, team mental models influence the team processes and the team performance (B. D. Edwards, E. A. Day, W. Arthur, & S. T. Bell, 2006, p. 727; S. Mohammed et al., 2010, p. 879).

Shared mental models are defined by J. A. Cannon-Bowers et al. (1993, p. 228)

> "... as knowledge structures held by members of a team that enable them to form accurate explanations and expectations for the task, and, in turn, to coordinate their actions and adapt their behaviour to demands of the task and other team members."

At first, there seems to be no differences between the understanding of shared mental models as defined by J. A. Cannon-Bowers et al. (1993), and team mental models as defined above. Based on this comparison, team mental models and shared mental models are the same, and they can be used interchangeably (see for instance S. S. Webber et al., 2000, p. 308). However, in their definition, J. Langan-Fox et al. (2001, p. 99) apply shared mental models to two individuals. They describe shared mental models as "...the extent to which a dyad of individuals possesses a similar cognitive representation of some situation or phenomenon" (J. Langan-Fox et al., 2001, p. 99; see also R. Klimoski & S. Mohammed, 1994, p. 414; J. Langan-Fox et al., 2004, p. 335). Besides, J. Langan-Fox et al. (2001, p. 99) stated, that a team mental model "refers to shared cognition in a team as a collectivity, not shared cognition among dyads of individuals". This definition is problematic if a team is defined as two (= dyad), or more persons as J. A. Cannon-Bowers et al. (1993) do. However, after consideration of R. Klimoski and S. Mohammed's (1994, p. 426) view of the team mental model, one possible difference appears, the individual versus group perspective of shared knowledge elicitation. J. Langan-Fox et al. (2001, p. 99) stress in their definition of shared mental models that the individual possesses similar cognitive representation. R. Klimoski and S. Mohammed (1994, p. 426) stress that team mental models are an "emergent characteristic of the group, which is more than just the sum of individual models". This leads to the assumption, that team mental models are overlapping cognitive structures, based on the individual mental models during, or after, the occurrence of team interaction. Therefore, the social part has an impact on the individual mental model. However, shared mental models are overlapping cognitive structures among individuals, without any team interaction. Based on this view, team mental models are related to the holistic approach of eliciting shared knowledge, and shared mental models to the collective approach of eliciting shared knowledge (see chapter 3.6). This distinction should be maintained when referring to the measurement approach of shared knowledge.

Thus, the following definition of a team mental model based on this will be used in this thesis:

Team mental models are based on idiosyncratic mental models. They are shared mental representations and understandings about key elements of the teams' relevant environment, and enable team members to predict the expectations as team members, to adapt to the team task and to other team members. They describe the extent of overlap in the idiosyncratic mental models.

Additionally, the term 'team mental model' will be used in this thesis

on a theoretical basis as a concept to describe overlapping cognitive structures at a team level,

on a methodical basis as a concept, referring to the holistic approach of eliciting shared knowledge (see chapter 3.6).

The term 'shared mental model' will be used in this thesis

on a methodical basis as a concept, referring to the collective approach of eliciting shared knowledge (see chapter 3.6).

2.2.3.3. Purpose of Mental Models and Team Mental Models

There are different model classifications (see for instance Normans`, 1983, model classification in the context of human-computer interaction, or Cannon-Bowers et al., 1993, model classification in context of team mental models). W. B. Rouse and N. M. Morris (1986, p. 350 f.) state that the development of a taxonomy of mental models is influenced by two components. One component is the background of the researcher (for example computer science, engineering, or psychology). The other component is the domain, which is being researched (for example system design, problem solving in physics, or making value judgments). This thesis is based on a psychological-management view (background), and it focusses on shared knowledge (domain). In other words, the objective of this thesis is to analyse idiosyncratic mental models in terms of their similarities; the research is methodologically based. Researching mental models starts in study I with the research field of cause-and-effect relationships in management (see chapter 4.1.1). Cause-and-effect relationships have the structure 'A $\rightarrow$ B'. This structure corresponds to concepts, and the linkage between concepts. Hence, mental models can have similar structures (see below). Therefore, using the definition of mental models given in chapter 2.2.3.1, mental models will be classified based on

- the content knowledge of the domain, hence the concepts, and
- the structure within the content, hence the relationships between concepts.

Mental models and team mental models are often defined in a **domain specific manner** (see J. A. Cannon-Bowers & E. Salas, 1997, p. 161; L. L. Levesque, J. M. Wilson, & D. R. Wholey, 2001, p. 135, and for instance the taxonomy by J. Rasmussen, 1986, p. 15). One reason for this is the assumption that humans can have various mental models at a time (J. A. Cannon-Bowers et al., 1993; R. Klimoski & S. Mohammed, 1994; L. L. Levesque et al., 2001; Johnson-Laird, 1985, cit. D. P. Spicer, 1998). In a team mental model context, J. A. Cannon-Bowers et al. (1993, p. 232 f.; see also J. A. Cannon-Bowers & E. Salas, 2001, p. 197) differentiate between four types of mental models: equipment model, task model, team interaction model and team model. They assume that these model types are useful for effective team performance. Equipment models include knowledge about features and limits of the equipment, and the implementation processes. The authors assume that equipment models are robust, because of the transfer of the interaction between operator and system to other situations. Task models include knowledge about environmental limits, procedures, task-related strategies, and actions. Based on the consideration that situational parameters differ between different tasks, leading to different operations, the task model is more unstable compared to the equipment model. The team interaction model includes knowledge about roles and responsibilities of the team members, as well as knowledge about communication channels, and role dependencies. This model is changeable in the same way as the task model, because of the dynamic in the roles, and responsibilities of the task. The team model includes knowledge, which helps the members to understand the idiosyncrasies of their team. It includes knowledge about skills, preferences, and ability, and it helps to "compensate for one another, predict each other's action, provide information before being asked and allocate resources according to member expertise" (J. A. Cannon-Bowers & E. Salas, 2001, p. 197). Because of the dependency on team members, tasks, and situations, this model is less robust when compared to the other three models.

The four types of models by J. A. Cannon-Bowers et al. (1993) are dependent. Further, this classification is not empirically validated (K. A. Smith-Jentsch et al., 2005, p. 524). Usually one or two of these dimensions are analysed by studying the effect on the efficiency of teams (see e.g. M. A. Marks, M. J. Sabella, C. S. Burke, & S. J. Zaccaro, 2002; J. E. Mathieu, T. S. Heffner, G. F. Goodwin, E. Salas, & J. A. Cannon-Bowers, 2005; B.-C. Lim & K. J. Klein, 2006; A. P. Banks & L. J. Millward, 2007). Anyway, this classification creates a possibility to analyse shared knowledge. Because this thesis focuses on the development of an aggregation method of idiosyncratic mental models to team mental models, only one view, the task view, will be used here.

The **structure of mental models** refers to the relationship between concepts. Two aspects of the structure carry the information. Firstly, it is the meaningful 'spatial arrangement' of concepts. This means the form by which concepts are arranged in the idiosyncratic mental models. Secondly, it is the value of the connections between concepts. The first applies mainly to hierarchical-structured mental models (see Figure 7, p. 30), where concepts are structured with a meaningful principle or ranking (see below). The second, the value of the connection, refers to the rule system, which relates the concepts to each other (see below).

Figure 7: Example of a Hierarchical-Structured Mental Model

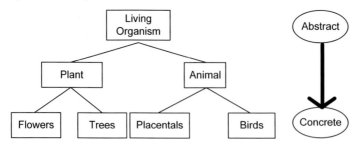

In hierarchical-structured mental models, principles for the arrangement vary in their purpose. Principles can be hierarchical positions, degree of importance, sequences, or degree of abstractness of the concepts. Figure 7 shows an example of abstractness of concepts with the more abstract or broader concepts placed at the top, and the more concrete or less inclusive concepts below them (J. D. Novak & D. B. Gowin, 1984, p. 15). This example is structured vertically in the form of a pyramid (see, for instance, also figure 4-1 by T. Mandl, 2000,

p. 38). However, the pattern could also be structured in the form of a decision tree (see, for instance, figure 4 by Y. G. Ji, 2001, p. 140). Another example showing the importance of the order of concepts is given in the study by M. A. Marks et al. (2000, p. 976, figure 2) where nomothetic concept maps of three team members in the form of a network structure are compared.

In strategic management, hierarchical structuring is important in order to understand how strategists view the competitive environment (A. S. Huff, 1990, pp. 23-25). That means:

> "Monitoring, adapting to, and pre-empting rivals that managers first assess interorganizational similarities and then distinguish between organizational friends and foes." (J. F. Porac & H. Thomas, 1994, p. 54);

In other words, hierarchical structuring helps to separate similarities and differences between competitors (A. Ginsberg, 1994, p. 166). With a hierarchical classification, different abstraction levels carry different degrees of information (see for instance E. Rosch, C. B. Mervis, W. D. Gray, D. M. Johnson, & P. Boyes-Braem, 1976a; see also chapter 4.5.1.2). Classification leads to a decrease in environmental complexity. An example of a study about hierarchical classification in strategic management research is shown by J. F. Porac, H. Thomas and B. Emme (1987, cit. Huff, 1990, p. 25; see also J. F. Porac & H. Thomas, 1994).

Concepts in non-hierarchical mental models are not ranked clearly. The concepts are equal and not ordered, and lack ranking. This implies that the connections between the concepts, such as arrows or lines with qualitative notations, carry mainly the information about the relationships (see for instance figure 1 by B. Vandenbosch & C. A. Higgins, 1996, p. 204). They are the key to reading and understanding the models.

In this thesis, participants will get a range of rules and different values for connecting concepts. Therefore, participants have a lot of freedom in structuring their mental models. Hence, there is no explicit rule about the way in which idiosyncratic mental models can be ordered. This thesis does not focus on hierarchical structure.

This chapter has outlined the theoretical underpinning of knowledge, shared knowledge constructs, as well as mental models, and team mental model constructs. It started with an introduction to different approaches to research in knowledge and shared knowledge. They are researched by way of an outline of the Structure Genesis Approach, which explains the emergence of knowledge and its development by individuals. The basic constructs 'knowledge' and 'shared knowledge' are defined using the Structure Genesis Approach. Knowledge refers to the individual perspective. It is defined as depending upon personal experience and previous knowledge, and results in different cognitive representations. Shared knowledge refers to the team level, and it is based on the individual's knowledge. It is defined as overlapping cognitive structures in the sense of common knowledge.

Because of the breadth of the knowledge and shared knowledge constructs, specific constructs for its operation are used. The more specific constructs used in this thesis are mental models and team mental models, which are called mediator constructs (chapter 2.2.3). Mental models are one kind of cognitive representation. They are the mediators between knowledge and the real world. Mental models include domain knowledge, and they are able to build up the structure of the domain. This property is important for understanding shared knowledge, because different structures of the content of the domain could lead to different decisions (see chapters 2.2.3.1 and 4.1.1). This property also makes mental models interesting for the research into cause-and-effect relationships (see chapter 4.1.1). Mental models are able to adopt the same structure as cause-and-effect relationships. Team mental models are based on individual models in the same way as shared knowledge. They are defined as the extent to which the individual mental models overlap. Taxonomies of mental models and team mental models are given, based on the definition of basic constructs and mediator constructs. The following section describes the methodical basis for measuring shared knowledge (see Figure 1, p. 8, square 'methodical bases').

3. Research Methodology

3.1. Research Paradigm

"What is most fundamental is the research question---research methods should follow research questions in a way that offers the best chance to obtain useful answers." (B. R. Johnson & A. J. Onwuegbuzie, 2004, pp. 17-18)

The research paradigm in this thesis uses a 'mixed method' approach (for the different meanings of paradigm see D. L. Morgan, 2007; D. M. Mertens, 2003). Mixed methods philosophy is pragmatism (see R. B. Johnson, A. J. Onwuengbuzie, & L. A. Turner, 2007, p. 113; J. W. Creswell & A. Tashakkori, 2007, p. 305), which is practical and applied,

> "...deconstructive paradigm that debunks concepts such as "truth"... and focuses instead on "what works" as the truth regarding the research questions..." (A. Tashakkori & C. Teddlie, 2003c, p. 713)

Pragmatism supports the use of qualitative and quantitative research, as well as eclecticism and pluralism, and rejects the choice between reasoning strategies (inductive, abductive, and deductive, see chapter 3.3). The research question dominates the methods and the paradigm. Therefore, the goal, rather than the source, is important (A. Tashakkori & C. Teddlie, 2003a, p. 75; C. Teddlie & A. Tashakkori, 2003, p. 21; A. Tashakkori & C. Teddlie, 1998, pp. 22-30; S. J. Maxcy, 2003, p. 75; B. R. Johnson & A. J. Onwuegbuzie, 2004, pp. 17-18, see this also for an outline of the general characteristics of pragmatism Table 1, p. 18).

The term 'mixed method' describes the use in qualitative and quantitative approaches of two types of

- research questions,
- sampling procedures,
- data (such as numbers and words),
- data collection techniques,
- data analysis procedures (such as statistical based or thematic based) and/or
- conclusion (such as objective and subjective)

(A. Tashakkori & J. W. Creswell, 2007, p. 4). Hence, the term 'mixed method' is used both in theoretical and practical sense. Firstly, it refers to the methods by which qualitative and quantitative data are collected and analysed (see chapter 3.2 Research Design Strategies). Secondly, it describes the methodology in terms of the integration of qualitative and quantitative research (A. Tashakkori & J. W. Creswell, 2007, p. 3; see also J. W. Creswell, R. Shope, V. L. P. Clark, & D. O. Green, 2006). This chapter is about the methodology.

J. W. Creswell and A. Tashakkori (2007) describe four different, but not mutually exclusive, perspectives for the mixed method approach. The first perspective focuses on the development and use of strategies for eliciting, analysing, and interpreting different qualitative and quantitative data. This is called the 'method perspective', and combines at least one quantitative and one qualitative method in a mixed-method design (J. C. Greene, V. J. Caracelli, & W. F. Graham, 1989, p. 256). Scientists, who support this perspective stress the independence of paradigms and qualitative and quantitative methods (J. C. Greene et al., 1989, p. 256; J. W. Creswell & A. Tashakkori, 2007, p. 304): Mixed method "...is a clean approach, untangled with philosophy and paradigms" (J. W. Creswell & A. Tashakkori, 2007, p. 304). This first perspective is criticised because of its oversimplification of qualitative and quantitative data types and collection techniques (J. W. Creswell & A. Tashakkori, 2007, p. 304).

The second perspective is methodological. Scientists, who support this perspective stress that method and paradigm are not separate. The method is part of the paradigm (J. W. Creswell & A. Tashakkori, 2007, p. 304). Hence, the design of mixed method research incorporates both methodology and method (J. W. Creswell et al., 2006, p. 1). The term 'methodology' refers to the philosophical underpinning and the basic assumptions of research. 'Methods' are techniques of data collection and analysis with quantitative and qualitative instruments. The research design is a strategy, which links the methodology and methods. The purpose for combining qualitative and quantitative methods is a better understanding of the research subject (J. W. Creswell & V. L. Plano Clark, 2007, pp. 4-5). Methodological perspective is criticised because both qualitative and quantitative approaches cannot be mixed easily, because they are both underpinned by different paradigms (J. W. Creswell & A. Tashakkori, 2007, p. 305). Both methods could lead to different possible outcomes (see for instance J. Brannen, 2005, p. 176; C. Erzberger & U. Kelle, 2003, p. 466; U. Kelle & C. Erzberger, 2005, pp. 304-307).

The third perspective about the mixed method approach, the paradigm perspective, is concerned with the philosophical assumption of the research, such as

"...what knowledge warrants our attention, how knowledge is learned, the nature of reality and values, and also the historical and sociopolitical perspectives that individuals bring to research." (J. W. Creswell & A. Tashakkori, 2007, p. 305).

The last, the practice perspective, relates to the use of mixed methods as a necessity for the on-going research process. Mixed methods are used to conduct research in the most comfortable perspectives for the researcher (J. W. Creswell & A. Tashakkori, 2007, p. 306).

This thesis takes a preference for the method perspective. Different strategies for eliciting and analysing qualitative and quantitative data will be used for the development of the methodological approach to aggregate idiosyncratic mental models to determine similarity and differences.

As a basis for defining mixed methods, R. B. Johnson et al. (2007) have analysed the definitions used by different researchers. They found five themes that were part of definitions (see for the following R. B. Johnson et al., 2007, pp. 118-123). The first investigates the meaning of 'mixed' in quantitative and qualitative research (see for instance the definition by H. Chen in R. B. Johnson et al., 2007, p. 119). The second questions "when or where in the design mixing is carried out ..." (p. 122), such as during the data collection, and/or data analysis stage (see, for instance, the definition by U. Kelle in R. B. Johnson et al., 2007, p. 120). The third describes the breadth of mixed research from mixed data collection to other variables (see for instance the definition by J. Creswell in R. B. Johnson et al., 2007, p. 119; R. B. Johnson and A. J. Onwuegbuzie in R. B. Johnson et al., 2007, p. 120). The fourth concentrates on the reasons why mixed research is carried out. They are, for instance, to produce more consistent and valid findings, to validate and explicate findings from other approaches, and to offer richer more meaningful and more useful answers to research questions (see also the definition by J. C. Greene et al., 1989, pp. 258-260; U. Kelle in R. B. Johnson et al., 2007, p. 120; for a typology of research purposes I. Newman, C. S. Ridenour, C. Newman, & G. M. P. DeMarco, Jr., 2003). The last refers to the orientation of mixed method research, such as a 'bottom-up' approach (where research questions drive the mixed method approach) or a 'top-down' approach (where mixed method approach is driven by the researchers' quest to conduct research). For an example of the top-down approach see the definition by D. Mertens in R. B. Johnson et al. (2007, p. 119).

Based on their analysis, R. B. Johnson et al. (2007, p. 123) offer a general definition of mixed method research as

> "...the type of research in which a researcher or team of researchers combines elements of qualitative and quantitative research approaches (e.g., use of qualitative and quantitative viewpoints, data collection, analysis, inference techniques) for the broad purposes of breadth and depth of understanding and corroboration."

Additionally, they distinguish between qualitative dominant mixed approach, pure mixed approach, and quantitative dominant mixed approach. The qualitative dominant research paradigm fits research projects, which are 'naturally' qualitative, but where quantitative features are included. Researchers conducting a pure mixed approach refer to the strategy of reasoning and philosophy of mixed method research. Quantitative and qualitative approaches are equally valid, and both contribute to the research. The quantitative dominant research paradigm fits studies, which are 'naturally' quantitative, but where qualitative features are included in the research process (R. B. Johnson et al., 2007, pp. 123-124).

This thesis follows a qualitative dominant research paradigm. The focus is on the development of an aggregation approach, in the manner of research into idiosyncratic mental models, their concepts, their relationships, and their similarity. Hence, the subject of this thesis is 'naturally' qualitative. Quantitative aspects of strategies for eliciting, aggregating, and analysing concepts and their relationships are used to gain deeper insights into the development process of the aggregation method.

3.2. Research Design Strategies

A. Tashakkori and C. Teddlie (1998, pp. 17-19) distinguish three major design strategies: 'monomethod studies', 'mixed method studies', and 'mixed model studies'. 'Monomethod studies' are conducted by researchers, who work within a quantitative or qualitative approach. The term 'mixed method study' refers to 'one research unit' or research process, which consists of one research question, a data collection stage, a data analysis stage, and an inference stage. It combines different quantitative and qualitative methods via triangulation techniques, and includes different design strategies (A. Tashakkori & C. Teddlie, 1998, pp. 17-19). Triangulation is the combination of several methods applied in a specific way, to exclude the weakness of the methods, and in order to strengthen the validity of the results (J. C. Greene et al., 1989, p. 256). An often cited taxonomy of triangulation is Denzins taxonomy (1970, cit. P. Downward & A. Mearman, 2007, p. 80; Denzin, 1978, cit. A. Tashakkori & C. Teddlie, 1998, p. 41). Denzins taxonomy refers to the combination of different data resources to analyse the same phenomenon (see chapter 3.4, A. Tashakkori & C. Teddlie, 1998, p. 41. For the different types of triangulation see, for instance, A. Tashakkori & C. Teddlie, 1998, p. 41; P. Downward & A. Mearman, 2007, p. 81; R. B. Johnson et al., 2007, p. 114).

The term 'mixed model study' refers to the combination of several 'research units'. The research process is a combination of different research questions, data collection and analysis stages and different inference stages in the following ways (A. Tashakkori & C. Teddlie, 1998, pp. 17-19, A. J. Onwuegbuzie & R. B. Johnson, 2006, p. 53; A. Tashakkori & C. Teddlie, 2003b):

- Concurrent
- Sequential
- Parallel

- Fully mixed
- Conversion

Meta-inference concludes the mixed model studies (compare Figures 26.5 until 26.10 in A. Tashakkori & C. Teddlie, 2003b, pp. 688-689).

In **concurrent mixed method design**, one research question is directed simultaneously to the quantitative and qualitative method approach (A. Tashakkori & C. Teddlie, 2003b, p. 686). Quantitative and qualitative data will be collected, analysed separately at the same time, and consolidated later for inference (A. J. Onwuegbuzie & R. B. Johnson, 2006, p. 53; A. Tashakkori & C. Teddlie, 2003b, p. 686; A. J. Onwuegbuzie & N. L. Leech, 2004, p. 780).

In **concurrent mixed model design**, two research questions are directed simultaneously towards one approach. Quantitative and qualitative data will be collected, analysed, interpreted separately at the same time, and consolidated later for meta-inference (Figure 26.6 in A. Tashakkori & C. Teddlie, 2003b, p. 688).

Sequential mixed method design is aimed at one research question. It starts with collecting and analysing one data type, for instance qualitative data. Depending upon the result of this stage, the quantitative data will be collected and analysed. Afterwards both results will be consolidated for inference (A. Tashakkori & C. Teddlie, 2003b, p. 687, see especially Figure 26.7, p. 688; A. J. Onwuegbuzie & R. B. Johnson, 2006).

Sequential mixed model design works in a similar way. Sequential design starts with collecting and analysing one data type. Depending on the inference at this stage, a second question will be directed to the second data type, including data collection, analysis, and interpretation. Based on both inferences, a meta-inference will be made for consolidation (Figure 26.6 in A. Tashakkori & C. Teddlie, 2003b, p. 688).

In **parallel mixed designs**, quantitative and qualitative data will be collected, analysed, and interpreted separately. Each source of data leads to its own inferences. The results will not be consolidated, as they are in concurrent designs (A. J. Onwuegbuzie & R. B. Johnson, 2006, p. 53).

Fully mixed designs are aimed at multiple research questions. Qualitative and quantitative aspects will be mixed during each step of the research process, during the collection, analysing, and/or inference stages. Afterwards, both inferences will be consolidated to meta-inference. Therefore, each stage influences the conceptualisation of the other approach (A. J. Onwuegbuzie & R. B. Johnson, 2006, p. 53; A. Tashakkori & C. Teddlie, 2003b, pp. 689-690).

Conversion mixed method designs focus on one research question. One data type will be collected using one method, for instance qualitative data (A. Tashakkori & C. Teddlie, 2003b, pp. 688-689; A. J. Onwuegbuzie & R. B. Johnson, 2006, p. 53). These data will be transformed into the other data type, for instance, qualitative data will be transformed into quantitative data. Afterwards both kind of data will be analysed separately (see Figure 26.9, A. Tashakkori & C. Teddlie, 2003b, p. 689) and then consolidated for a conclusion.

Conversion mixed model design refers to two research questions, one data collection stage, but with separate data analysis stages, and separate inferences. At the end of the process, both inferences will be consolidated again. According to A. Tashakkori and C. Teddlie (1998, pp. 128-130) both directions of data transformation are possible: qualitative data into quantitative data and vice versa. I do not agree with A. Tashakkori and C. Teddlie (1998, pp. 128-130) about this point. Transformation of data refers to a change in the level of data abstraction. Qualitative data (e.g. verbal) are changed into quantitative data (numerical) in another level of abstraction. However, during this transformation, qualitative data lose part of their meaning. A core of information will be preserved. The information of qualitative data is condensed; the data changes its shape but condenses the core information. A transformation of quantitative into qualitative data is not possible, because abstract figures cannot be assigned to meaning diversity (H. Witt, 2001, p. 2). Further discussion is possible as to whether the proposed transformation of quantitative data into qualitative categories, as suggested by A. Tashakkori and C. Teddlie (1998, pp. 128-130), is a transformation in the sense described above.

Research design in this thesis is a combination of sequential mixed model design, parallel mixed method design, conversion mixed method design, and conversion mixed model design. Idiographic-qualitative, idiographic-quantitative, nomothetic-qualitative and nomothetic-quantitative methods were triangulated during data collection stages and/or data analysis stages. 'Idiographic' and 'nomothetic' refer to different degrees of freedom, which participants had during the research process (see chapter 3.5). 'Qualitative' and 'quantitative' refer to the data type (words / numbers). Qualitative methods produce word-based data, which were analysed with qualitative word-based analysis methods in an interpretative way. Quantitative methods produced numerical data, which were analysed with statistical techniques (see chapter 3.5). Additionally, qualitative data were also analysed with quantitative methods, and therefore transformed into quantitative data.

During the data collection for study I, Structure-Formation-Technique was used, which included idiographic-qualitative and nomothetic-qualitative parts (see Figure 8, p. 40). Hence, idiosyncratic mental models were produced. The content of the mental models, hence the concepts, are produced idiographically; the structure between concepts was produced nomothetically because all participants received the same rules for the structuring process[5]. Both content and structure are qualitative, because their value is word based, not numerical. The same procedure was used for studies III, IV and V. Additionally in study III, a nomothetic-quantitative method was used. Participants were asked, with a standardised questionnaire, about the perceived teamwork. In study V, a nomothetic-quantitative and -qualitative questionnaire was used. Participants were asked about their preferences and opinions, for instance.

The data collection in study II is different. There, no data was collected. The purpose of study II was to aggregate the collected data of study I. Hence, the combination of study I and study II refers to a conversion mixed model design. In study II, the idiographic-qualitative data of study I were aggregated into further qualitative data. Afterwards, these data were analysed with idiographic-quantitative and idiographic-qualitative methods using a parallel mixed method design.

In all studies, data were analysed with idiographic-qualitative methods and idiographic-quantitative methods. Idiographic-qualitative methods were word-based; referring to the concepts used and related words. Idiographic-quantitative methods were frequency-based, referring to these concepts and related words.

Nomothetic-quantitative frequency analysis using chi^2-analysis (see, for instance, J. Bortz & C. Schuster, 2010) was used in study I referring to the frequency of cause-and-effect relationships. This frequency was transformed into quantitative data. This transformation uses a conversion mixed method design. In study III, a teamwork questionnaire was analysed in a nomothetic-quantitative way by ranking the extent to which items of the participants coincide. Study III was conducted as a parallel mixed model design. In study V, nomothetic-quantitative analysis described the sample and its evaluation, in terms of teamwork and different rule systems. In studies II and IV, the analysis concentrated on qualitative data only.

The objective of this thesis is to analyse idiosyncratic mental models in terms of similarity. Referring to different research unit steps (research question, data collection, data analysis, and inference stages; see above), data aggregation is an important and necessary step before the analysing stage. Aggregation of idiosyncratic mental models was done using the meaning relation tool. The meaning relation tool was developed during the different studies. Therefore, the process of developing this aggregation method is sequentially based.

---

[5] At this point, it would be correct to name the mental models as idiographic-nomothetic-mixed. However, it should be stressed that the content of the mental models is individual. During the Approach B, the analysis of nomothetic structure, hence the cause-and-effect relations, does not play a primarily role anymore (for reasons see chapter 4.3). Therefore, the term idiosyncratic mental models will be continued to be used.

Figure 8: Research Design Strategy

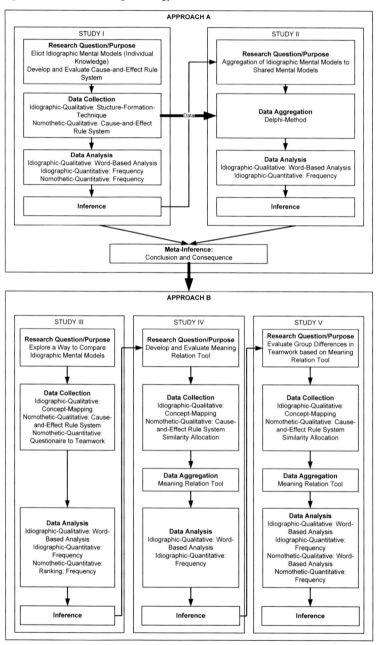

A Summary of the Performance of Conceptualisation

Sequential mixed model design: A sequential design is used when referring to the mixed model design, hence the combination of the different research studies. Each follow-up study starts with a new research question, which is based on the results and inferences of the earlier study. Comparing the relationship of both approaches, Approach B was developed because of the results and inferences of Approach A. This is, by definition, also sequential.

Conversion mixed model design: Approach A was conducted as a conversion mixed model design. Both studies started with their own research questions. In the second study, the data of the first study were used for the aggregation and analysis using qualitative and quantitative analysing methods.

Parallel mixed method design: Study III was conducted as a parallel mixed method design. During the data collection stage, a standardized questionnaire (nomothetic-quantitative) and concept mapping (nomothetic-qualitative: cause-and-effect rule system; idiographic-qualitative: idiosyncratic concepts) were used. The results of the (nomothetic-quantitative) questionnaire were analysed by ranking. The results of the qualitative data collection part were analysed with idiographic-qualitative word-based analysis and idiographic-quantitative frequency analysis.

Conversion mixed method design: In studies I, III, IV, and V idiographic-qualitative data were transformed into quantitative data for separate analysis procedures. This process uses a conversion mixed method design.

3.3. Strategy of Reasoning

"Reasoning is the ability to make inferences" (F. Portoraro, 2007)

Inductive, abductive, and deductive are different approaches of reasoning. They differ in starting points, steps in the reasoning process, and conclusion points (N. W. H. Blaikie, 2000, p. 24 f.). These strategies are linked differently in the context of discovery and the context of justification (R. Brühl, 2006, p. 182).

Induction starts with empirical data collection. It endeavours to generalise for all cases when given data from some cases (see, for instance, R. Brühl, 2006, p. 183; S. Psillos, 2000, p. 59; N. Lachiche, 2000, p. 107; N. W. H. Blaikie, 2000, p. 25). It is the "inference of the rule from the case and the result" (I. Niiniluoto, 1999, p. S437). The inference is called "inductive logic" (N. W. H. Blaikie, 2000, p. 25). It extends the content, because not all cases are collected, but all cases are used for the conclusion. Therefore, there is still some uncertainty about finding some cases, which do not fit the conclusion (R. Brühl, 2006, p. 183).

If some cases are found which do not fit the conclusion, a few promising hypotheses are formulated to explain why this is so (R. Brühl, 2006, p. 183; N. Rescher, 1978, p. 42). This reasoning is called abduction. Abduction gets its information from observed cases and the background knowledge of the researcher (N. Lachiche, 2000, p. 108; R. Brühl, 2006, p. 183). It includes new knowledge based on creativity (R. Brühl, 2006, p. 184). Therefore, abduction is seen as reasoning which generates "testworthy" (I. Niiniluoto, 1999, p. S441) hypotheses, which could explain certain phenomena (S. Psillos, 2000, p. 59). However, abduction does not provide "support or justification to a hypothesis" (I. Niiniluoto, 1999, p. S441). Therefore, abduction is also seen as extending the content because not all possible hypotheses are generated. This means that there is still some uncertainty about a possible missing hypothesis, which could prove to be a significant fit (R. Brühl, 2006, p. 183).

Whereas induction and abduction are aimed at inferring hypotheses based on empirical data (N. Lachiche, 2000, p. 107), deductive reasoning is aimed at inferring results based on rules and cases (I. Niiniluoto, 1999, p. S437; see R. Brühl, 2006, p. 185). Deductive reasoning starts with theoretical assumptions, concepts, or known rules (N. W. H. Blaikie, 2000, p. 25; J. Reichertz, 2004, p. 279), from which hypotheses will be deduced (N. W. H. Blaikie, 2000, p. 25). Following this, empirical cases will be collected. They either conform to the hypotheses, and in turn to the theory, or they do not support the hypothesis and therefore do not support the theory. In that case, the theory has to adapted or rejected before testing new cases (N. W. H. Blaikie, 2000, p. 25). In this sense, no new knowledge will be included (J. Reichertz, 2004, p. 279).

The distinction between the context of discovery and the context of justification can be traced back to H. Reichenbach (1938), and it describes different stages of the research process (R. Brühl & S. Buch, 2006, p. 4). The context of discovery focuses on the development of hypotheses. Therefore, induction and abduction are usually associated with this context (R. Brühl, 2006, p. 182). The context of justification aims at testing hypotheses, and is therefore associated with deduction (R. Brühl, 2006, p. 182).

This thesis focuses on a method development to aggregate idiosyncratic mental models. Therefore, it is in the context of discovery. Nevertheless, the development of a method cannot work without a content specific problem. It starts with asking participants about the competitive situation of their firm. Here, an inductive strategy was chosen (see study I, chapter 4.1). Nevertheless, the strategy of reasoning will become an abductive strategy to test hypotheses in study V (chapter 4.6), deduced from empirical data of studies III and IV.

3.4. Quality Indices

"The curious public (or peer reviewer or funding source) deserves to know exactly how the qualitative researcher prepares him- or herself for the endeavor, and how data is collected and analyzed." (J. Kirk & M. L. Miller, 1986, p. 72).

In developing a methodological approach, it is important that it satisfies standards, which allow a statement to be made about the validity of the approach. Such standards are established for the quantitative orientated research paradigm: reliability, validity, and objectivity (see R. Brühl & S. Buch, 2006, see for the standards established books of quantitative research such as J. Bortz & N. Döring, 2006; G. A. Lienert & U. Raatz, 1998). From the perspective of Y. Lincoln and E. Guba (1985, p. 290), these criteria serve to generate trustworthiness for the research. Such established standards are missing in the qualitative-orientated research (see R. Brühl & S. Buch, 2006). However, the literature about qualitative methods discusses several criteria, which can be expanded as needed, rewritten, or reduced (see for instance A. Tashakkori & C. Teddlie, 1998, chapter 4; or the discussion of the characteristics of qualitative research by P. Mayring, 2002, pp. 24-39). Because this thesis has a methodological objective to develop an approach for the comparability of idiosyncratic mental models (see chapter 1.2), and is rooted in a qualitative dominant research paradigm (see chapter 3.1), the trustworthiness of the methodological approach will be generated mainly through the following criteria:

- Validity through triangulation,
- Transparency of research,
- Research economics,
- Credibility of the results through communicative validation,
- Content validity as an indicator for credibility and trustworthiness,
- Validity through consensus,
- Credibility and trustworthiness of the meaning relation tool through experimental validation.

Triangulation is the combination of several methods in a specific way to exclude the weakness of the methods, and in order to strengthen the validity of the results (J. C. Greene et al., 1989, p. 256; S. Lamnek, 2010, p. 142). An often cited taxonomy of triangulation is Denzins taxonomy (1970, cit. P. Downward & A. Mearman, 2007, p. 80; Denzin, 1978, cit. A. Tashakkori & C. Teddlie, 1998, p. 41), which refers to the combination of different data resources to analyse same phenomenon (A. Tashakkori & C. Teddlie, 1998, p. 41). Denzin distinguishes four types of triangulation: data triangulation, investor triangulation, theoretical triangulation and methodological triangulation. Data triangulation refers to the elicitation of different types of data sources at different times and situations. Investor triangulation refers to the use of different researchers to elicit and analyse data. Theoretical triangulation refers to the interpretation of results using different perspectives. Finally, methodological triangulation involves the combination of different methodical approaches for collecting data (A. Tashakkori & C. Teddlie, 1998, p. 41; P. Downward & A. Mearman, 2007, p. 81). Referring to methodological triangulation, Denzin also distinguishes between within-method triangulation and between-method triangulation (R. B. Johnson et al., 2007, p. 114; P. Downward & A. Mearman, 2007, p. 81). Within-method triangulation refers to the use of a variation of the same method; between-method triangulation refers to the use of different methods, such as qualitative and quantitative methods. In this thesis, nomothetic-qualitative and –quantitative as well as idiographic-qualitative and -quantitative analysis methods are used to interpret the results. This is linked to a theoretical triangulation (see Figure 8, p. 40).

Transparency is given through outlining and justifying specific methods in the different studies. Methods to collect knowledge structures, as well as methods to analyse the results, will be explained when considering the research objective. The process of the development of the aggregation approach is outlined in chapter 4.

Research economics is traditionally an ancillary quality index in quantitative research paradigm. Methods are economic if they are not time consuming, are easy to use, need little material, and are quick and easy to evaluate (G. A. Lienert & U. Raatz, 1998, p. 12). The approach to aggregate idiosyncratic mental models to team mental models should meet this standard, in order to keep the burden for both the researcher and the participants as low as possible.

In the **communicative validation**, the validity of the results is assessed through consensus building (S. Lamnek, 2010, pp. 139 / 682). The results are checked again by asking the participants to judge the validity and consistency of the results (S. Lamnek, 2010). This was applied mainly in Approach A. In a "weak version" (C. Seale, 1999, p. 62) of a member check, participants of study I were asked to comment on the accuracy of the concepts. These concepts were prepared by the interviewer (see chapter 4.1.3.8). In study II, one participant of study I was asked to validate the experts' categories. The objective was to evaluate the credibility of the expert categories, based on comparison with the participants' evaluation (see chapter 4.2.2.2.5).

Content validity is, as with research economics, traditionally an ancillary quality index in a quantitative research paradigm, where content validity is used to check whether the items cover all major aspects (see for instance, J. Bortz & N. Döring, 2006, p. 200; M. Amelang & W. Zielinski, 2002, p. 160 f.). However, in this thesis, content validity will be re-interpreted. Method development in the context of qualitative dominant research paradigm cannot work without content specific problems. One reason is the finality of the mental model construct (W. B. Rouse & N. M. Morris, 1986, chapter 2.2.3.1). Hence, content validity can be used as an indicator of the quality of the aggregation approach. The question, which will be asked, is "How clear are the aggregated results?" This validation was used, especially in Approach A, by looking for ambiguous results in the aggregated mental models.

Consensus is an important construct of the interpersonal validation. It is regarded as evidence of validity when several people can agree on the credibility and meaning of the data (J. Bortz & N. Döring, 2006, p. 328). In this thesis, consensus is an important aspect, especially in team mental model building. It is reflected in the team mental model as a result of the discussion of the task in the team stages (see Approach B, chapters 4.4, 4.5, and 4.6). Hence, the evidence of validity is linked to the meaning of team concepts. Therefore, it is assumed that participants are able to make judgements about the relationship between the meaning of the idiosyncratic concepts and team concepts (see chapter 4.5.1.2).

In this thesis, an indirect way of method validation was used: the **experimental validation**. The research in study V considered whether individuals and teams differ in their performance (see Figure 36, p. 181), and whether there was a change in concept numbers between individual stages and team stages (see Figure 35, p. 180). In an experimental design with different levels of the factor 'type of group', the meaning relation tool was used to reveal differences between the groups. Such differences would support a meaning relation tool as a tool to adjust interrelations. Therefore, meaning relations tool is a tool that supports an approach focussing on the aggregation of idiosyncratic knowledge structures, and the representation of group differences (see Approach B, particularly chapter 4.6).

3.5. Research Techniques in (Shared)-Knowledge Research

3.5.1. Object of Investigation and its Implications in this Thesis

Methods to elicit and represent knowledge are distinct from methods to analyse knowledge. Elicitation techniques refer to the customization of knowledge (L. A. DeChurch & J. R. Mesmer-Magnus, 2010a, p. 2). Knowledge, which is personal in character, is not measurable as long as people do not transfer this knowledge into shareable symbols and signs. It is important to recognize, that not every kind of knowledge is transferable into signs by participants (see chapter 2.2.2). Moreover, elicitation techniques, symbols, and signs are interdependent. Other methods are required to elicit action knowledge based on behaviour, as opposed to conceptual knowledge based on language. Hence, the elicitation methods have to be adequate to the object under investigation (D. Silverman, 1993).

The object of investigation is the cognitive representation in the form of mental models. It has been mentioned that mental models include domain knowledge, and the knowledge about the structure of the domain, which result in concepts and their relationship (see chapter 2.2.3). Consequently, research techniques concentrate on the elicitation of signs and symbols, in the shape of concepts and their relationships. No behavioural analysis about shared knowledge in terms of activities will be made.

It is assumed that conceptual knowledge will be expressed in language. Similar to G. Lakoff and M. Johnson (1999, p. 244) statement

"Simple Ideas Are Words

Complex Ideas Are Sentences"

in their chapter "The Thought As Language Metaphor" (1999, pp. 244-246), concepts in mental models represent simple conceptual knowledge, hence simple domain specific knowledge. Concepts and the structure between these concepts represent complex conceptual knowledge, hence complex domain specific knowledge. Concepts describe experiences and illustrate the idiosyncratic knowledge of humans (see chapter 2.2). Based on a thinking process, mental models will be elicited.

In accordance with the mental model construct in chapter 2.2.3, there are two forms of elicitation (see Figure 9, p. 47). The first focuses on the elicitation of the content, and uses methods such as open interviews, Likert-Scale questionnaires, and similarity ratings (S. Mohammed & B. C. Dumville, 2001, p. 91). The second focuses on the structure as well. This is usually a two-step-approach: first to elicit knowledge, and second to construct the structure. Here, different mixed approaches exist. One approach includes methods, which elicit both content and structure such as concept mapping. The second approach uses a separate method for each step, such as a similarity rating for the content, and a pathfinder for the structure. These methods are independent and changeable.

The method of analysis depends upon elicited data. For qualitative data such as words, analytical methods such as qualitative content analysis (P. Mayring, 2010) or grounded theory (A. L. Strauss & J. Corbin, 1994, 1998) are used. Quantitative, numerical data will be analysed using statistical methods based on a measurement scale and other criteria, such as sampling size. Attention should be paid to the fact, that it is possible to transform qualitative into quantitative data (e.g. categorical based), and via interrater judgements to a higher degree of measurability (R. Brühl & S. Buch, 2006). Transforming quantitative into qualitative data is not possible because of the condensed information in the quantitative data (H. Witt, 2001, p. 2; see also chapter 3.2).

Figure 9: Elicitation Methods

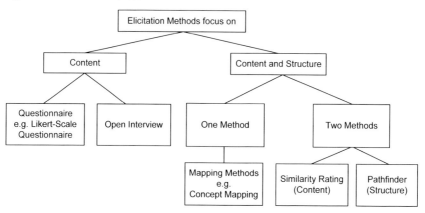

3.5.2. Nomothetic and Idiographic Mapping Methods

The distinction between nomothetic and idiographic is discussed in the context of the incompatibility of qualitative and quantitative approaches. In addition to other criteria such as deduction, explanation and measurement, 'nomothetic' is used to describe quantitative methods. Whereas, the term 'idiographic' is used in collaboration with other terms such as inductive, explorative, and descriptive in order to illustrate qualitative methods (see S. Lamnek, 2010, pp. 215-244; J. Bortz & N. Döring, 2006, pp. 298-302). Furthermore, all these terms are also used to distinguish between the context of justification and the context of discovery (R. Brühl & S. Buch, 2006; see chapter 3.3).

In fact, qualitative methods produce qualitative data, together with specific elicitation methods (for example interviews), which are analysed in an interpretative way (for example qualitative content analysis by P. Mayring, 2010). This encourages the discovery of phenomena rather than the testing of hypotheses (J. Bortz & N. Döring, 2006, p. 738). Quantitative methods produce, together with specific elicitation methods (for example questionnaires), quantitative (numerical) data, which are analysed with statistical techniques (for example ANOVA) to explore new effects on the one hand, and to test hypotheses on the other (J. Bortz & N. Döring, 2006, p. 738). Nevertheless, these distinctions are only tangential. Qualitative methods are used to test hypotheses, and quantitative methods are used to discover new phenomena (see mixed-methods concept, e.g. A. Tashakkori & C. Teddlie, 2003c; R. Brühl & S. Buch, 2006). Hence, the terms 'nomothetic' and 'idiographic' are ideal descriptions for methods, in which the participants have different degrees of freedom in the research process (G. W. Goodhew et al., 2005, p. 126). Idiographic methods, such as cognitive interviews, deal with the understanding of participants within a problem area. At this point, participants have the greatest influence on the research process. The possibility for participants to influence the research process in nomothetic methods is rather limited. Nomothetic methods are constrained by the researcher. A typical example of this is the questionnaire.

Because the term 'quantitative' is associated primarily with eliciting and analysing numeric material and 'qualitative' primarily with eliciting and analysing words, I will use the terms 'nomothetic' and 'idiographic' to stress the different degrees of freedom participants will have. This nomenclature is important because the participant will get a qualitative but nomothetic rule system during the different studies. The rule system is adapted from the Structure–Formation–Technique, which is a mapping method (see below and chapter 4.1.3.3). Therefore, the freedom for the participants to construct a structure, e.g. in form of cause-and-effect, is rather constrained in terms of given rules. However, participants will still have freedom to add missing rules. The concepts of the participants are idiographic, because participants use their own concepts for the construction process. Concepts and rule system have qualitative, concrete values. Therefore, the terms 'nomothetic' and 'idiographic' are better descriptions of the data type than the terms 'quantitative' and 'qualitative'.

There are many different kinds of mapping techniques. These techniques all have the structure of their results in common. M. Laukkanen (1994, p. 323) describes the structure for causal maps that are typical for mapping techniques:

> "The nodes stand for concepts, phenomena, which their owners, such as managers, subjectively seem to perceive in their domains. The arrows represent their beliefs about ... relationships among the phenomena." (M. Laukkanen, 1994, p. 323)

Differences arise from methodological implementation and from the context of the application.

A greater understanding of how the participants deal with a particular problem area is gained by using idiographic mapping techniques (Table 1, p. 49, row 1). Participants generate concepts (columns 2 and 3), and they construct the structure between these concepts themselves (column 4). Therefore, the constructed mental model is highly idiographic. It reflects the participant's view of the problem (column 5).

In nomothetic mapping techniques (Table 1, row 3), the researcher generates concepts by other sources, such as an expert's consultation (column 2). Therefore, if all participants receive the same concepts from the experts ("predefined categories" L. A. DeChurch & J. R. Mesmer-Magnus, 2010a, p. 5), these concepts are nomothetic (column 3). The structures of concepts could be created arithmetically (column 4). Based on similar judgements by participants of the concepts (column 5), computer programs, such as pathfinder, generate latent structures of the experience domain of participants (W. C. McGaghie, D. R. McCrimmon, G. Mitchell, & J. A. Thompson, 2004; T. E. Goldsmith, P. J. Johnson, & W. H. Acton, 1991; L. A. DeChurch & J. R. Mesmer-Magnus, 2010a, p. 5; see for instance the study by N. J. Cooke et al., 2007a, p. 152).

Table 1: Outline of Idiographic Mapping Methods, Mixed Form of Mapping Methods, and Nomothetic Mapping Methods

Row	Column				
	1	2	3	4	5
	Research Process Methods	Who Generates Concepts?	Concepts Are	Who Constructs the Structure Between Concepts?	Participants Focus on…
1	Idiographic	Participants	Idiographic	Participants	Generating concepts and structuring process
2	Mixed Form	Consultation of experts	Nomothetic	Participants	Structuring process
3	Nomothetic	Consultation of experts	Nomothetic	Computer program e.g. pathfinder	Similarity judgements of experts' concept

If participants create the structure by themselves (Table 1, column 4, row 2) based on the experts' concepts (column 2, row 2), or participants choose 'their' concepts out of a concept pool, this methodological approach would be a mixed form of idiographic and nomothetic methods (row 2). Concepts would still be nomothetic because participants did not generate them by themselves (columns 2 and 3, row 2).

Mapping methods are used in different contexts, and they differ in their purpose. Mind maps are used to build up cognitive associations. The structure has several branches. Starting from a central concept, mind mapping helps to restructure related concepts (see for instance T. Buzan & B. Buzan, 2005). Semantic networks represent information within texts, in the structure of networks (S.-P. Ballstaedt, H. Mandl, W. Schnotz, & S.-O. Tergan, 1981, p. 25). Other examples of mapping methods are concept mapping, cognitive mapping, and the Structure-Formation-Technique (see below).

Concept mapping is used in the context of educational psychology when describing meaningful learning (J. D. Novak & D. B. Gowin, 1984), and in the context of teamwork to study team mental models (S. Mohammed et al., 2000, p. 129; M. A. Marks et al., 2000; see e.g. the study by M. J. Pearsall, A. P. J. Ellis, & B. S. Bell, 2010). Concept mapping is used to externalize domain-specific knowledge. Concept maps symbolize meaningful relationships between concepts that are linked by words in a semantic unit (meaningful statements, M. Åhlberg, 2004, p. 1; W. Acar & D. Druckenmiller, 2006, p. 998). This unit is also called a proposition (J. D. Novak & D. B. Gowin, 1984, p. 15; M. A. Ruiz-Primo & R. J. Shavelson, 1996, p. 570). In a simple form, propositions include two concepts with one relationship (J. D. Novak & D. B. Gowin, 1984, p. 15; M. A. Ruiz-Primo & R. J. Shavelson, 1996, p. 570). Especially for meaningful learning, concept maps should have a hierarchical structure with broader concepts on the top, and concepts that are more concrete below them (see chapter 2.2.3.3). As mentioned in chapter 2.2.3.3, the hierarchical structure is also important in strategic management, in order to understand how strategists perceive similarities and differences between competitors (A. S. Huff, 1990, pp. 23-25; A. Ginsberg, 1994, p. 166).

Cognitive mapping is much more often used in management research. The label 'cognitive map' was first used by E. Toleman (1948, cit. P. B. Bell, T. C. Greene, J. D. Fisher, & A. Baum, 2001, p. 70; D. P. Spicer, 1998, p. 127), who described how rats had learned to map their environment (1948, cit. P. B. Bell et al., 2001; D. P. Spicer, 1998). Hence, the term 'cognitive map' stresses cognitive representations of environmental conditions (C. M. Fiol & A. S. Huff, 1992, p. 267). They may include different types of relationships. K. E. Weick and M. G. Bougon (2001, p. 311) specify relationships such as proximity, resemblance, and implications. Because of the environmental focus, cognitive mapping gained especially attention in managerial cognition research (see for instance D. P. Tegarden & S. D. Sheetz, 2003; M. Laukkanen, 1990), and many different variations of cognitive mapping were developed (see for instance a method by W. Acar & D. Druckenmiller, 2006, which they called comprehensive situation mapping). One special cognitive map is the causal map (K. E. Weick & M. G. Bougon, 2001, p. 311). Causal maps highlight the individual belief about causal relations in management (L. Markóczy & J. Goldberg, 1995; see also A. S. Huff, 1990, p. 28; B. B. Tylor & D. R. Gnyawali, 2009, pp. 97-98; see e.g. the study by V. Ambrosini & C. Bowman, 2005) such as competition and performance (A. Ginsberg, 1994, p. 166). Therefore, in the same way as concept maps, cognitive maps are representations of the construction and analysis of individual and team mental models (D. P. Spicer, 1998, p. 127ff).

Structure-Formation-Technique is founded in the theory and methodology of the 'Research Programme Subjective Theories' (Forschungsprogramm Subjektive Theorien, B. Scheele & N. Groeben, 1986; N. Groeben, D. Wahl, J. Schlee, & B. Scheele, 1988). They have a theoretical basis, which allows assumptions to be made about human characteristics, central terminology, methodical approach, and the possibilities for their modification. These give it a special status (D. Wahl, 1991, p. 53). Structure-Formation-Technique has a "2-phase model of the research structure" (B. Scheele & N. Groeben, 1988, p. 20). The first phase is "communicative validation" (B. Scheele & N. Groeben, 1988, p. 20). This is characterized by reconstructing concepts. Reasons for acts, intentions, and objectives will be described, based on dialogue-consensus. The second phase, which is called "explanative validation" ('explanative Validierung' B. Scheele & N. Groeben, 1988, p. 20), is qualified by examining the adequacy of the remodelled construct.

This thesis starts by using parts of the Structure-Formation-Technique (study I, see chapter 4.1) to elicit idiosyncratic mental models. During the research process, the mapping method was adjusted. There were two reasons for this. Firstly, the focus changed in the different studies, but always addressed to the same research question (see chapter 1.2). Secondly, in developing a methodological approach, it is important that this satisfies standards, which permit a statement to be made about the validity of the approach. One quality index is research economics (see chapter 3.4). Hence, during the development process, the mapping method was changed from the rather complex Structure-Formation-Technique to the simpler concept mapping method in studies III (chapter 4.4), IV (chapter 4.5), and V (chapter 4.6). This could be done because in the end, the results of all mapping methods have the same structure (see M. Laukkanen, 1994, p. 323).

3.5.3. Advantages and Disadvantages of Mapping Methods

There exists no consensus about which research approach – nomothetic or idiographic – would be best for eliciting mental models and team mental models (S. Mohammed et al., 2000, p. 155; J. R. Rentsch & R. Klimoski, 2001). Both approaches have advantages and disadvantages. The advantages are combined in "hybrid approaches" (G. P. Hodgkinson & M. P. Healey, 2008, p. 492).

Generally, mapping methods have the advantage that they visualize concepts and structures of mental models (M. Bonato, 1990, p. 33). Idiographic mapping methods reveal concepts and structures immediately, as they are in the mind of the participants (M. Bonato, 1990, p. 33; S. Mohammed et al., 2010, p. 885). In contrast to nomothetic mapping methods, the structure between concepts is clearly specified (S. Mohammed et al., 2000, p. 148). The elicitation process is not greatly influenced by the researcher. Additionally, as W. B. Rouse and N. M. Morris (1986) stated, mental models serve a special purpose; they are designed for a special task. Therefore, a high level of generalisation for these models can be assumed. Participants probably construct similar mental models with the same task in other interviewing situations. This means that idiosyncratic methods have a high external validity (see for external validity, for instance, J. Bortz & C. Schuster, 2010; J. Bortz & N. Döring, 2006).

However, a major disadvantage is that it is difficult to compare idiosyncratic mental models between different participants (S. Mohammed et al., 2010, p. 885; C. Eden & F. Ackermann,

1998, pp. 194-195; see chapter 3.7.3). One reason for this is the coding problem (L. Markoczy & J. Goldberg, 1995, p. 310). Another reason is biases within the rating (see G. P. Hodgkinson, 2002). For instance, K. Daniels et al. (2002, p. 41; see chapter 1.1) told their participants to evaluate the similarities based on comparing the maps of other participants to their own mental model. G. P. Hodgkinson (2002) criticised this procedure. Participants are not able to judge the overall similarity of complex maps; it will introduce bias into the rating.

Numerical comparability is a key objective of nomothetic methods (G. W. Goodhew et al., 2005, p. 126). The most commonly discussed examples are similarity and accuracy (see for instance L. L. Levesque et al., 2001; M. A. Marks et al., 2000; S. Mohammed, 2010, p. 885; see chapter 3.7.1). Similarity describes the extent to which mental models overlap (B. D. Edwards et al., 2006, p. 727; M. A. Marks et al., 2000, p. 973; J. E. Mathieu et al., 2005, p. 38; J. R. Rentsch, E. E. Small, & P. J. Hanges, 2008, p. 135). Accuracy describes the degree, to which the knowledge structures are adequately represented (M. A. Marks et al., 2000, p. 973; B. D. Edwards et al., 2006, p. 727; C. J. Resick et al., 2010, p. 175). However, even with both metrics, similarity and accuracy, it is not certain whether these methods elicit the specific mental model of participants, as idiosyncratic methods do (J. Langan-Fox et al., 2004, p. 338). Therefore, it is possible that other mental models could be constructed using idiographic methods. For that reason, this thesis focuses more on uninfluenced mental models of participants, and an idiographic elicitation approach is preferred.

3.6. Research Approach for Eliciting Shared Knowledge

Two general approaches to elicit shared knowledge are discussed in the literature: the holistic and the collective approach. Both are different but causally related (S. C. Schneider & R. Angelmar, 1993, p. 359). The holistic approach represents

> "...emergent properties of collectives, whereas aggregative measures are models about how individual contributions combine to create emergent properties."[6] (S. C. Schneider & R. Angelmar, 1993, p. 359).

The holistic approach (global measurement, S. C. Schneider & R. Angelmar, 1993, p. 356) surveys the team as an entity (N. J. Cooke et al., 2000, p. 157; N. J. Cooke, P. A. Kiekel, & E. E. Helm, 2001, p. 299; D. L. O'Connor, T. E. Johnson, & M. K. Khalil, 2004). Responses result from joint decision-making within the team (see Figure 10, p. 53). Hence, the holistic approach captures social interaction processes and communication (S. Mohammed et al., 2000, p.150). It is assumed that team knowledge is more than just the combined knowledge

---

[6] aggregative measures = collective appraoch

components of individual team members (R. Klimoski & S. Mohammed, 1994, p. 426; N. J. Cooke et al., 2000, p. 157). Therefore, the holistic approach has significant implications for team performance (see chapter 3.9).

Figure 10: Holistic and Collective Approach

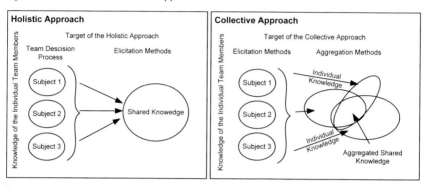

However, the contribution that would be attributable to the individual team members is no longer recognizable. This has implications for evaluating team members and for studying the idiosyncratic mental models of participants before social interaction occurs. Additionally, it should be noted that because of the joint decision-making process, the results could be influenced by aspects of group bias such as false consensus or groupthink (see for instance P. E. Jones & P. H. M. P. Roelofsma, 2000; to groupthink concept see I. L. Janis, 1972, 1983). False consensus "refers to the tendency to overestimate the degree of similarity between self and others and may result in biased judgements or decisions" (P. E. Jones & P. H. M. P. Roelofsma, 2000, p. 1134). The same is true with groupthink. Similar mental models may lead participants to think in a similarly, even if the mental models are not accurate (P. E. Jones & P. H. M. P. Roelofsma, 2000, p. 1142).

The collective approach (aggregate measurement, S. C. Schneider & R. Angelmar, 1993, p. 356) focuses on individual knowledge (see Figure 10). Therefore, this approach distinguishes between elicitation and aggregation methods (N. J. Cooke et al., 2000, p. 157). As a first step, the knowledge of each team member is measured separately. In the second step, the individual knowledge is aggregated to a global model ("scale up" to team cognition, N. J. Cooke et al., 2007a, p.146; N. J. Cooke et al., 2000, p. 157; N. J. Cooke et al., 2001, p. 299). Elicitation methods can include observations, surveys, and mapping techniques. Aggregation methods can include the minimum or maximum value, average, median value, sum, range calculations or similarity ratings (N. J. Cooke et al., 2000, p. 168; S. Mohammed et al., 2010, p. 885; for the methods see e.g. J. Bortz & C. Schuster, 2010; chapter 3.7.1).

With the collective approach, it is assumed indirectly that the contributions of group members are of equal importance (S. Mohammed et al., 2000, p.149; N. J. Cooke & J. C. Gorman, 2006, p. 271; S. Mohammed et al. 2010, pp. 885-888). However, this assumption can be questioned with heterogeneous groups, where some members may have more influence or have a deeper knowledge than others (N. J. Cooke & J. C. Gorman, 2006, p. 271; N. J. Cooke et al., 2007b, pp. 247-249; S. Mohammed et al., 2010, pp. 885-888). Additionally, S. Mohammed et al. (2000, p. 149) state "averaging across qualitatively different knowledge structures may distort the group average and obscure interpretable structures." Both have implications for the research question in this thesis, which is how can the similarity of idiosyncratic mental models be identified and presented (see chapter 1.1).

As stated in chapter 1, and as it will be outlined in the research project (chapter 4), mental models focus on important issues of a domain (chapter 4.1.1). An indication of the importance is the centrality of the concepts in a mental model. The centrality of a concept is expressed in two ways – firstly, the type of concept (cause-concept, effect-concept, mediating concept), and secondly, the number of in-arrows or out-arrows or both (see chapters 3.7.2 and 4.1.4.3.1). In idiosyncratic mental models, similar concepts may vary in both ways. One participant may use many concrete concepts in his idiosyncratic mental model, whereas another participant may use fewer abstract ones. By attempting to quantify this information, an overestimation of the mental model of the first participant could be made, with a corresponding underestimation of that of the second. In reality, the difference between both models may not be significant. This is discussed in chapter 4.5.1.2 (see Figure 25, p. 143), and is based on the work of E. Rosch et al. (1976a).

Because of the advantages and disadvantages of the holistic and the collective approach to the research question of studying similarity of idiosyncratic mental models, both eliciting approaches are used in this thesis. Approach A, which includes studies I and II, focuses on the collective approach. Study I refers to the elicitation process of idiosyncratic mental models. Study II refers to the aggregation process of the idiosyncratic mental models. Approach B, which includes studies III, IV, and V, combines both elicitation approaches. The collective approach is applied in the stage 1 of the studies, where the idiosyncratic mental models are collected, as well as in the aggregation part of the stage 2 in studies IV and V. Additionally, during the stage 2, which is based on the holistic approach, the team mental models are collected. Both the results of the eliciting approaches – hence the idiosyncratic mental models of the collective stages and the team mental models of the holistic stages – are used to deduce shared knowledge (see approaches for aggregating mental models below). This is done by using the meaning relation tool (for theoretical underpinning see study IV, chapter 4.5). The combination of the holistic and collective approach in Approach B is also the starting point to test the proposition 'the whole is more than the sum of its parts' as it was suggested by S. C. Schneider and R. Angelmar (1993, p. 360; see chapter 4.6).

3.7. Research Approach for Aggregating Mental Models

3.7.1. Similarity and Accuracy

Mental models elicited with nomothetic, mixed or idiographic mapping methods differ in the degree of idiosyncrasy of the individuals' mental models (see chapter 3.5.2). Ultimately, this determines the choice of the aggregation approach. For instance, if a nomothetic-quantitative elicitation approach is used, an aggregation method such as the minimum or maximum value, which would represent shared knowledge could be used "to the extent that knowledge was a function of the strongest or weakest team member" (N. J. Cooke et al., 2000, p. 168). Other aggregation methods are the average, median value, sum, or range calculations (N. J. Cooke et al., 2000, p. 168; for more details of the methods see e.g. J. Bortz & C. Schuster, 2010; see also chapter 3.6). However, if highly idiosyncratic mental models are under investigation, using idiosyncratic-qualitative elicitation methods, focusing on content and structure of these mental modes, such aggregation approaches are not appropriate. There are at least two reasons for this. Firstly, they do not capture the structure of the models; secondly, information about individual qualitative differences are lost (see L. A. DeChurch & J. R. Mesmer-Magnus, 2010a, p. 3; S. Mohammed et al., 2000, p. 149). Such information could explain differences in team performance (see chapter 1).

S. Mohammed et al. (2010, p. 885) note that most empirical studies on team mental models aggregate individual mental models by comparing them with each other using similarity ratings, or by comparing them with an expert model by focusing on accuracy. In the team mental model literature, similarity describes the extent to which mental models overlap (B. D. Edwards et al., 2006, p. 727; M. A. Marks et al., 2000, p. 973): Similarity is "the extent to which team members' mental models are consistent with one another" (J. E. Mathieu et al., 2005, p. 38; J. R. Rentsch, E. E. Small, & P. J. Hanges, 2008, p. 135). Accuracy describes the degree, to which the knowledge structures are adequately represented (M. A. Marks et al., 2000, p. 973; B. D. Edwards et al., 2006, p. 727; C. J. Resick et al., 2010, p. 175). The definition of similarity and accuracy is valid despite the fact that these two concepts are often researched differently (Edwards et al., 2006, p. 728; M. A. Marks et al., 2000, p. 973). One reason can be the object of investigation. Empirical studies usually focus on team process variables, such as communication and coordination (B. D. Edwards et al., 2006, p. 728; M. A. Marks et al., 2000, p. 973). For these variables, similarity has a higher impact on effective teamwork than accuracy. Another reason is conceptually based. Accuracy is usually determined by the comparison of the team mental model with an expert model (see for instance S. S. Webber et al., 2000; K. A. Smith-Jentsch, G. E. Campbell, D. M. Milanovich, & A. M. Reynolds, 2001; K. A. Smith-Jentsch et al., 2005; B. D. Edwards et al., 2006; B. C. Lim & K. J. Klein, 2006). This includes the one accurate expert model itself and excludes the possibility of different 'right' expert model results (M. A. Marks et al., 2000, p. 975; S. S. Webber et al., 2000, p. 312; J. E. Mathieu et al., 2005, p. 39).

Additionally, according to the definitions of similarity and accuracy, both concepts are not equally applicable within the contexts of discovery and justification (see chapter 3.3). The context of discovery aims to develop hypotheses. Therefore, the focus is to gain knowledge (see R. Brühl, 2006). The context of justification aims to test hypotheses. Therefore, the focus is to confirm knowledge (see R. Brühl, 2006). Accuracy, as it is used in team mental model studies, requires expert knowledge; participants' knowledge is then compared to expert knowledge. Hence, the focus is to confirm knowledge. Based on these considerations, accuracy is not applicable in the context of discovery, only within the context of justification. Similarity is applicable in both contexts. With similarity, 'reliable knowledge' is not a prerequisite. Hence, the accuracy of knowledge plays no role. Quite the contrary, as dysfunctionality in teams, which could be measured in different team performances, could result from similarities in knowledge structure within the team, caused by groupthink or false consensus (see for instance P. E. Jones & P. H. M. P. Roelofsma, 2000; to groupthink concept see I. L. Janis, 1972, 1983; chapter 3.6). Such similarities could be detected.

However, this thesis focusses on the development of an approach to compare and aggregate idiosyncratic mental models to shared knowledge. Hence, it is based in the context of discovery with a strong focus on similarity of the idiosyncratic mental models. Therefore, approaches researching the similarity of mental models will be reviewed next.

3.7.2. Similarity Approaches

3.7.2.1. Consensus and Consistency as Nomothetic-Quantitative Perspectives on Similarity

D. L. Medin, R. L. Goldstone and D. Gentner (1993, p. 254 f.) mention at least two different perspectives of similarity. The first considers similarity as an explanatory construct; the second considers similarity as a measurement tool. Although both views need a theoretical framework for the construct and for measuring the construct, the first view focuses more on the theoretical construct itself (e.g. similarity-based models of categorization, D. L. Medin et al., 1993, p. 255), whereas the second view considers similarity rather as a describing variable within a context.

An example of a study using similarity as a measurement tool is the one by S. S. Webber et al. (2000). S. S. Webber et al. (2000, p. 310 f.) differentiate similarity by referring to consistency and consensus. Consistency refers to an interrater-reliability based on a questionnaire, and reveals differences between rater-evaluation patterns. Figure 11 shows a hypothetical example. Participants 1 and 2 differ in their evaluation of the items. For instance, participant 1 agrees with the first item (the 'x' in Figure 11) whereas participant 2 does not agree with the first item (the 'o' in Figure 11).

Figure 11: Hypothetical Example for Consistency

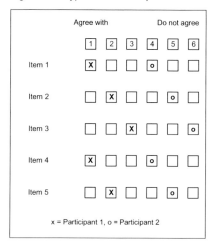

However, looking at the pattern for all items, both participants show similar evaluation behaviour. Both agree with the first and fourth item, and both do not agree with the third item. Therefore, participants differ in their judgement of all items, but they do have similar evaluation patterns. Similarly, differences in evaluation patterns could be obtained through inter-rater correlation. A high inter-rater correlation, for example based on an inter-class correlation coefficient, leads one to assume that there is little difference in evaluation patterns (S. S. Webber et al., 2000, p. 311; also L. L. Levesque et al., 2001, p. 137; for the methodology J. Bortz & N. Döring, 2006, pp. 277).

Consensus refers to the degree to which the rater makes the same judgements. This means the extent to which team members agree on a set of judgements (r_{wgs} statistic develops by James et al., 1984, cit. J. Langan-Fox et al., 2001, p. 103; S. S. Webber et al., 2000, p. 311; N. J. Cooke et al., 2000, p. 163; L. L. Levesque et al., 2001, p. 137; B. L. Kirkman, P. E. Tesluk & B. Rosen, 2001, p. 648). Figure 12 shows a hypothetical example for consensus of two participants. Both participants agree, and do not agree, on the same items to the same extent.

In this thesis, the similarity concept 'consensus' is part of the aggregation approach towards shared knowledge. It is consistent with the definition of shared knowledge as overlapping knowledge structures (see chapter 2.2.2.2). If two participants judge their idiosyncratic concepts to be the same as team concept, then the two participants agree. They have shared knowledge (for the theoretical underpinning see study IV, chapter 4.5).

Figure 12: Hypothetical Example for Consensus

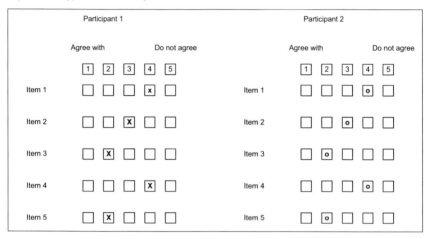

3.7.2.2. Correspondence Analysis as Nomothetic-Qualitative Approach in Analysing Similarity

Correspondence analysis is an explorative method for graphic and numeric analysis of a contingency table (J. Blasius, 2001, p. 6). The similarity between individual mental models can be analysed, for example the similarity between a participants' mental model and an expert mental model (A. A. Eckert, 2000, p. 143), or between two participants' mental models based on qualitative concepts. Therefore, this chapter focuses on correspondence analysis. It outlines the basics of correspondence analysis, and it sketches different grades of similarity. Both refer to nomothetic concept mapping. However, elements of correspondence analysis were applied in Approach A (see chapters 4.1 and 4.2).

Correspondence analysis examines corresponding concept pairs in different individual mental models. Corresponding means that there are the same concept pairs in two individual mental models[7]. Comparing these concept pairs, four cases are possible (see A. A. Eckert, 2000; Table 2, p. 60):

- Two concepts are connected in both mental models (cell +, +; column 2, row 2).
- Two concepts are not connected in both mental models (cell -, -; column 1, row 1).
- Two concepts are connected in the mental model of participant 1 but the same concept pair is not connected in the mental model of participant 2 (cell +, -; column 2, row 1).
- Two concepts are not connected in the mental model of participant 1 but the same concept pair is connected in the mental model of participant 2 (cell -, +; column 1, row 2).

For example, the following four concepts are given: advertising, money, staff, and customers. Two mental models in the form of causal chains were constructed by two participants (see Case 1):

Case 1: Correspondent and Not-Correspondent Concept Pairs (Hypothetical)

- Participant 1: money → advertising → customers → staff
- Participant 2: staff → advertising → customers → money

The arrow '→' means 'influences' and connects the concepts. Referring to the formula in Table 2, p. 60, (column 3, row 3), and four concepts, it is possible to build six concepts pairs:

- Money – advertising
- Money – customers
- Money – staff
- Advertising – customers

---

[7] The term 'individual mental model' stresses the construction of a mental model based on nomothetic, hence given concepts, and given rules. In nomothetic concept mapping methods, all participants receive the same concepts and rules, from which they can choose to construct an individual mental model (see chapter 3.5.2). Thus, the models do not differ in the content of concepts in general, but they probably differ in chosen concepts, or in the structure between these concepts. Therefore, these mental models are individual but not idiosyncratic. By contrast, the term 'idiosyncratic mental model' stresses the construction of a mental model based on idiosyncratic concepts as well as idiosyncratic or nomothetic rules. At this point, it would be correct to name the mental models examined in this thesis as mixed idiographic-nomothetic. However, to stress that the content of the mental models are individual, and because the nomothetic structure of the mental models will not be primarily analysed during Approach B, the term 'idiographic mental model' will continued to be used.

- Adverting – staff
- Customers – staff

Table 2: Correspondent and Not-Correspondent Concept Pairs in two Mental Models (following A. A. Eckert, 2000, p. 144, table 1)

			Column		
			1	2	3
			Mental Model of Participant 1		
			Not Connected Concept Pairs	Connected Concept Pairs	Σ
			–	+	
Row	Mental Model of Participant 2	1 / Not Connected Concept Pairs / –	Σ correspondent concept pairs, which are not connected in both mental models	Σ of correspondent concept pairs, which are connected in mental model of participant 1 but not connected in mental model of participant 2	Σ not connected concepts of mental models
		2 / Connected Concept Pairs / +	Σ of correspondent concept pairs, which are not connected in mental model of participant 1 but are connected in mental model of participant 2	Σ correspondent concept pairs, which are connected in both mental models	Σ connected concepts of mental models
		3 / Σ	Σ not connected concepts of mental models	Σ connected concepts of mental models	Σ of all possible connections: N(N-1)/2

Note i: N = concept numbers

Referring to the hypothetical Case 1 above, participants 1 and 2 differ in the connection of four corresponding concept pairs (see Table 3, p. 61). Participant 1 connected the concept pairs 'money – advertising' and 'customers – staff', whereas participant 2 did not (cell +, -). Participant 2 connected the concept pairs 'money – customers', and 'adverting – staff', but participant 1 did not (cell -, +). Participants agree on the connection of two concepts pairs. Both participants connected the concepts 'advertising – customers' (cell +, +), and both participants did not connect the concepts 'money – staff' (cell -, -).

The correspondence of two mental models is described with coefficient C, following the formula (A. A. Eckert, 2000, p. 144, Formula (1)):

Formula 1: Correspondence Coefficient

$$C = \frac{(cell-,-) + (cell+,+) - ((cell+,-) + (cell-,+))}{\Sigma \text{ of all possible connections}}$$

The range of C is between -1 and +1. -1 would mean 'no correspondence at all'; +1 would mean 'total correspondence'. For the given example, C = - 0.33. That means there are more non-correspondent concepts pairs than correspondent concept pairs.

Table 3: Example Correspondence analysis

		Mental Model of Participant 1		Σ
		Not Connected Concept Pairs	Connected Concept Pairs	
		−	+	
Mental Model of Participant 2	Not Connected Concept Pairs −	'Money' – 'Staff'	'Money' – 'Advertising' 'Customer' – 'Staff'	3
	Connected Concept Pairs +	'Money' – 'Customer' 'Adverting' – 'Staff'	'Advertising' – 'Customer'	3
	Σ	3	3	6

Based on the description above, it is possible to vary the stringency of the comparison (the following description refers again to A. A. Eckert, 2000). The simplest contrast is to prove that both mental models correspond to the connection of concept pairs (see Case 1, p. 59). The next step would be to analyse whether the direction of the connection is the same in both causal chains. For instance, both participants made the following connection in causal chains (see Case 2):

Case 2: Direction of the Connection (Hypothetical)

- Participant 1: money → customers → advertising → staff
- Participant 2: staff → advertising → customers → money

The concepts 'customers' and 'advertising' are still connected in both mental models, as was described in Case 1, but the concept pairs differ in the direction of the connection. Therefore, in Case 1 'same concepts are connected or not connected' the correspondent concept pairs are identical. For Case 2 'the direction of the connection', the correspondent concept pairs are not identical anymore, because participant 1 connected 'customers' → advertising', and participant 2 connected 'advertising → customers'. The comparison in Case 2 is strict because of the additional condition: connection and same direction.

The last case is to prove whether the connection between corresponding concept pairs in both mental models have the same value. In Case 1 and Case 2, the arrows '→' just mean influences. However, the influence could be positive '+ →' or negative '- →' (as well as other possible values). The comparison in Case 3 is identical, when compared to Case 2, despite the additional condition: connection and same value.

Summarizing the three degrees of similarity, the example of the concept pair 'advertising-customers' will be analysed based on Case 3 of causal chains:

Case 3: Value of the Connections (Hypothetical)

- Participant 1: money —→ advertising +→ customer +→ staff
- Participant 2: staff → advertising → customer → money

In Case 1 'correspondent in the connection', both mental models have correspondent units. Both participants connected 'advertising – customers'. In Case 2 'same direction of the connection', both mental models also have correspondent units. The direction in the connection is the same in both concept pairs: Advertising has an impact on customers (advertising → customers). In Case 3 'same value of the connection', both participants differ in their result, because the value of the arrow is different. Participant 1 stated a positive influence. Participant 2 simply stated an influence. The value of the arrow is a qualitative nuance.

The different degrees of similarity provide a first hint of the research similarity between single concept pairs. They will be used in Approach A for evaluating the similarity between idiosyncratic mental models, by using concepts and the structure between concepts (see chapter 4.2.3.4).

3.7.2.3. Complexity and Centrality as a Basis for an Idiographic-Qualitative Approach in Analysing Similarity

C. Eden et al. (1992, pp. 312-314) mention two approaches for analysing idiosyncratic mental models:

- The first focuses on the centrality of concepts.
- The second analyses the complexity of the mental models.

The **centrality of concepts** analyses the total number of in-arrows and out-arrows from each concept (C. Eden et al., 1992, p. 313). Hence, it focuses on the domain, by calculating the cause and effect of each concept or by analysing the property of hierarchy (C. Eden et al., 1992; C. Eden, 2004, p. 682).

The **complexity of the mental models** is a function of the total number of concepts and the total number of links. The more concepts and links in the mental model, the more complex is the mental model (C. Eden et al., 1992, p. 312). However, C. Eden et al. (1992, p. 312) note from their experience, that the number of constructs elicited during the interview depends upon the length of the interviews as well as the interviewer skills. Therefore, another approach would be to analyse the ratio of links to constructs (C. Eden et al., 1992, p. 313). A high ratio indicates a high level of cognitive complexity (C. Eden et al., 1992, p. 313; C. Eden, 2004, pp. 676-677).

With the analysis of the centrality of concepts, only parts of the mental models will be analysed; but it indicates the richness of meaning of each concept (C. Eden et al., 1992, p. 313). The evaluation of the similarity between different idiosyncratic mental models by focusing on their complexity is more structural than content based. However, in this thesis, both indicators, complexity and centrality, are applied in Approach A to compare the idiosyncratic mental models of the participants (see e.g. chapter 4.1.4.3).

3.7.3. Problems of Judging Similarity in Idiosyncratic Mental Models

The approaches described above are appropriate for mental models which have the same number of concepts and concepts that appear in each model. Both of these are unlikely to appear in idiosyncratic mental models. This is because of the freedom, which the participants have during the elicitation process (see also chapter 3.5.3) to use their own language and to add concepts or to delete them. The main problem in judging similarity in idiosyncratic mental models is to identify synonymous elements in the maps (C. Eden & F. Ackermann, 1998, p. 195). C. Eden & F. Ackermann (1998, p. 196) note that mental models

> "... elicited from an individual or group only acquire meaning when explored by that individual or group, or researchers, when they become ... part of the group. Although ... that the context of elements will help to illuminate their meaning, the implicit shared background and history of the group will always play a major part in determining the meaning of the map."

Hence, the process of comparing idiosyncratic mental models becomes difficult (see C. Eden & F. Ackermann, 1998, p. 195). Additionally, C. Eden & F. Ackermann (1998, p. 196) note that it is necessary for the interviewer, when constructing the aggregated model to understand fully the participants "words, language, jargon and shorthand vocabulary of the interviewees." Otherwise, it would be risky to identify concepts as synonyms (C. Eden & F. Ackermann, 1998, p. 196). However, C. Eden & F. Ackermann (1998, pp. 196-197) also mention different ways to compensate:

- Firstly, to let the participants review and evaluate the aggregated model, which was compared and constructed by the interviewer, in order to ensure reliability,
- Secondly, to elicit models from participants with similar cultural backgrounds, and
- Thirdly, to be familiar with the groups whose models will be compared.

C. Eden and F. Ackermann (1998, pp. 196-198) discussed the 'researcher approach' in determining similarity between idiosyncratic mental models. This thesis takes another stance. It focusses on the participants' view of detecting similarity between idiosyncratic mental models.

In Approach A, study II, which is based on the Delphi-Method, experts from the same organization as the participants in study I detected similarities between different idiosyncratic mental models. In this way, it differs from the researcher approach discussed by C. Eden and F. Ackermann (1998). The experts came from the same group and therefore shared the same organisational culture, with similar perceptions to the participants in study I (see chapter 4.2.2.1). Hence, it was assumed that the experts understood fully the participants' language. Additionally, as was also suggested by C. Eden and F. Ackermann (1998, p. 196; see above), the expert results were evaluated by one participant to ensure credibility (see chapters 3.4 and 4.2.3.5). The conclusion is that Approach A produced desired results, but not in the desired quality (sees chapters 4.2.4 and 4.3).

Approach B focussed on the development of an approach to compare highly idiosyncratic concepts using the participants' view. C. Eden & F. Ackermann (1998, p. 195) note, "detecting synonyms is essential" for comparing idiosyncrasies. Approach B does not focus solely on detecting synonyms within mental models. Approach B focusses on the development of rules including 'synonyms', 'hyponyms', 'incompatibilities' and 'antonyms' for evaluating semantics. These rules define the 'meaning relation tool' (see chapter 4.5.1.4). They are underscored with a theoretical basis within the categorization process (see chapter 4.5.1.2). Hence, in contrast to the researcher approach by C. Eden and F. Ackermann (1998), this approach is based on the evaluation of the meaning of the idiosyncratic concepts judged by the participants themselves. It reflects the view of the participants. This approach coincides with that of C. Eden and F. Ackermann (1998, p. 196) when they stress the importance of the history of the group in determining the meaning of concepts. Additionally, it takes into account the view of G. P. Hodgkinson (2002), when he states that participants are not able to judge the overall similarity of complex maps. With this approach, the researcher can draw conclusions about shared knowledge, based on the participants' evaluation of the meaning of concepts.

3.8. Shared Construct from a Methodological Perspective

Chapter 2.2.2.2 discussed the shared knowledge construct and its meaning from a theoretical perspective. This chapter highlights the meaning of shared knowledge from a methodological perspective, and discusses further implications.

In chapter 2.2.2.2, it was said that 'share' could have two different meanings: first, to divide something up, and second to have something in common (see R. Klimoski & S. Mohammed, 1994). It was also said that to have something in common could result in different degrees of overlapping. This will be explained using the example 'overlapped internal representation about teamwork of team members' different team types' (see Figure 13).

Team type is an independent variable (A); different levels of team type are, for instance, work teams and management teams. These different levels of team type should have different influences on the dependent variable (B) 'overlapping in internal representation'. Hence, the degree of overlapping of the internal representation about teamwork should be different with work and management teams (see Figure 13). The lines on which the ellipses are situated refer to the degree of overlapping within the team, as a continuum with the poles 'identical overlapped' (= 100%) and 'no overlapping' (= 0%). The closer the ellipses are situated to one of the poles; the more or less overlapped are the idiosyncratic mental models and team mental models. The research area in the given example is teamwork.

Figure 13: Example for One Type of Model (about Team Work) by two Different Team Types

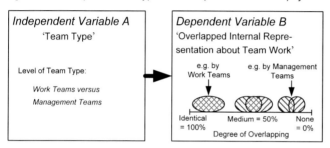

Another example for the dependent variable B is 'task related knowledge about environmental restitutions'. This results from the description by J. A. Cannon-Bowers et al. (1993), and by me in chapter 2.2.3.3 of the taxonomy of mental models.

Both examples focus on one model type. This view of sharing is one-dimensional. The multidimensional view of sharing is related to the interdependence or interaction of two or more variables, and to the assumptions that one person can have, rather than just one mental model at a time (J. A. Cannon-Bowers et al., 1993, p. 231 ff.). Different types of sharing exist, and these are illustrated below. N. J. Cooke et al. (2000, p. 156) state that a

> "...team member might hold compatible or complementary knowledge in addition to common knowledge (Cannon-Bowers & Salas, 1997; Klimoski & Mohammed, 1994). That is, there might be some knowledge overlap required among team members, but in addition, role-specific yet compatible knowledge is required."

In view of the assumption that the models of the taxonomy by J. A. Cannon-Bowers et al. (1993) are dependent, the multidimensional view is comparable to multivariate analysis (to multivariate analysis see, for instance, J. Bortz & C. Schuster, 2010). Multivariate analysis examines some of the dependent variables (for example B1, B2). These dependent variables are different types of mental models held at the same time. For example, B1 = task model with task-related knowledge, B2 = team model with team-related knowledge (see the dependent variable in Figure 14).

Figure 14: Example for Four Types of Dependent Models by two Different Team Types

Independent Variable A 'Team Type'	Dependent Variable B 'Overlapping of Internal Representation Refering to Team Work'			
		Work Teams ⟶ ⊘		
		Management Teams ⟶ ○		
	'Team Model'	Identical = 100%	No Overlapping = 0%	
Level of Team Type: 'Work Teams' vs. 'Management Teams'	'Team Interaction Model'	Identical = 100%	No Overlapping = 0%	Time of Measurement t_1
	'Task Model'	Identical = 100%	No Overlapping = 0%	
	'Equipment Model'	Identical = 100%	No Overlapping = 0%	
	Degree of Overlapping			

Figure 14 illustrates the meaning of the citation by N. J. Cooke et al. (2000, p. 156) in terms of coexisting mental models using the taxonomy of J. A. Cannon-Bowers et al. (1993, see chapter 2.2.3.3). This example shows hypothetically the influence of the independent variable upon a dependent variable. The independent variable (A) or 'team type' has two levels: work teams versus management teams. The dependent variable (B) or 'overlapping of internal representation' is analysed using the team model, team interaction model, task model and equipment model. In this example, work teams could be workers on the same engine in the same team. They work together closely. Members of management teams could be leaders of different divisions, such as financial and marketing, who have regular meetings. The shaded ellipse in Figure 14 sketches the team mental model of work teams, which includes different individual mental models. The white ellipse describes the team mental model of the management teams, which also includes different individual mental models. The lines on which the ellipses are situated refer to the degree of overlapping within the team as a continuum, with the poles 'identical' (= 100%) and 'no overlapping' (= 0%). The closer the ellipses are situated to one of the poles, the more or less overlapped are the idiosyncratic mental models and team mental models. The notion 'time of measurement t_1' expresses that types of mental models exist simultaneously, namely at the time when collecting the mental model (no explicit distinction is made between collective and holistic approaches, see chapter 3.6).

It is assumed, that the similarity of the mental models is constrained by the working environment. When asking workers about their task and team, they would probably have similar mental models. This contrasts with managers when asked the same about different managerial tasks and the management team. This is where the context has a significant influence (see G. P. Hodgkinson & P. R. Sparrow, 2002, p. 150; G. P. Hodgkinson & G. Johnson, 1994, p. 530; see also B. B. Tyler & D. R. Gnyawali, 2009, pp. 115-117). Assuming that work teams and management teams are asked the same questions about their teams and work in the example given above, the following hypothetical results would be possible. Members of management teams have less overlapped knowledge structures about the management team (team model) compared to work team members. The white ellipse (management teams) is not as close to the identical pole as the shaded ellipse (work teams, see Figure 14). Therefore, members of work teams share more knowledge. They know about the skills and preferences of their teammates, because of their common working experience. Additionally, work teams have similar views about the equipment they need for work, and the limitations of that equipment, when compared to the management teams. Managers know about their own equipment, for instance, a special financial programme, but they know less about the equipment of their team members, such as a special graphic programme. Additionally, in this example, it is assumed that management teams and work teams have similar knowledge about their team task related strategies and actions, and about the limits of different situational parameters (task model). Both ellipses are close to the identical pole. Referring to team interaction model, both teams do not differ in the degree of overlapping in terms of knowledge about roles and responsibility. The example in Figure 14 illustrates why it is unlikely that participants have identical or completely distinct knowledge (N. J. Cooke et al., 2000, p. 156). The different model types depend upon contextual factors and upon experience (see chapter 2.2.3.3). Taking together, they all form parts of knowledge. In this sense, J. A. Cannon-Bowers and E. Salas' (2001) statement about 'What do we mean by 'shared'' is understood. J. A. Cannon-Bowers and E. Salas (2001, p. 198 f.) suggest a taxonomy of four categories about the meaning of sharing (for the following see Figure 15). These categories are shared or overlapping, similar/identical, complementary or compatible and distributed.

Figure 15: Meanings of Sharedness based on Cannon-Bowers & E. Salas (2001)

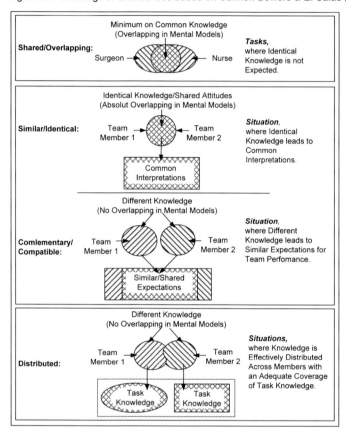

The first category 'shared or overlapping' is identical with the understanding of sharing given above. It means to have something in common. However, in contrast to this, J. A. Cannon-Bowers and E. Salas (2001, p. 198 f.) do not suggest a continuum, but rather categories. This is why they have a second category 'similar/identical', which I have placed at the end of the continuum in Figure 14. They make a distinction between both categories. They relate the first category, shared/overlapping, to tasks, where a minimum of knowledge has to be common to all team members in order to improve team performance, but where identical knowledge cannot be expected, such as in a surgeon-nurse-team. J. A. Cannon-Bowers and E. Salas (2001, p. 198 f.) relate this knowledge base as an example to 'certain attitudes and/or belief' (2001, p. 198 f.). For the second category 'similar/identical', J. A. Cannon-Bowers and E. Salas (2001, p. 198 f.) state that it is necessary to have identical attitudes and/or beliefs to get a common understanding, which results in effective team performance. The example they give is identical beliefs about the value of feedback for developing the team. The third category 'complementary or compatible' refers to different – or distributed – knowledge, which leads to similar not necessarily identical expectations for team and task (J. A. Cannon-Bowers et al., 1993, p. 235). An example of this understanding of sharing is expert knowledge in multidisciplinary teams (J. A. Cannon-Bowers & E. Salas, 2001, p. 198 f.). In their last category 'distributed', J. A. Cannon-Bowers and E. Salas (2001, p. 198 f.) refer to S. Mohammed and B. C. Dumville's (2001) understanding of sharing in the sense of dividing, adjusting the notion that an adequate coverage of task knowledge is necessary for adequate team performance. In this case, the mental models are different, but still compatible. The example given – military teams – is typical for situations, which are too complex for one person.

The objective of this thesis is to aggregate idiosyncratic mental models to a team mental model in order to determine their similarity. An important construct to determine the similarity in idiosyncratic mental models is the shared construct. 'Shared' is understood in this thesis in terms of overlapping knowledge structures, in the sense of common knowledge (see also chapter 2.2.3.3). In this sense, the understanding of 'shared' conforms to the outline of similar perspectives (see chapter 3.7.2). It is assumed that the overlapping in knowledge structures can take different degrees on the continuum, with the poles 'identical' and 'no overlapping'. Because this thesis focuses on the development of an aggregation method, only one type of mental model, the task view, will be used in the different studies to collect idiosyncratic mental models and team mental models (see the following chapter 4).

3.9. Team Performance from a Methodological Perspective

Study IV (chapter 4.5.3.4.3) outlines the analysis procedure of the idiosyncratic concepts of team members, based on the team mental model. During this procedure a new construct arose which will be called 'team performance'. E. Salas et al. (2005, pp. 556-557) note that a "number of researchers have conceptualized team performance as a function of each team member's individual input minus the process losses associated with working with others". Team performance is viewed differently in this thesis. Team performance is the output of the team, which is not explainable by earlier individual measurements. It is new knowledge based on new team concepts (see chapter 4.5.3.4.3). This derives from a combination of holistic and collective approaches. It produces the effect, as stated in chapter 3.6, that 'the whole is more than the sum of its parts' (see S. C. Schneider & R. Angelmar, 1993, p. 360; see chapters 3.6 and 4.6). This view of team performance is in line with the literature, because it focusses on the outcome, regardless of how the team accomplished the tasks. Therefore, it differs from the construct of 'team effectiveness' (see E. Salas et al., 2005, p.

557; E. Salas et al., 2007). The construct 'team performance', as it is defined and presented in this thesis, also reflects the influence of communication and social interaction, which are thought to enhance shared knowledge (S. Mohammed et al., 2010, p. 885; see the results in study V, chapter 4.6.5). Team performance will be validated by hypotheses in study V (chapter 4.6). This chapter discusses the construct 'team performance' mainly within the team mental model literature, and from the methodological perspective.

Team performance is influenced by many factors (see e.g. reviews by R. A. Guzzo & M. W. Dickson, 1996; C. R. Paris et al., 2000). Many frameworks are offered to describe such influences (see for instance schematic representation by S. I. Tannenbaum et al., 1996, p. 507; S. G. Cohen & D. E. Bailey, 1997, p. 244; or studies by D. R. Denison, S. L. Hart, & J. A. Kahn, 1996; M. A. Marks, J. E. Mathieu, & S. J. Zaccaro, 2001). As Mathieu et al. (2000, p. 273) find, frameworks have in common an '**input-process-output**' structure (R. Rico, M. Sánchez-Manzanares, F. Gil, & C. Gibson, 2008, p. 163).

The **input** refers to the conditions (J. E. Mathieu et al., 2000, p. 273), such as characteristics of the task and work, as well as characteristics of the individuals and teams. Examples of characteristics of individuals are mental models, personality, or motivation (S. I. Tannenbaum et al., 1996, p. 507; S. G. Cohen & D. E. Bailey, 1997, p. 244).

The **process** describes the way in which the team transforms inputs into outputs (J. E. Mathieu et al., 2000, p. 273). The team is influenced by internal and external processes, such as coordination and communication, as well as interventions (S. I. Tannenbaum et al., 1996, p. 507; S. G. Cohen & D. E. Bailey, 1997, p. 244).

The **output** is the result of the teamwork (J. E. Mathieu et al., 2000, p. 273). The results comprises

- changes at the team level, such as new rules, new communication or common knowledge,
- changes at the individual level such as motivation and knowledge, and
- changes about team performance, which includes, for instance, quality and quantity performance indices

(S. I. Tannenbaum et al., 1996, p. 507; S. G. Cohen & D. E. Bailey, 1997, p. 244). It is important that knowledge structures are part of the input, but they are also a result of the process. In this thesis, knowledge structures are researched as outputs. The idiosyncratic mental models and team mental models of participants about a specific problem were assessed and compared.

Performance indices can have different aspects. Typically, team performance is measured by task performance, completion or proficiency (L. A. DeChurch & J. R. Mesmer-Magnus, 2010a, p. 5; L. A. DeChurch & J. R. Mesmer-Magnus, 2010b, p. 34; C. R. Paris et al., 2000, p. 1057). Examples are the speed of task solving (see D. A. Harrison, S. Mohammed, J. E. McGrath, A. T. Florey, & S. W. Vanderstoep, 2003), scores for each solved task (see A. P. Banks & L. J. Millward, 2007) or as Timmerman has described it "the team's winning percentage at the end" (T. A. Timmerman, 2005, p. 29). There is mention of two classes of performance judgements:

- objective judgements, and
- subjective judgements

(L. A. DeChurch & J. R. Mesmer-Magnus, 2010a, p. 5; J. R. Mesmer-Magnus & L. A. DeChurch, 2009, p. 536; L. A. DeChurch & J. R. Mesmer-Magnus, 2010b, p. 34). These judgements differ how well they represent the total domain of team performance, and of how much they are influenced by irrelevant factors such as rater biases (deficiency and contamination, J. R. Mesmer-Magnus & L. A DeChurch, 2009, p. 536).

Objective judgements do not cover the whole team performance construct, but they are less influenced by other non-performance-relevant sources of variance, such as rater biases (J. R. Mesmer-Magnus & L. A DeChurch, 2009, p. 536). Examples are profitability, market growth, computer simulation scores, and number of targets hit (J. R. Mesmer-Magnus & L. A DeChurch, 2009, p. 539; L. A. DeChurch & J. R. Mesmer-Magnus, 2010b, p. 34). For instance, Marks et al. (2002, p. 7) used a computer simulation score. Team performance was based on the sum of the number of targets hit during each mission, and the team's time in minutes of 'alive time', averaged over two parallel missions. In an earlier study, Marks et al. (2000, p. 974 / p. 977) used a tank war-game simulation, viewing team performance as the number of pillboxes destroyed and pillboxes rebuilt. J. E. Mathieu et al. (2000, pp. 276-277) investigated team performance in a low-fidelity personal-computer–based simulation. Team performance was measured as the number of points earned during two missions. N. J. Cooke et al. (2003, p. 184) focussed on the mission completion rate, or the proportion of the mission tasks completed successfully. K. A. Smith-Jentsch (2005, p. 527) measured safety and efficiency based on safety incursions and flight delays, in an air traffic control environment. B. D. Edwards et al. (2006, p. 730) took a video game to measure team performance. The performance was measured as the average of total scores from two test games. A. P. J. Ellis (2006) investigated team performance by standardizing and combining offensive and defensive scores in a command-control simulation. A similar scoring was used by M. J. Pearsall, A. P. J. Ellis, and B. S. Bell (2010, p. 196) when investigating the effects of role identification behaviour on team cognition development and team performance. P. Banks and L. J. Millward (2007, p. 99) scored one point for each enemy tank successfully destroyed. Y. Zhou and E. Wang (2010, p. 433 / p. 436) investigated the effects of shared mental models on the relationship between team processes and performance, within a simulated construction project planning program. Team performance was measured by minimizing material and staff costs (Y. Zhou and E. Wang, 2010, p. 440).

Subjective judgements capture better the relevant team performance domain, but they are also more influenced by performance irrelevant content such as biases (J. R. Mesmer-Magnus & L. A DeChurch, 2009, p. 536; see also G. P. Hodgkinson, 2002). J. R. Mesmer-Magnus and L. A. DeChurch (2009, p. 539, L. A. DeChurch & J. R. Mesmer-Magnus, 2010b, p. 34) mention the evaluation of the performance by supervisors or teams. For instance, B. C. Lim and K. J. Klein (2006) used expert ratings of each team's performance based on a 7-point scale. K. Lewis (2003, p. 592) used electronic device kit which student teams had to assemble. The team performance was measured in two ways. Firstly, how accurately the team assembled the electronic (accuracy); secondly, how quickly they completed the assembly (time based). Each assembly error was punished with a 60-second penalty (K. Lewis, 2003, p. 595). F. W. Kellermanns, S. W. Floyd, A. W. Pearson, and B. Spencer (2008) investigated the effect of constructive confrontation on shared mental models and team performance. Team performance was defined as decision quality measured on a 7-point Likert-Scale evaluating the decision quality (2008, pp. 122-136). D. A. Harrison, et al. (2003, p. 648) used trained judges, who rated the viability and innovativeness of a team's solutions for campus problems suggested per minute. The final score was the product of mean viability and mean innovativeness. M. J. Waller, N. Gupta, and R. C. Giambatista (2004, p. 1539) scored an overall team performance index based on the evaluation of three trainers within a natural decision simulator environment (nuclear power plant). The trainers were licensed operators currently working as operator trainers in the organization. To evaluate team performance, trainers focussed on six categories: diagnosis of problems and conditions based on signals and readings, understanding of plant and system response, adherence and use of procedures, control board operations, crew operations, and communications.

Both, objective and subjective judgements described above, are outcome measures. C. R. Paris et al. (2000, pp. 1056-1057) distinguish between outcome and process measures and individual and team measures. They add that process measures generally depend upon observation by skilled raters. They include on an individual level e.g. the measures of cognitive processes, and on a team level e.g. information exchange, communication, supporting behaviour and team leadership. These additional differentiations reflect the applicability of team performance construct as developed in this thesis.

The measurement of team performance and the resulting team performance index, which is given in percentage terms (see chapter 4.5.3.4.3) differ from most measures and indices described above in the following ways:

1. Team performance conceptualized in this thesis is based on qualitative concept mapping techniques. It reflects cognitive structures based on qualitative concepts. Most indices described above are based on action and are measured with quantitative indices (e.g. mission completion rate, number of targets hit).
2. The index is independent from skilled raters, because it is derived from the concepts of individuals and teams. Therefore, it includes fewer non-performance-relevant sources of variance (rater bias), and is an objective measure.
3. The index reflects cognitive changes, which occur when work changes from an individual to a team. Hence, differences between individuals and teams can be analysed, but the input of the individual can also be compared to that of the team. Hence, team performance in this thesis also reflects communication and social interaction processes (process measures).
4. Therefore, the index is applicable to both an individual and a team level.

The disadvantage of this team performance construct is that the index is of relative value. Hence, at least, two measurement sessions are needed to achieve results. Additionally, the index is only informative, if changes occur, such as changes in the work situation (team versus individual), or if different groups are compared. From this perspective, team performance is not economic (see chapter 3.4).

4. Research Project 'The Comparability of Idiosyncratic Mental Models'

4.1. Empirical Study I: Eliciting Idiosyncratic Knowledge Structures (Approach A)

4.1.1. Outline of the Research Topic of Approach A

The research topic in study I is about cause-and-effect relationships. There are two reasons for this. **The first reason** refers to the basic construct. It is used as a platform for understanding shared knowledge. Cause-and-effect relationships can be represented in mental models. Both cause-and-effect relationships and mental models have a form, which allows a distinction to be seen between content and structure. This is important, because mental models focus on important issues of a domain. The choice of issues reflects the evaluation of their importance as judged by an individual. Additionally, team members could have the same content knowledge of a domain, but the structure, hence the linkages between concepts, could be different. This means that the same concepts in two different mental models are not linked. The value of the linkage could also be different (e.g. positive or negative). Therefore, mental models are different. Langan-Fox et al. (2004, p. 334) stated that mental models form the framework in which decisions take place, according to the perception of the individual (chapter 2.2.3.1). Hence, mental models determine the understanding of the domain. Therefore, different mental models might cause differences in understanding and decision making in teams (see J. Langan-Fox et al., 2004, p. 334). This can lead to misunderstandings, which could result in disasters, especially in risky, time-critical and dynamic situations, such as aviation. Here, the time between the wrong decision and the result is usually very short. This is why shared knowledge is central to team process research and man-machine-interaction settings (see studies by R. J. Stout et al., 1999; N. J. Cooke et al., 2003; A. P. Banks & L. J. Millward, 2007; J. Sauer et al., 2006; see chapter 1.1).

However, in management, the time between a wrong decision and its outcomes could be much longer (e.g. disinvestment decisions). The evaluation of the domain, based on the mental model held at the time of decision, is difficult to reconstruct in detail after a long period. Moreover, in terms of strategy, G. P. Hodgkinson and P. R. Sparrow (2002, p. 150) noted that company members in different roles are confronted by different environmental conditions. These variations, which depend on the position and responsibilities of the members in the company, lead to differences in individual knowledge. Nevertheless, a minimum of common knowledge between different company members is necessary in order to implement the strategic business goals and objectives of the company (I. Bamberger & T. Wrona, 2004, p. 368; see chapter 1.1). Therefore:

Content Specific Research Question 1: *What similarities exist in idiosyncratic mental models between members of a company?* (see Table 4, p. 78, row 4)

The second reason for focusing on cause-and-effect relationships relates to their fundamental importance in management accounting and strategy. The knowledge about cause-and-effect influences strategic planning and operational management, as well as the implementation of company goals. Often, corporate governance focuses on management decisions of short-term results, such as quarterly turnover. One reason for this is the link between salaries paid and monetary success. This can lead to an over-valuation of short-term results. A tool, which highlights the perspective of long-term goals, is the Balanced Scorecard (R. S. Kaplan & D. P. Norton, 1996a; R. S. Kaplan & D. P. Norton, 1996b, p. 75; F. Figge, T. Hahn, S. Schaltegger, & M. Wagner, 2002, p. 270; M. Chavan, 2009, pp. 395-396). It became well known through publications by R. S. Kaplan and D. P. Norton (1996a). It is a strategic management tool that can be used as a mediator between strategy development and strategy implementation (R. Brühl, 2009, pp. 431-432). The Balanced Scorecard provides additional information, rather than single reports. It includes financial measures (e.g. return on capital), non-financial measures (e.g. customer retention) and issues for the realization of strategic objectives (e.g. human capital and organizational capital; see R. S. Kaplan & D. P. Norton, 2004, p. 11; R. Brühl, 2009, pp. 434-436). Non-financial perspectives are specifically included in the Balanced Scorecard if they are part of a cause-and-effect chain. Such a chain would be an important element of the Balanced Scorecard (R. S. Kaplan, 2000; C. D. Ittner & D. F. Larcker, 2003; P. N. Bukh & T. Malmi, 2005, p. 88; I. M. Cobbold & G. J. G. Lawrie, 2002).

However, C. D. Ittner and D. F. Larcker (2003, p. 88) state that most companies fail to identify and analyse non-financial perspectives. In addition, they note that only 23% of the 157 companies surveyed always build and validate causal models (C. D. Ittner & D. F. Larcker, 2003, p. 91). P. N. Bukh and T. Malmi (2005, p. 90) mention that in Nordic Firms often "a rather simplified interpretation" (p. 90) of the Balanced Scorecard was implemented: "...scorecards are only composed of a collection of indicators sorted in four dimensions without any attempts to map the relationships between the indicators...". G. Speckbacher, J. Bishof, and T. Pfeiffer (2003) found that out of 42 companies in Germany, Austria, and Switzerland, which use a Balanced Scorecard, only 21 include cause-and-effect relationships. Consequently, it is difficult to simulate business models in the form of cause-and-effect relationships or as C. D. Ittner and D. F. Larcker (2001, p. 375) stated:

"...little is known about how (or if) companies develop explicit business models or how these models vary depending upon the organization's strategies, objectives, and organizational design."

Based on the assumption of formal and rational decision-making, strategy measures are planned with the objective of achieving long-term goals for the company (M. K. Welge & A. Al-Laham, 2003, p. 13). Nevertheless, as managerial research recognized, even managers are constrained by cognition. Therefore, a strategy is "...a set of hypotheses about cause and effect" (R. S. Kaplan & D. P. Norton, 1996a, p. 30). Hence, cause-and-effect relationships are propositions about factors, which influence the performance of companies (P. N. Bukh & T. Malmi, 2005, p. 96). Anyway, the knowledge about cause-and-effect relationships in a company is critically important for translating company strategies into action (R. S. Kaplan & D. P. Norton, 1996a). It is important to identify "value drivers in a causal chain of leading and lagging performance indicators" (C. D. Ittner & D. F. Larcker, 2001, p. 375; P. N. Bukh & T. Malmi, 2005).

Company members construct cause-and-effect relationships based on their knowledge and background, as well as information, which they get from their environment (from management accounting systems for example). Management accounting systems provide information about strategic and operational goals for managers. They have to insure that the input-output processes in the company help to achieve these goals. Therefore, managers need information about what has happened and what is expected to happen. If necessary, in order to adjust the processes, they have to analyse the variances and take appropriate action (R. Brühl, 2009, Chapter 2). Nevertheless, information is of no benefit, if managers do not understand the processes, or do not have an "understanding of cause and effect" (R. Simons, 2000, p. 63). This understanding is equally relevant in management accounting and strategic management. Management accounting provides information, which managers in strategic management need for decision-making. Hence, management accountants work in a gatekeeping role (see K. Lewin, 1947). They judge the importance of information, and decide what information will be passed on to the next level of management. Hence, they must construct mental models of the processes in the company. For the same reason, strategic managers need to have this understanding as a basis for strategic decision-making. For this reason, the second content specific research question in study I is:

Content Specific Research Question 2: *What kind of cause-and-effect relationships do individuals perceive within an organization?* (see Table 4, p. 78, row 5)

Table 4: Outline of Research Question, Method Objectives and Content Specific Questions of Study I

		Column	
		1	2
Row	1	Research question (Approach A and B) (see chapter 1.1)	How can the similarity of idiosyncratic mental models be identified and presented?
	2	Method objective 1 of study I (see Figure 2, p. 9)	Elicit idiosyncratic mental models
	3	Method objective 2 of study I (see Figure 2, p. 9)	Develop a rule system to build up cause-and-effect relationships
	4	Content specific research question 1	What commonalities exist in idiosyncratic mental models between members of a company?
	5	Content specific research question 2	What kind of cause-and-effect relationships do individuals perceive within an organization?

4.1.2. Outline of the Research Setting of Approach A

The research setting in Approach A concerns the resources and internal processes of the firm. In terms of cause-and-effect relationships two questions arise. What resources are of concern to managers (content related), and what is the relationship between these resources (structure based)? The reason for focussing on this is that they impact greatly on the competitiveness of a company. This is clearly important for successful firms. Two dimensions, the internal and external, are critical for strategic management tool SWOT-analysis. The internal view considers the strengths and weaknesses of the company (J. Barney, 1991, p. 100; see for instance M. Kutschker & S. Schmid, 2008, p. 842). The firm's resources, and the way in which they are used, are relevant (J. Barney, 1991). According to the resource-based view, resources can be both tangible and intangible assets, which would include capabilities as well as organisational procedures (B. Wernerfelt, 1984, p. 172; J. Barney, 1991, p. 101). The external view looks at relevant environmental factors, especially the opportunities for, and threats to the company (J. Barney, 1991, p. 100; see, for instance, M. Kutschker & S. Schmid, 2008, p. 842). This view comes from the competitive forces model of Porter (M. E. Porter, 1985; J. Barney, 1991). The Balanced Scorecard has no explicit perspective on competitors. However, it focuses on resources from two directions: learning and growth (perspective of potential), as well as internal business processes (process perspective). The learning and growth perceptive is mainly about resources and capabilities. Internal business processes are mainly about the specific ways in which resources are combined. It is the output of the combination of resources and capabilities (see the cause-and-effect relationship in R. S. Kaplan & D. P. Norton, 1996a). Both perspectives are closely linked. Therefore, based on a Balanced Scorecard scenario, the research setting for this study includes resources and capabilities, as well as opportunities for and threats to a firm.

4.1.3. Method

4.1.3.1. Participants

Five participants of a small company were asked for an interview. Four participants agreed – three males and one female. Participant 1 and 4 were in similar positions in the company, as were participant 2 and 3. Because of the company small size, no demographic data were collected. The company is in the knowledge management and service industry.

4.1.3.2. Research Design

Table 5 outlines the research design. Study I was designed in three parts. In stage 1, the participants (N = 4) were interviewed using a semi-structured interview (column 1, row 2). In stage 2 (column 3, row 2), participants constructed their mental model using cause-and-effect relationships. In the 'between stages'-part (column 2, row 2), the interviewer prepared the concepts for the construction process in stage 2 (column 3, row 2). The participants in stage 1 were the same as in stage 2 (row 1).

Table 5:   Study I – Design

Row		Column		
		1	2	3
		Stage 1	Between Stages	Stage 2
1	Sample Group	S1		S1
2	Stage Objective	Participants were interviewed.	Interviewer prepared concepts for stage 2.	Participants constructed mental models.

4.1.3.3. Data Collecting Approach: Structure-Formation-Technique and its Application in this Thesis

Concepts form an essential part of the participants' mental model. Therefore, they have to be generated by the participants, according to their subjective evaluation of the concept's importance for a domain. Consequently, predefined concept lists, which are normally used in the nomothetic approach, are not suitable (see chapter 3.5.2). Additionally, the construction of mental models should be done by the participants themselves, to reflect their view of the domain (see chapters 2.2 and 4.1.1). For this reason, a Structure-Formation-Technique was used. This is a pool of methods to externalize knowledge. These are graphical methods, which have the objective to structure domain-specific knowledge in a simple form. A special Structure-Formation-Technique is the Heidelberger-Structure-Formation-Technique (HSFT), which was first presented 1979 by B. Scheele and N. Groeben (M. Bonato, 1990, p. 35).

This technique is founded in theory and methodology in the "Research Programme Subjective Theories" (Forschungsprogramm Subjektive Theorien, B. Scheele & N. Groeben, 1986; N. Groeben, D. Wahl, J. Schlee, & B. Scheele, 1988; for the construct of subjective theories see N. Groeben et al., 1988; B. Scheele & N. Groeben, 1988; N. Groeben & B. Scheele, 2000; H.-D. Dann, 1992; further R. K. Merton, 1968). It has a two-stage-approach (M. Bonato, 1990; B. Scheele & N. Groeben, 1988). In stage 1, the content of the domain is surveyed. In stage 2, the structure is modelled on the content. The disconnection of content inquiry and structure modelling is the basic principle of this Structure-Formation-Technique, whereby the core of the technique is structuring. B. Scheele and N. Groeben (1986; 1988, p. 37) suggest a semi-structured interview with three different questions in stage 1. Firstly, researchers should ask open, non-directed questions. Secondly, based on hypotheses, they should ask open, directed questions. Lastly, they should ask questions, which compare two statements. After completion of stage 1, the main concepts of the participants will be written down on concept cards. In stage 2, the core point of this technique, participants get a rules system, which they use to construct and structure their mental model. The rule system has to be adequate to the object of investigation, so that the participants are able to map their mental model (M. Bonato, 1990; D. Silverman, 1993).

Two versions of the technique exist (for the following M. Bonato, 1990, pp. 35-39). In the original version, researcher and participant construct the structure based on the concepts of stage 1. This is an active process for the participants and for the researcher. The researcher becomes part of the study, because he also constructs a cognitive map of the participant. Both maps frame the basis for the discussion that follows. The aim of the discussion is to construct adequately the mental model of the participant. This part is called "dialogue-consensus" (Dialog-Konsens). It is the validation of the results (B. Scheele & N. Groeben, 1986; 1988, p. 37).

The second version, the monological version, is used for surveying domain-knowledge. The interview can be omitted. Concepts could be written down directly on concept cards. Moreover, a dialogue-consensus would not be necessary, because of the domain-knowledge (B. Scheele & N. Groeben, 1986; M. Bonato, 1990, p. 38).

Research in this thesis is derived from the tradition of the knowledge-rich and domain-specific research about mental models. Individuals use mental models in their reasoning about phenomena in the everyday world (see the overviews in D. Gentner & A. L. Stevens, 1983; Y. Rogers, A. Rutherford, & P. A. Bibby, 1992; J. Oakhill & A. Garnham, 1996). Mental models are representations of the cognitive system of individuals (see chapter 2.2.2). For that reason, they are subjective, because they are represented in their minds. In Approach A, participants will be confronted with complex and poorly structured phenomena. They have to build models of their organisation and organisational problems. Because participants face many different entities and their relationships, they need a knowledge structure, which copes with this complexity. This knowledge structure will be called 'idiosyncratic mental model' in this thesis.

One of the basic positions of qualitative research is that the method has to be adequate to the object under investigation (D. Silverman, 1993). H. A. Simon (1992, p. 156) stated that real decision-making situations are often characterized by inconsistent information. Decisions are made because of a trade-off between the speed of decision-making and the accuracy of the decision, based on the 'best of knowledge':

> "... They do the best they can to achieve their goals according to the knowledge they can bring to mind, and the inferences that knowledge supports, in the time allowed." (S. J. Payne, 2003, p. 138).

Therefore, it was decided to adjust the method. Instead of the dialogue consensus character, the "monological application" (B. Scheele & N. Groeben, 1986, p. 535) of Heidelberger-Structure-Formation-Technique was used. Hence, there were no discussions about mental models between interviewer and participant. The decision to use the monological version was made because the participants should have maximum control. They should spontaneously and by themselves create the concepts as well as the structure. This procedure provides the chance to elicit mental models that are not biased because of the interventions of other individuals. These individual mental models reflect the internal structure of knowledge, which the participants use in their daily lives. When participants make decisions in their organisational environment, they do this using their own mental model. If researchers are interested in team mental model building, this procedure will detect differences in the idiosyncratic mental models. These individual differences can be dealt with in a procedure, which opens up a discussion about similarities and differences between the mental models of team members (see for instance C. Eden & F. Ackermann, 2002). Additionally, the rule system was adjusted to build cause-and-effect relationships. The rules represent different types of relationships between concepts, to ensure that the mental models of the participants will be covered fully.

4.1.3.4. Stimulus Material for Collecting Data including the Rule System

It is important for constructing mental models that there is an adequate rule system, which investigates the structure of the concepts, so that the participants are able to map their mental model (M. Bonato, 1990). As the research questions are aimed at resources and capabilities as well as opportunities for and threats to organisations, the rule system has to reflect those relationships. Therefore, the rule system represents different categories of relationships between concepts (e.g.): 'concept A effects concept B'; 'A has a positive (negative) effect on B'; 'A is an opportunity/benefit (threat/disadvantage) for B'. Moreover, some grouping and clustering rules were included: 'A is part of B'; 'A effects group (B, C, D)'; 'group (A, B, C) effects D'; as well as a listing rule, and an 'or'-rule (see Appendix 1). These rules were developed from the taped interview of participant 1 (Table 5, p. 79, column 1) as well as from the researcher's views.

A semi-structured interview of four questions, about the research setting of resources and internal processes, was developed for stage 1 (see chapter 4.1.1). The focus of participants was directed towards their organisation. They were asked to describe competitive resources and capabilities of their organization. The participants were also asked to reflect on their possible contribution towards the competitive advantage of their organisation. Particularly, they were asked:

- Which of your company's resources must remain for it to be competitive in the long term?
- To what extent do abilities play in a role?
- What opportunities and risks do you see for maintaining or increasing the competitiveness of your company?
- To what extent do you believe every individual can contribute to maintaining and building competitiveness?

4.1.3.5. Screening of Data During the Research Process

Method objective 2 is the development of a rule system to build cause-and-effect relationships (see Table 4, p. 78). For that reason, during stage 2, participant 1 was observed as to how he coped with the method. B. Scheele and N. Groeben (1988) stated that dealing with rule systems could be difficult for those who are not used to this method. One problem could be the unintended interruption by participants. Thus, it was the aim to find out if participants use all rules, omit some rules, or if they are not able to deal with the rule system at all. A first screening took place looking for significant problems. As a result, rules were fine-tuned for further research in study I. Additionally, the elicitation stage was extended, with a small preparatory exercise, for the other participants. Using the preparatory exercise, the participants became acquainted with the rules. By the end of stage 2, each participant was asked for his impression. This was important because the participants, who were supposed to be interviewed in further research, were probably not used to this kind of qualitative research.

4.1.3.6. Data Analysis Approaches

The idiosyncratic mental models were analysed in two ways:

- Quantitative analysis: nomothetic-quantitative and idiographic-quantitative
- Qualitative analysis: idiographic-qualitative

Quantitative analysis referred to the frequency of the cause-and-effect-rules which were used (nomothetic-quantitative analysis), as well as the centrality of concepts (idiographic-quantitative analysis). The analysis of cause-and-effect rules focussed on two questions (see chapter 4.1.4.2). Firstly, what kind of rules participants used for constructing the idiosyncratic mental models. Secondly, in which way do participants differ in the frequency with which they use the cause-and-effect-rules. Centrality of concepts was analysed based on the frequency of the in-arrows and out-arrows from the idiosyncratic concepts (chapter 4.1.4.3.1) as suggested by Eden et al. (1992, p. 313; see chapter 3.7.2.3). Frequency analysis of central-cause and central-effect concepts was done for comparing similar, important concepts in idiosyncratic mental models.

Qualitative analysis was word-based, focussing on linked, hence connected, concepts (idiographic-qualitative analysis). It was focussed on capabilities and resources, in particular the example of Human Resources, as well as opportunities and risks. Hence, chapter 4.1.4.3.2 sketches the content specific questions 'What kind of cause-and-effect relationship do members perceive within their organisation?' (content question 2, Table 4, p. 78) as well as 'What commonalities exists?' (content question 1, Table 4, p. 78).

4.1.3.7. Equipment

The interviews of stage 1 were recorded on audio tape. The construction process of stage 2 was taped on video. The participant used a flipchart for constructing mental models and paper and pencil for drawing the connections between concepts. To retain this, the mental models were taped to flipchart paper. Moreover, the mental model, which was the result of the construction process, were photographed, and later transferred to VISIO, a graphic software tool.

4.1.3.8. Research Process

The study took place between November 2004 and March 2005. The interviews were conducted within the organisation in German. The interviewer was the same in all interviews. The semi-structured interview described above (see chapter 4.1.3.4) was conducted during stage 1, and lasted for about one hour. It was finished as soon as the participants had nothing more to say.

After stage 1, the interviewer prepared concepts, based on the tape recordings. Some reasons for taking up a concept were:

- Special emphasis,
- Enumerations, examples, and
- Detailed descriptions.

An example of a detailed description given by one participant was:

> "Yes. Well, if I – I don't know- if I lived in Asia for a few years, then went to another Asian country, where the culture is nevertheless very different, it would probably not be as difficult for me, as it would be if it were my first time etc." (Participant 2)

Here, the concept 'intercultural experience' was generated. The generated concepts were the basis for constructing the participant's mental models.

In stage 2, participant 1 received the cause-and-effect rules on paper. The rules were explained by the interviewer. The participant was told to use the rule 'opportunity/benefit' whenever he saw an opportunity or a benefit, and the rule 'threat/disadvantage' whenever he saw a threat or a disadvantage. The procedure for explaining the mental model construction using cause-and-effect rules changed for the other three participants. At the beginning of stage 2, the participants got a preliminary exercise. They were asked to construct a mental model 'lifecycle' using the concepts 'water', 'tree', 'growth', 'lifecycle', 'leaves', 'bananas', 'apples', and 'children'. At this point, the cause-and-effect rules were explained. Participants were introduced to the procedure 'how to construct mental models'.

Following the introduction to the cause-and-effect rules, all four participants were asked to check the concepts, which were prepared by the interviewer. This check was made to ensure participants agreed with these concepts. This procedure is part of the communicative validation (see chapter 3.4). Additionally, during stage 2 with participant 1, it was noticed that the participant wanted to cluster concepts. Thus, participants were allowed to cluster concepts, if they thought concepts belong together. The main idea for clustering concepts is to gain an overview, and to reduce complexity for the participant. Additionally, C. Eden and F. Ackermann (1998, p. 201) note that clusters are focussed on specific areas. These can be compared with those from other participants within the same area.

After concepts were checked, participants started to construct their mental models. At this stage, participants were allowed to add rules if they felt that rules were missing. Stage 2 was finished when participants ended the construction of the mental models. This took about one to one and a half hours.

4.1.4. Results

4.1.4.1. Method Objective 1: Idiosyncratic Mental Models

Method Objective 1 was to elicit idiosyncratic mental models (Table 4, p. 78). This chapter introduces the method for reading these mental models. Figure 16 shows the simplified mental model of participant 4. Circles symbolize original concepts. Because of the need for anonymity, not all original concepts are reported (empty circles). Cause-and-effect rules, hence the relations between concepts, are pictured with arrows. Arrows also include the values of the rules. For instance, the rule 'positive effect' has an arrow with a plus sign. 'Zero' at the start or end of an arrow symbolizes an effect on a group of concepts (see Appendix 1). As an example, Figure 16 shows one cluster 'human resources' that includes the concepts 'management administration', 'top management' and 'general administration'. Five clusters with 14 concepts affect the cluster 'human resources': The cluster 'internalize the idea of the company', 'intercultural work' and 'above use' has a positive effect on the cluster 'human resources'. In turn, 'human resources' has a positive effect on two other concepts, 'strengthening of research and development' as well as 'products'.

This mental model shows no feedback-loops. Linear structures of relations between concepts predominate in all four mental models (for the mental model of participant 3 see Appendix 2).

Figure 16: Study I – Mental Model by Participant 4

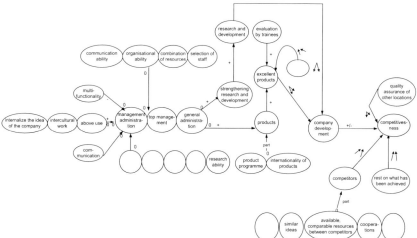

4.1.4.2. Method Objective 2: Results to the Cause-and-Effect Rule System

Method Objective 2 was to develop cause-and-effect rules (Table 4, p. 78). This chapter outlines observations, which were made during the development process, as well as the results.

Participant 1 performed well during stage 2 because of the instruction. Remarkably, the participant took more than one hour to construct the mental model. He was not willing to work on the model after that. In addition, it turned out that the rules were incomplete. Therefore, it was decided to change the introduction. Hence, participants 2, 3 and 4 were told to cluster the concepts if they wanted to. Additionally, the rule system was expanded to include more rules (for a concept A and a group {B, C, D} as well as a group {A, B, C} and a concept D): 'A affects the group' and 'the group affects D'. Table 6 shows a detailed record of the rules used by the participants.

Table 6: Study I – Used Rules a Participant (in Absolute Quantities)

Row	Participant \ Rules	Column 1 Participant 1 (Pre-Test)	Column 2 Participant 2	Column 3 Participant 3	Column 4 Participant 4
1	Concepts	47	53	42	35
2	Rules (overall 11)	9	10	9	9
3	Cluster	4	11	8	6
4	Single concept	34	10	13	13
5	Rule 'effects'	9	11	6	3
6	Rule 'positive effect'	24	25	4	7
7	Rule 'negative effect'	3	7	0	2
8	Rule 'part of'	5	12	11	2
9	Rule 'necessary'	6	18	2	0
10	Rule 'benefit'	4	6	5	3
11	Rule 'disadvantage'	1	3	2	3
12	Use of the rule 'or'	No	No	No	No
13	Use of the rule 'A effects'	Yes	Yes	Yes	Yes
14	Use of the rule 'group effects'	No	Yes	Yes	Yes

Note ii: Rules connecting clusters counted once; Double concepts counted once

Because the rules were developed based on the interview of participant 1 and the researcher's views, the results of participant 1 are described as pre-test results (column 2). Column 1 refers to different aspects of concepts such as 'cluster' (row 3), and 'single concepts' (row 4) as well as to the rules such as 'positive effect' (row 6) and 'part of' (row 8). Columns 3, 4 and 5 depict the results for participants 2, 3 and 4. For instance, participant 1 used 34 single concepts and four clusters. Participant 4 used 13 single concepts, but six clusters. Concepts, which were clustered, were not counted as single concepts.

It is worthwhile noticing that the four participants did not differ substantially in the number of rules used (row 2). On average, nine out of eleven rules were used. The rule 'or' was not used. Participants differed in the number of single concepts ($\chi^2_{emp}=21.09$, $p < 0.001$[8]*, row 4). Furthermore, participant 1 (pre-test) did not use the rule 'group effects', unlike the other participants.

There are some qualitative differences between participants. For instance, participant 2 used the rule 'necessary' 18 times, whereas participant 4 never used this rule ($\chi^2_{emp}=16.00$, $p<0.001$[9]**,[10]***). Similar results are found for the following rules:

- 'Part of': participant 2 used this rule 12 times whereas participant 4 used it only twice ($\chi^2_{emp}=9.20$, $p=0.027$*; $\chi^2_{emp}=7,28$, $p =0.026$**,[11]****),
- 'Positive effect': participant 2 used this rule 25 times whereas participant 3 used it four times ($\chi^2_{emp}=19.08$, $p<0.001$*; $\chi^2_{emp}=21.50$, $p<0.001$**,****).

It is noteworthy that Participant 2 used some rules more often than the other participants, such as the rules 'negative effect' (row 7) and 'necessary' (row 9).

Table 7 outlines the results of the rule 'cluster' in Table 6, row 3. Table 7 shows how often participants formed clusters (column 2-5), and how many concepts participants assigned to a cluster (column 1, row 1-7). It is notable that in contrast to the other participants, participant 2 developed clusters, which included many concepts, such as one cluster with nine concepts and one with seven concepts.

Table 7: Study I – Quantities of Clusters and Concept in a Cluster

Row	Column 1 Participant / Group	Column 2 Participant 1 (Pre-Test)	Column 3 Participant 2	Column 4 Participant 3	Column 5 Participant 4
1	Group with 2 concept	1	6	3	1
2	Group with 3 concept	1			2
3	Group with 4 concept	2	1	3	1
4	Group with 5 concept		1	1	2
5	Group with 6 concept		1	1	
6	Group with 7 concept		1		
7	Group with 9 concept		1		

[8] *Sign. 1-dim. Chi-square-test (four participants) $\chi^2_{crit\ (3,\ 95\%)}=7,81$
[9] **Sign. 1-dim. Chi-square-test (three participants) $\chi^2_{crit\ (2,\ 95\%)}=5,99$
[10] *** one case is zero
[11] **** Participants 2-4

4.1.4.3. Content Specific Questions: Description of the Results of the Elicitation of Knowledge

Method Objective 1 was to elicit idiosyncratic knowledge (Table 4, p. 78). This is the basis for the aggregation to shared knowledge (study II, chapter 4.2). However, Figure 16, p. 85, and Appendix 2 show the high complexity of the idiosyncratic mental models. It is therefore necessary to focus more strongly on the analysis of important issues about differences and similarities between idiosyncratic mental models. Therefore, it was decided to explore single concepts first by analysing their centrality. Hence, the focus is content-related and based on examples of central cause- and central effect-concepts (chapter 4.1.4.3.1) as suggested by Eden et al. (1992, p. 313; chapter 3.7.2.3). This is followed by an outline of similarities of the idiosyncratic mental models to linked concepts within the example of Human Resources, and its capabilities, opportunities and risks (chapter 4.1.4.3.2).

4.1.4.3.1. Central Cause-Concepts and Central Effect-Concepts

Table 8, p. 89, shows, which concepts (columns 1 and 4) of the participants (columns 1-3 and 4-6) have the most in-arrows ('IA', influenced by, columns 2 and 5), and out-arrows ('OA', affects other, columns 3 and 6). Additionally, it outlines which concepts influence most other concepts (row 'cause concept'), and which concepts are most often influenced by other concepts (row 'effect concept'). Hence, it reveals the most important sources and targets, and therefore central concepts (C. Eden et al., 1992, p. 313). Table 8 reveals three different types of concepts:

- Central cause-concepts
- Central effect-concepts
- Mediating concepts

Central cause-concepts are at the beginning of a causal chain. Therefore, they have out-arrows and no in-arrows such as the concepts 'internationality' (participant 1, five out-arrows, column 3, row 1), 'certification' (participant 1, three out-arrows, column 3, row 2), 'finance' (participant 3, four out-arrows, column 3, row 9), 'communication' (participant 4, one out-arrow, column 6, row 10), and 'company contacts' (participant 3, three out-arrows, column 3, row 10).

Central effect-concepts have in-arrows and no out-arrows such as the concepts 'competitiveness' (participant 3, 22 in-arrows, column 2, row 11), 'company' (participant 3, seven in-arrows, column 2, row 12), and 'marketing' (participant 3, five in-arrows, column 2, row 13). Central effect-concepts are at the end of a causal chain.

Table 8: Study I – Concepts, Which often Influenced by other Concepts and Causes other Concepts

Row	Participant / Concepts	Participant 1 (Pre-Test)			Participant 2		
		Concepts	IA	OA	Concepts	IA	OA
1	Cause concepts	Internationality	-	5			
2		Certifications	-	3			
3	Mediating concepts	Programs for top manager	3	3	Linguistic abilities	22	20
4		Knowledge	5	1	Intercultural experience*	22	19
5		Research	4	1	Cultural influences*	23	19
6		Programs for becoming top manager	3	1	Reputation	31	2
7					Ability to pursuance of a job	28	18
8					Specialisation	24	19

Row	Participant / Concepts	Participant 3			Participant 4		
		Concepts	IA	OA	Concepts	IA	OA
9	Cause concepts	Finance	-	4	Internalize the idea of the company*,**	-	1
10		Company contacts	-	3	Communication*,**	-	1
11	Effect concepts	Competitiveness	22	-			
12		Company	7	-			
13		Marketing	5	-			
14	Mediating concepts	Research	2	3	Cluster 'employees' (top management, general management, management administration) each	14	2
15					Cluster 'employees' (top management, general management, management administration) each	14	2
16					Products	5	1
17					Competitiveness	4	1

Note iii: IA = in-arrows; OA = out-arrows; Arrows which effects groups are counted separately; *Example, more than three concepts got the same number of arrows; ** Concepts were included in the table because the mental models of participant 3 and participant 4 were evaluated referring there similarity (see below).

Mediating concepts have in-arrows and out-arrows. They influence other concepts, and they are influenced by other concepts, such as the concept 'product' (participant 4, column 4, row 16, five in-arrows, and one out-arrow). Among these central mediating concepts are once which were given identical names by participants, such as the concept 'competitiveness' (participant 3, column 1, row 11, and participant 4, column 4, row 17) and given similar names, such as the concepts 'internationality' and 'intercultural experience' (participant 1, column 1, row 1, and participant 2, column 4, row 4).

4.1.4.3.2. Example of Linked Concepts Using Cause-and-Effect Rules

This chapter highlights related or linked concepts. The focus is on

- capabilities and resources, and in particular, human resources as well as
- opportunities and risks.

In three mental models (participant 1, 3 and 4), **human resources and/or its capabilities** are central resources. Table 9 shows a selection of concepts chosen by participants when referring to human resources and its capability.

Table 9: Study I – Examples for Human Resources and its Capability Concepts, Named by Participants

Concepts / Participant	Participant 1 (Pre-Test)	Participant 2	Participant 3	Participant 4
Human Resources	Top management		Young top management	Top management
	Staff		Employee	General management
	Management administration		Management administration	Management administration
Capabilities	Adaptability	Informed abilities	Competitiveness	Communication abilities
	Network ability			Organisational abilities
	Research ability			Competitiveness
	Coordination ability			Five anonymous concepts

Usually, capabilities were linked directly to human resources, such as:

- Participant 1: 'management administration' effects 'network ability' and 'intercultural competence' has a positive effect on 'management administration',
- Participant 3: 'best performance of employees' is necessary for 'competitiveness' and 'creativity of the employees/space' is an opportunity for 'competitiveness',
- Participant 4: 'organisational ability' effects 'management administration' and 'communication' effects 'management administration'.

These examples show a remarkable similarity. However, participant 2 has developed the most complex model, but had a weaker view of human resources. Only the concept 'informed abilities' – about the entire company – is part of human resources in a wider sense. Nevertheless, participant 2 was the only one who took the customers' view in the mental model – the trainees, with their capabilities. Participant 2 stated:

- 'Intercultural experiences' are necessary for an 'ability do a job',
- 'Linguistic abilities' affect 'cultural influences'.

A first hint of how participants linked **opportunities and risks** to resources and capabilities is revealed in Table 6, p. 86. The rules 'benefit' and 'disadvantage' are especially important. In summary, the four participants used these rules almost equally often. Participant 4 linked most of these rules to the competitive position of his organisation ('benefit' three times, 'threats' twice; see Figure 16, p. 85):

- 'Quality of assurance of other location' is a benefit for the 'competitiveness'. Similarly, 'excellent products', 'research and development' are benefits for 'company development',
- 'Competitors', 'rest on what has been achieved' are threats for 'competitiveness'.

By contrast, participant 1 linked three out of five of these rules to resources or capabilities of resources ('benefit' three times), such as:

- 'Trained staff' are a benefit for 'management administration',
- 'IT' is a benefit for the 'general management',
- 'Temporary help' is a benefit for 'top management'.

The other participants mixed the rules between resources, competitive position, and other important aspects for the competitive capabilities of their organization. For instance:

- 'Cooperation with other companies' is a benefit and a threat for the 'application orientated approach' (Participant 2),
- 'Reputation' is a benefit for 'personal contacts' (Participant 2),
- 'Rapid growth of the company' is a threat to 'competitiveness' (Participant 3),
- 'Employees as representatives of the company' are benefits for 'marketing' (Participant 3).

4.1.5. Interpretation and Discussion

The Method Objective 2 in this study was to develop a rule system to build cause-and-effect relationships. Generally, participants did not have problems with the rules. Only participant 4 asked for a rule 'no connection'. Thus, the rule system worked well. Adequate methods concerning the object of investigation is one important basic position of qualitative research (D. Silverman, 1993; see chapter 4.1.3.3). However, Table 6, p. 86, reveals that almost all rules were used a couple of times by each participant except for the rules 'necessary' (participant

4) and 'negative effect' (participant 3). Only the rule 'or' was not used. It could be that these rules are not part of the mental model of the participants. It is also possible that the participants got tired, or that the task was too difficult, so they were unable to recognize these rules. Participants were not used to this method of research. Nevertheless, it is significant that in total the rule 'negative effect' is used less often (twelve times) than the rule 'positive effect' (57 times).

It is also remarkable that participant 2 used many rules, and constructed many different clusters (see Table 7, p. 87). This could be evidence for a highly developed and highly differentiated mental model. The degree to which the rules were used is noticeable (row 5 until 11, Table 6, p. 86). They are a qualitative nuance of the structure of the mental model. The average application of these rules with all four participants is about 46 times (with participant 2, 3 and 4 it is about 44 times). Participant 2 used these rules 82 times; this is way above the average. In addition, participant 2 was the only one who connected concepts within the cluster. Participant 2 took the longest time with stage 2. Therefore, it is not clear how many of the differences between participant 2 and the other participants are caused by the mental model of participant 2, or caused by other attributes, such as higher motivation, deeper interest in the research area, or having no time constraint. In addition, it may be that participant 2 had a different mental model because of his work in the organisation. Participant 2 and participant 4 had the same roles in the company, but in different areas. It could be that participant 2 needed detailed organisational knowledge for his job. This would support the notion that differences in responsibility could have an impact on the knowledge structures (see G. P. Hodgkinson & P. R. Sparrow, 2002, p. 150; G. P. Hodgkinson & G. Johnson, 1994, p. 530). However, for reasons of anonymity, it is not possible to clarify this, because of the size of the organisation.

The difference in numbers of clusters and single concepts between participant 1 and the other participants can be traced back to the change in the introduction for the cause-and-effect rules. Participants 2, 3 and 4 were told to cluster concepts, if they wanted to. They were told this because participant 1 wanted to cluster. Furthermore, it is critical that the rule system was adjusted because of the results of participant 1. The rule system might have been changed if other participants had had the lead position. In addition, Structure-Formation-Technique makes great demands on participants, in terms of communication and abstraction (H.-D. Dann, 1992).

The methods used must be adequate for the object of investigation (D. Silverman, 1993; see chapter 4.1.3.3) which includes the research process. Four participants were interviewed in one organisation, for about 10 hours in total. In that time, they revealed their idiosyncratic mental models about the organisation. Reflecting on the results of the comparison of the idiosyncratic mental models, it should be noted that they were highly idiosyncratic, but also had common qualities. For instance, three participants weighted human resources as a central resource, but each in an idiosyncratic way. One might guess from these findings that mental models have common qualities, which are not shared by all members of an organisation (see C. Eden et al., 1992, pp. 314-315). From a review of the literature, it can be assumed that the nature of mental models is still an open question: Are there similarities between mental models, or are they highly idiosyncratic? Looking at the findings of study I, in line with the reported differences and similarities of the results by G. P. Hodgkinson and G. Johnson (1994) and R. K. Reger and A. S. Huff (1993), both may be true.

However, firstly, it should be stressed that the empirical findings depend on how concepts and their relationships were elicited (see chapter 3.5). The qualitative approach gave participants a high degree of control. They generated their own concepts, and based on these concepts, they constructed their mental model. The interview was conducted with a minimum of direction. This leads to the issue of comparability of the concepts, and in turn of the mental models. However, this lack of comparability is not as compelling as is the advantage of getting an uninfluenced mental model. As mentioned in the introduction (see chapter 1), in most studies participants do not have full control when constructing their mental model (see also K. E. Weick & M. G. Bougon, 2001, p. 320). In this study, the eliciting process focussed on examining idiosyncratic mental models. Therefore, in line with the study by K. Daniels et al. (2002), it was decided to give the participants maximum control in this process.

Evaluating the importance of concepts with the quantity of relationships in a mental model (see chapter 4.1.4.3) would appear to be a simple matter (P. Cossette & M. Audet, 1992, p. 341). However, counting concepts and relationships gives a hint of the complexity of the mental model and the central concepts (C. Eden et al., 1992, p. 313; K. E. Weick & M. G. Bougon, 2001, p. 320; C. Eden, 2004, p. 677).

In accordance with the results in other studies (see e.g. J. A. M. Vennix, 1999, p. 381; J. K. Doyle, M. J. Radzicki, & W. S. Trees, 2008, p. 283; the study by B. Fokkinga, I. Bleijenbergh & J. Vennix, 2009, cit. after M. Schaffernicht & S. N. Groesser, 2011), feedback-loops were rarely used by the participants. For these findings, Weick and Bougon (2001, p. 321) summarize different explanations and tendencies (K. E. Weick & M. G. Bougon, 2001, p. 321):

- Uncertainty situations:

"...there is evidence that people who normally perceive loops ignore them and impose a clear, categorical, lineal structure on their experience when there is uncertainty..." (K. E. Weick & M. G. Bougon, 2001, p. 321)

- Indeterminate situations:

"...executives often pick the simplest and most direct arguments that offer immediate, tangible results, and favour the dominant coalition." (K. E. Weick & M. G. Bougon, 2001, p. 321)

- Stress conditions:

"Since uncertainty produces stress and since organizations operate under uncertainty much of the time, we might expect to find relatively simple, nonrecursive structures in dominant cause maps." (K. E. Weick & M. G. Bougon, 2001, p. 321)

- To bring things to an end

"...in a world where there is so much turnover that the effects of an action seldom affect the originator." (K. E. Weick & M. G. Bougon, 2001, p. 321)

- Situations which are explored:

"...they take several actions, only some of which have consequences." (K. E. Weick & M. G. Bougon, 2001, p. 321)

All of these are possible explanations for the missing loops in the current study.

The results could have been affected by the fact that participants did not write down the concepts themselves. It is possible that not all concepts were taken up by the interviewer, or that some were taken up which were not important to the participant. The subjective reality of the interviewer could have influenced the results. In qualitative research, the researcher is always part of the process, and can take an active role. On the one hand, this active role was restricted, to allow the participant to construct a model without being influenced. On the other hand, the interviewer wrote up the concepts, based on audiotapes in stage 1, paying attention to emphasis, enumerations, detailed descriptions, and examples (see chapter 4.1.3.8). Nevertheless, this could raise the question as to whether concepts really reflect the subjective reality of the participants who were interviewed. However, the participants looked at the concepts at the beginning of stage 2. If they did not agree with the concepts they could add, change, or delete cards even during the modelling process.

Additionally, the strict monological application of Heidelberg-Structure-Formation-Technique could have been used, where the participants wrote the concepts themselves (see M. Bonato, 1990). However, a different method was applied. During the pre-test interview of participant 1, it was realised quickly that conducting the interview and while the participant was writing up the concepts, was asking too much. The process seems to have been too complex. Asking participants to take part in three different stages (1. being interviewed, 2. listing to their audiotapes and writing the concepts, 3. constructing mental models) would overtax them. Therefore, this process was the best way to develop concepts. It provides overall support for, yet avoids overtaxing the participant. Additionally, the concepts are supported because of validation by participants at the beginning of stage 2 (communicative validation, S. Lamnek, 2010; C. Seale, 1999; see chapter 3.4).

As a result of the above, it can be concluded that the rule system adequately reflects cause-and-effect relationships. Additionally, the adapted form of Structure-Formation-Techniques elicits idiosyncratic mental models. They show individual characteristics, but also commonalities, which can now be analysed in a structured way.

4.2. Empirical Study II: The Delphi-Method for Analysing Idiosyncratic Mental Models in Terms of Similarity (Approach A)

4.2.1. Introduction

The literature about shared knowledge discusses the elicitation of individual knowledge based on quantities (e.g. J. Langan-Fox et al., 2000), as well as the use of aggregation methods to generate collective representations and shared mental models (N. J. Cooke et al., 2001, p. 299; N. J. Cooke et al., 2007b; S. Mohammed et al. 2010, see chapter 3.7). In the previous study, an idiographic approach was preferred (see chapter 3.5.2). It looked at the idiosyncratic mental models of participants. Hence, participants used their own concepts to construct their mental model. The disadvantage of this approach is the lack of comparability between idiosyncratic mental models (S. Mohammed et al., 2010, p. 885).

However, the results in study I revealed common qualities in the mental models of the participants (see chapter 4.1.4). For instance, participant 1 generated a concept 'coordination ability' (see Table 9, p. 90), and participant 3 generated a concept 'coordination process' (see Appendix 2). Because of such similarities, it should be possible to compare these concepts, for instance, if the names of these concepts are adjusted to abstract categories. The original concepts of the idiosyncratic mental models would still be available. Through the abstract categories, the overlap in knowledge structure would become apparent. This would confirm the statement by S. Mohammed et al. (2000, p. 149) that about the obscuring of interpretable structures (see chapter 3.6). Hence, if there are similar concepts in different idiosyncratic mental models, adjusted to same abstract category, similarity in content and structure of the idiosyncratic mental models could be compared. The challenge is to summarize in one category concepts which have the same meaning but different names. Concepts which have virtually identical verbal tags, but which differ in meaning, would not be included (C. Eden et al., 1981, pp. 41-42; P. E. Jones & P. H. M. P. Roelofsma, 2000, p. 1142; see chapter 1.1). The aim of study II was therefore to find out, if and to what extent it would be possible to assimilate the individual language of idiosyncratic mental models. Hence, study II took a closer look at the common qualities of the idiosyncratic mental models, which were elicited in study I. This leads to

Method Objective 3: *to aggregate idiosyncratic mental models to shared mental models using abstract categories* (see chapter 2.2.3.2)

There is for this method objective the

Content Specific Research Question: *What are the similarities in the idiosyncratic mental models in study I when they are expressed in terms of concepts with different names?*

The concepts of the idiosyncratic mental models are transformed into more abstract ones, hence into categories. Thereby, common ground is found between the mental models of different participants. The animal example in Figure 17, p. 97, and the school example in Appendix 3 indicate that the participants' idiosyncratic concepts might differ in their degree of abstraction. The task for the participants is therefore to assign specific concepts, such as canary, ostrich, shark, and salmon (Figure 17), into more abstract categories, such as bird, fish, and animals. In the end, the number of subcategories generated is irrelevant (such as 'skinny legs → ostrich → bird'), or how *many* categories are omitted (such as 'skinny legs → bird'; see also chapter 4.2.2.1).

Table 10 contrasts the relationship between study I and study II with respect to the study focus, method object and the results of studies, which compared study I and study II of Approach A.

Table 10: Study II – Overview about the Relationship between Study I and Study II

	Study I	Study II
Study Focus	Idiosyncratic mental models	Similar content in the idiosyncratic mental models
Method Object	To elicit idiosyncratic mental models To develop cause-and-effect rules	To aggregate idiosyncratic mental models to shared mental models focussing on common meaning of the concepts
Results	Four idiosyncratic mental models	Comparability of the idiosyncratic mental models

Figure 17: Study II – Example 'Animal' (Example following J. R. Anderson, 2001)

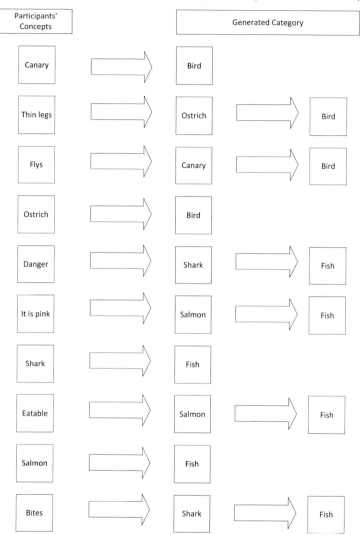

4.2.2. Method

4.2.2.1. Adapting the Delphi-Method for Qualitative Expert Aggregation

The Delphi-Method is a specific form of written interview. It was developed and used scientifically in the 1950s by RAND Corporation (A. Linstone & M. Turoff, 1975/2002a, p. 10; C. Buckley, 1995, p. 16; C.-C. Hsu & B. A. Sandford, 2007, p. 1; M. Häder, 2009, p. 32). Its "… object is to obtain the most reliable consensus of opinion of a group of experts." (N. C. Dalkey & O. Helmer, 1963, p. 458). The Delphi-Method is characterized among other things, by anonymity, iteration and aggregation of group responses. An essential feature of the approach is controlled feedback (N. C. Dalkey & O. Helmer, 1963, p. 458; V. Story, L. Hurdley, G. Smith, & J. Saker, 2001, p. 489; M. Häder, 2009, p. 25). In the Delphi-Method, all expert proposals are gathered centrally for solving a problem, and are summarised and analysed by a panel. The anonymous proposals are returned to the experts. Afterwards, each expert has the option to modify and adjust his proposal after considering the proposals of other experts. The proposals are likewise gathered centrally and analysed again. This anonymous interviewing process is repeated until the experts agree on one proposal for a solution to the problem (see for instance J. Bortz & N. Döring, 2006; V. Story et al., 2001; for examples of the application of the method see the edited book by H. A. Linstone & M. Turoff, 1975/2002b; different types of Delphi-Method are also described in M. Häder, 2009).

The advantage of the Delphi-Method is that the individual experts are influenced very little by their group. Direct confrontation between the experts is avoided, and group dynamics and the effect of status are minimised (see, for instance, N. C. Dalkey & O. Helmer, 1963, p. 458; P. M. Mullen, 2003, p. 49). Additionally, the Delphi-Method gathers expert opinions efficiently (C. Buckley, 1995, p. 16). Moreover, P. C. Howze and C. Dalrymple (2004, p. 179) mention that compared to face-to-face meetings, participants were spared long meetings, leaving more time for productive thinking about the issues. For this reason, the Delphi-Method is suitable in this study (for further discussion of the advantages and disadvantages of Delphi-Method, see for instance P. M. Mullen, 2003).

The Delphi-Method was chosen in study II in order to adjust the participants' language. In study I it was observed that participant 1 generated a concept 'coordination ability' and participant 3 generated a concept 'coordination process'. 'Coordination' may be proposed as the common ground between both. Hence, based on the concepts of the idiosyncratic mental models of the participants, the experts could assign categories to similar concepts. The more concepts of different mental models, which are assigned to the same category, the more likely these models are to be similar. The participants would then have shared knowledge. The Delphi-Method is used as a framework for the generation and decision-making process for categories. Based on the participants' mental models in study I, the experts generate categories, and compare these categories with those of the other experts, until a consensus is reached for a set of categories. However, this procedure requires some prerequisites. The experts need to have

- similar perceptions to the participants of study I about the abilities, chances, risks, and disadvantages of the company, and
- an understanding of the tasks in study I.

Experts are frequently the subject of investigation (see, for instance, for the decision-making research J. Shanteau, 1992a, and for the expertise research K. A. Ericsson & J. Smith, 1991). However, there is no coherent definition of 'experts'. Some scientists characterise 'experts' as having a couple of years of experience (K. A. Ericsson & J. Smith, 1991, p. 7; M. F. Cassidy & D. Buede, 2009, p. 455) or as persons who have theoretical academic knowledge and practical experience (R. Bromme & R. Rambow, 2001, p. 542; R. Bromme, R. Jucks, & R. Rambow, 2004, pp. 180-181). Other researchers describe 'experts' as people who have more domain knowledge than non-experts, which is structured by active and reflective experience (H. A. Mieg, 2001; M. T. H. Chi, 2006). J. Shanteau (1992a, p. 5) sums this up by saying that there are as many definitions of 'expert', as there are scientists in this field. He suggests, therefore, defining 'expert' only within his domain. This is especially important because experts lose their special skills outside their area of expertise (J. Shanteau, 1992b, p. 3).

The domain in this study is defined as the abilities, chances, risks, and disadvantages of the company. It has a strong focus on the internal processes and resources of the firm (see chapter 4.1.1). Therefore, it also includes aspects of company strategy and culture. The experts are required to simulate as if they were in the positions of the participants when they form categories. The knowledge about and the perception of the company are the basis for the experts to understand the participants' idiosyncratic mental models. Based on this understanding, they find categories, which can be assigned to similar concepts of different mental models. Thus, the focus is on understanding the models and not on the evaluation of whether models are correct or false, or good or bad models for the company. Hence, the experts are insiders working within the firm (see C. Eden & F. Ackerman, 1998, p. 196). Therefore, three colleagues of the participants in study I were recruited, two male and one female. One had a psychology background, one a business management background, and one a mixed background of business management and engineering. The experts came from the same division of the company as participants 1, 3, and 4 in study I. Neither the experts nor the participants knew who the others were. This ensured a high degree of anonymity.

The experts were introduced to the research field of study I: 'Construction of mental models pertaining to chances, risks, abilities, and skills of the company in competition'. Experts generate categories pertaining to the idiosyncratic concepts of participants in study I. It was therefore necessary that they had an understanding of the participants' task, the procedure and the results in study I. Therefore, key facts were explained, and an example of a mental model was shown to them. This was done to introduce the experts to their task: the generation of meaningful categories for each idiosyncratic concept of the participants' idiosyncratic mental models. For a better understanding of this task, the experts were given two examples of different themes. Figure 17, p. 97, shows the animal example (for the second example 'school' see Appendix 3; see also chapter 4.2.1). The words 'canary', 'legs', etc. on the left hand side in Figure 17 represent participants' idiosyncratic concepts in their idiosyncratic mental models. These words are participants' concepts, which will be presented to the experts. In the middle, following the first arrow is one possible category, which the experts could generate, based on the concept chosen by the participant. A second arrow following the first main category suggests the possibility of generating a further main category. For instance, one main category of the concept 'canary' is 'bird'; a possible main category for the concept 'skinny legs' could be 'ostrich' followed by another main category 'bird'. The fact that for the concept 'skinny legs' a more abstract category 'ostrich' could be generated, may become obvious in the list of participants concepts, one of which is ostrich. Generating the concept 'bird', however, would be an additional action, because the category 'bird' is not listed.

However, data was analysed at two different stages during the research process:

- Aggregation stage
- Analysis stage

During the **aggregation stage**, analysis was completed as part of the Delphi process, when the experts generated and allocated main categories to the participants' idiosyncratic concepts (see research process, chapter 4.2.2.2). This analysis was necessary to respond to the experts about their different viewpoints.

During the **analysis stage**, the results of the aggregation process were analysed, after the experts had reached a final solution for the replacement of a participants' concept by an expert category (see results, chapter 4.2.3). At this point, the similarities of the idiosyncratic mental models were analysed within the framework of the experts' categories. A quantitative frequency analysis was conducted on the number of categories generated by the experts. A qualitative word-based analysis was used for the similarity evaluation. In addition, one participant of study I was asked to compare the categories generated by experts with his own mental model. This is part of the communicative validation (see S. Lamnek, 2010; C. Seale, 1999; chapter 3.4).

4.2.2.2. Research Process

Study II took place in September and November 2005. The interviews were conducted in German within the organisation at the workplace of the experts. The introduction to the topic, as described above, took place at the beginning of stage 1. The interviewer, who was the same in all interviews, was present all the time, to answer any question. The interviews proceeded in single stages with paper-and-pencil. A description of the material and task used, and other conditions, such as the preparation for next stages are described subsequently.

4.2.2.2.1. Stage 1 – Process of Free Generation

In stage 1, experts received a list of all concepts, which participants of study I had generated for their idiosyncratic mental models. The list was chosen to help the experts. Thus, they had the concepts of the idiosyncratic mental models but not the relationships between them. The experts were asked to generate categories for these concepts. More than one category could be generated for each concept. When no category was found, concepts could be omitted. Hence, experts had freedom with the generation process. For this task, they needed between 30 and 60 minutes. Answers were written down next to the participants' concepts.

4.2.2.2.2. Stage 2 – Initial Feedback about the Mental Model of Participant 4

After the experts had generated these categories, they were gathered together. Because of the total number of categories, which were generated for each participant's concept, it was necessary to reduce this number for feedback in stage 2. The categories were chosen based on:

- At least two experts generating the same category, e.g. category 'employee' was generated by experts 1 and 3,
- One category with a content similar to that of another category was mentioned more often, e.g. category 'adaptation' (expert 2) was mentioned 2 times; therefore this category was used instead of the category 'change management' (mentioned once by expert 1),
- One category is a part of a second category, e.g. category 'practical orientation' (expert 1) can be seen as a part of 'practical' (expert 2).

Table 11, p. 102, shows an example of the list of the idiosyncratic concepts of participant 4 (column 1, rows 1, 2 and 3), and the categories, which the experts had generated for each concept (columns 2, 3 and 4, rows 1, 2 and 3). Appendix 4 shows all categories used in stage 2. For instance, for the participant's concept 'similar business models of other companies' (column 1, row 1), expert 1 had generated a category 'competitor' (column 2, row 1) and expert 2 a category 'competition' (column 3, row 1). The categories gathered together were used for stage 2.

Table 11: Study II – Excerpt from the List for Assigning Concepts by Participant 4 to Free Generated Categories by Experts

Row	Column			
	1	2	3	4
	Concepts of the Mental Model of Participant 4	Categories of Expert 1	Categories of Expert 2	Categories of Expert 3
1	Similar business models of other companies	Competitor	Competition	
2	Selection of staff	Quality management	Employee	
3	Internalize the idea of the company	Corporate identity (CI) / Public relations (PR)		Identification with the company

The categories summarized were arranged around each mental model. Thus the expert categories framed the participant's mental model (see Figure 18[12], p. 103). Afterwards the interviewer connected each participant's concept (see Figure 18, middle) to the expert generated category to which it belonged (see Figure 18, frame). This connection was based on the results of stage 1, where experts had generated categories from the participants' concepts.

For instance, the concept 'selection of staff' (Table 11 column 1, row 2) is a concept from participant 4 (see Figure 18; this concept is in the middle and has two lines to the categories in the perimeter). Expert 1 generated for this concept a category 'quality management' (Table 11, column 2), and expert 2 a category 'employee' (Table 11, column 3). Expert 3 (Table 11, column 4) did not generate a category for this concept. Therefore, the cell is empty. However, the expert categories 'quality management' and 'employee' were connected by a line to the concept 'selection of staff' as it is shown in Figure 18. This process started with the idiosyncratic mental model of participant 4.

The connection of the participants' concepts to the experts' categories, based on the results of stage 1, took a considerable time. Moreover, the orientation within the mental model with all the connecting lines was complicated. Therefore, it was decided to respond to the experts'

---

[12] Figure 18 is intended to show just how the material was returned to the experts.

results of one participant model before starting to classify another mental model. The aim was to find out how the experts would react to this information.

Figure 18: Study II – Example for the Mental Model with the Experts' Categories of Participant 4

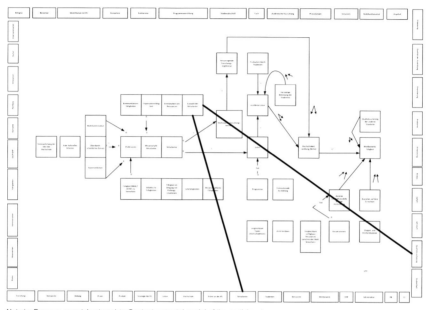

Note iv: Frame = experts' categories; Content = mental model of the participant

To avoid overloading the experts, the expert result of the model of participant 4 was edited and divided. At this point, the experts received four copies of the model of participant 4. Each sheet included the experts' categories for a maximum of 10 idiosyncratic concepts of participant 4. Hence, 10 idiosyncratic concepts were linked to categories, which were suggested by the experts in stage 1. The experts' evaluations were given back in the way shown in Figure 18. Additionally, each expert got one sheet of paper with the mental model of participant 4, which was framed with the categories generated by the experts, but without any lines.

The experts were asked to allocate each participant concept to one expert category. In this part of the interview, it was important that the experts concentrated on the value of the connection between the participant's concepts. For instance, participant 4 connected in his idiosyncratic mental model:

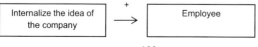

This means: Internalize the idea of the company has a positive effect on employees.

In stage 1, the experts had generated for the participant's concept 'internalize the idea of the company' the categories 'Corporate Identity', 'Public Relations', and 'Identification with Company'. For the participants' concept 'employee', all experts had generated the category 'employee'. Now, the experts had to decide which of the experts' categories would fit the participant's model. The experts likewise needed 30 to 60 minutes for this task.

4.2.2.2.3. Stage 3 – Further Feedback about the Mental Model of Participant 4

The analysis of the results of stage 2 was conducted in the same way as for stage 1. The researcher connected each participant concept with each expert category, based on the results of the expert evaluation in stage 2.

In stage 3, the experts received a list of all concepts of participant 4, where the experts had not been able to agree on the same expert category. Besides each concept, the alternative experts' categories were listed. Additionally, the experts received a copy of the mental model of participant 4 for support and orientation purposes.

The experts were asked to decide on one category, or to state whether two categories meant the same. If two categories meant the same, the experts should decide, which category they would prefer. For instance, one expert generated the category 'employees'. Another generated a similar category 'members of staff'. Here the experts were asked to state whether the categories meant the same and on which they would finally decide. The experts needed 10 to 15 minutes for this task.

4.2.2.2.4. Stages 4 and 5 – Feedback about the Mental Model of Participant 3

Because of the time and workload demands on the experts, it was decided to conduct an expert evaluation using the Delphi-Method for just *one* more model. The model of participant 3 was chosen because of its size (42 concepts). However, only two experts agreed to do this, one with a business management background, and one with a mixed background of business management and engineering. A further expert was not ask to participate, because categories were used which had been the results of the stage 1 'process of free generation'. Another expert could have generated other categories.

In order to avoid overload in stage 4, the experts received four different copies of the model of participant 3. Each sheet included the experts' evaluation for a maximum of 13 concepts of participant 3. Hence, 13 participant's concepts were connected to each category that was suggested by the experts in stage 1. In stage 5, the experts received a copy of the mental model of participant 3, enclosing the experts' evaluation where the experts did not agree on the same category in stage 4. The experts' evaluations were given back, in the same way as it is shown in Figure 18, p. 103. In addition, each expert got sheets of paper with the mental model of participant 3, which was framed with the experts' main categories without any lines (see Figure 18). The experts also received a copy of the mental model of participant 4. This was necessary because experts were asked to use categories consistent with those, which they had used for the idiosyncratic mental model participant 4 when allocating each participant concept to one expert category. The experts likewise needed up to 60 minutes for this task.

4.2.2.2.5. Stage 6 – Evaluation of the Experts' Categories by Participant 3

Subsequently, after the analysis of the results of stage 5, a small (quasi external) evaluation of the categories was conducted. The objective was to evaluate the credibility of the expert categories, by comparing them with the participant's evaluation of these categories (see chapter 3.4). For this stage, participant 3 agreed to another interview.

The objective of study II was to adjust the concept names of the participants' idiosyncratic mental models, using categories to compare them in terms of content and structure. Therefore, participant 3 was asked to judge the experts' categories by comparing them with his concepts. He received the experts' categories and his own original mental model as shown in Figure 18, without lines. The task was to allocate his mental model concepts to the experts' categories with pencil lines. Afterwards, the participant evaluated which experts' categories had similar meanings. The experts' concepts, given to participant 3, had not been grouped in any way. Because of the number of categories, it is possible that participant 3 would assign concepts to the next best suitable category. Then, in the mind of participant 3, the process would have been complete, although other connecting links might still have been possible.

However, for this task, participant 3 needed about 60 minutes, although there was an external time constraint. Therefore, for the similarity judgments of the expert categories, only the categories relevant to the model of participant 3 were investigated. Categories, which had been allocated neither by the expert nor by participant 3, were not investigated. The participants' answer about the similarity was recorded on the researcher's paper with numbers: Similar numbers meant a similar meaning of the categories. This stage involved only participant 3, who was interviewed at his workplace.

4.2.2.2.6. Summary of the Research Process

Table 12 summarises the research process. Column 1 refers to the single consecutive points in time. Column 2 outlines the interviewees at the respective points in time, and column 3 the subject of analysis. Column 4 describes the way and the basis in which the subject was illustrated to the experts. Column 5 briefly states the tasks and methods posed to the interviewees.

Table 12: Study II – Summary of the Research Process

Column				
1	2	3	4	5
Stage (S)	Number of Interviewees	Subject of Analysis	Way in which the subject is illustrated	Task and Method
S 1	3 Experts	Concepts of all four participants	List of participants concepts	Free generation of categories
S 2	3 Experts	Mental model of participant 4	Mental model of participant 4: Participant's concepts are connected to the experts' categories, which were suggested for each concept Basis: Results of S1 (free generation process)	Allocating participant's concepts to experts' categories with lines
S 3	3 Experts	Mental model of participant 4	List of controversial concepts, where the experts' did not agreed on the same category, and respective alternative categories Basis: Results of S2	Stating, which categories are similar or have the same content; Decide in favour of category
S 4	2 Experts	Mental model of participant 3	Mental model of participant 3: Participant's concepts are connected to the experts' categories, which were suggested for each concept Basis: Results of S1 (free generation process)	Allocating participant's concepts to experts' categories with lines
S 5	2 Expert	Mental model of participant 3	Mental model of participant 3: Participant's controversial concepts, where the experts' did not agreed on the same category Basis: Results of S4	Allocating participant's concepts to experts' categories with lines
S 6	Participant 3	Mental model of participant 3	Mental model of participant 3: Participant's concepts are not connected with the experts categories	Allocating participant's concepts to experts' categories with lines; Grouping similar categories

4.2.3. Results

This chapter outlines the results of the research process (see chapter 4.2.2.2, aggregation stage) as well as the results of the final replacement of participants' concepts with expert categories (see chapter 4.2.3, analysing stage). It is subdivided into six chapters with different viewpoints (see Figure 19).

Figure 19: Study II – Overview of the Results

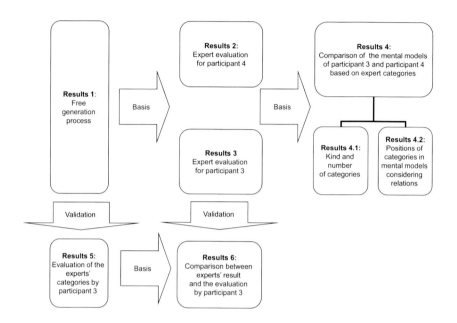

The results of the free generation process (stage 1) will be described first (see Figure 19, result 1; chapter 4.2.3.1). The next section describes the results for the replacement of participants' concepts by expert categories using the model of participant 4 (Figure 19, result 2, chapter 4.2.3.2), and then by participant 3 (Figure 19, result 3, chapter 4.2.3.3). The order of this report was chosen for two reasons. Firstly, the order corresponds to that of the research process: evaluating the mental model of participant 4 first, then the mental model of participant 3. The second reason refers to the fact that participant 3 agreed to an evaluation of the experts' categories. However, the results of the models of both participants 4 and 3 are necessary for this thesis (see 1.2), as was the development and exploration of a method, which investigates the comparison of idiosyncratic mental models, by referring to the similarities (Figure 19, result 4, and chapter 4.2.3.4). This comparison is based on the results of the expert evaluation. The last two chapters refer to the validation process. Firstly, the results of the validation are reported (Figure 19, results 5, chapter 4.2.3.5). Lastly, the expert results are compared with those of participant 3 (Figure 19, result 6, chapter 4.2.3.6).

4.2.3.1. Results 1: Free Generation Process

The experts generated on average 27.33 categories, with a range from 11 (expert 2, see Appendix 6) to 50 (expert 1, see Appendix 5). In addition, the experts differ in the frequency of the nomination of their generated categories (within-expert-view; seeAppendix 5 for expert 1, Appendix 6 for expert 2, and Appendix 7 for expert 3). The four most common categories of the experts are shown in Table 13. For instance, expert 1 assigned 29 participants' concepts to the category 'USP' (unique selling point). Expert 2 did the same with 33 participants' concepts to the category 'traineeship'.

Table 13: Study II – Most Frequent Categories per Expert

	Expert 1	Expert 2	Expert 3
Category Name and Frequency in Times	CI: 18 times PR: 20 times Products: 25 times USP: 29 times	Company: 29 times Staff quality: 23 times Trainee: 26 times Traineeship: 33 times	Portfolio: 11 times Traineeship: 8 times Risk: 5 times Competition ability: 5 times

Table 13 and Table 14 also indicate categories common among the experts (between-expert-view).

Table 14: Study II – Common Categories and their Frequency of Nomination

Row	Column					
	1	2	3	4	5	6
	Expert 1	Frequency	Expert 2	Frequency	Expert 3	Frequency
1	Graduates	1			Graduates	2
2	Research department	1	Research department	9	Research department	4
3	Company	2	Company	29		
4			Traineeship	33	Traineeship	8
5	Employee	12			Employee	2
6	Practical contact	8	Practical contact	5		
7	Resources	4			Resources	1
8	Trainees	3	Trainees	26		
9	Competition	9	Competition	3		
10	Internationality	2			Internationality	2

For instance, the category 'research department' was generated by all experts (see Table 14, columns 1, 3 and 5, row 2). Nine categories were generated by at least two experts, such as the category 'traineeship' (columns 3 and 5, row 4). The total number of categories generated by only one expert is 72.

Table 15 shows an outline of similar categories generated by experts (column 2, 4 and 6), the frequency of their nomination, hence how often participants' concepts were assigned to these categories (column 3, 5 and 7), and which categories were used as a basis for the

Delphi process in stage 2 and stage 4 (column 1). The experts also generated categories, which are similar in meaning but have different names. For instance, expert 1 generated a category 'danger' (column 2, row 13), and expert 3 a category 'risk' (column 6, row 13). Similar results were also found within the categories of one expert. For instance, expert 1 generated two concepts with similar content, 'quality' (column 2, row 14) and 'quality management' (column 2, row 15). Expert 2 generated the concepts 'staff' (column 4, row 1) and 'staff quality' (column 4, row 2). Expert 3 generated the concepts 'abilities' (column 6, row 4) and 'competition ability' (column 6, row 5).

Table 15: Study II – Section about Similar Categories and their Frequency of Nomination between and within the Experts

Row	Column						
	1	2	3	4	5	6	7
	Category*	Expert 1	F	Expert 2	F	Expert 3	F
1	Employee			Staff	19	Clerk	2
2				Staff quality	23	Cooperation	2
3	Offer	Offer	2			Offer of the company	1
4	Abilities, Competition					Abilities	4
5		Competition Situation	1			Competition ability	5
6		Competitor	3				
7	Strategy of the company	Company development	1	Strategy of the company	11		
8		Member development	1				
9	Practical contacts	Practical orientation	2	Practical	1	Contacts	4
10		Company contact	2				
11	Network	Former employees	1				
12		Network	8				
13	Danger, Risk	Danger	11			Risk	5
14	Quality of products, Quality of management	Quality	6			Quality of products	1
15		Quality management	14				
16	Products, Portfolio Alignment of the products	Products	25			Portfolio	11
17		Product palette	2				
18		Alignment of the products	2				
19		Detailed products	9				
20	CI Identification with the company	CI	18			Identification with the company	1
21	Companies brand name					Companies brand name	4
22	Adaptation	Change management	1			Adaptation	2

Note v: *Category (column 1) = category used for stages 2 and 4 during the Delphi process; F = frequency

4.2.3.2. Results 2: Expert Evaluation for Participant 4

After stage 3 was finished, the original concepts of participant 4 were replaced by the experts' categories. The only concepts, which were replaced by experts' categories, were ones, which experts agreed should be in the same category. The experts agreed on common categories for 16 out of 35 concepts. That is about half of all concepts. In total, experts assigned 16 concepts to seven categories. This is about 2.3 concepts per category. Figure 20 shows the mental model of participant 4 including the replaced categories. The categories are:

- Abilities
- Employee
- Networks
- Products
- Competition
- Identifying with the company
- PR

Figure 20: Study II – Mental Model of Participant 4 with Replaced Categories (Experts View)

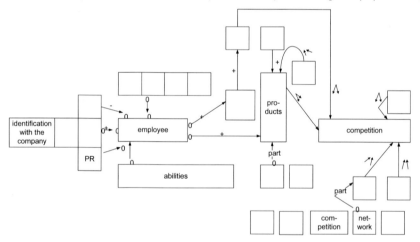

4.2.3.3. Results 3: Expert Evaluation for Participant 3

The same procedure was done after stage 5 for the concepts of participant 3. Here, 34 out of 42 concepts were replaced by experts' categories. This is about 80% of all concepts. The only concepts, which were replaced by categories, were those, which the experts agreed to be in the same category. In total, experts assigned 34 concepts to 14 expert categories. This is about 2.4 concepts per category. The categories are:

- Abilities
- Company

- Competition
- Danger
- Identifying with the company
- Internationality
- PR
- Quality management

- Corporate identity
- Employee
- Infrastructure
- Practical contacts
- Products
- Trainees

Figure 21 shows the mental model of participant 3. The squares symbolize the expert categories. Circles symbolize original concepts by the participant 3, which were not replaced with an expert category.

Figure 21: Study II – Mental Model of Participant 3 with Replaced Categories (Experts View)

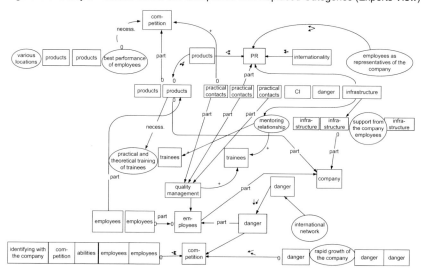

It is notable that the experts underwent a learning process as they progressed with the evaluation of the mental model of participant 3. The evaluation of the mental model seemed to be much easier to them, as they gained experience in reading mental models. Both experts reported this.

4.2.3.4. Results 4: Comparison of the Mental Models of Participants 3 and 4 Based on the Experts' Categories (Content Question 1)

4.2.3.4.1. Type and Number of Categories

When depicting expert categories in the mental models of participants 4 (see Figure 20, p. 110) and 3 (see Figure 21, p. 111), it is important to know that big boxes include more participants' concepts than small boxes. This was done, because experts assigned more whole clusters to the same category. Hence, this category included all concepts. For instance, the category 'abilities' from participant 4 includes five concepts (see Figure 20), while the category 'internationality' from participant 3 (see Figure 21) includes only one concept.

With regard to participant 4, the experts agreed on common categories for 16 out of 35 concepts, which they assigned to seven categories (see Table 16, column 2). With participant 3, the experts agreed on 34 out of 42 concepts, which they assigned to 14 categories (see Table 16, column 1). Six of the experts' categories are the same for both participants. These are 'PR', 'employees', 'identifying with the company', 'competition', 'abilities', and 'products'.

Table 16: Study II – Overview Expert Categories for Participants 3 and 4

Column	
1	2
Expert Categories for Participant 3	Expert Categories for Participant 4
PR	PR
Employees	Employees
Identifying with the company	Identifying with the company
Competition	Competition
Abilities	Abilities
Products	Products
Corporate identity	Networks
Company	
Trainees	
Quality management	
Internationality	
Business contacts	
Danger	
Infrastructure	

Therefore, the following chapter 4.2.3.4.2 highlights these concepts, while comparing the mental models of participants 3 and 4, and the relationships between these concepts. The comparison is based on the outlines of the similarity concept for analysing mental models in terms of the different grades of similarity (see chapter 3.7.2.2, p. 58 ff.).

4.2.3.4.2. Commonalities in Mental Models Considering Relations

Both participants have six categories in common (see Table 16). Referring to the different grades of similarity described in chapter 3.7.2.2, with the first grade of similarity 'same connected categories' (see Table 17, row 1), both participants have six concept pairs in common, and one connection including three concepts. With the second grade of similarity 'same direction of the connection' (Table 17, row 2), both participants have four concept pairs in common, and one connection including three concepts. With the last grade of similarity 'same value of the connection' (Table 17, row 3) participants have nothing in common.

Table 17: Study II – Overview of Connected Categories, Same Direction of the Connections and the Same Value of the Connections

Row	Similarity referring to	Column 1 Participant 3	Column 2 Participant 4
1	Same connected categorie's: A and B	'Employees' – 'Products'	'Employees' – 'Products'
		'Products' – 'Competition'	'Products' – 'Competition'
		'Abilities' – 'Employees'	'Abilities' – 'Employees'
		'Employees' – 'Products'	'Employees' – 'Products'
		'Products' – 'Competition'	'Products' – 'Competition'
		'Identification with the company' – 'Employees'	'Identification with the company' – 'Employees'
		'Employees' – 'Products' – 'Competition'	'Employees' – 'Products' – 'Competition'
			'Employees' – 'Competition'
2	Same direction of the connection: A → B	'Employees' → 'Products'	'Employees' → 'Products'
		'Products' → 'Competition'	'Products' → 'Competition'
		'Employees' → 'Products'	'Employees' → 'Products'
		'Products' → 'Competition'	'Products' → 'Competition'
		'Employees' → 'Products' → 'Competition'	'Employees' → 'Products' → 'Competition'
			'Employees' → 'Competition'
3	Same value of the connections	None	None

Taking a closer look at the categories in the mental models of participants 3 and 4, the following may be important (compare Figure 20, p. 110, and Figure 21, p. 111). Based on the experts' categories, both participants connected the concepts 'products' and 'competition' (Table 17, row 1). Both participants stated that 'products' have an effect on 'competition' (Table 17, row 2). However, participants differed in the value of the connections (Table 17, row 3). Participant 3 stated that 'products' are necessarily part of 'competition'. Participant 4 stated that 'products' offer an opportunity or an advantage for 'competition'. This perception comes from inside the company. The opposite perception, 'competition' has an effect on 'products', is also possible. This would depict an outside perspective, like that of the market in which the company operates.

Both participants also connected the concepts 'products' and 'employees' in the same direction (Table 17, rows 1 and 2) but with different values. Participant 3 viewed employees as 'part' of the products whereas participant 4 considered them to have a 'positive influence' on the products. Compared to 'positive influence', 'part' is a clearly a much stronger connection with the product. It is inseparability, or a condition: If employees were to be separated from products, the products would be incomplete. Participant 4 viewed products, and the possibility to influence them, from an active or outside perspective.

Participant 4 connected indirectly the concept 'employees' with the concept 'competition', yet did this via the concept 'products'. That is to say, 'employees' have a positive influence on the 'products' and this is an advantage or an opportunity for 'competition'. Participant 3 connected directly and indirectly 'employees' and 'competition'. 'Employees' are indirectly a part of the 'products', which are in turn part of the 'competition'. 'Employees' have a direct advantage or opportunity for 'competition'.

Another connection between the two concepts exists between the categories 'employees', and 'abilities'. Participant 4 connected the concepts 'employees' with 'abilities'. That is to say, all 'abilities' have an effect on 'employees'. They can only exist with employees – not with the organisation. Participant 3 linked 'employees' and 'ability' with the conjunction 'and' (bottom left, Figure 21, p. 111).

4.2.3.5. Results 5: Evaluation of the Experts' Categories by Participant 3

Participant 3 assigned 33 of his concepts in study I to 27 of the experts' categories of study II. This is about 80% of all concepts. Figure 22, p. 115, shows the mental model of participant 3 with the replaced experts' categories, based on the evaluation of participant 3. The squares symbolize replaced concepts. These positions are now expert categories. Circles symbolize the original concepts of participant 3.

Table 18, p. 115, shows how participant 3 assigned his concepts to the experts' categories. Several concepts were assigned to more than one category, such as the concept 'level of trainees' to the categories 'abilities' (row 1) and 'trainees' (row 27), or the concept 'top management' to the categories 'alignment' (row 3), 'employees' (row 11) and 'research department' (row 23).

Figure 22: Study II – Mental Model of Participant 3 with Replaced Categories (Participant View)

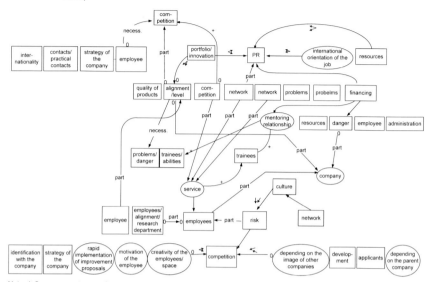

Note vi: Squares = category of experts replaced by participant 3; Circles = the original concepts by participant 3 (no assignment of concepts to categories)

Table 18: Study II – Allocation of the Participant 3's Concepts to the Experts Categories by Participant 3

Row	Experts Categories	Participants 3 Concepts (Evaluation)				
1	Abilities	Level of trainees				
2	Administration	Administration				
3	Alignment	Top management			Anonymous	
4	Applicant	Quality of the applicants/ Potential of the applicants				
5	Competition	Fairs			Competitiveness	
6	Competitor	Competitiveness				
7	Contacts	Practical				
8	Culture	Cultural differences				
9	Danger	IT				
10	Development	Rapid growth of the company				
11	Employees	Employee	Support from the company employees	Best performance of employees	Top management	Management administration
12	Finance	Budget				
13	Identification with the company	Attitude / Satisfaction of employees				
14	Innovation	Further product development				
15	Internationality	Various locations				
16	Level	Anonymous				

Row	Experts Categories	Participants 3 Concepts (Evaluation)		
17	Network	International network	Internships mediation	Practical contacts of the company
18	Portfolio	Further product development		
19	PR	Marketing / Public relations		
20	Practical Contact	Practical		
21	Problems	Reputation "unknown" company in germany	Name of the company	Practical and theoretical training of trainees
22	Quality of products	Training		
23	Research department	Top management		
24	Resources	Equipment / Rooms (resources)		Employees as representatives of the company
25	Risk	Coordination processes		
26	Strategy of the company	Products as core competence		Small company
27	Trainees	Training periods of trainees		Level of trainees

Moreover, participant 3 judged following categories as similar:

- Employees, staff, resources,
- Danger, problems, risks,
- Competition, competitor,
- Competence, abilities,
- Infrastructure, applicant.

4.2.3.6. Results 6: Comparison between Experts' Results for the Mental Model of Participant 3, and the Evaluation of the Experts' Categories by Participant 3

The comparison of the evaluation of the categories by participant 3 (participant view, see Figure 22, p. 115) and the allocation of his concepts to the experts' categories (expert view, Figure 21, p. 111) revealed identical assignments, as is shown in Table 19, p. 117. For instance, 'competitiveness' is an original concept from participant 3 (see Appendix 2). Both participant 3 and the experts assigned this concept (Table 19, column 1) to the category 'competition' (Table 19, column 2).

Table 19: Study II – Identical Assignments of Concepts of Participant 3 to Expert Categories by Participant 3 and Experts

Column	
1	2
Participants Original Concept	Experts Generated Category to the Concept
Competitiveness	Competition
Marketing	Public relations
Reputation "unknown" company in germany	Danger
Level of trainee	Trainee
Training periods	Trainee
Coordination processes	Danger
Management administration	Employee
Top management	Employee
Employees	Employees
Attitude / Satisfaction of employees	Identifying with the company

Figure 23 illustrates this assignment by the way of the original mental model from participant 3. The squares symbolize common categories (participant 3 and the experts), and circles symbolize original concepts of participant 3.

Figure 23: Study II – Common Categories Replaced by Experts and Participant 3

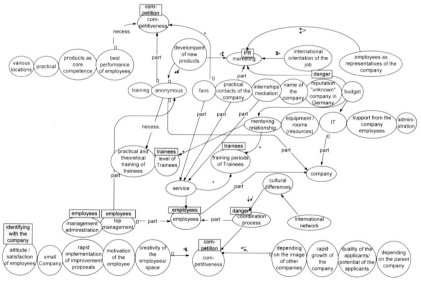

Note vii: Squares = common category of experts and participant 3; Circles = the original concepts by participant 3

The experts and participant 3, both assigned ten out of a total of 42 concepts[13] to six categories. The categories are (see Table 19, column 2):

- Competition,
- PR,
- Danger,
- Trainee,
- Employee,
- Identifying with the company.

This is under 25% of the original number of concepts of participant 3.

4.2.4. Discussion

Looking at the concepts of participants 3 and 4, and comparing them with the experts' categories, a problem is apparent. Comparing idiosyncratic concepts independently of the experts' categories, similarities appear. Participant 3 stated that 'employees as representatives of the company' present an opportunity for 'marketing' (Table 20, columns 1-3, row 1). Participant 4 stated that 'communication' has an effect on 'top management' (Table 20, columns 4-6, row 1).

Table 20: Study II – Comparison of Statements by Participant 3 and Participant 4 and Their Fit in Different Meanings

Row	Concepts and Scenarios	Column					
		1	2	3	4	5	6
		Participant 3			Participant 4		
		Cause Concept	Relationship	Effect Concept	Cause Concept	Relationship	Effect Concept
1	Original Concepts	'Employees as representatives of the company'	Opportunity for	'Marketing'	'Communication'	Effect on	'Top management'
2	Scenario 1 suggested by Expert 1	'Competition'	Opportunity for	'PR'	'PR'	Effect on	'Employees'
3	Scenario 2 suggested by Expert 2	'Employees'	Opportunity for	'PR'	'PR'	Effect on	'Employees'

---

[13] The concept 'competition' was counted once. To keep an overview, participant 3 replicated this concept in study I.

With the concepts of participant 4, the experts agreed on the category 'employees' (column 6, rows 2, and 3) for the concept 'top management' (column 6, row 1), and they agreed on the category 'PR' (column 4, rows 2, and 3) for the concept 'communication' (column 4, row 1). With the concepts of participant 3, the experts' agreed that the concept 'marketing' (column 3, row 1) should fall into the category 'PR' (column 3, rows 2, and 3). 'Marketing', 'communication' and 'PR' have a close relationship to each other. However, when participant 3 referred to the concept 'employees as representatives of the company', experts did not agree on the same category. During both stages, stages 4 and 5, expert 1 stated 'employees as representatives of the company' (column 1, row 1) refers to the category 'competition' (column 1, row 2). Expert 2 stated that this same concept refers to different category 'employees' (column 1, row 3). In fact, both scenarios in the mental model of participant 3 would fit. 'Competition' is an opportunity for 'PR', and 'employees' are an opportunity for 'PR' (see Table 20, p. 118). Scenario 2 is more of an inside view of the company (columns 1-3, row 3). Scenario 1 is more of an outside view of the company (columns 1-3, row 2).

Comparing the original concepts of participants 3 and 4, when scenario 2 suggested by expert 2 ('employees' are an opportunity for 'PR', columns 1-3, row 3) is applied to the statement of participant 3, the statement of participant 3 ('employees as representatives of the company' present an opportunity for 'marketing', columns 1-3, row 1) appears to be similar to the statement of participant 4 ('communication' has an effect on 'top management', columns 4-6, row 1), and to the experts' categories for participant's concepts ('PR' has an effect on 'employees', columns 4-6, row 3). The statements are similar in terms of content, but differ in terms of direction, and the values of the connections. When scenario 1 suggested by expert 1 ('competition' is an opportunity for 'PR', columns 1-3, row 2) is applied to the statement of participant 3, the statement of participant 3 ('employees as representatives of the company' present an opportunity for 'marketing', columns 1-3, row 1) appears not to be similar to the statement of participant 4 ('communication' has an effect on 'top management', columns 4-6, row 1), and to the experts' categories for participant's concepts ('PR' has an effect on 'employees', columns 4-6, row 2). The statements are not similar in terms of content, direction and the values of the connections.

It is not clear, which scenario would better match the meaning of the statement of participant 3, because the thought processes behind that statement are unknown. It is also not clear, which meanings are behind the categories 'employees' and 'competition' when given by the experts (Table 20, p. 118, row 2 and row 3). There is no more context information to conclude which scenario would fit best. To consider the mental model of participant 3 from the inside or outside perspective would not increase the trustworthiness of the result (see chapter 3.4; for validity in qualitative research see, for instance, R. Brühl & S. Buch, 2006; Y. Lincoln and E. Guba, 1985). This is because in the model of participant 3, there are concepts from both the inside and outside view. Examples from the inside view are concepts and connections such as "'attitude/satisfaction of employees', 'small company', 'rapid implementation of improvement proposals', 'motivation of the employee', 'creativity of the employees' are opportunities for 'competition'". Examples from the outside view are concepts and connections such as "'depending on the image of other companies', 'rapid growth of the company', 'quality and potential of the applicants', 'depending on the parent company' as a threat for 'competition'" (see Figure 23, p. 117). The inside and outside views are part of the interview question (see chapter 4.1.3.4). For that reason, it is necessary to find other, more reliable and valid ways to compare different idiosyncratic mental models, in terms of their similarity. Due to the lack of knowledge about the context, the information in the mental models – as well as the fact that the experts came from the same organization as the participants – are not enough for comparing seemingly similar concepts in the idiosyncratic mental models based on 'expert' evaluations as it was done here (see C. Eden & F. Ackermann, 1998, p.198). Hence, the content validity as it is understood in this thesis for Approach A is low (see chapter 3.4).

The views of participant 3, when assessing the experts' categories, appeared to be reasonable. The objective was to test the credibility of the expert results (see chapter 3.4; S. Lamnek, 2010). During the interview with participant 3, it was observed that he assigned concepts only to the category 'staff', but not to the category 'employees'. It was assumed that staff and employees meant the same. When he finished the assignment, he was asked to group together those categories, which have similar meanings. He grouped 'staff' and 'employees' together with 'resources'.

The contrast between the classification of concepts of participant 3 to the experts' categories, and the grouping of the experts' categories in terms of similarity by participant 3, also shows that there are discrepancies. For instance, during the judgement of the similarity of the expert categories by participant 3 (see chapter 4.2.3.5, last paragraph) the categories 'competence' and 'abilities' were linked by participant 3 as was expected. However, when concepts were assigned to the categories, participant 3 assigned the concept 'level of trainees' to the category 'trainees' *and* to the category 'abilities' (see Table 18, p. 115). These two categories were not grouped together by participant 3 during the similarity judgement of the expert categories (see chapter 4.2.3.5, last paragraph). Therefore, it cannot be assumed that both categories have a similar meaning for participant 3. Hence, it could be possible that participant 3 viewed 'abilities' more on the organisational than on the individual level within the company. The experts, who had generated the categories, could view 'abilities' more on the individual level. This leads to the conclusion that the participant's concept, which is assigned to different expert categories, is multidimensional. Moreover, the categories could also be multidimensional. In the quantitative research paradigm (see chapter 3.1), it is a prerequisite to reflect on this multidimensionality as a condition of the development of valid tests (see S. Buch, 2007; K. A. Bollen & R. Lennox, 1991, as well as books about test theory and test construction such as J. Rost, 2004; J. Krauth, 1995). However, the multidimensionality of concepts and categories was not taken into account in the current study. It was considered when generating different words with similar meanings. Therefore, it was assumed that the purpose of the construction of a mental model (see W. B. Rouse & N. M. Morris, 1986) would include enough information to reach much clearer results for the generation of categories, and the assignment of concepts to categories. However, it was not assumed that generating different categories with different meanings would fit into the original participant mental model (see Table 20, p. 118). The reduction of categories by clustering also did not lead to clear results, since more than one category is possible for a participant's concept. Nevertheless, it is apparently a relevant factor in the generation and depiction of common categories. All this taken together lowers the trustworthiness of the results, as well as the validity of the approach of expert evaluation (see chapter 3.4; Y. Lincoln & E. Guba, 1985).

The assignment of the concepts 'competitiveness' to the category 'competition', and 'marketing' to 'PR' seems plain. 'Marketing' can be part of 'PR'. 'Competitiveness' can be seen as a component of 'competition'. Another component might be 'competitors', for without them competition is unnecessary and impossible. The assignment of the concept 'coordination processes' to the category 'danger' is less obvious. It should be pointed out that the task was to generate 'main' categories. It would be more understandable to link 'coordination processes' with 'coordination' or 'processes'. However, experts and participant 3 unanimously linked 'coordination processes' with 'danger'. This allocation is far removed from the original concept 'coordination processes'. Participants with educational backgrounds other than business administration would probably make an assignment that is semantically closer, such as 'coordination'. A similar phenomenon can be seen with the concept 'attitude and satisfaction of employees' when assigned to the category 'identifying with the company'. Here, the assignment of the concept 'attitude and satisfaction of employees' to the category 'employees' would be possible. However, the assignment of the category 'identification' is not so far off, as contented employees are more likely to identify with their company. However, further research must be done as to whether an abstract allocation may be an indicator for situational awareness in companies (see e.g. M. R. Endsley, 2000) or for a comprehensive mental model about the company.

4.3. Conclusion of Approach A and Consequences for Approach B

The objectives of study I were to elicit idiosyncratic mental models, and to find adequate rules to construct mental models in strategic management and management accounting. Study II focussed on the aggregation of idiosyncratic mental models using Delphi-Method. The aim of study II was to find out if it would be possible to aggregate concepts by different participants to the same categories. This would permit the identification of overlapping knowledge structures. The analysis of the results of the studies reveals that some modifications need to be done. In summary, the main issues focus on methodological objectives in both studies:

- Eliciting idiosyncratic mental models: The interview and the concepts
- Aggregating idiosyncratic mental models: The process to make the idiosyncratic mental models comparable

The **interview** was semi-structured, which produced useful information. Some of these results are not reported in this thesis, such as how participants think about their own possibilities to strengthen the competitive advantage of their organisation. This was decided because the participants did not return to this topic during the second phase of the interview. Therefore, they did not integrate this view into the models. In future, participants could be asked to integrate their reflections into their mental model. However, this would extend the study, and probably make the process even more difficult for the participants.

Participant 1 was asked to write down the most important concepts during the interview. Unfortunately, he forgot about it. When he started to answer the 'open' interview question, he was speaking freely. By reminding the participant to write down the concepts, he lost the thread. Hence, the interviewer stopped reminding the participant, and prepared the concepts based on the tape recordings. This leads to the possibility that the interviewer could have influenced the results, by focussing on concepts during the preparation stage. A modification could be to change the interview by including more domain-orientated tasks. For instance, tasks could require participants to write answers down (B. Scheele & N. Groeben, 1986, p. 535). This would reduce the time taken both for the participants and for the interviewer. Moreover, the concepts would not be influenced by the interviewer's views.

Study II shows that it is indeed possible to render **comparable different idiosyncratic mental models** by using the Delphi-Method. There are matches in the assignments of experts and in the evaluation of participant 3 (see chapter 4.2.3). There are both advantages and disadvantages with this. Primarily, it poses a great cognitive challenge to the experts by immersing them in each mental model, and then assessing the relationships between the individual concepts. The fact that the experts came from the same company did not make the task any easier for them. However, a learning process was noted, during the evaluation of the second model. A practice unit may alleviate the problem. On the other hand, the time constraint is already considerable.

Furthermore, the assignment of idiosyncratic concepts to expert categories is ambiguous, because of the evaluation by the experts and the evaluation of participant 3. This means that comparability is limited, because context knowledge is missing (see chapter 4.2.3). Therefore, it seems important to include more context knowledge into the next study. For that reason, the design should be changed. There could be a face-to-face discussion between participants (and / or experts), to ensure that the same meanings were agreed for the concepts and categories.

Study II also indicates that one dimension, which is relevant for generating categories, could be the semantic similarity between the individual concepts and categories. Semantic similarity was not indicated by the examples given to the experts, when explaining the task (see Figure 17, Appendix 3). Therefore, semantic similarity could be identified when making comparisons between idiosyncratic mental models. In essence, the Delphi-Method has produced the desired result. That is to say, mental models are comparable. However, the results were not of the desired quality.

4.4. Empirical Study III - Developing a Method to Aggregate Idiosyncratic Mental Models in Terms of Similarity (Approach B)

4.4.1. Introduction to Study III: Preliminary Thoughts

Approach A uncovered methodological problems about the comparability of idiosyncratic concepts, although the Delphi-Method produced the desired results. The idiosyncratic mental models of two participants were partly comparable. However, the Delphi-Method exposed disadvantages. Firstly, this method is exhausting for the experts. It is a cognitive challenge for the experts to immerse themselves in the participants' mental models. Secondly, it is time-consuming. Although P. C. Howze and C. Dalrymple (2004, p. 179) stated that compared to face-to-face meetings, the participants felt free of long meetings, and they retained more time for productive thinking, the lack of time was the reason why only two experts agreed to take part in a second research process, researching the mental model of participant 3. Nevertheless, more importantly, the assignment process of idiosyncratic concepts to expert categories is equivocal. The results revealed that different categories with different meanings would fit the participant's mental model. There are no trends for one certain category because of the lack of context information. Therefore, the research design must adapt, moving away from aggregating concepts with methods from the 'outside' perspective as with the Delphi-Method. The next approach should consider two points:

- The approach has to enable the research of idiosyncratic knowledge.
- The aggregation of the idiosyncratic concepts should be done by the participants themselves.

The objective of this study is therefore

Method Objective 4: *to explore a way to compare idiosyncratic concepts by participants themselves.*

Therefore, the aim of this study was to find out what type of options result, when decisions are left to the participants. Hence, the approach was to change the process so that participants could state the meaning of concepts. Taking into account the conclusions and consequences in chapter 4.3, the idea was to combine a collective and holistic approach (for the approaches see chapter 3.6). Since the aim is to compare idiosyncratic knowledge, the collective approach comes first. This approach enables the participants to construct an uninfluenced mental model, as was done in study I. The holistic approach follows, and gives the participants the opportunity to find commonalities based on idiosyncratic knowledge. Hence, participants aggregate their individual knowledge to shared knowledge, by comparing their idiosyncratic mental models. Figure 24 shows the combination of both approaches in time. However, the focus in this study was on knowledge content, rather than on knowledge structure.

Figure 24: Study III – Combination of Collective and Holistic Approach

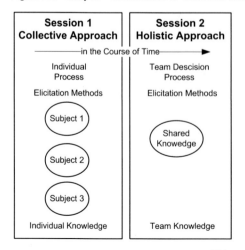

Additionally, in study II (see chapter 4.2.4), it was observed that experts and participants linked 'coordination processes' with 'danger'. This allocation is far removed from the original concept 'coordination processes'. It was assumed that participants with educational backgrounds other than business administration would probably make an assignment that is semantically closer. Hence, it could be that such abstract allocation may be an indicator for situational awareness in companies (see e.g. M. R. Endsley, 2000). This should be researched. However, before such research can be done, it is necessary to find out

Study Objective: *how non-business economists solve business administration problems.*

4.4.2. Method

4.4.2.1. Participants

This study was conducted with a small sample. Three female participants majoring in different fields of study (History/German, Law, and Biology) were recruited. There are several reasons for a heterogeneous sample. Firstly, students majoring in different fields were used to explore how participants without management knowledge would solve management tasks, and discover what problems would occur. This was of interest in study II, where the experts as well as participant 3, all with a management background, assigned the concept 'coordination processes' to the category 'danger'. Other categories such as 'coordination' or 'process' would have been possible, and perhaps more likely, with participants who had no management background (in addition see the review to heterogeneity and performance by R. A. Guzzo & M. W. Dickson, 1996, pp. 311-312). Secondly, no student with a major in business administration was selected to have 'expert status' in stage 2 (team stage; see chapter 4.4.2.2). Another consideration was that it could be positive for the team process, if the participants knew each another (see the review to familiarity and performance by R. A. Guzzo & M. W. Dickson, 1996, p. 312). It is possible that because of the new topic, participants who did not know each other would avoid embarrassment by not discussing the topic. For the same reason, it was decided to ask participants from the same gender, in order to exclude gender bias. Therefore, three participants of the same gender with different backgrounds were selected. On average, the students were 25 years old, with a range of 22 to 27 years. They were studying on average for 10 semesters with a range of 5 to 15 semesters. All participants had work experience. On average, they had worked for four different firms with a range of 3 to 5 firms. Students received EUR 35.00 for their participation in the study.

4.4.2.2. Design

Table 21 shows the study design. Based on the combination of the collective (column 1 and 3) and holistic (column 2) approach (see chapter 3.6), this study was designed with repeated measures. In stage 1 (column 1), the idiosyncratic mental model was derived in a single stage (collective approach). Stage 2 was conducted as a team stage. It focussed on the team mental model (column 2). The last stage (column 3) focussed on the idiosyncratic mental models again.

Table 21:   Study III – Design

			Column		
			1	2	3
			Stage 1	Stage 2	Stage 3
Row	1	Measurement Approach	Collective	Holistic	Collective
	2	Focus on	Idiosyncratic mental models	Team mental model	Idiosyncratic mental models
	3	Stage Size	Single sessions	Team session	Single sessions
	4	Aim — Part I	Elicitation process	Elicitation process	Elicitation process
	5	Aim — Part II			Discovering similarity between the results of stage 1 and stage 2

The idiosyncratic mental models elicited in stages 1 and the team mental model elicited in stage 2 (Table 21, row 4, part I) were used for the similarity judgement, which were added in stage 3 (row 5, part II).

4.4.2.3. Procedure

Table 22 shows the plan, including the three stages. Between stage 1 (single) and stage 2 (team) as well as stage 2 (team) and stage 3 (single) there was a gap of at least seven days. The study took place in December 2005 and January 2006. The participants were in the apartment of the interviewer. Therefore, the interviewer was present all the time to answer questions. The interviews were conducted in German.

Table 22:   Study III – Plan

	Stage 1			Stage 2	Stage 3
	Week 1	Week 2	Week 3	Week 4	Week 5
Chrono-logy	Participant 1			Team	Participant 1
	Participant 2				Participant 3
			Participant 3		Participant 2

The research process was subdivided into two parts. The first part concentrated on the elicitation process with repeated measurements (Table 21, p. 126, row 4, part I). Therefore, the material and tasks in this process will be described in chapter 4.4.2.3.1. The second part focussed on the aggregation of the idiosyncratic mental models (Table 21, row 5, part II). Therefore, the material and task will be described in chapter 4.4.2.3.2. The last chapter outlines the data analysis (chapter 4.4.2.3.3).

4.4.2.3.1. Collecting Idiosyncratic Mental Models and Team Mental Models: Stimulus Material, Tasks and Data Collection (Stages 1, 2 and 3)

Following an initial greeting, participants were given their task. A Balanced Scorecard scenario was developed, which allowed the participants to write down their answers directly. This process was based on the monological version of the Structure-Formation-Technique (see B. Scheele & N. Groeben, 1986, p. 535; M. Bonato, 1990, p. 38). The scenario was described as follows (estimated translated):

> "In the first meeting, you should use the Balanced Scorecard (BSC), which is described on another sheet, to improve suggestions for objectives for managing your university cafeteria. Please read the information about Balanced Scorecard now. You can also read them at any time!
>
> The university cafeteria has the following problems:
>
> - Decline in customer numbers because of food quality and sulky service,
> - High staff turnover,
> - Decrease in turnover, and in the last quarter for the first time, a negative profit.
>
> Using Balanced Scorecard and your proposals, these problems should be solved, and a sustainable structure of the cafeteria should be generated."

The Balanced Scorecard was described briefly with its history, function, and structure, and with its four perspectives 'financial', 'internal business process', 'potential' and 'customer' (following Figure 1-1, R. S. Kaplan & D. P. Norton, 1996a, p. 9), including objective, mean and measurement. The perspectives were introduced with short questions, such as

- What do we want to offer our investors? (financial perspective)
- How should our customers perceive us? (customer perspective)
- In which processes should we achieve excellence? (internal business process perspective)
- How can we maintain our flexibility? (perspective of potential)

An example was given for each perspective, such as growth in turnover or profitability (financial perspective), customer satisfaction (customer perspective), developmental period (internal business process perspective), and staff morale (perspective of potential). The difference between 'objectives' and 'means' was explained using examples (see Appendix 8).

After stage 1, the material was modified. This was done to avoid repetition in stage 2 of answers given in stage 1. Hence, an extended scenario was given. The challenge was to explore problems of the expanded cafeteria, such as further resources required for the supply for schools, as well as a high proportion of students from abroad (see Appendix 9). In addition to their mental model of stage 1 and the scenario, the students also received the Balanced Scorecard description again.

In stage 3, the participants received the description of the problems, and the Balanced Scorecard, which they had in stage 2, as well as the cause-and-effect rule system. This time the participants did not receive their idiosyncratic mental model or team mental model.

The tasks were constant over the three stages. The first task asked the participants to identify 12 to 20 objectives for the cafeteria, based on the four perspectives of the Balanced Scorecard for future success. The second task was about the cause-and-effect relationship between different objectives. For this task, participants received the cause-and-effect rule system (see Appendix 1). The last task was concerned with means and their verification (see Appendix 10). For a better understanding of the tasks, an example was given, based on the library (see Appendix 11).

The participants needed about 2 to 2 ½ hours to complete the tasks in all three stages. It was up to the participants to write the answers down on concept cards, or on a sheet of paper using the structure of the Balanced Scorecard. All participants chose the paper.

4.4.2.3.2. Aggregation Process: Stimulus Material, Task and the Process of Discovering Similarity in Stage 3

Following the problem-solving task in stage 3, the participants received

- their suggestion of a Balanced Scorecard of stage 1, the original idiosyncratic mental model,
- a list of idiosyncratic concepts of their Balanced Scorecard result of stage 1, including the objectives, means and their verification, which the participants had suggested,
- the Balanced Scorecard result of stage 2, the team mental model in its original form,
- a list of all concepts of the team result, including the objectives suggested by the team, means, and their verification.

Lists were made to arrange their answers on an extra sheet, because they had chosen to write on sheets of paper. Concept lists were prepared during stage 2 and stage 3. Because of the time, which participants needed each stage to complete the task, and the time required for preparing the concept lists, it was decided to focus on the idiosyncratic concepts of stage 1 and the team concepts of stage 2 during stage 3. These results were given to the participants to support the following task.

They were asked to judge the similarity in meaning of their idiosyncratic concepts from stage 1 with the team result in stage 2. They were also asked to report motives and reasons for the judgement. The assigned individual and team concepts were glued on to a sheet of paper. The rules and motives of the judgement were written down next to the fixed concepts. In addition, participants 2 and 3 were given the comparison rules of idiosyncratic concepts and team concepts formed by participant 1 for comment. For this task, each participant took about 30 to 45 minutes.

Stage 3 was finished after the participants completed a short questionnaire about perceived teamwork and some socio-demographic data (Appendix 12). In this questionnaire, participants used a ratio scale with a length of 10 centimetres, answering questions such as

- How right they felt during solving the task in each stage (from very insecure to very secure),
- How they felt about the teamwork (from very bad to very good),
- How they produced new ideas (from very bad to very good),
- How many new ideas they could produce (from very little to very much).

Although a statistical analysis was not undertaken because of the group size, this questionnaire should give an impression of how a participant progressed with unfamiliar tasks and situations.

4.4.2.3.3. Data Analysis

The analysis was done to discover different features, and was therefore exploratory. The main issues were to explore rules for similarity judgements, and if participants had problems with management tasks. Analysis of the idiosyncratic mental models was completed by referring to idiographic- and nomothetic-quantitative frequency analysis, and idiographic-qualitative word-based analyses. The nomothetic-quantitative frequency analysis was done using the perceived teamwork questionnaire to illustrate differences between participants. Idiographic-quantitative frequency analysis focussed on rules generated for judging the similarity between idiosyncratic concepts and team concepts. Idiographic-qualitative analysis involved a short validation of the consistency of similarity judgements, and their credibility.

4.4.3. Results, Discussion and Conclusion

4.4.3.1. To the Perceived Teamwork

Participants 1 and 3 felt the same way about task solving, and teamwork (see Table 23, p. 130, item 1-4). On the interval scale (last column of each participant), there was no difference between them. Both received the same value. Looking at the ratio scale (first column of each participant), and the ranking (second column of each participant), both participants had interchangeable ratings. At one time, participant 1 gave the highest value, another time it was participant 3.

Participant 2 was different. She had the same value as both other participants in item 1 for stages 2 and 3 (teamwork stage) on the interval scale, and the same values as participant 3 on the ratio scale and ranking (item 1, stages 2 and 3). The other values were always lower. In stage 1, with item 1, she scored the lowest value on the ratio scale (ratio = 0.3 centimetre), which is almost 'very insecure'.

Table 23: Study III – Results of the Questionnaire about Perceived Teamwork

		Participant 1			Participant 2			Participant 3		
		RS *	Rang **	IS ***	RS *	Rang **	IS ***	RS *	Rang **	Is ***
Item 1: How right did you felt during solving the task?	Stage 1 Single	4	1	2	0,3	3	1	2,5	2	2
	Stage 2 Teamwork	5,4	1	3	5	2,5	3	5	2,5	3
	Stage 3 Single	4,3	3	3	5	1,5	3	5	1,5	3
Item 2: How do you felt about the teamwork?		6,8	2	4	5	3	3	7,8	1	4
Item 3: How did you produce new ideas?		6,3	1	4	3,2	3	2	6,2	2	4
Item 4: How many new ideas you could produce?		4,6	2	3	3,1	3	2	5,3	1	3

Note viii: * RS = ratio scale; ** Rang = ranking; Highest value = 1, lowest value = 3 based on ratio, *** IS = interval scale; Transformed into interval scale: 0 centimetres to 2 centimetres are equivalent to a 1 on the interval scale; 2.1 centimetres to 4 centimetres are equivalent to a 2; and so on

4.4.3.2. To Method Objective 4 and Study Objective: The Similarity Allocation of the Idiosyncratic Concepts to Team Concepts

The objective of this analysis was

- to explore how non-business economists solve management tasks, focusing on concept numbers for the objective level (O), mean level (A)[14], and measurement level (M) within the perspectives of the Balanced Scorecard and
- to explore how participants compare idiosyncratic concepts by themselves.

Table 24, p. 131, compared **concepts numbers** of the individual stages (stage 1, stage 3) for each level (O, A, M) and for each perspective of the Balanced Scorecard. Table 24 reveals that the level 'measurement' (rows 3, 6, 9, and 12) was omitted

- partially during the stages by participant 1 in stage 1 (column 1, row 12), and participant 3 in stage 3 (column 6, row 3), or
- completely by participant 1 in stage 3 (column 2, row 3, row 6, row 9, row 12), and participant 3 in stage 1 (column 5, row 3, row 6, row 9, row 12).

Only participant 2 generated for each objective a package of measures in both sessions.

Table 24: Study III – Number of Concepts Generated in Individual Sessions

			Column					
			1	2	3	4	5	6
			\multicolumn{6}{Concept Numbers Generated}					
Row	PS	L	Participant 1		Participant 2		Participant 3	
			Stage 1	Stage 3	Stage 1	Stage 3	Stage 1	Stage 3
1	Financial	O	5	4	3	4	3	3
2		A	9	6	4	3	3	5
3		M	4	None	1	3	None	None
4	Process	O	3	4	3	2	2	3
5		A	3	7	4	3	2	4
6		M	4	None	2	2	None	1
7	Potential	O	2	4	3	3	4	3
8		A	3	7	3	7	5	6
9		M	1	None	4	3	None	1
10	Customer	O	3	4	4	5	5	3
11		A	6	7	4	5	5	3
12		M	None	None	2	4	None	2

Note ix: PS = perspective; L = level within the perspective

Participant 1 used five different rules to **compare idiosyncratic concepts** with team concepts (Table 25, row 1). She used the rule 'part' eight times (three times as a financial perspective, three times as an internal business process, twice as a customer perspective). The

---

[14] Mean = arrangement, therefore 'A'

rule 'synonym' was used three times (financial and customer perspective). Participant 1 stated (Appendix 13):

- 'Increase in revenue' (single concept) is a part of the team concept 'improving the financial situation' (financial perspective),
- 'Advertising and promotion to attract' (single concept) is part of the team concept 'promotion activities' (customer perspective),
- 'Creating extensive range of daily menus' (single concept) is a synonym for the team concept 'extensive offering' (customer perspective).

Table 25: Study III – Outline of Similarity Allocation Rules

Row	P	Perspective							
		Financial		Internal Business Process		Potential		Customer	
		Rule	No	Rule	No	Rule	No	Rule	No
1	1	Part	3	Part	3	None	None	Part	2
								Synonym	2
		Synonym	1	Exactly the same	1			Same	1
								Expanded	1
2	2	Part	3	None	None	None	None	Synonym	5
3	3	Part	4	Part	2	None	None	Part	4
								Synonym	2
		Synonym	1	Result	1			Result	1

Note x: P = participant; No = number (frequency of use)

In a similar way, participants 2 and 3 used or adapted the rules 'synonym' and 'part' (see Table 25, rows 2 and 3). They stated for instance (see Appendix 13):

- Participant 2: 'good food' (idiosyncratic concept) is a synonym for 'qualitative good food' (team concept; customer perspective),
- Participant 2: 'fair prices' (idiosyncratic concept) is a synonym for 'good price-performance ratio' (team concept; customer perspective),
- Participant 3: 'nice staff' (idiosyncratic concept) is a synonym for 'friendly service' (team concept; customer perspective),
- Participant 3: 'reduce spending' (idiosyncratic concept) is a synonym for 'restriction of expenditure' (team concept; financial perspective),
- Participant 2: 'low production costs, but good quality' (idiosyncratic concept) is a part of 'restriction of expenditure' (team concept; financial perspective),
- Participant 3: 'to offer the customer fresh food for more money' (idiosyncratic concept) is a part of 'customer growth' (team concept; customer perspective).

Participant 1 and participant 3 used additional rules. These rules are 'exactly the same', 'expanded', 'same' and 'result':

- Participant 1: 'in addition to training and professional qualification, regular team meetings (once per month)' (idiosyncratic concept) is exactly the same as 'having a say', 'social events', 'promotion of team spirit' and 'employee of the Month' (team concepts; process perspective),

- Participant 1: 'responsibility for the spatial design for employees or provide dedicated staff' and 'attractively decorated' (idiosyncratic concepts) is expanded to 'advice on design' (team concept; customer perspective),

- Participant 1: 'customer satisfaction' (idiosyncratic concept) is same as 'customer satisfaction' (team concept; customer perspective),

- Participant 3: 'change the shopping list and order list' (idiosyncratic concept) results in 'menu card' (team concept; customer perspective),

- Participant 3: 'prepare food consisting of at least 5 menus (taking into account individual needs such as vegetarian, diet, allergies, etc.)' (idiosyncratic concept) results in 'wholesalers / modification of the shopping list' (team concept; process perspective).

The participants did not seem to have any difficulties with the assignment of the idiosyncratic concepts to the team concepts. Participant 1 was able to talk about the reasons for the assignment and the motives behind them. She had generated all the rules herself. For participant 2, it was difficult to talk about motives. Therefore, she was given rules suggested by participant 1, with the offer to use these rules, if she wanted. Participant 2 used two of these rules. Participant 3 used the rules of participant 1, and adapted or extended them. It was easier for participant 3 than for participant 2 to talk about the assignment process. However, this task was probably much easier for participant 1, because she was majoring in German. By chance, this participant was always the first one to be interviewed in the stages (see Table 22, p. 126).

The rules used most often by all participants were the rules 'synonym' and 'part of'. The result of the similarity assignment supported the idea – as already seen in study II – for using rules based on lexical semantics. Similarity rules based on lexical semantics could be a valuable approach.

However, the similarity analysis of idiosyncratic concepts and team concepts was based on the number of assigned concepts for the objective level (O), mean level (A), and measurement level (M), within the perspectives of the Balanced Scorecard. A word-based content analysis was used, focusing on the consistency of the results (see validity through triangulation, chapter 3.4). Table 26, p. 134, outlines the concept numbers generated by participants 1, 2, and 3 during individual stage 1 (column 4, 6, 8) as well as team stage 2 (column 2). The concept numbers were counted for each level (O, A, M, column 1) and for each perspective.

Participants assigned idiosyncratic concepts to team concepts from the customer, financial and process perspectives. No one used the perspective of potential. Most idiosyncratic concepts were assigned to the customer perspective (see Table 26, rows 10-12). In the objective level 'O' (row 10), six (column 3) out of nine (column 2) team concepts were used for the similarity assignment by all participants. For the mean level 'A' (row 11), four out of seven team concepts were used and one out of three team concepts in the measurement level 'M' (row 12).

Additionally, Table 26 shows the columns 'used in stage 3 for similarity judgement' for each participant (columns 5, 7, 9). These columns outline the number of idiosyncratic concepts of stage 1, which were used by each participant for the assignment of the idiosyncratic concepts to the team concepts (column 3). Column 3 (team stage) outlines how many of the team concepts were used for this assignment. For instance, participant 1 generated five concepts for the objective level from a financial perspective in stage 1 (column 4, row 1). Two (column 5, row 1) of these five concepts (column 4, row 1) were assigned by participant 1 to two concepts of the team stage (column 3, row 1). Four concepts were generated in the team stage (column 2, row 1).

Table 26: Study III – Number of Concepts Generated and Assigned

Row	Perspective	Level	Column								
			1	2	3	4	5	6	7	8	9
				Concept Numbers							
				Team		Participant 1		Participant 2		Participant 3	
				Generated in Stage 2 in total	Used in Stage 3 for Similarity judgement*	Generated in Stage 1	Used in Stage 3 for Similarity judgement	Generated in Stage 1	Used in Stage 3 for Similarity judgement	Generated in Stage 1	Used in Stage 3 for Similarity judgement
1	Financial	O		4	2	5	2	3	1	3	2 (+2)
2		A		6	2	9	1	3	None	3	3 (-2)
3		M		None	None	4	None	1	None	None	None
4	Process	O		7	2	3	None	3	None	2	2
5		A		8	3	3	3	4	None	2	None
6		M		1	None	4	None	2	None	None	1
7	enti	O		6	None	2	None	3	None	4	None

Row	Perspective	Level	Column								
			1	2	3	4	5	6	7	8	9
			Concept Numbers								
			Team		Participant 1		Participant 2		Participant 3		
			Generated in Stage 2 in total	Used in Stage 3 for Similarity judgement*	Generated in Stage 1	Used in Stage 3 for Similarity judgement	Generated in Stage 1	Used in Stage 3 for Similarity judgement	Generated in Stage 1	Used in Stage 3 for Similarity judgement
8	Customer	A	7	None	3	None	3	None	5	None
9		M	1	None	1	None	4	None	None	None
10		O	9	6	3	4	4	4	5	6
11		A	7	4	6	2	4	None	5	3
12		M	3	1	None	None	2	1	None	None

Note xi: O = objective, A = mean, M = measurement; *By all participants

There is one difference apparent in Table 26. Participant 3 (column 8 and 9) assigned two concepts of the mean level to the objective level. This means that participant 3 used three arrangement concepts, but two of these three concepts (signed as 3(-2)) were assigned to the objective level (signed as 2(+2)).

Participant 2 assigned her idiosyncratic concepts of stage 1 to the team concepts from the customer perspective (column 7, rows 10 and 12) and financial perspective (column 7, row 1), and declined to assign idiosyncratic concepts to the other two perspectives 'process' and 'potential' because she was unable to make any appropriate comparison. She stated that she had realized she had mixed up 'perspective of potential' and 'process perspective' during the stages. Therefore, it is not possible to compare her idiosyncratic concepts with the team concepts from both perspectives. However, this statement could also be the reason why her evaluation in the perceived teamwork questionnaire was lower than the evaluation of the other two participants (see chapter 4.4.3.1).

Additionally, the analysis of the Balanced Scorecard results of the three stages revealed some uncertainties in the assignment of the idiosyncratic concepts to Balanced Scorecard perspectives. Table 27 outlines two examples for the perspective of potential and the process perspective. For instance, the concept 'motivation' was generated from the perspective of potential by participants 1 and 3 in single stages (stages 1 and 3, columns 1 and 3; rows 1 and 3; see Table 27).

Table 27: Example 'Motivation' and 'Personal Training'

Row	Partici-pant	Column 1	Column 2	Column 3	Column 4	Column 5	Column 6
		Perspective of Potential			Process Perspective		
		Stage 1 Single	Stage 2 Team	Stage 3 Single	Stage 1 Single	Stage 2 Team	Stage 3 Single
1	1	Staff motivation		Staff motivation		Staff motivation	Staff motivation
2	2						
3	3	Motivation promotion		Motivation promotion			
Row	Partici-pant	Perspective of Potential			Process Perspective		
		Stage 1 Single	Stage 2 Team	Stage 3 Single	Stage 1 Single	Stage 2 Team	Stage 3 Single
4	1				Personal training		
5	2				Development of the staff		Personal training
6	3			Employee training			

Moreover, participant 1 also generated this concept from the process perspective in stage 3 (column 6, row 1). During the team stage (stage 2, column 5, rows 1-3), this concept was generated from the process perspective. Participant 2 did not generate such a concept before or after the team stage for either of these two perspectives.

Similar results were found for the concept 'personal training'. Participants 1 and 2 mentioned 'personal training' and 'development of the staff' in stage 1 from the process perspective (column 4, rows 4 and 5). Participant 2 mentioned it also in stage 3 (column 6, row 5). During stage 3, participant 3 introduced a concept 'employee training' . Participant 3 generated this concept from the perspective of potential (column 3, row 6). However, during the team stage such concepts were not generated, neither from the perspective of potential nor for the process perspective. Other concepts such as 'nice service', 'friendly personnel' or some similar concept only came up from the customer perspective for all participants during the team stage (stage 2) and stage 3. Summarizing the results, especially of participant 2, for the four perspectives of the Balanced Scorecard, it can be assumed that the perspectives 'financial' and 'customer' were perceived by the participant as quite distinct, and the perspectives 'process' and 'potential' as more homogenous. However, the misunderstandings about the perspectives of the Balanced Scorecard could be an example of a group specific problem, since all participants had other training backgrounds. The Balanced Scorecard was new to all of them. Nevertheless, the confusion about perspectives could also be caused by the explanation in the handouts given to the participants (see Appendix 8). Slide 3 in Appendix 8 shows how the process perspective and perspectives of potential were explained. The process perspective was explained as 'In which processes should we achieve excellence?' Some examples were given, such as development time, and error-prone processes. The perspective of potential was explained as 'How can we maintain our flexibility?' Examples for that perspective were employee 'satisfaction' and 'continuous training'. The process perspective refers to production and processes, which are critical for reaching objectives, such as innovation and operation processes (R. S. Kaplan & D. P. Norton, 1996a, chapter 5). The perspective of potential contributes to learning and growth of organisations, and to employee development (R. S. Kaplan & D. P. Norton, 1996a, chapter 6). It might be that the difference between both perspectives was not explained clearly enough for participants not majoring in business.

There is also very little difference between objectives and measurement, particularly with regard to the generation of indices, a typical error of the Balanced Scorecard (see, for instance, J. Löbel, H.-A. Schröger & H. Closhen, 2005, p. 129). All perspectives in the Balanced Scorecard are related to each other. It is possible that cause-and-effect relationships were identified but not implemented, because of confusion between the process perspective and the mean level. For instance, the process perspective of the Balanced Scorecard for the team stage includes the objectives und means listed in Table 28, p. 138, such as 'motivation of the employees' (column 1, row 1) and 'having a say' (column 2, row 1).

The objectives 'motivation of employees' and 'building up permanent workforce' (column 1, row 1 and 2) are employment focussed. These objectives belong more to the perspective of potential. The two objectives 'advertising' and 'consumer increase' (column 1, row 3 and 4) focus more on a customer perspective. The last objective 'no supply bottleneck' is one of the process perspectives. Nevertheless, all objectives could be reinterpreted as processes. Objectives are state of affairs, which are to be desired (R. Brühl, 2009, p. 16). Future conditions will be achieved using means for changing processes. Changing processes are a potential for further development. Therefore, it might be possible that the process perspective is mixed up with means for changing processes and / or perspectives of potential. With regard to the content, the difference between objectives and means is not always clear (see, for instance, J. Löbel, H.-A. Schröger & H. Closhen, 2005, p. 129). For example, in stage 1, participant 3 generated for the customer objective perspective the statement 'reorganisation of the university cafeteria' (see Appendix 14). Participant 3 wrote about the same point from the objective level '→ redesign from cold to warm'. Hence, the part '→ redesign from cold to warm' is an explanation for the further objective 'reorganisation of the university cafeteria'. However, a closer look at the explanation of the objective reveals that this could be interpreted as a mean. Her suggested mean was to consult a professional adviser, and to drive to IKEA (see Appendix 14).

Table 28: Results for the Process Perspective of the Team (Stage 2)

Row	Column 1 Objectives	Column 2 Means	Column 3 Measurement
1	Motivation of employees	Having a say Social events Promotion of team spirit Employee of the month	
2	Building up permanent workforce	Correspond to contractual arrangements Probationary Prepare substantial food consisting of at least 5 menus (Taking into account individual needs such as vegetarian, diet, allergies, etc.)	
3	Advertising		Numbers of customers
4	Customer increase		
5	No supply bottleneck		

Furthermore, participant 3 sometimes used very abstract terms, such as 'in places where money can be saved, no money should be wasted' (participant 3, stage 3, financial perspective). Such abstract terms could be caused by a lack of knowledge about precise places where money could be saved. This would mean that their work experience was not enough to solve the task, and the information given in this case may not have been detailed enough. The only way to find out more about this would be to repeat the study with the same task and conducting processes, with management students, managers or other people, with a greater work experience, or people who have experience with Balanced Scorecards.

The lack of difference between objectives and means could also be caused by the process itself. The fact that participants had a free choice in structuring the task (writing on card files as opposed to writing on a sheet of paper for the Balanced Scorecard) proved difficult. Participants chose the paper form, probably because they were more used to writing on paper. The greatest problem was the limited space. They tried to write down their answers on one sheet of paper, even though they could have used as many as they wanted. Additionally, the space problem was caused partly by the task itself. The structure was given for the objectives, means, and measurements of the Balanced Scorecard (slide 2, see Appendix 8). However, at the beginning of the tasks (see Appendix 10) they focussed on the objectives of all four perspectives. Later, the focus was on the means and measurement. As a result, the distinction between mean and measurement was not clear for participant 1 (see Appendix 15). Just a small arrow makes the difference. The result for the Balanced Scorecard from participant 3 is similar (see Appendix 14). Here, as described above, there was no difference between objectives and mean (see for instance J. Löbel, H.-A. Schröger, & H. Closhen, 2005). The arrows are used for explanations such as 'it is less waste food' and 'portions with different prices = customer friendly' as explanations for 'save waste by offering the food in portions'. The second explanation 'portions with different prices = customer friendly' is also partly a mean. Moreover, participant 3 had no measurements, probably because her style was to explain everything. Participant 2 solved the structural problem by writing one item below another in order (see Appendix 16).

The method of recording answers on paper caused another problem: preparing the participants' concepts for the similarity assignment. During stage 3 for participant 1, it was realized that there would be no time to prepare the individual concepts of the last stage, in the same way as was done with the concepts in stages 1 and 2. Nevertheless, this would have been necessary to keep everything constant. The individual concepts of stage 1 and team concepts of stage 2 were listed at the beginning of stage 3 on new sheets of paper. The individual concepts, which the participants assigned to team concepts for each perspective of the Balanced Scorecard, were cut out. Then participants glued the assigned individual concepts and team concepts on a separate sheet. However, this also means that eliciting idiosyncratic mental models during stage 3 was not necessary. When participant 1 had finished stage 3, it was decided not to change the process, but to collect the data of the other two participants in stage 3 as well. Moreover, the participants also needed a long time for the assignment process. Therefore, in study IV the process of preparing data for the assignment process and the process of assignment itself should have been changed. Faced with these problems, no choice would be given to the participants in study IV. Participants would write down answers on file cards, so it would be possible to conduct Structure-Formation-Technique, as was done in study I.

All together, the results indicate that the Balanced Scorecard scenario given in this study needs

- deeper knowledge about the Balanced Scorecard tool itself, and
- deeper management knowledge.

To make sure that participants have a deeper knowledge of the Balanced Scorecard tool, a practice similar to the one in study I, for the cause-and-effect rule system on the life cycle example, should be done with the Balanced Scorecard task, especially for participants majoring in fields other than management.

The only way to make sure that participants have deeper management knowledge is probably to ask managers or management students themselves to take part, or to give participants training in the task field, which would lengthen the procedure. This has to be set against the objective to reduce the time taken by the participants (research economics, see chapter 3.4).

It could probably be reduced if the design and task were changed by writing answers on file cards.

Reconsidering the group of participants and the task, I have to say, that it is probably unlikely that participants with backgrounds other than management would have to solve such management problems in the real world, without having any preparation time. Even people majoring in different backgrounds are designated to projects on which they work in heterogenic teams using their specialist knowledge. However, the realisation of this difficulty was not the aim of this study, which was to explore a way for comparing idiosyncratic knowledge in the form of similar concepts. The results suggest that semantics could be investigated in further research.

4.5. Empirical Study IV – Idiosyncratic Mental Models and Semantic Relations

> "The study of "externalized language" ... treats language as an external artifact used by human beings, and seeks to characterize its properties as part of the external world with which humans interact. By contrast, the study of "internalized language" ... treats language as a body of knowledge within the minds/brains of speakers, and seeks to characterize its properties within the context of a more general theory of psychology."
>
> (R. Jackendoff, 1996, p. 539)

4.5.1. Theoretical Assumptions

4.5.1.1. Introduction

The results of study III about the similarity assignment of idiosyncratic concepts to team concepts supported the idea of working with semantic relations. Semantics deal with the meaning of language (J. J. Katz, 1972, p. 1). It is the "theory of the relation between language and the world" (R. Jackendoff, 1996, p. 539). One research field of semantics, the lexical semantic, is concerned with the meaning of words. Researching word meaning is done in different ways. One way is to look at word meaning within a group of similar words. For instance, the meaning of the word 'river' within the group of similar words 'stream', 'waterway', 'brook', and 'canal'. Nevertheless, researching word meaning is also done by looking at the relationship between different words. Here, semantic relations such as synonyms, antonyms, and hyponyms play a major role in the research.

The objective in this study is to develop a system of rules, which enable participants to map their idiosyncratic concepts to team concepts based on the participants' perceived meaning of the concepts. It combines the collective and the holistic approach (see chapter 3.6). Several presumptions are made about this objective:

1. Concepts are idiosyncratic. They are part of idiosyncratic mental models and reflect the constancy of experience and knowledge (see chapter 2.2).

2. In a holistic session, a task related conversation between team members takes place. The conversation results in a solution for the task, based on a group decision-making process. The solution is the team mental model, which consists of concepts and the relationships between them.

3. Participants are able to map their idiosyncratic concepts to team concepts. Participants do the assignment based on a propositional categorisation process (see chapter 4.5.1.5). Regarding structural theoretical assumptions of basic level effects and prototype effects (G. Lakoff, 1987), it is assumed that similarly judged concepts are related to each other (see Figure 28, p. 148; E. Rosch et al., 1976a. For the importance of prototype theory in linguistics see, for instance, N. Dörschner, 1996; G. Kleiber, 1998; M. Mangasser-Wahl, 2000a; M. Mangasser-Wahl, 2000b). Firstly, concepts are related in terms of a semantic constitution (see chapter 4.5.1.2.1). Concepts differ in their degree of abstraction (vertically, see chapter 4.5.1.2; see Figure 7, p. 30; additionally chapter 2.2.3.3). Secondly, concepts are related in terms of family resemblances. Concepts differ in the degree to which they represent a category (horizontally, see chapter 4.5.1.2.2; see for instance N. Dörschner, 1996, p. 45). For that reason, it is possible that participants use concepts with different names, but which refer to the same category. Hence, these concepts are similar in meaning and have a similar function in the mental models.

4. Because concepts are idiosyncratic, with idiosyncratic mental models on the one hand, and team members discussing solutions for the task during the team stages on the other, participants are able to judge the similarity of idiosyncratic concepts and team concepts (similar C. Eden & F. Ackermann, 1998, p. 196).

4.5.1.2. Categorization

> "...categorization...the main way that we make sense of experience." (G. Lakoff, 1987, p. xi)

Categorization is an essential aspect of cognitive organizing (G. Kleiber, 1998, p. 4). Categorizing things or abstract entities is done because they have qualities in common (G. Lakoff, 1987, p. 5 f.; E. Rosch & B. B. Lloyd, 1978). Assuming there is an ability to generalize about individual entities; categorization stabilizes the perceived environment (G. Kleiber, 1998, p. 4 f.). Things are grouped together based on the common attributes of entities (G. Lakoff, 1987,

p. 5; G. Kleiber, 1998, p. 4). Hence, categorization investigates the classification rules. These classification rules are attributes, which are shared by all representatives (G. Kleiber, 1998, p. 5). According to "experience realism" (Erfahrungsrealismus, G. Kleiber, 1998, p. 5) corresponding to prototype theory (G. Kleiber, 1998, p. 5), not all attributes have to be shared by all entities. It is assumed that classification is based upon global similarities between entities (G. Kleiber, 1998, p. 5). Two basic principles are assumed to be important. The first is cognitive economy, which refers to the function of category systems affording maximum information with minimum cognitive effort (E. Rosch, 1978, p. 28). The second principle is the perceived world structure. The structure of the information is "provided and asserts that the perceived world comes as structured information rather than as arbitrary or unpredictable attributes" (E. Rosch, 1978, p. 28). This means that what is perceived is so organised that it makes sense. How it will be perceived depends upon many factors, such as culture. Both principles have an impact on the abstraction level of the categories developed by participants (E. Rosch, 1978, p. 29).

4.5.1.2.1. Vertical Dimension of Categories: Semantic Constitution

In experiments with natural categories such as furniture, fish and clothing (E. Rosch et al., 1976a, p. 388, Table 1), E. Rosch et al. (1976a) gave participants lists of concepts (for a detailed description of the experiments see E. Rosch et al., 1976a). The concepts were categorized on three levels of a hierarchical taxonomy (see Figure 25, p. 143): superordinate level, basic level, subordinate level (E. Rosch et al., 1976a, p. 388, Table 1). Categories are defined by E. Rosch et al. (1976a, p. 383) as a number of objects, which are seen to be equivalent, such as bicycle for the basic level in Figure 25. The category 'bicycle' includes different kinds of bicycles: racing bikes, city bikes, light ones, heavy ones, etc. This means that the category includes every vehicle, which would be perceived to be a bicycle. The relationship between categories at different levels, which are related to each other by class inclusion, is defined by E. Rosch et al. (1976a) as taxonomy such as 'vehicle – bicycle – racing bike' or 'vehicle – truck – SCANIA' (see Figure 25).

Figure 25: Study IV – Inner Structure of Taxonomies

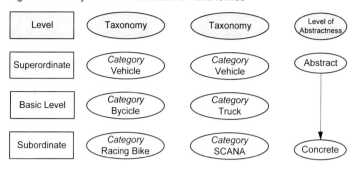

The level of abstraction is related to the degree of inclusiveness of a category. At the superordinate level, in Figure 25 and Figure 26 the category 'vehicle' has the highest level of abstraction and therefore the greatest inclusiveness. The superordinate level includes basic level objects, such as bicycles, trucks, and motorbikes, as well as subordinate level objects, such as Honda, Suzuki, and MAN (indicated with the line in Figure 26). However, a lower level does not include an exhaustive list of higher-level objects. For instance, basic level objects as 'motorbike' includes superordinate level objects 'vehicle', but it does not include all objects in the category 'vehicle', such as 'truck'. Nevertheless, 'truck' and 'motorbike' are basic level objects of the same superordinate level 'vehicle'. Categories such as 'motorbike' and 'truck' are perceived as completely distinct. However, objects within categories are perceived as very similar. Racing bikes and city bikes are very similar (see G. Lakoff, 1987, p. 52). This perception can be traced back to the concept of 'cue validity', which is defined as the probability "that an object is in a particular category given its possession of some features" (G. Lakoff, 1987, p. 52). The best cues are ones, which work for all categories in that level (G. Lakoff, 1987, p. 52). For instance, a cue for the example in Figure 26 is 'moving'. 'Moving' is an attribute for all three basic level categories 'motorbike', 'bicycle', and 'truck'.

Figure 26: Study IV – Example for Inclusiveness of Categories

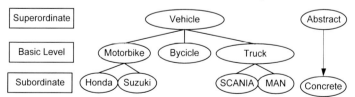

Basic level objects carry the most information. Objects at this level have the highest attribute numbers in common, and have similar motor movements (e.g. from an experimental instruction: "...write down the muscle movements that you make when you use or interact with that

object...", E. Rosch et al., 1976a, p. 394), similar shapes (E. Rosch, 1978, pp. 32-33), and "can be identified from averaged shapes of members of the class" (E. Rosch et al., 1976a, p. 382). Basic level objects are used most often. They are the ones learned and named first by children, and are the most essential in language (E. Rosch et al., 1976a, p. 435).

4.5.1.2.2. Horizontal Dimension: Family Resemblances

> "...categorical judgements become a problem only if one is concerned with boundaries..." (Rosch, 1978, p. 36, in reference to Wittgenstein, 1953)

The horizontal dimension in the categorization process is related to the term 'prototype' (see for instance E. Rosch, 1978). The prototype is the best entity of a category. It is very representative because it reflects the most common attributes (E. Rosch, 1978, p. 37; G. Kleiber, 1998, p. 52). The prototype is not defined by only one individual. It depends on the concurrent judgment of those who use the word (N. Dörschner, 1996, p. 44). Rosch (1973, p. 133) showed in experiments with natural categories that, based on concurrent participants' judgements, 'apple' is very representative for the category 'fruit', 'chemistry' for the category 'science', 'football' for 'sport', and 'robin' for 'birds'. In contrast to these, 'olive', 'history', 'weight lifting', and 'ostrich' are bad representatives for their categories.

The prototype itself does not describe a theory of representation of categories, or a theory of learning categories. The prototype is learned. Therefore, it depends on other issues, such as cultural factors. The empirical results reflect judgement behaviour like the degree to which it is a prototype (see also T. B. Seiler, 2001a, p. 131). The prototype itself acts as a "cognitive reference point" (G. Lakoff, 1987, pp. 40-46) for inference processes. Hence, G. Lakoff (1987, pp. 40-46) argues that it is better to speak of prototype effects rather than a prototype. Additionally, it was found that results of the categorization processes depend on situational, contextual and pragmatical conditions (T. B. Seiler, 2001a, p. 139). Anyway, categories

> "...must have additional internal structure of some sort that produces these ... ratings. Moreover, that internal structure must be part of our concept of what a bird is..." (G. Lakoff, 1987, p. 45).

4.5.1.2.3. Conclusion of Categorization, and Further Consequences for the Thesis Research Process

In this thesis, a within-a-level-structure is assumed, including the prototype as core, and other entities organized around it. Figure 27 shows how the structure around a prototype could be organised. In the middle is the entity 'apple', which is highly typical for the category 'fruit'. Around the entity 'apple' are other entities, which become less typical for the category 'fruits'. They are less typical the greater the distance from the prototype. That means entities, which are situated closer to the prototype, have a higher degree of representation for this category. Therefore, these entities are more similar to the prototype than entities on the periphery. As a result, category borders are not sharp (N. Dörschner, 1996, pp. 44-45).

Figure 27: Study IV – Fictional Example for Horizontal Dimension (Categories are taken from E. Rosch, 1973, p. 133, Table 1)

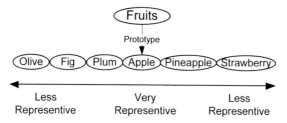

This principle can be traced back to L. Wittgenstein's family resemblances (L. Wittgenstein, 1953/2001). Based on the example of games (for instance board games, ball-games, L. Wittgenstein, 2002, p. 27c, p. 66), L. Wittgenstein argued that it is not possible to define universal attributes for all different types of games. Hence, it is not possible to define sharp borders for categories. Family resemblances refer to a structure where the entities do not need to have all attributes in common in order to belong to the same category (G. Kleiber, 1998, p. 36). This is often described with an 'AB, BC, CD, DE'-example (see for instance E. Rosch, S. Carol, & S. R. Miller, 1976b, p. 493). Here, only the neighbours have at least one common attribute as a minimum for family bonds (N. Dörschner, 1996, p. 46). However, this also means that A and E can be categorized in the same category, without having an obviously common attribute.

Therefore, in this work, it is assumed that entities, which are judged by participants to be similar, are bounded by a structure. This structure refers to the semantic constitution or family resemblance, or a combination of both. Here, two aspects are stressed:

- Judgements by participants
- Structure among concepts

In the collective and holistic stages, participants receive domain specific tasks. During the collective stage, participants solve the task by themselves. The result is the objectified idiosyncratic mental model of the participant (see chapter 2.2.2). The concepts of an objectified idiosyncratic mental model symbolize simple personal conceptual knowledge. They are knowledge about the domain content of the task. During the holistic stage, participants solve the same task in a team, based on a discussion process. Here, participants again rely on their personal knowledge. In study III, the discussion was part of the task and was therefore observed during the holistic stage (see chapter 4.4). The result of the task of the holistic stage is the objectified team mental model. Because of discussion during the team session, and because of the objectified idiosyncratic concepts of the collective session, it is assumed that **participants are able to judge** the relationship between the meaning of the idiosyncratic concepts and team concepts.

It cannot be excluded that during the holistic stage participants discuss other things in the team beside those focussed on during the collective stage. This could happen if, for instance, misunderstandings occur. This was the case with participant 2 in study III (see chapter 4.4). Nevertheless, this would confirm the assumption that participants are still able to judge the relationship of meaning between different concepts. Participant 2 showed it when she declined to assign her idiosyncratic concepts to the team concepts. The only way to minimize the discussion of other aspects of the task is to keep the tasks constant throughout the different stages.

A **structure between idiosyncratic concepts** of the collective stages and team concepts of the holistic stage is not necessarily obvious to third persons. For them they would be simply concepts, but not necessarily with special meanings in the task solving process. Therefore, it might not be possible for them to understand why the participant used a particular concept (see C. Eden & F. Ackermann, 1998, p. 196; chapter 3.7.3).

Idiosyncratic concepts and team concepts could be at the limit of a with-in-level-structure where the boundaries are not sharply defined between categories. Whether these concepts are part of the same category would be judged by the participants, when comparing their idiosyncratic concepts and the team concepts. It is not clear which concepts, the idiosyncratic ones or the team concepts, would act as a cognitive reference point (see G. Lakoff, 1987). However, in both stages, the collective and holistic stage, participants rely on personal knowledge.

The interpretation of the meaning of participants' concepts by a third person depends upon the third person's personal knowledge, their assumptions about the meaning of participants' concepts, and / or their learned prototypical reference points (see above). The reason for this is the missing context knowledge caused by idiosyncratic concept mapping methods. Therefore, a third person might generate different categories. An example of this is the validation by participant 3 in study II (see chapter 4.2.3.5 and 4.2.3.6) where

- Participant 3 did not assign all her idiosyncratic concepts of study I to the experts' categories of study II, and moreover

- Participant 3 and the experts did not match all the assignments of the idiosyncratic concepts to categories.

However, participants would still be able to stress slight differences in the meaning of their idiosyncratic concepts or important information, when generating categories on a basic or a superordinate level. The participants' intention for using idiosyncratic concepts will not be lost. Figure 28, p. 148, shows the possibility of finding different basic level concepts, where not all subordinate concepts would fit in. For instance, lemon, fig, and strawberry are concepts on subordinate level. Mediterranean, oily, and sweet are higher abstract concepts on a basic level, and fruit is based on a superordinate level. Lemon is not salty or sweet but it is a Mediterranean fruit. Olive is a Mediterranean fruit, oily, but not sweet. Strawberry is probably not really perceived as a Mediterranean fruit. Nevertheless, all have a superordinate level in common because they are fruits. However, if it is the task to construct a model about 'fruits you like', it is not useful to generate a superordinate level 'fruit' to compare different fruits, which were generated by different participants. Important information would get lost where participants differ.

The problem of choosing the right meaningful category on a superordinate or basic level for an idiosyncratic concept occurs as it did in study II (see chapter 4.2.4) when two informative categories on a basic or superordinate level, would fit the idiosyncratic mental model. For example, olive as it is sketched in Figure 28 would fit into both basic levels: oily and Mediterranean. A category Mediterranean and oily would not be plausible at a subordinate level with concept 'lemon', which is a Mediterranean fruit but not oily. Therefore, in such an ambiguous situation, generating categories of higher abstraction could lead to uncertainties in terms of the concept meaning, when they are generated by someone other than the participant (see C. Eden & F. Ackermann, 1998). Additionally, a third person could also categorize concepts, based on other common attributes, which a fourth person would not do. Referring to the principle of cognitive economy, one influencing factor is also culture (see above). Another point is that different categories such as sweet, oily, and Mediterranean in Figure 28 could have other prototypes. Prototypical for Mediterranean could be olive, for sweet fruits maybe strawberry. This would lead to different cognitive reference points (see above), hence to different inference processes, and hence to different idiosyncratic mental models.

Therefore, the judgement about the similarity of idiosyncratic concepts and team concepts, which can also include generating other abstract categories, should be done by the participants themselves. This is important because both concepts, the idiosyncratic and the team concepts, rely on the knowledge of the participants.

Figure 28: Study IV – Combination of Vertical and Horizontal Structure based on Fruit Example

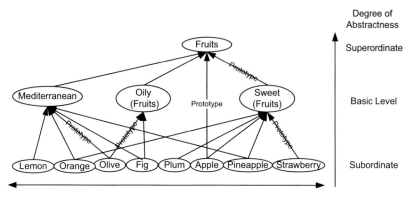

4.5.1.3. Categorization and Lexical Semantics

As explained above, a participant could choose less representative examples when constructing idiosyncratic mental models. Even if the task for constructing idiosyncratic mental models is focussed on a specific problem, different people could generate different categories, with a different degree of abstractness of the entities. This means that participants themselves could also give different examples for the same category, as was observed in study I; for instance, 'management administration', 'top management' and 'general administration' (participant 4, study 1, Figure 18, p. 103). The value of the dimension 'family resemblance' is the assumption that two idiosyncratic concepts could be placed in the same category, even if they are placed toward the limits of the category, such as olive and strawberry as assumed in Figure 27, p. 145 (see also Figure 28). This means, these concepts are linked together by a loose family bond. The judgement by participants, that two or more concepts should be placed in the same category, could originate from different sources. Such sources are, for instance, the discussion process in the holistic session, where participants discuss concepts or logical inferences based on other entities with the same attributes. For example,

> Strawberries were discussed and categorized in the team stage as being sweet.
>
> <u>Oranges as part of idiosyncratic mental model of a participant are sweet.</u>
>
> Oranges are categorized by the participant as being sweet.

Such logical inferences are discussed by P. N. Johnson-Laird (1983). However, this is not the purpose of this work. For this thesis, the assumption is important, that participants are able to judge the similarity of idiosyncratic concepts and team concepts no matter how they do this. For this process, participants need a tool to communicate how the similarities or differences appear. In other words, they need a tool to express the semantic constitution and family resemblances, if concepts have similar meanings. For this reason, this study reverts to semantic relations, which are part of lexical semantics, without intending to formulate a new semantic theory (see chapter 4.5.1.4).

It is an important assumption that for the interpretation of shared knowledge two participants could use words which differ in their abstractness or prototypicality, but which are placed in the same category. This leads to the assumption that the intended use of these concepts was similar or the same. This means that even if one participant used an abstract concept and another participant a concrete concept, both participants have shared knowledge. They just differ in the way they objectify their knowledge.

4.5.1.4. Meaning Relation Tool based on Semantics

The 'meaning relation tool' helps participants to communicate relationships between different concepts. Based on the two dimensions 'family resemblance' and 'semantic constitutions' (see chapter 4.5.1.2), four rules seem to be adequate: 'synonym' or 'interchangeable', 'antonym', 'hyponym' or 'part of something', and 'incompatible'.

Synonym and antonym refer to the horizontal, family resemblance. Synonym describes the equal relationship between two or more entities (A. C. Schalley, 2004, p. 27). It is based upon contextual factors (J. Lyons, 1995, p. 463). Two concepts are synonymous if they have the same meaning. For instance, if a person A says 'I am buying bread in a shop', and person B is buying bread in the shop (J. Lyons, 1995, p. 463). Differences in the degree of synonymy, hence entities can be more or less synonymous, and the dimension of synonymy related to cognitive and emotive synonymy, will not be made here (see D. A. Cruse, 1986, chapter 12; J. Lyons, 1995, chapter 10.2; D. Geeraerts, 2010, pp. 84-85).

Antonym is the expression for a word, which describes the opposite of another word (J. Lyons, 1995, p. 473). Notwithstanding the fact that semantic researchers distinguish between many kinds of opposite (see for instance A. C. Schalley, 2004, p. 27 f.; D. A. Cruse, 1986, chapter 9; J. Lyons, 1995, chapter 10.4), the term will be used in this work in its "most frequently encountered sense" (D. A. Cruse, 1986, p. 204) to illustrate all types of lexical opposites (D. A. Cruse, 1986, p. 204). Examples are, for instance, 'light vs. heavy', 'healthy vs. ill', and 'light vs. dark' (A. Cruse, 2011, pp. 155-156; D. Geeraerts, 2010, pp. 85-86).

Hyponym refers to the vertical, semantic constitution dimension. Hyponym is concerned with class inclusion. A more specific, concrete concept is part of a more abstract concept. For instance, the meaning of the term 'rose' is included in the meaning of the term 'flower', but the term 'flower' includes more entities than the term 'rose', such as 'tulip' and 'lilac' (J. Lyons, 1995, p. 464; A. C. Schalley, 2004, p. 28; A. Cruse, 2011, p. 134; D. Geeraerts, 2010, p. 82).

Incompatibility concerns contradiction or discrepancy between concepts. One concept negates another. An example of incompatible concepts is colours. Colours are alternatives. A book, which is blue, cannot be red (D. A. Cruse, 1986, p. 93; A. Cruse, 2011, p. 151).

4.5.1.5. Semantic and Propositional Categorization in Mental Models

Two kinds of cognitive categorization are important in this work: The first is the propositional categorisation that "where a (named) entity is explicitly placed into a named category" (D. Edwards, 1991, p. 519). Examples are a 'plant is a living organism' or 'trees are plants'. The second categorization is the semantic. Entities such as a sentence – or parts of mental models – are categorized in terms of events, objects, time, or definiteness and spatial locations (D. Edwards, 1991, p. 518 f). The difference between both categorizations is intentional. It is assumed that propositional categorization is intentional, therefore used "as objects of thought" (G. Lakoff, 1987, p. 335). Whereas semantic categorization is assumed to be unconscious and automatic in terms of a schema-driven cognition (D. Edwards, 1991, p. 519), therefore "used in thought" (G. Lakoff, 1987, p. 335; D. Edwards, 1991, p. 519). Semantic categorization supplies a cognitive basis for propositional categorisation (D. Edwards, 1991, p. 519).

The differentiation between semantic and propositional categorization is important. Semantic categorization is assumed to be demonstrated in the form of the idiosyncratic mental models. The idiosyncratic mental models are the result of solving tasks, therefore of thinking. The propositional categorization is what the participants are supposed to do when using semantic relations. It is the judgement that two entities, the concepts of the idiosyncratic mental model and the concepts of the team model, mean the same.

Attention should be paid to the distinction between the semantic categorization and semantic relations. Semantic categorizing originates from cognitive psychology and refers to the thinking. Semantic relations originate from linguistics. Here, research is conducted on the relationship of meaning between words. Therefore, semantic relations are, in this thesis, a tool for propositional categorization. Propositional categorizing refers to the vertical and horizontal structure of words.

4.5.1.6. Mental Models and Semantic Constitution

Mental models and semantic constitution are sometimes not sharply distinct. A mental model was defined as an internal (cognitive) representation of a dynamic system. It is used by humans, to describe the system, to explain the function of the system and to predict future states of the system, based on experience and previous knowledge (R. Brühl & S. Buch, 2005; see chapter 2.2.3.1). The reference point in this definition is the dynamic system. It consists of different entities, which are organized and structured in some way. Chapter 2.2.3.3 stresses how these structures could look. This implies the assumption that objectified mental models represent complex cognitive knowledge structures. The term 'structure' refers to the frame of mental models, to its architecture in which concepts are fitted. Therefore, the structure of a mental model refers to the relationship between entities and concepts. Concepts themselves can be perceived as very different or very similar in meaning. For instance, the concepts 'finance' and 'customer' could be assigned to different categories, based on the perception of the participants, and based on the task. In mental models, which focus on content and structure, both concepts could be related in some way, such as the way in which a customer affects the finance of a company.

Semantic constitution refers to the relationships in meaning between concepts. For instance, the concept 'communication' can be seen as a part of 'PR'. Another example would be the concepts 'river' and 'waterway', which could mean the same depending on the task. If it is the task to construct domain specific knowledge, such as 'living organism', with subcategories such as plants and animals, as was shown in Figure 7, p. 30, then the mental model is identical to the semantic constitution.

4.5.2. Summary about the Objectives

In study I, participants of a small company were asked for their views about the competitive situation of their company. Idiosyncratic mental models with common qualities were found in accordance with the reported results in the literature (see for instance G. P. Hodgkinson & G. Johson, 1994; B. B. Tyler & D. R. Gnyawali, 2009; see chapter 1). In study II, these idiosyncratic mental models were adapted to their similarities using the Delphi-Method. The results of study II indicated that participants themselves should evaluate the similarity of their idiosyncratic mental models (see chapters 4.2.3 and 4.3). For that reason, study III explored a way for participants to compare idiosyncratic concepts. Based on the experiences of study III, a design and similarity judgement process was developed using semantic relations in study IV. Both design and judgement processes now differ from those in Approach A. Therefore, it was decided to repeat studies I and II with the current design, focussing on eliciting and comparing idiosyncratic mental models and team mental models.

The methodical objectives are therefore

Method Objective 5: *to elicit idiosyncratic mental models and team mental models based on the adapted study design*, and

Method Objective 6: *to develop and improve the meaning relation tool based on semantics.*

The study specific objectives are

Study Objective 1: *to underpin theoretically the meaning relations tool,* and

Study Objective 2: *to apply the meaning relation tool, based on the adapted study design, to see if it works and with what results.*

4.5.3. Method

4.5.3.1. Participants

Study III focussed on the question how non-business economists solve business administration problems. This was of interest because of the results of study II with regard to the categorization process (see chapter 4.2.4). The results of study III, which were based on a Balanced Scorecard scenario, indicated that deeper knowledge about the Balanced Scorecard and deeper management knowledge would be necessary (see chapter 4.4.3). None of the participants of study III had management training. In study IV, participants who took part were non-economist in background, but had received management training.

Study IV was conducted with two different groups:

- one group 'Natural Project Teams' and
- one group 'Experimental Teams'.

Members of the **'Natural Project Teams'** were studying a business administration master programme. This programme was designed especially for non-business administration students. They had a university degree but in fields other than business administration. Because of the different educational backgrounds, project teams were classified as heterogeneous (see the reasons for the distinction between homogeneous and heterogeneous groups in this study in chapter 4.5.3.5 Presumptions). Additionally, these teams were a quasi-experimental group. The term 'quasi-experimental' refers to the fact that the project teams already existed before conducting the study. Therefore, this group was also called a 'Natural Project Team'. However, four Natural Project Teams took part in this study, one team with three participants and three teams with two (N=9; three male and six female). Participants were delegates of their normal project groups. The project groups worked on real problems. They had to solve these problems as part of their management study. Their average age was

25 years, with a range from 22 to 28 years. They differed in the length of work experience, from none to 2 ½ years. All participants were members of the international business administration master programme for non-economists described above. Additionally, they came from different countries in Europe. Therefore, German was not the mother tongue for all participants. However, they all spoke German fluently, which was an entry requirement for the master programme. For their participation in this study, each team received a bottle of sparkling wine at the end of stage 2.

The group **'Experimental Teams'** was made up randomly from members of an international business administration doctoral programme. They were placed in five teams each with two participants (N=10; n^{15}=2, six male and four female). Participants of the Experimental Teams were mostly business economists. Eight of the ten participants had a business administration related background. Therefore, three homogeneous teams (with a business administrational background) and two heterogeneous teams (one participant with and one without a business administration background) were formed. Two teams of this group, one homogeneous and one heterogeneous, were used for the preliminary test. The average age within the Experimental Teams was 26.5 years, with a range from 25 to 28 years. The range reflected their working experience was from zero to two years. Four participants did not give an answer when asked about the length of their work experience. Their mother tongue was German.

Table 29, p. 153, summarizes the sample size used in this study, in terms of team composition (homogeneous and heterogeneous, row 1 and 2), the nature of the teams (quasi-experimental and experimental, column 1 and 2) and the number of the teams per cell.

It should be noted that the Natural Project Team was not homogenous, because members came from a special master programme for non-economists (see above). Therefore, they came from different backgrounds.

Table 29: Study IV – Outline of the Sample Size

Row	Nature of the Group Team Composition	Column 1 Natural Project Teams (quasi-experimental)	Column 2 Experimental Teams (experimental)
1	Homogenous		3
2	Heterogeneous	4	2

---

[15] n = Team size

4.5.3.2. Design

This study was conducted during a time when Natural Project Teams had to solve company-consulting projects, which were part of the curriculum. Company consulting projects are about real company related interests, such as the development of market strategies. They lasted for 5 weeks, and were full time for the students. Because of this demanding time schedule during the university project, the research was limited to two sessions. Stage 1 for the Natural Project Teams started in the third week of the company consulting project period. Stage 2 was scheduled in the last week of the project period. In both groups – Natural Project Teams and Experimental Teams – there were at least two weeks between stage 1 and stage 2. Table 30 shows the research design.

Table 30: Study IV – Research Design

Row		Objective	Column 1 Stage 1	Column 2 Stage 2
1		Measurement Approach	Collective	Holistic
2		Focus on	Individual mental models	Team mental models
3		Stage Size	Single sessions	Team session
4	Aim	Part I	Elicitation process	Elicitation process
5		Part II		Similarity mapping

Based on the combination of collective (column 1, row 1) and holistic (column 2, row 1) approaches (see chapter 3.6), this study was designed with repeated measures. In stage 1 (column 1), the idiosyncratic mental model was derived in a single stage (collective approach). In stage 2 (column 2), the team mental models were collected (holistic approach). The objective of stage 2 was subdivided into two parts: Firstly, to elicit the team mental model (column 2, row 4), and secondly, to evaluate the similarity between the idiosyncratic concepts of stage 1 and the team concepts of stage 2 (column 2, row 5).

4.5.3.3. Equipment

Stage 1 was conducted with paper and pencil. Participants had a free choice of different paper sizes and file cards. Most chose the paper for constructing their idiosyncratic mental model. Stage 2 was conducted exclusively with file cards, and the flipchart was used for the construction of the team mental models. The flipchart was also used for the similarity evaluation of the idiosyncratic concepts and team concepts. Using the meaning relation tool, similarity between idiosyncratic concepts and team concepts was written down on the team cards. To preserve them, the team mental models and the assigned idiosyncratic concepts were taped to the flipchart paper. Moreover, the results of the construction process were transferred in VISIO.

4.5.3.4. Procedure

Study IV was conducted during May and August 2006 for the Experimental Teams and in June 2006 for the Natural Project Teams. The interviews were performed mainly by a student apprentice under direction of the author. The interviewers were present all the time to answer any questions, and the interviews were conducted in German. The following chapter 4.5.3.4.1 describes the data collection including stimulus material, task and conducting process. Chapter 4.5.3.4.2 describes the aggregation process made by the participants, especially stimulus material, tasks, and the method adopted. Chapter 4.5.3.4.3 highlights the analysis process.

4.5.3.4.1. Collection Stage: Stimulus Material, Task and Data Collection of the Elicitation Process in Stage 1 and Stage 2

At the beginning of stage 1, teams of both groups received a paper, which introduced the organisational contents of the study. Because of the two sessions, each participant got a personal code, which was composed of

- The first letter of their mother's first name,
- The last letter of their father's first name and
- The participant's birthday.

These codes were important to identify participants' idiosyncratic concepts, which they got back in stage 2. Therefore, this introduction was given back again to the participants at the beginning of stage 2 to remind them. Additionally, each group received a number. Therefore, it could be seen who worked with whom.

Participants of the Natural Project Teams were asked about their project work. They received questions about the:

- Main objectives of the project,
- Problems that will be solved in the project,
- Opportunities for the solution of these problems as well as the resulting consequences and
- Cause-and-effect relationships between objectives, problems and opportunities.

For the Experimental Teams a specific logistics problem was designed. The cover story was:

"Berlin-Brandenburg has a total of 6 million inhabitants. Approximately, 3.4 million of them live in the city of Berlin. For an adequate supply for the city, it is necessary that 1.4 million vehicles per day bring in freight and business goods to the metropolitan area

Berlin-Brandenburg. The metropolitan area receives 460 million tonnes a year. In addition, industrial goods amounting to 242 million tons will be produced and shipped out. Seventy percentages of industrial goods are carried out by road transport. As a result, there is considerable strain on road transport, with different bottlenecks and congestion."

The main reason for designing one special problem for all Experimental Teams was that doctoral students became specialist in different fields, such as marketing, finance, or strategy. During the team session, they were randomly composed and constructed a team mental model. Based on this, participants judged the similarities between idiosyncratic concepts and team concepts. However, the focus in this study was not to find out about how the views of participants differed. The objective was to find out how the similarity evaluation, using the meaning relation tool, would work, and if it would be possible to come to conclusions about shared knowledge. For that reason, one problem was designed for use by all participants. Anyway, participants had complete freedom to generate concepts. They were only restricted to a defined domain.

The Experimental Teams received similar questions to the Natural Project Teams. They were asked about

- Problems that could occur,
- Solution of these problems and
- Cause-and-effect relationships between problems and solutions.

The focus in study IV was on the similarity judgement process, not on the cause-and-effect relationships. Therefore, to keep the process simple, participants of *both groups* received only two rules ('A has a positive effect on B' and 'A has a negative effect on B', see Appendix 1). Nevertheless, participants always had the freedom to create their own cause-and-effect rules.

The task was the same in all stages in both groups. All that changed was the size of the groups from individual stage to team stage. Participants of both groups needed about 30 minutes for stage 1. For stage 2, the teams needed between 1½ and 2 hours.

4.5.3.4.2. Aggregation Stage: Stimulus Material, Task and Conducting of the Similarity Evaluation in Stage 2

After the teams had finished their team mental model in stage 2, participants got a task for the similarity evaluation. They received a detailed description of the meaning relation tool, based on the semantics they were supposed to use for the judgement process (see Appendix 17). After reading the explanation, each participant received the idiosyncratic concepts of stage 1 with the task to use semantic relations for the similarity judgement process. Concepts were identical to the concepts of the idiosyncratic mental models of stage 1; the interviewees made no choices. For this task, participants needed about 15 minutes to 30 minutes. Teams were not separated.

4.5.3.4.3. Analysis Process

The analysis was done by focussing on concept numbers under consideration of the meaning relations used by the participants. Therefore, the analysis in this study focuses more on a quantitative than on a qualitative view (idiographic-quantitative). Idiographic-qualitative word based analyses were made to the validation of the result, to judge their credibility (see chapter 4.5.5; see triangulation, chapter 3.4).

The evaluation of similarity is founded upon the team concept, and is based on ratio analysis. The process will be described using the example of participants 14 and 15, who took part in this study. Both were economists, and doctoral students. Below is an outline of

- firstly, the analysis of the mapping of idiosyncratic concepts to the team concepts focussing on each participant (intra-individual view),
- secondly, the analysis of shared and distributed concepts and team performance (see below) focussing on the teams (n=2) and groups (homogeneous versus heterogeneous; inter-individual view).

The **intra-individual view** describes the assignment of the idiosyncratic concepts to the team concepts. It is a between-stage view. Based on the results of stage 1 and stage 2, this view focuses on how one participant mapped his own idiosyncratic concepts to team concepts. The analysis procedure will be explained, using the result of the team with participant 14 and 15 (see Table 31).

Table 31: Study IV – Example for the Analysis of the Allocation of the Idiosyncratic Concepts to the Team Concepts

				Column			
		1	2	3	4	5	6	7
Row	PN	Total Concept No in S1 (IMM)	Total Concept No in S2 (TMM)	Concept No of S1 which have Similar Meaning as Concepts of S2 (S1->S2)	Concept No of S2 which have Similar Meaning as Concepts of S1	Percentage Concepts of S1 which have Similar Meaning as Concepts of S2	Percentage Concepts of S2 on which concepts of S1 have Similar Meaning
1	14	23	19	15	9	65%	47%
2	15	10	19	9	6	90%	32%

Note xii: PN = participant number; No = number; IMM = idiosyncratic mental model; TMM = team mental model; S = stage

In stage 1, participant 14 constructed an idiosyncratic mental model based on 23 concepts (see Table 31; column 2, row 1). Participant 15 constructed his based on 10 concepts (column 2, row 2). In stage 2, both participants constructed a team mental model based on 19 team concepts (column 3, rows 1 and 2). These were the basis for the assignment of the idiosyncratic concepts. Therefore, the 19 team concepts are used as the base line of one hundred percentage (see Figure 29; team concepts), and the number of the idiosyncratic concepts assigned to team concepts by participants was analysed.

Figure 29: Study IV – Schematic Representation of the Projection of idiosyncratic Concepts to Team Concepts

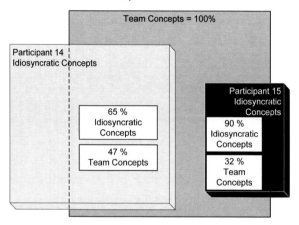

Participant 14 mapped 15 out of 23 idiosyncratic concepts in stage 1 (see Table 31; column 4, row 1) to nine out of 19 team concepts in stage 2 (see Table 31; column 5, row 1). Participant 15 did the same with nine out of ten idiosyncratic concepts in stage 1 (see Table 31; column 4, row 2) to six out of 19 team concepts in the team stage (column 5, row 2). In total, participant 14 mapped 65% of his own idiosyncratic concepts (15 out of 23 idiosyncratic concepts) to 47% of the team concepts (nine out of 19 team concepts). Figure 29 symbolizes these percentages (see also and Figure 32, p. 161). The light grey square on the left side in Figure 29 is the result of participant 14. The medium grey square in the middle refers to the base line, hence to the team. The overlapping of the squares is expressed in percentages. Participant 15 mapped 90% of the idiosyncratic concepts to 32% of the team concepts. The overlapping of the dark grey square on the right side in Figure 29 and the medium grey square in the middle symbolizes this. The idiosyncratic concepts of stage 1 are used for similarity evaluation using meaning relation tool on the team concepts in stage 2.

The **inter-individual view** is a within-stage view, which analysed common and distributed concepts. The analysis referred to two levels. Firstly, the analysis was done using the team level, which focussed on the results of the team members (n=2). Secondly, it referred to the group level, which focussed on the results of homogeneous and heterogeneous groups (three teams for each group). The basis of the analysis will be explained in the example of the team with participants 14 and 15 (see Figure 30, p. 159, Figure 31, p. 160, and Table 32, p. 160).

Figure 30 shows the result of the assignment of the idiosyncratic concepts to the team concepts by both participants. The team concepts are shown in light grey boxes. The concepts of participant 15 are in dark grey boxes. The concepts of participant 14 are in white boxes (see legend). The team model (stage 2) was the basis for this analysis. Both participants used the same four team concepts (see Table 32, p. 160, column 1), 'alternative routes', 'movement of customers to competitors', 'traffic jam interception', and 'delivery delay'. These represent 21% of the team concepts (Table 32, column 3) and are defined as 'shared concepts'.

Figure 30: Study IV – Team Concepts used by Both Participants (Shared Concepts)

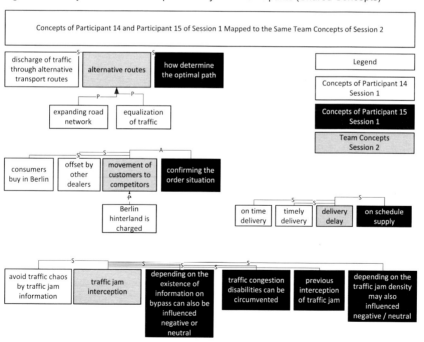

Figure 31, p. 160, shows the result where just one participant had assigned its idiosyncratic concept to team concepts. Hence, seven team concepts were used by just one of the participants for the assignment process (Table 32, column 4). In total, this represents 37% of the team concepts (Table 32, column 5). These concepts are defined as 'distributed concepts'. For instance, participant 14 assigned his own idiosyncratic concepts 'additional cost' (white concept, Figure 31) to the team concept 'additional costs due to delivery failures' (dark concept, Figure 31).

Table 32: Study IV – Analysis of Shared and Distributed Concepts

Column				
1	2	3	4	5
Number of Shared Used Team Concepts by Participant 14 and Participants 15	Total Number of Team Concepts	Percentage of Shared used Team Concepts	Total Number of Distributed Used Team Concepts by Participant 14 and Participants 15	Percentage of Different Used Team Concepts
4	19	21%	7	37%

Figure 31: Study IV – Distributed used Team Concepts

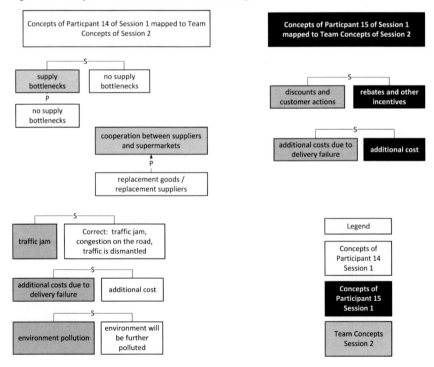

Figure 32, p. 161, shows the schematic representation of shared and distributed used team concepts. The white square represents the shared used concepts. It includes part of the team concept square and parts of the squares of participants 14 and 15. The overlapping of the light-grey square (participants 14) and the medium-grey square (team concepts) as well as the overlapping of the dark grey square (participant 15) and the medium grey square (team concept) represent the number of distributed used team concepts. Parts of the light grey square (participant 14) and dark grey square (participant 15), which are not overlapped with other squares, represent concepts, which do not have a correspondence in other models.

Summarizing, 21% of team concepts are used by both participants, and 37% are used by just one of them. This is a total of 58%. However, this also means that 42% of the team concepts are new concepts. They were generated during stage 2. Therefore, they cannot be explained by previous measurements such as memory performance. It can be assumed, that these 42% can be traced back to the output of the team, therefore to the team performance.

Figure 32: Study IV – Schematic Representation of Shared used and Distributed used Team Concepts

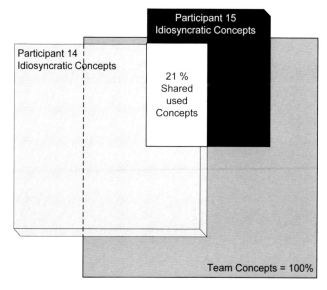

Hence, in this thesis,

> Team performance will be defined as the output of the team, which is not explainable through earlier measurements of individual sessions. Team performance will be viewed as new knowledge based on new team concepts. New team concepts are such concepts, which are without any similarity judgements of concepts further stages using meaning relation tool.

Team performance defined like this (see also chapter 3.9), can be represented by using the following formula:

Formula 2: Formula for Calculation Team Performance in Percentage based on Team Mental Models using Meaning Relation Tool

$$TP\% = \left(1 - \left(\frac{TCP1 + TCP2 - TCC}{TCIT}\right)\right) \bullet 100$$

The formula expressed in words:

Team Performance in % = (1 − (Number of Team Concepts used by Participant 1
   + Number of Team Concepts used by Participant 2
   − Number of Team Concepts used by both Participants)
   : Number of Team Concepts in Total) · 100

The 'number of team concepts used by participants 1' (=TCP1) and the 'number of team concepts used by participant 2' (=TCP2) are the distributed concepts. The 'number of team concepts used by both participants' (=TCC) are the shared concepts. The 'number of team concepts in total' (=TCIT) includes all team concepts of stage 2.

4.5.3.5. Presumptions about Homogeneous and Heterogeneous Teams and Team Performance

The presumptions were developed during the first few eliciting stages of the team concepts, because differences in the results of the similarity judgement between homogeneous and heterogeneous teams were observed.

The analysis described above is standardized on team concepts. Based on team concepts, the values are defined for shared used and distributed used concepts. Shared used concepts, distributed used concepts, and team performances are related to each other, because idiosyncratic concepts and team concepts have limited concept numbers. For the formulation of new hypotheses within the context of discovery, it could be important to prove if homogeneous and heterogeneous groups differ in the use of shared used concepts, distributed used concepts, and team performance. The presumption is that the idiosyncratic mental models of participants of homogeneous teams should be more similar because of their common education, and therefore common knowledge background, than those of participants in heterogeneous teams. A comparison between homogeneous and heterogeneous groups when evaluating these similarities would imply:

- Participants of homogeneous teams should have more shared used team concepts than participants in heterogeneous teams (see Figure 33, p. 163, dark squares by heterogeneous and homogeneous).

- Therefore, participants of homogeneous teams should have less distributed used team concepts than participants in heterogeneous teams (see in Figure 33 the white squares by heterogeneous and homogeneous teams).

- Additionally, because of the relationship between shared used concepts, distributed used concepts and team performance, it is assumed that participants of heterogeneous teams have a higher team performance than participants in homogeneous teams (see in Figure 33 the medium grey squares of heterogeneous teams compared to the medium grey squares of homogeneous teams).

Figure 33: Study IV – Presumption about Similarity, Distribution, and Team Performance

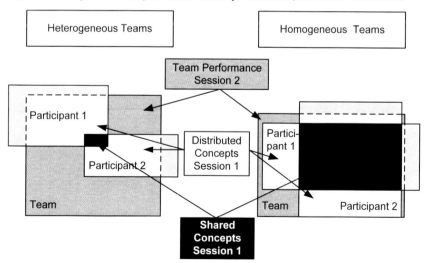

The last presumption refers to new team concepts. Heterogeneous teams should generate more new concepts than participants in homogeneous teams. It is assumed that this is because participants of the heterogeneous group have a higher potential knowledge than participants of the homogeneous group (W. Scholl, 2004, p. 118; in the broad sense J. R. Mesmer-Magnus & L. A. DeChurch, 2009, p. 535). Higher potential knowledge is an opportunity to increase knowledge (W. Scholl, 2004, p. 140). The increase in knowledge is one parameter for effectiveness (W. Scholl, 2004, Chapter 5), which is governed by performance (U. Klocke, 2004, p. 6, pp. 10-11). The verification of such presumptions could also be an indicator for the quality of the methodological approach, assuming that such differences really exist.

However, the difference between homogeneous and heterogeneous groups was made because of the observations different similarity judgements. Therefore, it should be seen as a covariate-similar to covariates in quantitative research paradigm. A covariate is a variable which could have an impact on the result of a study but which is not of primary interest in a study (see e.g. The Cambridge Dictionary of Statistics, 2010, p. 104, by B. S. Everitt & A. Skrondal). It should be also noted that this study is still in context of discovery (see chapter 3.3). Hence, the presumptions made here are no hypothesis.

4.5.4. Results

4.5.4.1. Sample

Six out of nine teams were analysed. Two teams started as preliminary teams, one homogeneous and one heterogeneous. Both teams came from the Experimental Group. The first heterogeneous, preliminary team was studied in just one session. This team was not analysed. The second homogenous, preliminary team was included in the analysis. Additionally, two out of four Project Teams were not included in the analysis. One team with three participants and one team which did not participate in stage 2. Therefore, in total, three homogeneous groups and three heterogeneous groups were analysed. Four of the six groups were from the group 'Experimental Teams'.

4.5.4.2. Method Objective 6 and Study Objective 2: Meaning Relation Tool

In total, the semantic term 'synonym' was used 66 times during the similarity judgement process. On average, this is 5.8 times per participant, with a range from zero (participant 11) to ten concepts (participant 14). For instance, participant 10 judged the idiosyncratic concept 'macro- and microanalysis' as a synonym for the team concept 'environmental analysis' (see

Appendix 18 for an outline of the number of participants, number of used relations, and examples for the similarity judgement of team concepts and assigned idiosyncratic concepts).

The next most frequently used semantic relation is hyponymy. Hyponymy was used 47 times, on average 3.9 times per participant, with a range from zero (participants 11 and 15) to nine concepts (participant 3). For instance, participant 14 judged 'no shortage of goods' as a part of 'supply bottlenecks'. One team (with participants 3 and 4) generated concept 'air pollution'. Both participants of this team had used this concept for similarity mapping of their idiosyncratic concepts 'ecological problems' (participant 3) and 'environmental pollution' (participant 4). This means that both participants had generated abstract concepts during stage 1. During the team stage, the concept was more concrete.

The semantic terms 'antonym' and 'incompatibility' were not used so frequently. Antonym was used seven times by four participants. One participant used this term four times, and three participants once. For instance, participant 8 judged his idiosyncratic concept 'Infonet is not often used' as an antonym for the team concept 'increase the use of the legal part of Infonet'. Another example is the idiosyncratic concept of participant 19 'bypassing the truck toll duty', which he had mapped as an antonym for the team concept 'general toll for all traffic routes'.

The term 'incompatible' was used twice. It was used by participants 8 and 18. Participant 8 mapped the team concept 'improve the structure and organization of the legal part of the infonet' as incompatible with the idiosyncratic concept 'poor construction of infonet'. Participant 18 used this rule for the mapping of the concepts 'use of other transport routes' (team concepts) and 'supply from all directions' (idiosyncratic concept).

The difference in the frequencies of the use of the meaning relations, which was tested with the non-parametric Friedman test for j matched groups, is significant (x^2= 24.09, df=3, p<.001). The Friedman test is a test for dependent variables, which determines whether the ranking points of dependent groups differ significantly from each other (to the Friedman-Test see for instance J. Janssen & W. Laatz, 2006, p. 556; J. Bortz & G. A. Lienert, 2008, pp. 203-208; W. L. Hays, 1988, pp. 832-833).

4.5.4.3. Evaluation of the Presumptions: Intra-Individual View – Between-Stage Results

The intra-individual view refers to the similarity judgement of the idiosyncratic concepts of stage 1 and the team concepts of stage 2. This analysis is subdivided into

- the team-based analysis of all teams (n=2) and

- the group-based analysis between homogeneous and heterogeneous groups.

The **team-based analysis** was done as described in chapter 4.5.3.4.3. Table 33, p. 166, outlines the results itemised

- Team number (column 1) and group (homogeneous vs. heterogeneous teams, column 2),
- Total concept numbers, which participants had generated in idiosyncratic stage 1 (column 4),
- Total number of team concepts, which participants had generated in stage 2 (column 5),
- The number of idiosyncratic concepts of stage 1, which have similar meanings compared to team concepts of stage 2 (column 6), in percentage terms (column 8), and
- The number of team concepts of stage 2, which have similar meanings compared to concepts of stage 1 (column 7), in percentage terms (column 9).

Table 33: Study IV – Results – Analysis of the Allocation of the Idiosyncratic Concepts to the Team Concepts over All Teams

Column								
1	2	3	4	5	6	7	8	9
T	Group	P	Total Concept No in S1	Total No of Team Concepts in S2	No of Concept in S1, which have Similar Meanings Compared to Concepts of S2	No of Concept in S2, which have Similar Meanings Compared to Concepts of S1	Percentage Concepts of S1, which have Similar Meanings Compared to Concepts of S2	Percentage Concepts of S2, which have Similar Meanings Compared to Concepts of S1
1	Homo	3	16	16	13	7	81.3%	43.8%
		4	11	16	8	9	72.7%	56.3%
2	Het	8	17	23	15	8	88.2%	34.8%
		9	14	23	12	9	85.7%	39.1%
3	Het	10	7	23	7	7	100.0%	30.4%
		11	12	23	0	0	0.0%	0.0%
4	Homo	14	23	19	15	9	65.2%	47.4%
		15	10	19	9	6	90.0%	31.6%
5	Het	16	16	15	10	7	62.5%	46.7%
		17	30	15	12	8	40.0%	53.3%
6	Homo	18	12	30	9	9	75.0%	30.0%
		19	11	30	11	9	100.0%	30.0%
	Average		14.9	21.0	10.1	7.3	71.7%	36.9%

Note xiii: T = team; Homo = homogenous; Het = heterogenous; P = participant number; No = number; S = stage

In stage 1, participants generated an average of 14.9 idiosyncratic concepts (Table 33, column 4, last row). In stage 2, participants generated an average of 21 team concepts (column 5, last row). Therefore, each participant assigned an average of 10.1 idiosyncratic concepts from stage 1 (column 6) to 7.3 team concepts of stage 2 (column 7). These represent 71.7% of the idiosyncratic concepts (column 8) to 36.9% of the team concepts (column 9).

It is interesting to note that the average and the range of values changed for the total number of concepts generated for stage 1 (individual session, see Table 33, column 4) when compared to stage 2 (team session, column 5). The average became higher in the team session (last row). The range became narrower (compare the columns). The total numbers of concept in stage 1 ranged from seven (team 3, participant 10) to 30 (team 5, participant 17) with an average of 14.9 (column 4). For stage 2, the range was from 15 (team 5) to 30 (team 6) with an average of 21 (column 5, last row). This change was tested with the nonparametric Wilcoxon test for two matched samples, and parametric t-test for matched samples (for the Wilcoxon test see J. Bortz & G. A. Lienert, 2008, pp. 191-200; W. L. Hays, 1988, pp. 827-829). The Wilcoxon test showed a significant result (z=-1.957, p=0.05, 2-tailed). The t-test for matched samples shows marginal differences between stage 1 and stage 2 (t=-2.124, df=11, p=0.057, 2-tailed). This means that the concept numbers of stage 1 differs from the concept numbers of stage 2. The following analysis was done **group-based** between homogeneous and heterogeneous groups and their differences (see Table 34).

Table 34: Study IV – Analysis of the Allocation of the Idiosyncratic Concepts to the Team Concepts Related to Group Compositions

Team	Group		P	Total No of Concepts in S1	Total No of Concepts in S2 Team	Concept No of S1, which have Similar Meanings Compared to Concepts of S2	Concept No of S2, which have Similar Meanings Compared to Concepts of S1	Percentage Concepts of S1, which have Similar Meanings Compared to Concepts of S2	Percentage Concepts of Stage 2, which have Similar Meanings Compared to Concepts of Stage 1
	1	2	3	4	5	6	7	8	9
									10
1	Homo	Ex	3	16	16	13	7	81.3	43.8
			4	11	16	8	9	72.7	56.3
6	Homo	Ex	18	12	30	9	9	75.0	30.0
			19	11	30	11	9	100.0	30.0
4	Homo	Ex	14	23	19	15	9	65.2	47.4
			15	10	19	9	6	90.0	31.6
	Average Homo			13.8	21.7	10.8	8.2	80.7	39.8
	Min Homo			10.0	16.0	8.0	6.0	65.2	30.0
	Max Homo			23.0	30.0	15.0	9.0	100.0	56.3

1	2	3	4	5	6	7	8	9	10
Min-Max Difference Homo				13.0	14.0	7.0	3.0	34.8	26.3
5	Het	Ex	16	16	15	10	7	62.5	46.7
			17	30	15	12	8	40.0	53.3
2	Het	NPT	8	17	23	15	8	88.2	34.8
			9	14	23	12	9	85.7	39.1
3	Het	NPT	10	7	23	7	7	100.0	30.4
			11	12	23	0	0	0.0	0.0
Average Het				16.0	20.3	9.3	6.5	62.7	34.16
Min Het				7.0	15.0	0.0	0.0	0.0	0.0
Max Het				30.0	23.0	15.0	9.0	100.0	53.3
Min-Max Difference Het				23.0	8.0	15.0	9.0	100.0	53.3

Note xiv: Homo = homogenous; Het = heterogeneous; Ex = experimental team; NPT = Natural Project Team; PN = participant number; No = number; S = stage

During stage 1, heterogeneous teams generated on average more idiosyncratic concepts (ø=16) compared to homogeneous teams (ø=13.8, Table 34, column 5). However, homogeneous teams mapped more idiosyncratic concepts of stage 1 (ø=10.8, column 7) to more team concepts of stage 2 (ø=8.2, column 8) compared to heterogeneous teams (stage 1 ø=9.3, stage 2 ø=6.5, columns 7 and 8). In addition, homogeneous teams generated more concepts in stage 2 (ø=21.7) than heterogeneous teams (ø=20.3, column 6). Nevertheless, there is one case where the minimum-maximum difference was greater for homogeneous teams than for the heterogeneous teams. This is in stage 2: 'the total number of team concepts' (column 6). This means that the values in homogeneous teams vary more than with heterogeneous teams.

4.5.4.4. Evaluation of the Presumptions: Inter-Individual View - Within-Stage Results

The inter-individual analysis was made

- firstly, by looking at the team results for shared and distributed concepts,
- secondly, for homogeneous and heterogeneous groups, and
- thirdly, for the team performance for all teams.

The analysis of **shared and distributed concepts** of team members, Table 35, p. 171, shows

- The total number of generated team concepts of stage 2 (column 5),
- The number of team concepts of stage 2, which have similar meanings compared to the idiosyncratic concepts of stage 1 (column 6),

- The number of team concepts used by all participants (column 7), also as a percentages (column 8),

- The number of distributed team concepts, used by either participant in the team (column 9), also as a percentages (column 10),

- The total number of shared and distributed concepts in percentages (column 11), and

- Concept numbers generated only within the team (new concepts[16], column 12), also as a percentages (column 13).

With the idiosyncratic concepts for all teams, there was an average of 39.6%[17] of the idiosyncratic concepts of stage 1, which have similar meanings compared to team concepts of stage 2, and are shared concepts of both participants. From the view point of the team concepts, that is about 20.6% (Table 35, p. 171, column 8), on average of 4.0 concepts for each participant (column 7), ranging from zero to eight team concepts (team 3 and team 2). 32.1% of the team concepts (column 10) are distributed among the team members. This is an average of 6.5 concepts (column 9), ranging from one to eleven team concepts (teams 2 and 6). Therefore, an average of 52.7% of the team concepts (column 11) is explainable through stage 1. 47.3% of the team concepts are newly generated concepts in stage 2 (column 13), which average 10.5 concepts (column 12). The range is from four (team 5) to 16 concepts (teams 3 and 6). Therefore, these concepts reflect the **performance of the team**.

Participants of **homogeneous and heterogeneous groups** shared on average four of the team concepts (Table 36, p. 172, column 5). However, both groups differ in the range of the number of shared concepts. In homogeneous teams, the range was from three to five concepts. This is a minimum-maximum difference of the values of two concepts. In heterogeneous teams, the range was from zero to eight shared used concepts, which is a minimum-maximum difference of eight concepts. Weighted with the total concept numbers (column 6), the shared used concepts range from 10.0% to 31.3% in the homogeneous teams, with an average of 20.8%, and from zero to 34.8% in the heterogeneous teams, with an average of 20.5%. Homogeneous teams also used more different team concepts (ø=8.0, column 7) than heterogeneous teams (ø=5.0, column 7). The minimum-maximum difference in the homogeneous teams is lower (five concepts) compared to the heterogeneous teams (six concepts,

---

[16] New concepts = team performance
[17] Column 7, Table 35, p. 156, divided on column 6, Table 33, p. 151, = 4 (number of common used team concepts used by both team members) / 10.1 (numbers of concepts in stage 1 which have similar meanings compared to concepts of stage 2).

column 7). Homogeneous teams generated fewer new concepts (ø=9.7, column 10) than heterogeneous teams (ø=11.3; **team performance**, column 10).

Comparing the numbers of concepts in Table 36, p. 172, in terms of the presumptions (see chapter 4.5.3.5), it can be said that

- as was mentioned, participants in heterogeneous teams have a higher team performance than participants in homogeneous teams (11.3 concepts to 9.7 concepts; 52.4% to 42.2%). This would confirm that heterogeneous groups have a higher potential knowledge (see W. Scholl, 2004, p. 118).
- There is no difference in the number of shared used concepts between homogeneous and heterogeneous teams (4.0 to 4.0 concepts). Weighted with the total number of team concepts, there is a small difference between homogeneous and heterogeneous teams (20.8% to 20.5%) in the direction mentioned.
- However, as was not mentioned, participants in homogeneous teams also have more distributed concepts than participants in heterogeneous teams (8.0 concepts to 5.0 concepts; 37.0% to 27.2%).

Table 35: Study IV – Results – Analysis of Shared and Distributed Concepts over All Teams

Column 1	Column 2	Column 3	Column 4	Column 5	Column 6	Column 7	Column 8	Column 9	Column 10	Column 11	Column 12	Column 13
Row	Team	Homogenous vs. Heterogeneous	Participant No.	Total Number of Team Concepts (Stage 2)	Numbers of Concept in Stage 2, which have Similar Meaning Compared to Concepts of Stage 1	Number of Shared Used Team Concepts by both Team Members	Shared used Concepts in % per Team^{1*}	Number of Distributed Used Team Concepts, Sum of both Participants per Team^{2*}	Distributed used Concepts in %^{3*}	Shared and Distributed Concepts in Total in %^{4*}	Team Performance in Numbers of Concepts^{5*} = New Concepts	Team Performance in %^{6*}
1	1	homo	3	16	7	5	31.3	6	37.5	68.8	5	31.3
2			4	16	9							
3	2	het	8	23	8	8	34.8	1	4.3	39.1	14	60.9
4			9	23	9							
5	3	het	10	23	7	0	0.0	7	30.4	30.4	16	69.6
6			11	23	0							
7	4	homo	14	19	9	4	21.1	7	36.8	57.9	8	42.1
8			15	19	6							
9	5	het	16	15	7	4	26.7	7	46.7	73.3	4	26.7
10			17	15	8							
11	6	homo	18	30	9	3	10.0	11	36.7	46.7	16	53.3
12			19	30	8							
Average				21	7.3	4	20.6	6.5	32.1	52.7	10.5	47.3

Note xv:
1* Number of shared used team concepts by both team members (column 7) / total number of team concepts (column 5) (stage 2) * 100
2* Concept numbers of stage 2 on which concepts of stage 1 were projected of participant 1 (e.g.: column 6, row 1, team 1) + concept numbers of stage 1 were projected of participant 2 (column 6, row 2, team 1) - 2* number of shared used concepts by both team members (column 7)
3* Number of distributed used team concepts by both participants (column 9) / total number of team concepts (Stage 2) (column 5) * 100
4* Shared used concepts in % (column 8) + distributed used concepts in % (column 10)
5* Total number of team concepts (stage 2) (column 5) - number of shared used team concepts by both team members (column 7) - number of distributed used team concepts by both participants (column 9)
6* Team performance in numbers of concepts (column 12) / total number of team concepts (Stage 2) (column 5)
Results may have rounding differences.

Table 36: Study IV – Analysis of Shared and Distributed Concepts Related to Group Composition

1	2	3	4	5	6	7	8	9	10	11
Team	Group		PN	No of Shared Used Team Concepts by both Team Members	Shared used Concepts in % per Team	No of Distributed Used Team Concepts, Sum of both Participants per Team	Distributed used Concepts in %	Shared and Distributed Concepts in Total in %	Team Performance in Numbers of Concepts = New Concepts	Team Performance in %
1	Homo	Ex	3	5	31.3	6	37.5	68.8	5	31.3
			4	5	31.3	6	37.5	68.8	5	31.3
6	Homo	Ex	18	3	10.0	11	36.7	46.7	16	53.3
			19	3	10.0	11	36.7	46.7	16	53.3
4	Homo	Ex	14	4	21.1	7	36.8	57.9	8	42.1
			15	4	21.1	7	36.8	57.9	8	42.1
Average				4.0	20.8	8.0	37.0	57.8	9.7	42.2
Min				3.0	10.0	6.0	36.7	46.7	5.00	31.2
Max				5.0	31.3	11.0	37.5	68.8	16.0	53.3
Min-Max Difference				2.0	21.3	5.0	0.83	22.1	11.0	22.1
5	Het	Ex	16	4	26.7	7	46.7	73.3	4	26.7
			17	4	26.7	7	46.7	73.3	4	26.7
2	Het	NPT	8	8	34.8	1	4.3	39.1	14	60.9
			9	8	34.8	1	4.3	39.1	14	60.9
3	Het	NPT	10	0	0.0	7	30.4	30.4	16	69.6
			11	0	0.0	7	30.4	30.4	16	69.6
Average				4.0	20.5	5.0	27.2	47.6	11.3	52.4
Min				0.0	0.0	1.0	4.4	30.4	4.0	26.7
Max				8.0	34.8	7.0	46.7	73.3	16.0	69.6
Min-Max Difference				8.0	34.8	6.0	42.3	42.9	12.0	42.9

Note xvi: Homo = Homogenous; Het = Heterogeneous; Ex = Experimental Team; NPT = Natural Project Team; PN = Participant Number; No = Number

The question that now arises is to prove whether these differences are statistically significant. As this thesis is written in the context of discovery (see chapter 3.3), two nonparametric techniques were used for the analysis of the presumptions, which lead to the formulation of hypotheses: the Mann-Whitney test, and the median test. The tests show whether two samples come from the same distribution (here homogeneous and heterogeneous groups). The Mann-Whitney test is the non-parametric alternative to the t-test for independent samples. It is used for small samples, but is less powerful if there are ceiling effects and if one sample has a higher dispersion. In that case, the median test should be used (J. Bortz & G. A. Lienert, 2008, p.142; to the tests see for instance W. L. Hays, 1988, pp. 825-827, pp. 829-832; J. Bortz & G. Lienert, 2008, pp. 140-151). As teams and participants differ in the number of idiosyncratic concepts generated and team concepts (see Table 33, p. 166), and linearity in terms of the amount of concepts cannot be assumed, two indicators were considered:

- Numbers of team concepts used as unweighted indicators and
- Number of used team concepts relative to the number of generated team concepts as a weighted reference point.

Based on this, the analysis of these two nonparametric tests was done. The observed differences between homogeneous and heterogeneous teams are not significant (see Appendix 19, and Appendix 20).

Figure 34, p. 174, illustrates the relationship between idiosyncratic concepts of stage 1 and team concepts of stage 2 in homogeneous and heterogeneous groups. Heterogeneous teams had generated more new concepts ($\varnothing=52.4\%$, dark grey = stage 2) as opposed to the shared and distributed used concepts ($\varnothing=47.6\%$, light grey = stage 1). Homogeneous teams had generated more concepts, which originated in stage 1 ($\varnothing=57.8\%$, light grey) than concepts which are new ($\varnothing=42.2\%$, dark grey = stage 2). However, the ratio between the number of old and new concepts is not significant in either groups (for the homogeneous group: $z=-1.069$, $p=0.285$, 2-tailed, Wilcoxon test).

Figure 34: Study IV – Relation between Shared and Distributed Concepts along with Team Performance

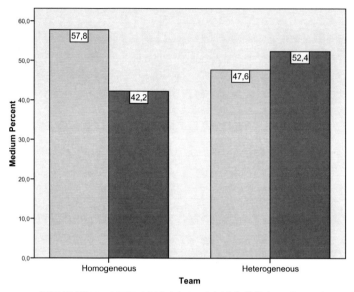

Note xvii: Light grey: shared and distributed concepts in total in %; Dark grey: team performance in %

4.5.5. Discussion and Limitations

Study IV aimed at developing a rules system, which enables the participants to judge similarities of the idiosyncratic concepts and team concepts, based on participants' perceived meaning of the concepts. The results of the use of the meaning relation tool revealed that participants used all four suggested rules, but with different frequencies. The most often used were 'synonym' and 'hyponym', followed, a long way behind, by 'antonym' and 'incompatible'. Synonym and hyponym characterize equality, hence comparable judgements about concepts. Antonym and incompatibility refer to judgements about differences in the value of concepts (e.g. positive and negative basic perception, see below). The frequency of the use of the meaning relations is significantly different. However, it is necessary to keep all rules, because they enable participants to judge the similarity of concepts even though concepts have different values. For instance, participant 16 generated an idiosyncratic concept 'supply security' during stage 1, which is a positive point of view. In the team session, this concept changed into 'supply bottleneck'. Bottleneck is a situation, which should be avoided. Hence, it is a negative point of view. This change can happen, if participants modify their basic perception about a theme. It is not a change of opinion. The first, basic perception refers to a thinking style. The second, opinion refers to an evaluation process. Thinking styles are characterized through

> "...directed perception with appropriate intellectual and fair processing of the percipience..." ["...gerichtetes Wahrnehmen mit entsprechendem gedanklichen und sachlichen Verarbeiten des Wahrgenommenen..."] (L. Fleck, 1980, Orig. 1935, p. 130)

Further, characteristics of thinking style include common attributes of the problems, judgements, adopted methods, as well as being accompanied by "technical and literate style of the knowledge system" (["...technischer und literarischer Stil des Wissenssystems."] L. Fleck, 1980, Orig. 1935, p. 130). Therefore, the thinking style determines what will be perceived in a specific context during a specific time (M. C. Waibel, 2002, p. 16). However, concepts such as 'supply security' and 'supply bottleneck' have a similar meaning when referred to the superordinate concept 'supply'. This thesis did not consider whether both concepts have the same function in the mental model and team mental model.

Based on the similarity judgement process of idiosyncratic concepts to team concepts, it was the objective to decide about shared and distributed knowledge in terms of shared used and distributed used concepts. The task did not change from stage 1 to stage 2 (see chapter 4.5.3.4). Therefore and because of the observation of differences in the results of the similarity judgement between homogeneous and heterogeneous teams during the first few eliciting stages, the implicit assumption was that the group composition (homogeneous versus heterogeneous) could have an impact on the sharedness of concepts (see chapter 4.5.3.5). W. Scholl (2004) mentioned that participants of heterogeneous groups have higher potential knowledge, which is an opportunity to increase knowledge. This could be reflected in a higher team performance, measured on the number of newly generated concepts in stage 2. However, no significant differences were found between homogeneous and heterogeneous groups (see chapter 4.5.4). There are some reasons for this. One reason could be the sample size. The analysis was done by comparing two groups with three teams each. The non-parametric Mann-Whitney test, which was used here because of the small sample size, analyses the ranks of the various observations (W. L. Hays, 1988, p. 825). The test will be significant ($p=.05$) at a sample size of three teams each group, if one group includes the lower ranks and the other group the higher ranks. Then the Mann-Whitney U would be zero, and the corresponding probability would be (1-tailed) $p=.05$ (for a detailed description how to conduct the test see J. Bortz & G. Lienert, 2008, pp. 140-151). In the current study, this would have been the case, if the teams in the homogeneous group had received the ranks one, two and three based on their results; and the teams in the heterogeneous groups would have received the ranks four, five, and six (or the other way around).

In fact, based on the data received in this study, the ranks were mixed up between homogeneous group and heterogeneous group; team 5 received a maverick value (see Table 37, p. 176). Based on the observed database, the value for Mann-Whitney is U=3 with the corresponding p=.35, 1-tailed (see Appendix 19).

Table 37: Study IV – Data Base for Mann-Whitney Test for Distributed Used Concepts in % (see Table 36)

	Rank	1	2	3	4	5	6	Rank $\sum$
Observed Value	Homogeneous Group			36.7	36.8	37.5		3+4+5=12
	Heterogeneous Group	4.3	30.4				46.7	1+2+6=9
	Team	2	3	6	4	1	5	

One reason for the maverick value of team 5 in this example was the weighting of the number of different team concepts used against the total number of team concepts generated (see Table 35, p. 171). The seven distributed team concepts of team 5 (column 9) were weighted by 15 of their generated team concepts (column 5). Team 3 also had seven distributed team concepts. With team 3, the seven disturbed team concepts of team 3 (column 9) were weighted by 23 of their generated team concepts (column 5). This explains the difference in the percentages of the distributed concepts, even though the number of different concepts used in both teams was the same (seven concepts). However, because of the different basic rate in team concepts generated, it is believed that the weighted value (in percentages) is the better value, because it reflects the whole number of team concepts. This also leads to the possibility of evaluating this value, and deducing sharedness or distributions. For instance, team 5 distributed 46.7% more concepts than team 3 with 30.4%. This contrast would not be possible when based on the concept numbers, because both teams used seven distributed concepts.

Another reason for the maverick value of team 5 was that this team was an Experimental Team, which was composed randomly. This team received the logistic problem (see chapter 4.5.3.4.1). The other heterogeneous teams were Natural Project Teams, which were asked about their existing projects. It could be that participants of the Natural Project Teams had already reflected about objectives and problems before conducting the study, because this was part of the solution to the company consultancy projects. The Experimental Team had to consider this, when they received the task. Maybe therefore, this is why the Experimental Team only generated 15 concepts during stage 2. However, an analysis of the content of the results from the Experimental Group is not possible because of the different themes in the company consultancy projects. Furthermore, it is a problem that the design was not balanced because there were no homogeneous Natural Project Groups. Besides that, it could be assumed that there were differences in motivation for task solution. Natural Project Teams received marks for their company consultation projects. The Experimental Teams did not receive anything. Therefore, the results could be determined by the motivation for task solving, which could also be a reason why team 5 had only generated 15 concepts during stage 2. Whereas, the heterogeneous teams 2 and 3 had generated 23 concepts each.

Moreover, the heterogeneous team 5 (with participants 16, and 17) is different when compared to the both other heterogeneous teams. In team 5 one participant had a business administration background and another had a non-business administration background. The task they had received was a business administration related task. This could explain why the non-economist had generated 16 concepts (participant 16), and the economist had generated 30 concepts during stage 1 (participant 17). Nevertheless, this concept number (30 concepts) is also remarkable compared to the other Experimental Teams (homogeneous teams 1, 4 and 6). Looking at the project tasks of the Natural Project Groups and comparing them with the one of team 5 (heterogeneous Experimental Team), it could be assumed that these projects were familiar or unfamiliar to the team members in equal measure, because they were participating in a master programme for non-economists. The team composition of team 5 and the difference in familiarity of the task could have made it easier or harder for this team to generate team concepts. However, it is also possible that participant 17 is a maverick because of the 30 generated concepts in stage 1. On the other hand, it could also be argued that the homogeneous team 6 is a maverick group because this group had generated 30 concepts during stage 2. These uncertainties and problems could be resolved by repetition with a much larger sample size.

However, the aim of this study was to elicit idiosyncratic mental models and team mental models based on the new design (Method Objective 5) as well as to develop and to improve a meaning relation system for similarity judgements (Method Objective 6). The analysis was done more on numerical facts than on content differences, with the aim of generating hypotheses. Further study should be repeated with a bigger sample size and comparable groups. Comparable groups refer to groups of the same composition: Natural Project Teams or Experimental Teams. In this case, it could be possible to trace differences within both homogeneous and heterogeneous groups.

An interesting result of this study is the significant change of numbers of generated idiosyncratic concepts during stage 1, compared to the team concepts in stage 2 (Wilcoxon test $z=-1.957$, $p=0.05$, 2-tailed). The increase of numbers of concepts was observed in both homogeneous and heterogeneous groups. The team performance concept was developed through the analysis of shared used and distributed used team concepts. Team performance was defined as the output of the team when referring to new concepts. Operationally, these concepts are not explainable through results of the earlier session, because participants did not assign any idiosyncratic concepts of stage 1 to these new team concepts in stage 2 using meaning relation tool. The new concepts are new facts or ideas. However, the team performance concept and the measure used here raise two questions. Are the differences found in the concept numbers between single stage and team stages (defined as team performance) caused by the team? Can the influence of the team be demonstrated? These questions are addressed in study V.

4.6. Empirical Study V – Evaluation of the Meaning Relation Tool

4.6.1. Introduction

The objective of study I was to elicit idiosyncratic mental models, and to develop and evaluate a rule-system to build up cause-and-effect relationships between idiosyncratic concepts in idiosyncratic mental models. Hence, it focussed on the content and the structure of idiosyncratic mental models. The objective of study II was to compare idiosyncratic concepts of different idiosyncratic mental models using Delphi-Method. Hence, it focussed on comparing idiosyncratic mental models. Because of the results of study II, Approach B has been adjusted accordingly.

Firstly, the object of investigation itself changed from comparing content and structure of different idiosyncratic mental models, to comparing idiosyncratic concepts of different participants. This was done because of the ambiguous results in study II. Therefore, Approach B addressed the questions of how idiosyncratic concepts could be compared in a more appropriate way. The focus of Approach B was the aggregation of idiosyncratic concepts, which resulted in the development of the meaning relation tool.

Secondly, the approach for eliciting shared knowledge in general (see chapter 3.6) and the similarity judgement process for idiosyncratic concepts were adjusted. Approach A, which included studies I and II focussed on a collective approach. Study I referred to the elicitation of idiosyncratic mental models including concepts and structure. Study II referred to the aggregation of idiosyncratic concepts. Approach B, which included studies III and IV, focussed on a combination of a collective and holistic approach. In each study, there were at least two stages. Stage 1 was the collective approach, where idiosyncratic mental models were collected. Stage 2 was the holistic approach, where the team mental models were collected. The meaning relation tool was used for the evaluation of similarity between the idiosyncratic concepts of stage 1 and the team concepts of stage 2. This procedure was the aggregation part of the collective approach.

In determining shared and distributed concepts, study IV revealed concepts of the idiosyncratic mental models and the team mental models, which did not correspond to one of the two models. This meant that there were some parts of the idiosyncratic mental models, which did not correspondent in meaning to the team mental model (see the *grey* parts of the idiosyncratic mental models in Figure 33, p. 163). Nevertheless, there were also some concepts in the team mental models, which did not correspond in meaning to the idiosyncratic mental models (*medium grey* parts of the team mental models in Figure 33, p. 163). Additionally, the number of concepts generated increased significantly from the individual (stage 1) to the team stage (stage 2). Therefore, it was assumed, that this increase could be traced back to teamwork. The number of newly created concepts was scored as a result of this teamwork, and was labelled in study IV as team performance.

All of this raises an important question. Can these two factors be a result of team performance?

1. An increase in numbers of concepts from stage 1 to stage 2
2. Some concepts of the team mental models did not correspond to concept of the idiosyncratic mental models

Studies usually focus on the influence of different factors on team performance, or on the connection between factors and the team performance itself. An example of this is the study by C. A. Bolstad and M. R. Endsley (1999) focussing on the influence of team mental models and shared displays on team performance. M. A. Marks et al. (2000) researched the influence of leader briefing and team-interaction training on team performance. Another example is the study by D. A. Harrison et al. (2003) researching the influence of different team types on team performance. M. Higgs (2006b) explored factors associated with team performance. Such inputs within the meaning of an independent variable, as in quantitative studies, are not the main focus of this thesis. This thesis focuses on the knowledge structures of participants. Here, knowledge structures are researched as outputs, because the idiosyncratic mental models and team mental models of participants about a specific problem were appraised using qualitative elicitation methods (see chapter 3.9). The term 'team performance' was suggested because of the results of the elicited output process (see chapter 4.5), where new concepts were observed during the team stage (to the team performance construct see also chapter 3.9).

One reason why the significance of inputs was not included in this thesis is the planning and implementation of the studies in the context of discovery (see chapter 3.3). The objective of this thesis is the development and exploration of a method, which investigates the comparison of idiosyncratic mental models, by studying similarities and differences. Hence, further development of the aggregation process was required. This strategy of reasoning is described as being inductive (see chapter 3.3).

To elicit idiosyncratic knowledge structures, idiographic methods were used to avoid influencing participants by suggestions (see chapter 3.5). As outlined in chapter 3.5, idiographic methods are usually related to qualitative methods, which produce mainly qualitative data, as here in this thesis. However, qualitative data can be transformed into quantitative data for further analysis – for example, by detecting differences in the outcome between different teams and groups based on statistical analysis. This was done in study IV, by analysing results of homogeneous and heterogeneous groups as a first screening for the evaluation of the methodical approach of aggregating idiosyncratic knowledge structures. This validation was carried out in the context of discovery (see chapter 3.3).

The consideration of independent variables, such as distinguishing between homogeneous and heterogeneous groups, was included initially in the analysis in study IV. This was done because in study IV differences in the results of the similarity judgement between homogeneous and heterogeneous teams were observed (see chapter 4.5.3.5). However, there were several reasons why no differences between them were found (see chapter 4.5.5). Nevertheless, significant differences were found between stages, when changing from an individual to a team elicitation approach. This is a change in the sample composition. The question is whether this change could have made a difference to the number of concepts generated between stages, by comparing the results from individuals with those from teams. Alternatively, one can ask whether this difference in numbers appeared by chance. This question is dealt with the context of justification (see chapter 3.3). If the change in the composition of the sample between stages made a difference in the number of generated concepts, then, where there is no change in the composition of the sample, there would be no difference in the number of concepts generated (see chapter 4.6.2). This was researched in a 'within-group-between-stage-view' (see Figure 35) by including different levels of factor 'type of group' – individual (control group 1), mixed (experimental group) and team level (control group 2; see also Table 38, p. 183).

Figure 35: Study V – Within-Group-Between-Stages-View

	Control Group 1	Experimental Group	Control Group 2
Stage 1			
Stage 2	↓		
Stage 3			

However, this thesis focuses on shared knowledge identified through mapping and evaluation processes between different stages. The participants in the individual stage are also members of the team stage (mixed group). Therefore, the concepts generated in the team stage are influenced by the earlier individual stage. Additionally, newly generated concepts were observed during the team stage, concepts unrelated to the individual mental model (see study IV). For that reason, the construct 'team performance' was developed. The performance of the team was defined methodologically as the outcome of the team stage, adjusted by the outcome of the individual stage. Similar meanings were excluded by using meaning relation tool. Hence, the number of newly generated concepts is the indicator for team performance (see chapter 3.9). The literature reports that teams contribute significantly to performance in organizations (chapter 2.2.3.2). Therefore, it is assumed that individuals and teams differ in their performance (between-group-within-stages-view, see Figure 36).

Figure 36: Study V – Between-Group-Within-Stages-View

	Control Group 1	Experimental Group	Control Group 2
Stage 1	→		
Stage 2			
Stage 3			

Teams should have a higher level of performance than individuals. Because team performance, as it is defined in this thesis (see chapter 4.5.3.4), is only of relative value, it would be seen particularly in the mixed group. Here, the performance would be higher than with other groups, because the mixed group changes from an individual stage to a team stage. With the other types of group 'individual' and 'team' which are not mixed, the performance would probably not change significantly between stages (within-group-between-stages-view, see Figure 35). However, the team group would already have a higher number of concepts compared to the individual group. Therefore, significant changes in concept numbers from individual to team stages in mixed group could reveal how performance changed. This would support the meaning relation tool as a tool for the adjustment of interrelations. Further, it supports the meaning relation tool as a method for focussing on the aggregation of idiosyncratic knowledge structures and on the representation of group differences. Because these presumptions are based upon empirical observation (see study IV), this strategy of reasoning is called abductive (see chapter 3.3).

The objectives of study V are

Method Objective 7: *to examine if the observed differences in study IV can be traced back to teamwork*

Method Objective 8: *to use the meaning relation tool as a means of validation.*

The study specific objectives are

Study Objective 1: *to explore if individuals and teams differ in their concept numbers,* and

Study Objective 2: *to test if individuals and teams differ in their performance.*

4.6.2. Hypotheses

Based on the above and the results of study IV, this chapter outlines the hypotheses about the evaluation of Approach B referring to two group indices. The first index refers to concept numbers. Hypotheses will be made for differences in the increase of concept numbers within-group-between-stages (Figure 35, p. 180) and between-group-within-stages (Figure 36, p. 181). The second index refers to group differences in terms of team performance (see chapter 4.6.2.2). Hence, this index is the result of stages 2 adjusted by the results of stage 1 by using the meaning relation tool.

4.6.2.1. Method Objective 7 & Study Objective 1: Group Differences Referring to Concept Numbers

Within-Group-Between-Stage Hypotheses: Concerning the Increase in Concept Numbers (see Figure 35)

If the observed increase of the concept numbers from stage 1 to stage 2 in study IV can be traced back to teamwork, then in study V significant differences in the concept numbers should occur in the mixed group. The mixed group is the experimental group, within the meaning of the quantitative approach (see Table 38, column 2, rows 1 / 2). Here, the group composition changes from the individual to the team stage. Further, it is assumed that this change in the sample composition will have an influence on the concept numbers in stage 3 (rows 2 / 3).

Table 38: Study V – Outline of the Within-Group-Between-Stage Hypotheses

Row	Group Stage	Column					
		1 Control Group 1 Individual Group (IG)		2 Experimental Group Mixed Group (MG)		3 Control Group 2 Team Group (TG)	
1	Stage 1	Individual measures	= (No change)	Individual measures	< (Increase)	Team measures	= (No change)
2	Stage 2	Individual measures	= (No change)	Team measures	< (Increase)	Team measures	= (No change)
3	Stage 3	Individual measures		Individual measures		Team measures	

However, there should be no significant change to the concept numbers in the control groups, where there is no change to the sample composition (columns 1 and 3). Two control groups ought to be used to compare their results with those of the mixed group. The first control group consists of individuals for all stages (column 1). The second control group consists of teams for all stages (column 3). Based on this, no significant differences to concept numbers should occur, either during the stages in the individual group (Table 38, column 1, rows 1 / 2 and 2 / 3) nor in the team group (Table 38, column 3, rows 1 / 2 and 2 / 3). Hence, the following hypotheses based on a three-stage design (see chapter 4.6.3.2) are formulated (see Table 38 for an outline of the hypotheses):

H1: The concept numbers increase during the stages for the mixed group (experimental group; repeated measurements).

→ $\mu_{Stage1MG} < \mu_{Stage2MG} < \mu_{Stage3MG}$

H2: The concept numbers will not change during the stages for the individual group (control group 1; repeated measurements).

→ $\mu_{Stage1IG} = \mu_{Stage2IG} = \mu_{Stage3IG}$

H3: The concept numbers will not change during the stages for the team group (control group 2; repeated measurements).

→ $\mu_{Stage1TG} = \mu_{Stage2TG} = \mu_{Stage3TG}$

Between-Group-Within-Stage Hypotheses: Concerning the Change in Concept Numbers when Comparing Groups (see Figure 36)

Because an increase in concept numbers from the individual to the team stage was observed in study IV, it is suspected that there is a significant difference in concept numbers between the team groups and individual groups. Teams will have generated more concepts than individuals. Hence, the following hypothesis for stage 1 is formulated:

H4: In stage 1, participants who work in teams (control group 2) will generate more concepts than participants who work in individual groups (mixed group; control group 1).

$\rightarrow \quad \mu_{Stage1TG} > \mu_{Stage1MG}, \mu_{Stage1IG}$

In stage 2, the composition of the mixed group changes from an individual to a team stage. Therefore, for stage 2, the following hypothesis is formulated:

H5: In stage 2, participants who work in teams (control group 2; mixed group) will generate more concepts than participants who work in individual groups (control group 1).

$\rightarrow \quad \mu_{Stage2TG}, \mu_{Stage2MG} > \mu_{Stage2IG}$

In stage 3, the composition of the mixed group changes again from a team to an individual stage. However, it is assumed that the work in teams (stage 2) will have an influence on the number of concepts generated during the following stage (stage 3) in mixed groups. Nevertheless, it is not clear how exactly the number of concepts will change in the mixed group, but it is assumed that the number in the mixed group will be less than in the team group. This leads to the next hypothesis:

H6: In stage 3, participants who work in teams (control group 2) will generate more concepts than participants who work in individual groups (mixed group; control group 1).

$\rightarrow \quad \mu_{Stage3TG} > \mu_{Stage3MG}, \mu_{Stage3IG}$

4.6.2.2. Method Objective 8 & Study Objective 2: Group Differences in Performance, Using the 'Meaning Relation Tool' to Adjust Interrelations between Stages

If the change of sample composition in study IV caused the increase in concept numbers, then in the current study there should be more new concepts generated by the mixed group in stage 2 than by the control groups. There should be fewer similarity mappings of idiosyncratic concepts to team concepts in the mixed group (experimental group) than in the control groups. Hence, the performance in the mixed group should be higher than in the control groups. This also includes the assumption that in all groups there will be an increase in the number of concepts, for instance, because of learning effects. Hence, team performance and learning effects are not clearly distinct. However, if the performance index in the mixed group is significantly higher than in the control groups, it could be concluded that performance was affected more by the work of the team than by learning effects. As this assumption demonstrates, team performance, as it is defined in this work, is only of relative value. For reasons of the performance construct, which refers to teams, only the mixed group and team group will be included in the analysis. Hence, the following hypothesis is formulated:

H7: The performance of the mixed group is higher than the performance in the team group (control group 2).

4.6.3. Method

4.6.3.1. Participants

Twenty-three students and one employee of Lancaster University, UK, took part in this study. Eleven were female and 13 male. Their age ranged from 20 to 42 years, with an average of 26.7 years. The participants were recruited mainly from the areas of IT, management, and psychology. Twelve participants were English native speakers. The other participants were two German, one Greek, one Chinese, one Arab, one Nigerian, one Malaysian and five participants with various Indian languages. They all spoke English fluently. Participants differed in their educational levels. One participant had an A-Level, five had a Bachelor Degree, and seventeen a Master Degree, one a PhD. Most participants will gain further qualification. After stage 3, all participants received an allowance of £ 40.00 for their expenses.

4.6.3.2. Design and Dependent Variables

This study was planned as a classic experimental design with three repeated stages. Table 39 shows the design. The independent variable is the 'type of group', with three levels; 'individual', 'mixed', and 'team groups'. There were eight participants in each group (see Table 39, row 4) and each was interviewed three times (see Table 39, stages).

Table 39: Study V – Experimental Design

Row	Stage	Type of Group		
		Control Group 1 Individual Group	Experimental Group Mixed Group	Control Group 3 Team Group
1	Stage 1	Si1=8	Si2=8	St3=4
2	Stage 2	Si1=8	Si2=8	St3=4
3	Stage 3	Si1=8	Si2=8	St3=4
4	N	n=8	n=8	n=8

Note xviii: Si = sample individual group; St = sample team group

There were two control groups. The first was composed of individuals (Table 40, column 1). Therefore, in this group only idiosyncratic mental models were collected throughout the three stages (Table 40, rows 1, 2 and 3; collective approach, see chapter 3.6).

Table 40: Study V – Outline of the Kind of Measures

Row	Stage	Column		
		1 Control Group 1 Individual Group	2 Experimental Group Mixed Group	3 Control Group 2 Team Group
1	Stage 1	Individual measures	Individual measures	Team measures
2	Stage 2	Individual measures	Team measures	Team measures
3	Stage 3	Individual measures	Individual measures	Team measures

The second control group consisted of four teams, each with two participants (see Table 40, column 3). Hence, based on the holistic approach (see chapter 3.6), the team mental models were collected in all three stages (Table 40, row 1, 2 and 3). The third group was the mixed group (Table 40, column 2), which was the experimental group. In stage 1 (Table 40, row 1) with the mixed group, the idiosyncratic mental models of the participants were collected in an individual stage (collective approach). Stage 2 (Table 40, row 2) was conducted as a team stage and focussed on the team mental model (holistic approach). Stage 3 (Table 40, row 3) focussed on the individual mental models again (collective approach). Study V was designed with a break of at least two weeks between stages 1 and 2, and a break of at least one week between stages 2 and 3.

Study V included two dependent variables (see Table 41). The first was the number of concepts generated in each stage (column 2, row 1). Therefore, the number of concepts generated was collected three times (column 2, rows 2, 3 and 4). The second dependent variable was the performance of the group (column 3, row 1). The performance of the group has been described above (see chapter 4.6.2). The results of stage 2 were adjusted with reference to stage 1 (performance-stage 1), and the results of stage 3 were adjusted with reference to stage 2 (performance-stage 2). Therefore, performance was measured twice (column 3, rows 3 and 4).

Table 41: Study V – Outline of the Dependent Variables

Row	Column		
	1	2	3
1	Stages	Number of Generated Concepts	Performance
2	Stage 1	Stage 1	
3	Stage 2	Stage 2	Performance-Stage 1
4	Stage 3	Stage 3	Performance-Stage 2

4.6.3.3. Stimulus Material

This study took place in cooperation with a master student at Lancaster University, who used the data for his thesis in Psychology. The study was financed by a large electronics company, whose interest was in an issue at the interface between psychology and technology. For this reason, the task used had a psychological-technical focus and was concerned about user experience and the usability of technologies. Both are important and relevant to marketing. The marketing focus was chosen in study V to evaluate the meaning relation tool. Here, it was important that each participant was able to answer questions regardless of educational background. For this reason, a marketing issue was chosen, where the personal preferences and opinions of the participants were asked. In particular, the issue was the general understanding of 'world class user experience' (WCUE). For the company and the master student, 'world class user experience' was subdivided into the categories 'usability', 'brand issues', 'point of sale', 'marketing', 'after sales care', and 'technical support'. For this reason, questions related to these categories. The idea was to let the participants generate as many aspects about 'world class user experience' as possible. Afterwards, these were applied to the example of a smart phone.

Additionally, it was assumed that participants' interest in, and involvement with mobile phones, especially smart phones would differ (see H. Meffert, 1998, p. 107, about the aspects that influence the involvement). Involvement is the extent of engagement of a participant to be interested in something (H. Meffert, 1998, p. 107):

"A person's perceived relevance of the object based on inherent needs, values, and interests." (J. L. Zaichkowsky, 1985, p. 341).

To get as many aspects as possible about 'world class user experience' and usability, independent of the smart phone, questions were asked about product features and the purchasing experience of high-involvement and low-involvement products or purchases. High-involvement purchases are complex decision-making purchases, because they are important for the customer. Low-involvement purchases go hand in hand with limited decision-making (H. Meffert, 1998, p. 107). In particular, it was asked:

- Which aspects are important when participants would buy or have bought an expensive product, over which they had to deliberate – such as a car (high-involvement).

- Which aspects give the best usability to a consumer electronic product, which they own.

- Why a participant bought a specific brand (referring to usability).

- What information in advertising would be looked at, or was sought, before purchasing new products.

- What do participants expect at a sales point, with very expensive products, or normal everyday products.

To find out about the important aspects of a smart phone, participants received the following questions and tasks. Firstly, they were asked to choose from the aspects generated, what a new mobile phone needs to have, in terms of usability and purchasing experience. This should be underlined with a red pen when written down on an Interactive Whiteboard (see chapter 4.6.3.4). Additionally, participants were asked which aspects of the chosen object would be 'nice to have', in terms of usability and purchasing experience. This should be underlined with a blue pen. After this task was finished, participants were asked to repeat the task again for a smart phone. The importance of the features was defined by participants using a hierarchal order. The most important feature received the number one, the second the number two and so on. The last tasks were the construction of idiosyncratic mental models and team mental models (see for the questionnaire Appendix 21). The cause-and-effect rule system for constructing the structure among aspects was, in this study, subdivided into two parts. During the first task, participants were asked about constructing the structure of concepts using the logical rules of the cause-and-effect rule system (see Appendix 22). In the last task, they were asked to do the same with rules such as positive or negative effect, and opportunity or threat (see Appendix 23). The tasks and the order of the tasks did not change with the stages. In stage 2, participants also received the task to map similarity between idiosyncratic concepts of stage 1 to team concepts of stage 2, using the meaning relation tool (see Appendix 24). To solve this task, they received their generated concepts, hence the usability aspects, of stage 1. This task was repeated in stage 3. Here, the participants mapped the similarity between concepts in stages 2 and 3 concepts.

4.6.3.4. Procedure

This study took place in cooperation with Lancaster University in June and July 2007 and used one of their seminar rooms. The author conducted the study and was present all the time to answer any question. Participants needed between 1½ and 2 hours for the single stage and between 2 and 2 ½ hours for the team stage. Interviews were conducted in English.

4.6.3.4.1. Pilot Study: Equipment and Task Testing

There was one pilot study with two participants. The first reason for running a pilot study was to test how the equipment was working. For conducting the study, and especially for saving the data, the Interactive Whiteboard by SMART Technologies was used. It is a display that is connected to a computer and projector, and displays the computer screen. The whiteboard met all the technical requirements necessary for the running of concept mapping techniques. It allows participants to write on the display, to save the handwritten concepts of the participants simultaneously, and to change the position of handwritten concepts for constructing idiosyncratic mental models and team mental models.

The second reason for running a pilot was to find out if participants had difficulties with the tasks. This was done, because the focus of the task changed from a strategy and controlling (studies I, II, III and IV) to a marketing focus. Now, usability and user experience related concepts had to be connected.

4.6.3.4.2. Elicitation Process

Table 42, p. 189, outlines a detailed description of the procedure of the study and the materials. At the beginning of stage 1 (row 1), participants received a paper, which introduced the structure of the study. It explained the personal code for the identification of participants in later stages (Appendix 25). After they had noted their personal code on the interactive whiteboard, they received the task to practise the rule system (Appendix 24) and the use of the interactive whiteboard (row 2). The task was standardised. Each step was explained. Participants also received the logical rule system, which was named as rule system 1 (Appendix 22) as well as the risk-chance rule system, named as rule system 2 (Appendix 23). For this task, participants needed about 30 minutes.

After the practice task, they received the main tasks about the questions of 'world class user experience' and usability (see Appendix 21, tasks 1 until 22), as well as both systems of rules (row 3). The last two tasks (tasks 18 and 21, see Appendix 21) were about the construction of the idiosyncratic mental models with the two different rule systems (rule system 1 and rule system 2). For these tasks, the concepts, which were numbered (tasks 16) and / or underlined in red and blue were used. Although 2 hours was predicted for this, teams needed much longer, and sometimes individuals less time.

Table 42: Study V – Outline of the Procedure

Row	Stage	Phase	Materials
1	Stage 1	Starting	Introduction into the study (Appendix 25)
2	Stage 1	Practise task	Task to practise the rule system (Appendix 24) Logical rule system – rule system 1 (Appendix 22) Risk-chance rule system – rule system 2 (Appendix 23)
3	Stage 1	Usability task	Word class user experience and usability task (Appendix 21 Logical rule system – rule system 1 (Appendix 22) Risk-chance rule system – rule system 2 (Appendix 23)
4	Stage 2	Usability task	Word class user experience and usability task (Appendix 21) Logical rule system – rule system 1 (Appendix 22) Risk-chance rule system – rule system 2 (Appendix 23)
5	Stage 2	Similarity task	Similarity task with the sense relations (Appendix 26) Concepts from stage 1
6	Stage 3	Usability task	Word class user experience and usability task (Appendix 21) Logical rule system – rule system 1 (Appendix 22) Risk-chance rule system – rule system 2 (Appendix 23)
7	Stage 3	Similarity task	Similarity task with the sense relations (Appendix 26) Concepts from stage 2
8		Demography	Follow up questionnaire (Appendix 27)

The process with the usability task was always repeated in each stage (rows 4 and 6). Additionally, in stage 2 and stage 3, participants received the task for the similarity evaluation (see Appendix 26), which included the meaning relation tool, and the participants' concepts of the previous stage (row 5 and row 7). They solved this task by themselves. Team members were separated. Hence, team members and participants of the mixed group did not see the similarity judgement results of their teammates. For the similarity mapping process in stages 2 and 3, they used the constructed idiosyncratic mental model and the team mental model of the last task 21. They needed about 20 minutes for this. Stage 2 finished after completing the similarity evaluation. Stage 3 finished after a demographic questionnaire was completed. This included questions about the person, chosen products during the generating phase, team work and work with the Interactive Whiteboard, as well as questions about the three rule systems (logical rule system, risk-chance rule system, meaning relation tool), and any intention to purchase a mobile phone or experience of having bought one (see Appendix 27).

4.6.3.4.3. Aggregating Process

The results of task 21 were used for the aggregation of stage 1 concepts to stage 2 concepts, as well as stage 2 concepts to stage 3 concepts. The team mental models of stage 2 (mixed group, team group) were used to test hypothesis 7 (team performance). This was done for two reasons. Firstly, the mixed group worked in teams in stage 2, and individually in stages 1 and 3. Secondly, the analysis process, as described in chapter 4.5.3.4.3, is based on team concepts. Therefore, stage 2 models were used for all levels of the factor 'type of group' for aggregation and for analysing performance differences.

For the aggregation process, the results were copied into VISIO format. Figure 37, p. 191, shows, as an example, the result of the aggregation process of stage 1 to stage 2 ('ST1-2' in the figure) for participant JE11. He was a member of the mixed group, working in stage 2 with partner JJ19. The grey squares in the figure, such as 'user menu' are concepts of stage 1. These concepts are idiosyncratic concepts. The blank squares, such as 'price', are concepts of stage 2. These concepts are based on the team mental model.

The connections of different squares with similar patterns, such as two or more connected grey squares, which are labelled with an '+' or '-', represent the structure between these concepts. Concepts and the structure of concepts represent the idiosyncratic mental model and the team mental model. They are the result of task 21. White squares, such as 'technology', are cluster names given by the author for better orientation within the aggregated figures. They show the similarities between the different stages of the same participant, including concepts of stages 1 and 2. The connection of two squares with different patterns, for example, one grey and one blank square, which is labelled with 's' (synonym) or 'p' (part of) is the result of the similarity judgement using the meaning relation tool. Appendix 28 shows the original mental model from JE11, stage 1, Appendix 29 the original mental model by JE11, stage 2, and Appendix 30 the result of the similarity evaluation of stage 1 concepts to stage 2 concepts by participant JE11. Appendix 31 shows the original mental model from JE11, stage 3, and Appendix 32 the result of the similarity evaluation of stage 2 concepts to stage 2 concepts by participant JE11.

Figure 37: Study V – Aggregation of the Results of Stage 1 and Stage 2 for Participant JE11

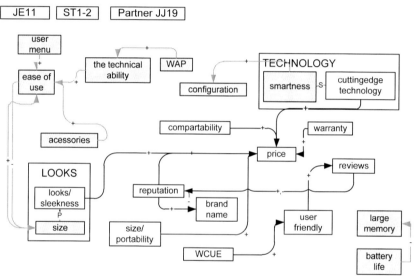

This aggregation was done for each idiosyncratic mental model and team mental models of each participant. For teams, the aggregation was summarized on one sheet of paper, as shown in Figure 38, p. 193, for the team ND10-DN04. The initials of the participants were used for identification of the similarity evaluation. For instance, participant ND10 stated that the concept 'technical support' of stage 1 and concept 'customer support' of stage 2 are synonyms. Therefore, he named this allocation as a synonym ('s'). Whereas participant DN04 stated that 'technical support' is part of 'customer support' and labelled this allocation with a 'p' (part of). For easier orientation and analysis, this cluster was labelled as 'support'. The thick dotted lines, which are labelled with '+' or '-' show, in this example, similarities in the connection between concepts when compared at different stages.

4.6.3.4.4. Analysis Process

Data analysis was done using nomothetic- and idiographic-quantitative frequency analyses, as well as nomothetic-qualitative and idiographic-qualitative word-based analyses. The nomothetic-quantitative and nomothetic-qualitative analysis was done using the follow up questionnaire to describe participants. With the hypotheses, within-group-differences over the stages and between-group-differences within stages were analysed using idiographic-quantitative frequency analysis (see Figure 8, p. 40) for the two dependent variables 'number of generated concepts' and 'performance' of the group (see chapter 4.6.3.2).

The dependent variable 'number of generated concepts' was collected three times (see Table 41, p. 186, column 2, row 2 until 4) by counting the concepts used for the construction of both idiosyncratic mental models and the team mental model. Hence, only concepts were used for the analyses process if they were connected to other concepts by at least one cause-and-effect rule. This analysis was the basis for testing hypotheses 1-6.

The second dependent variable 'performance' was used as described before. The concepts of the team mental models of stage 2 were adjusted for the concepts of the mental models and team mental models of stage 1 (performance-stage 1). The concepts of the mental models and team mental models of stage 3 were adjusted for the concepts of stage 2 (performance-stage 2), each using the meaning relation tool. With hypothesis 7, the performance was calculated for each team of the mixed group and team group for performance-stage 1 based on Formula 2, p. 162. Hence, the analysis of this variable was done once during measurement point 2 by analysing the use of meaning relation tool. Idiographic-qualitative word-based analysis, using the meaning relation tool (performance-stages 1 and 2), was used for the interpretation of the results (see also chapter 3.4 Quality Indices).

Figure 38: Study V – Aggregation of the Results of Stage 1 and Stage 2 for Team of Participants ND10 and DN04

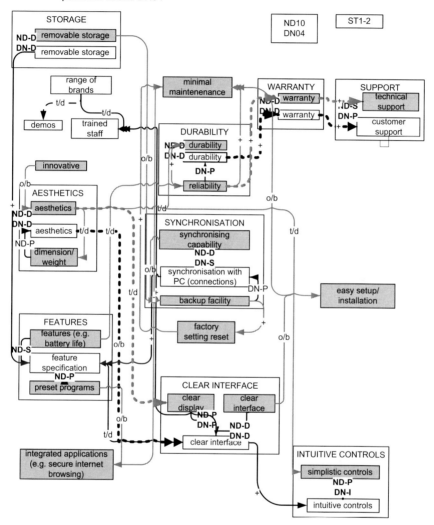

4.6.4. Results

4.6.4.1. Results of the Follow up Questionnaire

Two questions were asked about the usability aspects: 'Have you brought a technical product which was really expensive and that you had to deliberate over...', and 'Which consumer electronic product do you have at home, which you feel gives you the best usability ...'. The first question referred to a high involvement product, the second question to products with good usability experience. The most frequently named products for these two questions in all three stages were Computer/Laptop (first question: 40 times; second question: 17 times), Console and Play Station (first question: nine times; second question: twelve times), TV (first question: seven times; second question: eleven times), and Mobile Phone (first question: eight times; second question: ten times).

Referring to the first question, ten out of 24 participants stated that they have thought about the same product in all three stages. Here the computer was the most named product. All other participants changed their product during one of the three stages.

For the second question, nine out of 24 participants said that they thought about the same product in all three stages. TV was the most frequently mentioned product here. Again, all other participants changed their product during one of the three stages. Only four participants changed their product in neither the first nor the second question.

All participants said that they liked working in teams. Eight participants (three of the team group and five of the mixed group) declared that the teamwork was very good. Four participants of the team group and only two of the mixed group judged their teamwork as good, and one participant in each group said the teamwork was ok.

Referring to the team mental model construction in stage 2 (team group and mixed group), five of each group (in total ten participants) stated that 50% of their ideas in this stage were included in the team mental models. Six of these ten participants judged the teamwork as very good, three said the teamwork was good, and the last one said that the teamwork was ok. One participant in each group stated that they included 45% (mixed group) and 40% (team group) of their ideas in the team mental models. A participant from the mixed group said the teamwork was ok. A participant from the team group found the teamwork good. The last two participants of the mixed group stated that 70% of their ideas were included in the team mental model. The last two participants of the team group stated 79% and 100% of their ideas were included in the team mental models. These last four participants found the teamwork good or very good. It is notable that the participant, who included 100% of his own ideas in the team mental model, evaluated the teamwork only as good.

All participants stated that they liked to work with the Interactive Whiteboard. Seven participants liked to write on it. Sixteen liked to change the position of the concepts on the Interactive Whiteboard.

All participants of the individual group and the mixed group, and six participants of the team group liked the logical rule system (rule system 1). 13 of these stated that this was the easiest of the three rule systems. Two stated that this rule system was the hardest one, and seven found it medium hard. One of the team group members did not like it at all. He found it to be medium hard. The last participant was ambiguous about whether he liked it, stating that this rule system was the easiest one.

Based on Cramér's Index and Contingency Coefficient, there are significant relationships between group variables (individual, team and mixed group) and the statement of the participants to like or to dislike a rule system 2 (CI = .59, $p < .05$; CC = .51, $p < .05$). 13 out of 24 participants liked the second rule system, six from the individual group, six from the mixed group and one from the team group. Most participants of the team group did not like rule system 2.

Another significant relationship refers to the ranking of this rule system as easiest or hardest, and to the statement of the participants to like or to dislike rule system 2 (CI = .67, $p < .005$; CC = .56, $p < .005$). Participants, who did not like this rule system, were more likely to rank it as harder. Thirteen participants said they liked rule system 2. Seven found rule system 2 medium hard, five found it easy, and one hard. Eight out of eleven, who did not like this rule system, stated that it was the hardest. Only one participant said it was easy.

17 out of 24 participants liked the meaning relation tool, seven of the individual group and five each of the team group and the mixed group. Six participants stated not to like this rule system (three participants in the mixed group, two in the team group and one in the individual group). One participant of the team group was ambiguous about liking or disliking it. The same participant was also ambiguous about the first rule system, which he thought was medium hard. Seven participants said that this rule system was easy, and six of them liked it. Nine said that this rule system was ok, and eight judged it to be hard. Five of these eight did not like the rule system. This relationship is also significant (CI = .47, $p < .05$, CC = .55, $p < .05$).

4.6.4.2. Main Results

4.6.4.2.1. Method Objective 7 & Study Objective 1: Group Differences Referring to Concept Numbers

Within-Group-Between-Stage Hypotheses: Concerning the Increase of the Concept Numbers (see Figure 35)

In the first hypothesis (H1), it was stated that the concept numbers would increase over the stages in the mixed group. They should increase from stage 1 to stage 2 and from stage 2 to stage 3. This was tested with the non-parametric Friedman-Test. This is a test for dependent variables, which determines whether the ranking points of dependent groups differ significantly from each other (for the Friedman-Test see for instance J. Janssen & W. Laatz, 2006, p. 556). The test showed that the ranking points for the concept numbers including all three stages of the mixed group are only marginally different ($\chi^2_{(2, 95)}$=4.222, p_{emp}^{18}=0.065, 1-tailed, N=8, n_{teamMG}=4[19]; effect size: large, w=0.726; for effect size see J. Cohen, 1992, p. 157; J. Bortz & N. Döring, 2006, p. 606; B. Rasch, M. Friese, W. F. Hofmann, & E. Naumann, 2009, pp. 181-182; M. Ziegler & M. Bühner, 2009, pp. 265-266).

The graphical analysis revealed an increase in the number of concepts during the stages (stage 1 average: 12.50; stage 2 average: 15.25; stage 3 average: 18.00). The nonparametric Wilcoxon test for two matched samples (for the Wilcoxon test see J. Bortz & G. A. Lienert, 2008, pp. 191-200; W. L. Hays, 1988, pp. 827-829) revealed no significant differences when comparing stage 1 and stage 2 (z=-1.185, p=0.118, 1-tailed; effect size: medium, r=0.419; for effect size see A. Field, 2009, p. 550). Nevertheless, there are marginal differences when comparing stage 2 and stage 3 (z=-1.476, p=0.07, 1-tailed; effect size: large, r=0.522), as well as significant differences in the number of concepts when comparing stage 1 and stage 3 (z=-2.032, p=0.021, 1-tailed; effect size: large, r=0.718). However, according to hypothesis 1, there is no significant increase of concept numbers with the participants of the mixed group for all three stages (see Appendix 33 for a schematic representation).

Summarizing, hypothesis 1 (H1) cannot be accepted as valid.

In the second hypothesis (H2), it was stated that the concept numbers would not change significantly during the stages in the individual group (control group 1), either from stage 1 to stage 2 or from stage 2 to stage 3. The desired hypothesis 2 corresponds with hypothesis 0 (H0), which will be tested statistically. Significant differences in concept numbers between the different stages are not desired. This means it is not the alpha but the beta error, which is significant, as is usual in statistical tests. Alpha error is the rejection of the hypothesis 0, but this hypothesis is actually true. Beta error is the rejection of an alternative hypothesis (H1), but this hypothesis is actually true (see J. Bortz & G. A. Lienert, 2008). To cover the beta error, J. Bortz & G. A. Lienert (2008, p. 146) suggests increasing the significance level of alpha. He said to keep an alpha error of 25% (α=25%) is sufficient to ensure the beta-error probability. The acceptance of hypothesis 0 will be difficult (for further explanations see J. Bortz & G. A. Lienert, 2008). The non-parametric Friedman-Test showed no significant main effects ($\chi^2_{(2, 75)}$=2.250, p_{emp}=0.325, N=8, n_{teamIG}=4[20]; effect size: large, w=0.530), because p_{emp}=0.325>p_α=

---

[18] emp = empirical
[19] N = total number of participants, n_{teamMG} = number of teams of mixed group in stage 2
[20] n_{teamIG}=number of teams of individual group in stage 2

0.25. There is no significant increase of the concept numbers over all three stages (see Appendix 34 for a schematic representation).

Summarizing, hypothesis 2 (H2) can be accepted as valid.

In the third hypothesis (H3), it was stated that the concept numbers would not change significantly over the stages in the team group (control group 2), either from stage 1 to stage 2 or from stage 2 to stage 3. The basis for testing this hypothesis was the results of three teams instead of four. The reason is that team MN11-AS14 did not work as a team in stage 2. Therefore, the results of this team were not included in the analysis of hypothesis 3. The desired hypothesis 3 also corresponds with hypothesis 0 (H0), which will be tested statistically (see above). Therefore, the alpha error will be increased to 25%. The non-parametric Friedman-Test showed significant effects ($\chi^2_{(2, 75)}=9.82$, p=0.007, N=6, $n_{teamTG}=3$[21]; effect size: large, w=1.279) because $p_{emp}=0.007<p_{\alpha}=0.25$. Accordingly, in all three stages, there are significant differences in the number of concepts.

The nonparametric Wilcoxon test for two matched samples (for the Wilcoxon test see J. Bortz & G. A. Lienert, 2008, pp. 191-200; W. L. Hays, 1988, pp. 827-829) showed no significant differences in the number of concepts, when comparing stage 1 and stage 2 (z=-.743, p=0.458, 2-tailed[22]; effect size: medium, r=0.303). However, there are differences in the concept numbers when comparing stage 2 and stage 3 (z=-2.220, p=0.026, 2-tailed; effect size: large, r=0.906). Additionally, the Wilcoxon test shows a significant difference when comparing the concept numbers of stage 1 and stage 3 (z=-2.271, p=0.023, 2-tailed; effect size: large, r=0.927). The graphical analysis (see Figure 39) reveals that in stage 2 the teams had generated the lowest concept numbers (average 15.33), followed by the number of concepts generated in stage 1 (average 16.00). The greatest number of concepts was generated in stage 3 (average 20.33).

Summarizing, hypothesis 3 (H3) cannot be accepted as valid.

---

[21] n_{teamTG}=number of teams of team group, analysed for this hypotheses
[22] Because the hypothesis is undirected, a 2-sided significance is tested.

Figure 39: Study V – Concept Numbers of Control Group 2 (Team Group)

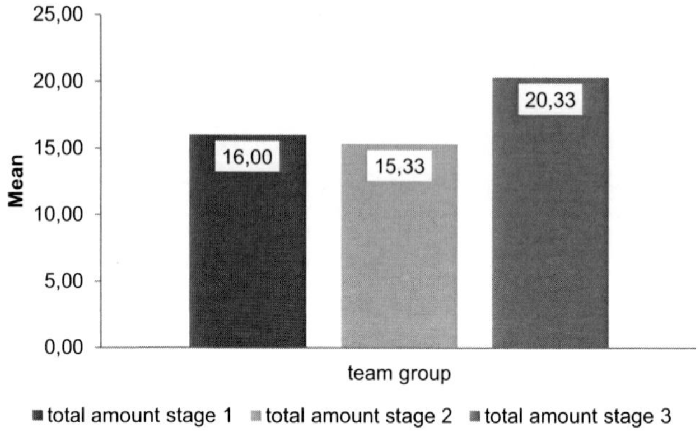

[Bar chart showing team group with three stages: total amount stage 1 = 16.00; total amount stage 2 = 15.33; total amount stage 3 = 20.33]

■ total amount stage 1   ■ total amount stage 2   ■ total amount stage 3

Between-Group-Within-Stage Hypotheses: Concerning the Change in Concept Numbers when Comparing Groups (see Figure 36)

The fourth hypothesis (H4) stated that participants in stage 1, who worked in teams, would generate more concepts than participants in the individual groups. This hypothesis was tested with the Mann-Whitney test. The Mann-Whitney test shows whether two samples come from the same distribution (here teams and individuals). It is the non-parametric alternative to the t-test for independent samples (to the Mann-Whitney test see J. Bortz & G. A. Lienert, 2008, pp. 140-151; W. L. Hays, 1988, pp. 825-827). The Mann-Whitney test for the fourth hypothesis is significant ($z=-3.043$, $p=0.001$, 1-tailed; effect size: large, $r=0.621$). This means, the groups do differ in the number of concepts. Hence, there is a significant difference in the distribution location of the groups.

The graphical analysis (see Figure 40) reveals that participants working in teams had generated more concepts (on average 16.25) than the participants working in individual groups (single group: 11.38; mixed group: 12.5; on average 11.94).

Additionally it was tested how the three groups (individual, mixed and team) do differ in the number of concepts. This was tested with the Mann-Whitney test. The test showed no significant results comparing individual and mixed group ($z=-0.803$, $p=0.42$, 2-tailed, $N=16$; effect size: small, $r=0.2$), and significant results comparing individual and team group ($z=-2.900$, $p=0.004$, 2-tailed, $N=16$; effect size: large, $r=0.725$), as well as comparing mixed and team group ($z=-2.351$, $p=0.019$, 2-tailed, $N=16$; effect size: large, $r=0.588$).

Summarizing, hypothesis 4 (H4) can be accepted as valid.

Figure 40: Study V – Mean Total Concept Numbers of Different Groups in Stage 1

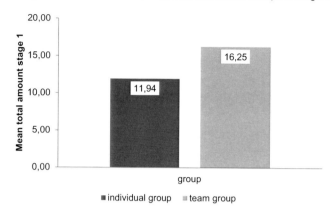

The fifth hypothesis (H5) stated that participants in stage 2 working in teams (control group 2; mixed group) would have generated more concepts than participants working in individual groups (control group 1). The basis for testing this hypothesis was the results of three teams of the team group, four teams of the mixed group and eight participants of the individual group. The reason for a lower number of participants in the team group is that team 'MN11-AS14' did not work as a team in stage 2. Therefore, the result of this team was not included in the analysis for this hypothesis. Hypothesis 5 was tested with Mann-Whitney test, which showed no significant results ($z=-0.826$, $p=0.20$, 1-tailed, $N=22$, $n_{team}=3$; effect size: small, $r=0.176$). This means that the groups do not differ in the number of concepts. Hence, there is no significant difference in the distribution location (see Appendix 35 for schematic representation).

Summarizing, hypothesis 5 (H5) cannot be accepted as valid.

The sixth hypothesis (H6) stated that participants in stage 3, who work in teams (control group 2) would have generated more concepts than participants, who work in individual groups (mixed group; control group 1). This hypothesis was tested with the Mann-Whitney test, which showed significant results ($z=-1.969$, $p=0.03$, 1-tailed, $N=24$, $n_{team}=4$; effect size: medium, $r=0.402$). This means, groups differ in the number of concepts. There is a significant difference in the distribution location.

The graphical analysis (see Figure 41) reveals that participants working in team groups generated more concepts (on average 19.75) than the participants working in individual groups (single group: 12.75; mixed group: 18.00; on average 15.38).

Additionally it was tested how the three groups (individual, mixed and team) do differ in the number of concepts. This was tested with the Mann-Whitney test. The test showed that the results comparing individual and mixed group are marginally different (z=-1.738, p=0.082, 2-tailed, N=16; effect size: medium, r=0.44). The results comparing individual and team group are significantly different (z=-2.220, p=0.026, 2-tailed, N=16; effect size: large, r=0.555). The results comparing mixed and team group are not significantly different (z=-1.167, p=0.24, 2-tailed, N=16; effect size: medium, r=0.291). Even this contrast reveals no significant differences between mixed group, working alone, and team group, the hypotheses is significant, as predicted.

Summarizing, hypothesis 6 (H6) can be accepted as valid.

Figure 41: Study V – Mean Total Concept Numbers of Different Groups in Stage 3

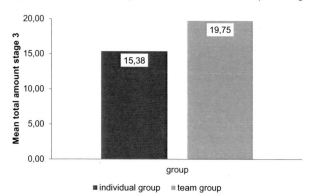

4.6.4.2.2. Method Objective 8 & Study Objective 2: Group Differences in Performance based on the Meaning Relation Tool to adjust Inter-relations between Stages

The last hypothesis (H7) stated that the performance of the mixed group is higher than the performance of the team group (control group 2). This was tested with the nonparametric Mann-Whitney test, which analyses the ranks of the various observations (see chapter 4.5.4.4). The basis for the analysis of this hypothesis was the team mental models of stage 2 of the mixed group, including four models by eight participants, and the team mental model of stage 2 of the team group, including three models by six participants. The Mann-Whitney test showed no significant result (z=-1.070, p=0.14, 1-tailed; effect size: medium, r=0.404). This means, the groups do not differ in their performance (see Appendix 36).

Summarizing, hypothesis 7 (H7) cannot be accepted as valid.

Table 43 summarises the results of the hypotheses.

Table 43: Study V – Overview of the Effects

Hypotheses	Effects Referring to the Concept Numbers		Result	Conclusion
	Level of Significance			
	Results Should be			
Hypothesis 1 Mixed group: Increase over the time	5%		Marginal differences Predicted direction	H 1 cannot be accepted as valid.
	Significant			
Hypothesis 2 Individual group: No increase over the time	25%		Not significant Predicted	H 2 can be accepted as valid.
	Not significant			
Hypothesis 3 Team group: No increase over the time	25%		Significant Not predicted	H 3 cannot be accepted as valid.
	Not significant			
Hypothesis 4 Stage 1: Individual group, mixed group < team group	5%		Significant Predicted direction	H 4 can be accepted as valid.
	Significant			
Hypothesis 5 Stage 2: Individual group < mixed group, team group	5%		Not significant Not predicted	H 5 cannot be accepted as valid.
	Significant			
Hypothesis 6 Stage 3: Individual group, mixed group < team group	5%		Significant Predicted direction	H 6 can be accepted as valid.
	Significant			
Hypothesis	Effects Referring to the Performance		Result	Conclusion
	Level of Significance			
	Hypotheses Should be			
Hypothesis 7 Mixed group > team group	5%		Not significant Not predicted	H 7 cannot be accepted as valid.
	Significant			

4.6.5. Interpretation, Discussion and Conclusion

In study IV, it was observed that the number of concepts generated increased significantly from the individual to the team stage. Therefore, it was assumed, that this increase in concepts can be traced back to teamwork. The number of newly generated concepts was detected by using the meaning relation tool, and was scored as the result of this teamwork. This was called 'team performance' in study IV. Both the increase in the number of concepts and the performance were aimed at verifying in an experimental design in study V, by studying different types of groups (Study Objective 1 and Study Objective 2). One group was always treated individually, the second group as a team, and the mixed group worked in turns individually and in teams. To verify that the increase of concepts can be traced back to teamwork, differences within the group over the different stages, and differences between groups within one stage were analysed. From the results, no clear conclusions can be drawn. Additionally, there is no significant difference when comparing team groups and mixed groups, concerning the new concepts, as this was called 'team performance'. However, results have to be interpreted carefully. Study design and procedure could be the reasons why results are affected.

The analysis of the concept numbers was based on idiosyncratic mental models and team mental models, hence, on concepts, which were connected with at least one cause-and-effect rule. One reason for focussing on them was that the participants often repeated concepts during the different elicitation tasks. Repeated concepts are not new concepts within the same stage. For instance, team DF06-ST01 duplicated 'price' and 'warranty' during the different tasks of stage 1. Team AS14-MN11 wrote down 'guarantee' three times during stage 1 and participant PS26 used 'user friendly' and 'user satisfaction' twice, and 'durability/durable' three times during one stage. During the construction task (tasks 18, and 21) of the idiosyncratic mental models and team mental models such repetitions were excluded. Therefore, it was decided to count only those concepts which were in the models. Single concepts, which were not repeated and were not part of the models, were excluded. However, this might also have influenced the results.

Different reasons could have caused repeated concepts within the same stage. For instance, the tasks were similar (see Appendix 21). They only referred to different objects, such as high involvement and low involvement products. Therefore, it could have been easier to repeat concepts within the different tasks, than to think about new aspects in following tasks. However, it is also possible that the repeated aspects are general aspects, hence important or stable aspects referring to world-class usability experience. This should be examined in a new investigation.

Another reason could be that participants liked writing on the Interactive Whiteboard. They were told to use concepts, which had been written down already instead of writing these concepts again, if they wanted to. However, participants did not often take this opportunity. Because of the freedom in the research process, it was decided to let the participants do 'whatever they wanted to'. This was done in all stages. In the follow up questionnaire, 16 participants stated that they liked to move concepts, and only seven participants said that they liked writing on the interactive whiteboard. However, moving concepts was 'main objective' of the construction process during tasks 18 and 21. It cannot be excluded that moving concepts was attributed mainly by the participants to this tasks, hence to the construction process.

Statistical results, based on the average number of concepts generated from a small sample size, were analysed with non-parametric methods. In total, 24 participants were interviewed three times, eight participants per group. This sample size was at the limit of feasibility because of cognitive overload and time expenditure for the participants, and because of the aggregating procedure of the qualitative data. Additionally, the analysis of the team group was based on the average concept number of three teams, because one team dropped out. During stage 2, this team worked in single stages because of scheduling problems.

The analysis of the data revealed variances in concept numbers (see Table 44).

Table 44: Study V – Range of Concept Numbers and their Difference in Range

Row	Stage	Range of Concept Numbers and their Difference	Individual Group	Mixed Group	Team Group[23]
		Column 1	Column 2	Column 3	Column 4	Column 5
1	Stage 1	Range	9-17	7-17	12-17
2		Difference in Range	8	10	5
3	Stage 2	Range	5-18	7-26	11-17
4		Difference in Range	13	19	6
5	Stage 3	Range	6-21	10-33	18-22
6		Difference in Range	15	23	4

In general, teams have the smallest range of concept numbers over all three stages (column 5, rows 2, 4, and 6). In stage 1, there was a difference of five concepts between the teams with the most and the least number used for the construction of their team mental model. In stage 2, there was a difference of six concepts, and in stage 3 only four concepts. However, in stages 1 and 2, teams started with a lower level of concept numbers compared to stage 3 (column 5, row 1, 3, and 5). The difference between participants with the greatest and the least number of concepts used for the construction of idiosyncratic mental models is much higher, and increases throughout the stages in the individual group (column 3, row 2, 4, and 6) and in the mixed group (column 4, row 2, 4, and 6) when compared to the team group. There could be different reasons for these variations.

During the first interview in stage 1, some unexpected things happened, which were not observed during the pilot study. Team 'ST01-DF06' (Table 45, team 1) were the first participants to be interviewed in the study (stage 1). During stage 1, this team had generated 61 concepts (including repetitions). 49 concepts were underlined as important for a smart phone (task 14). In task 16, it was said:

> "Bring these concepts into a hierarchy and write a "1" on the most important concept, a "2" on the 2nd most important, a "3" on the 3rd most important concept, and so on. There can be no joint most important concept, so each number should only be used once. ..."

---

[23] Based on 4 teams.

Table 45: Study V – Concept Numbers of Team Group

Nr. VP	Team	VP	Concept Numbers			Sum	Mean
			Stage 1	Stage 2	Stage 3		
17	1	ST01	12	17	19	48	16
18		DF06	12	17	19	48	16
19	2	GD16	17	17	20	54	18
20		MD28	17	17	20	54	18
21	3	ND10	19	12	22	53	18
22		DN04	19	12	22	53	18
23	4	MN11	17	12	18	47	16
24		AS14	17	11	18	46	15
		Sum	130	115	158	403	
	Average Team 1-4		16.25	14.38	19.75	50.38	
	Average Team 1-3		16.00	15.33	20.33	51.67	

Because it seemed impossible to construct a team mental model with 49 concepts within the allotted time, this team was told to use only ten concepts for evaluating the importance of a smart phone. These ten most important concepts were then used as a basis for the construction of the team mental model. In the end, they had used twelve concepts in stage 1 (see Table 45, stage 1). This was fewer than the other three teams, who had used between 17 and 19 concepts. Other participants and teams were told to use the underlined and/or numbered concepts for judging the importance of concepts, and constructing the models. In the end, it was up to the participants to choose concepts for the constructing process of the mental models and team mental models.

A similar pattern can be observed during stage 2 in the team group ND10-DN04 (team 3, Table 45, stage 2). Whereas this team had used 19 concepts in stage 1 to construct a team mental model, and in total 22 concepts in stage 3, they used only 12 concepts in stage 2 (Table 45, stage 2). It is not clear why they had lower concept numbers. It could be that interpersonal factors played a role. The results of the teamwork questionnaire reveal that both participants had stated that they liked teamwork. Nevertheless, whereas the other teams judged that their teamwork was very good or good, (based on school grades team ST01-DF06: grade 2; GD16-MD28: grade 1; MN11-AS14: grade 1.5), team ND10-DN04 judged that their teamwork was good or ok (grade: 2.5). Hence, their judgement of teamwork was slightly worse than the judgement by other teams. The judgement of teamwork was an evaluation of all stages.

In addition, the results in stages 1 and 3, team MN11-AS14 was disregarded in stage 2. Both members of this team did not work in stage 2 because of scheduling problems. This is also the reason why this team had different concept numbers in stage 2 (Table 45, stage 2, MN11: 12 concepts; AS14: 11 concepts, dark grey cells). The average of the team group (all teams together) based on the result of three teams (teams 1, 2 and 3) was used for the within-group analysis and hypothesis 5.

The results of stage 1 (Table 45, team 1) and of stage 2 (Table 45, team 3) were the reasons why the average number of the groups was much lower than in stage 3. At least for stage 1, it could be assumed that the average concept numbers would have been much higher than was seen if there would have been no limit to the concept numbers given by the interviewer. Hence, it is possible that the hypothesis 3 'the concept numbers will not change over the stages within the control group 2' could be valid. This should be examined in further study.

Hypothesis 1 stated for the mixed group, that concept numbers should increase during the stages, because it was assumed that working in a team has an impact on the number of the generated concepts in the stage 3, which follows. The analysis revealed a marginally different result in the predicted direction. The analysis of the single data of the mixed group (see Table 46, p. 205) over three stages shows results to the concept numbers by participants. For the participants KD08, JJ19, a continuous increase of concept numbers over all three stages was observed. There is no change in concept numbers at all by participant JE11. Participants JY21, ZM05, who worked in the same team, had the lowest concept numbers during the team stage. However, in stage 3, both were on about the same level with concept numbers as in stage 1. Participants MH11 (team 1 in stage 2) and DH03 (team 4 in stage 2) had the highest concept numbers during the team stage. Nevertheless, the concept numbers used by both participants for the construction of the individual mental models in stage 3 is higher than in stage 1. For participant RK08 it was observed that concept numbers increased from stage 1 to stage 2, and stayed on that level in stage 3.

It is not clear why these different developments are observed. It could be that they are a result of sample size. Only eight participants took part in this group. Additionally, these eight worked in only four groups. This is a small and not representative sample size and could explain the marginally different result (see above). On the other side, the size is important, because this small sample produced results with large effects (see results to Hypotheses 1). Hence, working in teams seems to have a noticeable effect. This was apparent at a later stage, when individuals worked alone (see the contrast to Hypothesis 6, see below).

Table 46: Study V – Concept Numbers of Mixed Group

Nr. VP	Team	VP	Concept Numbers			Sum	Mean
			Stage 1 (single)	Stage 2 (team)	Stage 3 (single)		
9	1	MH11	17	26	20	63	21
10		KD08	16	26	33	75	25
11	2	JE11	10	10	10	30	10
12		JJ19	7	10	22	39	13

Nr. VP	Team	VP	Concept Numbers			Sum	Mean
			Stage 1 (single)	Stage 2 (team)	Stage 3 (single)		
13	3	JY21	13	7	14	34	11
14		ZM05	15	7	13	35	12
15	4	RK08	11	18	18	47	16
16		DH03	11	18	14	43	14
		Sum	100	122	144	366	
		Average	12.50	15.25	18.00	45.75	

Anyway, a further qualitative concept based analysis, including cause-and-effect relationships in idiosyncratic mental models and team mental models, as well as considering the meaning relation tool, could open up new evidence for these reasons. Figure 42, p. 207, represents a section of an aggregated mental model and the team mental model of team 3.

The thick-bordered concepts with thick, bordered broken lines (warranty, brand, popularity, and reliability) are concepts of the team stage (stage 2). Concepts, which are light grey (brand, experience, popular) are concepts of participant JY21 in stage 1 (individual stage). Concepts with horizontal stripes (brand, stock on display, durable) are concepts of participant ZM05 in stage 1 (individual session). Dark grey concepts (brand, popular, offer, reliable, warranty) are concepts of participant JY21 in stage 3 (individual session). Lastly, concepts with white letters (reliability, price) are concepts of participant ZM05 in stage 3 (individual stage). The big squares 'brand', 'popular', and 'reliability' are cluster names given by the author for better orientation within the aggregated figures.

The cluster 'popular' is part of the mental model of participant JY21, who generated this concept in stages 1 and 3 (light and dark grey concept; individual session), and additionally in stage 2 (thick, bordered broken lines; team session). Participant JY21 also generated a concept 'brand' in stage 1 and 3 (light and dark grey concept; individual session). Participant ZM05 generated a concept 'brand', too, but only during stage 1 (horizontal striped concept). Brand was also part of the team mental model (stage 2, thick, bordered broken lines). The concept 'reliably' was generated by participant ZM05 during stage 1 (synonym durable; horizontal striped concept) and during stage 3 (diagonal striped concept). Additionally, this concept was generated during the team session, when participant ZM05 worked together with participant JY21. However, participant JY21 had generated this concept only in stage 3. Hence, it could be assumed, that participant JY21 remembered this concept from the previous stage, and therefore the team stage, influenced the concept generating of this individual in stage 3.

Figure 42: Study V – Section of the Aggregated Mental Models and the Team Mental Model of Team 3

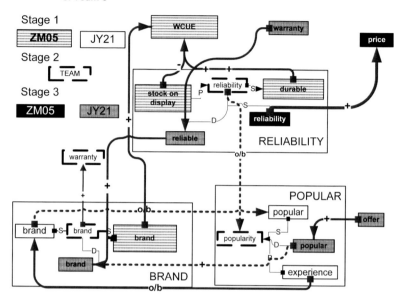

However, the cause-and-effect relations are more interesting. For the following comments, refer to the dotted lines in Figure 42. 'Popular' was connected by participant JY21 in stage 1 with 'brand' (shadowed concepts). During the team stage (stage 2), the team had connected 'popularity' with 'reliability' (thick, bordered broken lined concepts). During stage 3, participant JY21 again connects 'popular' with 'brand'. Summarizing, the concept 'popular' connected by participant JY21 with the concept 'brand' corresponds with the connection in stage 1 and stage 3. Nevertheless, during the team stage (stage 2, holistic approach; see chapter 3.6) such a connection is missing. Here, the team had connected 'popularity' with 'reliability'. Hence, a concept, which can be traced back to the individual mental model of participant JY21 (collective approach, see chapter 3.6), was connected with a concept that is more part of the individual mental model of participant ZM05 (collective approach, see chapter 3.6). Therefore, it could be assumed that team members had influenced each other in constructing the team mental model (see C. Eden et al., 1981, pp. 41-42; T. B. Seiler, 2003, p. 42; T. B. Seiler & G. Reinmann, 2004, p. 18; R. Brühl & S. Buch, 2005, p. 9). Maybe because of the combination of holistic and collective approach, as it was done in this study, it is possible to visualize the social interaction processes and communication (see S. Mohammed et al., 2000, p.150). However, this influence was less strong during stage 3 when team members worked in individual stages again. This also raises the question of the stability of mental models and team mental models contents (see J. A. Cannon-Bowers et al., 1993, p. 232 f.; J. A. Cannon-Bowers & E. Salas, 2001, p. 197; chapter 2.2.3.3).

The meaning of content stability will be explained using a section of the task model by participants ND10 and DN04 over all three stages (see Figure 43, p. 209). Figure 43 is separated into two parts. The first shows a section of the team mental model, including cause-and-effect rules ('+', 'o/b') of stage 1 (white concepts) and stage 2 (dark concepts). The second shows a section of the team mental model of stage 2 (dark concepts), and stage 3 (shadowed concepts). Additionally, both sections sketch the meaning relations of the team members, hence the assignment of concepts in stage 1 to concepts in stage 2, as well as concepts in stage 3 to concepts stage 2, using meaning relation tool (for instance, 'D'= duplicated, see below). The big squares 'reliability/durability', 'warranty', and 'support' are cluster names given by the author for better orientation within the aggregated figures.

In the team mental model of stage 1 (white concepts), the team connected 'reliability' and 'warranty' as well as 'warranty' and 'technical support'. They labelled these relationships as positive (e.g., 'warranty' has a positive effect on 'technical support'). In stage 2 (dark concepts), the team constructed similar units, namely, 'durability' has a positive effect on 'warranty', and 'warranty' has a positive effect on 'customer support'. During the meaning relation task (task 23, see Appendix 26) in stage 2 (see Table 42, p. 189, row 5), both participants assigned 'warranty' in stage 1 as a duplicate of 'warranty' in stage 2. 'Technical support' was assigned by participant ND10 as a synonym to 'customer support', whereas participant DN04 stated that 'technical support' is a part of customer support. Both participants also assigned 'durability' in stage 1 as a duplicate of 'durability' in stage 2, but only participant DN04 had assigned 'reliability' in stage 1 as part of 'durability' in stage 2. During stage 3 (shadowed concepts), a similar cause-and-effect chain was constructed. 'Reliability' had a positive effect on 'warranty', which was an opportunity or benefit for 'customer support'. During the similarity judgement task, both participants stated 'durability' as being a part of 'reliably', and 'warranty' as a duplicate of 'customer support' as well. Throughout three stages, it looks as though these sections of team mental models at different stages are robust. The team connected similar concepts with those of similar value in the same direction (see chapter 3.7.2). Both team members stated the meanings of the concepts in a similar way.

Figure 43: Study V – Section of Team Mental Models of Stages 1, 2 and 3 by Team 3

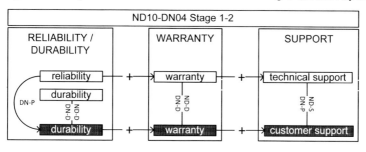

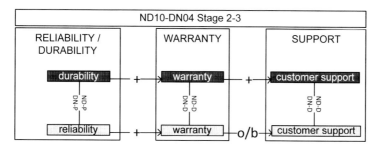

In contrast to this result, J. A. Cannon-Bowers et al. (1993, p. 232 f.), and J. A. Cannon-Bowers and E. Salas (2001, p. 197; chapter 2.2.3.3) assumed, that task models have a moderate content stability. This is because situational parameters differ between different tasks, which also lead to different operations. Situational parameters are for instance workload and time pressure (J. A. Cannon-Bowers et al., 1993, p. 232). However, in this study, workload and time pressure was constant over the three stages, which may explain the stability.

However, another question arises: Why did only participant DN04 allocate 'reliability' to 'durability'? The presumption is that participant ND10 stopped looking for other solutions when he found a fit between a concept in stage 1 and a concept in stage 2. To stop looking for other pattern is typical for working under stress condition (H. L. Thompson, 2010, p. 145). Hence, this might have caused confusion because of information overload in the workplace (see for this and further stressors J. A. Cannon-Bowers & E. Salas, 1998, pp. 19-20). Figure 44 shows the result of participant ND10 for the similarity evaluation task in stage 1 and stage 2 concepts. Figure 44 also illustrates the highly complex processes with which participants had to cope. For a better orientation, stage 1 concepts were presented in a different colour to stage 2 concepts. Nevertheless, orientation could have been difficult for the participant. However, the influence of the equipment (interactive whiteboard vs. paper-and-pencil) on cognitive processing should be tested. In the same way, it could be that the missing link between 'reliability' and 'durability' from participant ND10 reflects the knowledge structures of this participant. Consequently, there is no clear explanation, and it should therefore be examined in a further study.

Figure 44: Study V – Original Database of the Similarity Allocation Task by Participant ND10 (Stage 1-2)

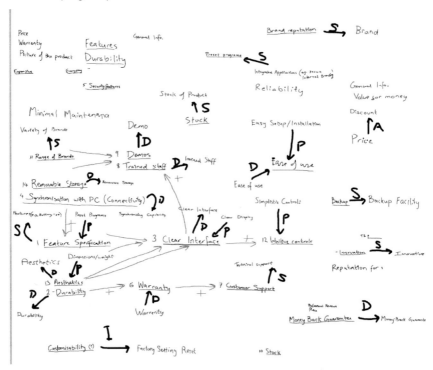

Summarizing, the lower concept numbers of the team group, together with the high range of concept numbers in mixed groups, explains why hypothesis 5 could not accepted being valid.

Additionally, it could be argued that teams needed more time than individuals, and therefore generated more concepts than individuals. This seems not to be true. Participants of the mixed group worked during stage 2 in teams. However, during stage 3, they had generated most concept numbers, when they worked individually again. Therefore, it seems that working in teams had an effect on the individual stage, which followed.

The last reason why results should be interpreted carefully concerns the meaning relation tool. In the last hypothesis, it was stated that the performance of the mixed group was higher than the performance of the control group 2 (team group). This was tested with nonparametric Mann-Whitney test, which showed no significant result. The basis for the analysis was the team mental models of stage 2 of the mixed group and the team group. Team performance was defined (see chapter 4.5.3.4.3, additionally Formula 2, p. 162) as

> "...output of the team, which is not explainable through earlier measurements of individual sessions. Team performance will be viewed as new knowledge based on new team concepts. New team concepts are such concepts, which are without any similarity judgements of concepts further stages using meaning relation tool."

Participants received four rules 'synonym', 'part of', 'antonym', and 'incompatible' for similarity assignment. During stage 1 of the evaluation task, it was sometimes observed that participants did not allocate same concepts of stage 1 to the concepts of stage 2. Figure 45, p. 212, shows an example by participant WG22. He was a member of the individual group. Grey concepts are stage 1 concepts. White concepts are stage 2 concepts. Big squares with unbroken lines such as 'price', and 'service' are cluster names given by the author. Squares with broken lines without a name show the same concepts of stage 1 and stage 2 which were not assigned by the participant, for instance 'brand' of stage 1 (grey concepts) and 'brand' of stage 2 (white concepts). It was not clear why the participants did not assign such concepts. When it was noticed, they were asked why they did not assign such concepts, and if they would use one of the other rules. Sometimes they used one of the four rules and sometimes, as with participant WG22, they denied using one of the rules. It was the tenth participant in stage 2 who started a discussion about it. He explained that a rule 'synonym' would not cover an allocation 'brand' to 'brand', because synonym means similar, but not the same. His suggestion was to include a rule 'duplicated', which was picked up by the following participants and teams. However, half of the participants and teams had already finished by that time. With regard to the definition of the performance indicator, it is critical whether the concepts were assigned or not, especially if concepts were part of the models. Therefore, this study should be repeated to test hypothesis 7 because it was not accepted as being valid.

Figure 45: Study V – Result of the Similarity Allocation Task of Stage 1 Concepts to Stage 2 Concepts by Participant WG22 (Individual group)

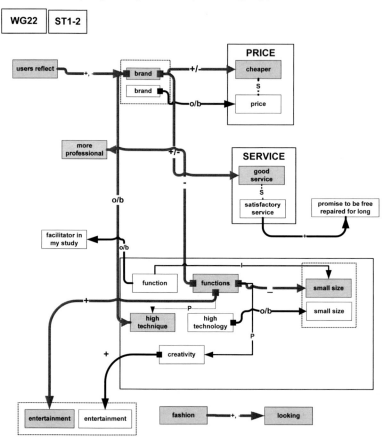

5. Discussion and Conclusion

5.1. Discussion of the Research Methods, including their Limitations

5.1.1. What is the Research Contribution?

This thesis provides a methodological contribution for researching shared knowledge. Within the range of quantitative and qualitative based methods used to elicit, aggregate and analyse knowledge and shared knowledge (see e.g. J. Langan-Fox et al., 2000; N. J. Cooke et al., 2000; S. Mohammed et al., 2000; S. Mohammed et al., 2010; see also chapter 3.5), a concept mapping technique was used to elicit *highly idiosyncratic* mental models. An approach to compare such models with each other has been developed.

Highly idiosyncratic mental models form the framework in which decisions take place (J. Langan-Fox et al., 2004, p. 334). They are the basis for team mental model building (see chapter 2.2.3.2). Most team mental model studies aggregate individual mental models by comparing them with each other, in terms of similarity (S. Mohammed et al., 2010, p. 885) e.g. via participant or expert rating. This procedure is criticised by G. P. Hodgkinson (2002) because participants are not able to judge the overall similarity of complex maps, and it will introduce bias into the rating. In addition, with ratings it is assumed indirectly that contributions of the group members are equally important. This is questionable for heterogeneous groups and for teams where the members have different deep knowledge (S. Mohammed et al., 2000, p. 149; N. J. Cooke & J. C. Gorman, 2006, p. 271; N. J. Cooke et al., 2007b, pp. 247-249; S. Mohammed et al., 2010, pp. 885-888; see chapters 1.2, and 3.6). Furthermore, similarity-rating scales capture levels of knowledge and obscure the knowledge structure (L. A. DeChurch & J. R. Mesmer-Magnus, 2010a, p. 3). However, the interpretability of the knowledge structure is also important, because knowledge structures are also part of the framework in which decisions take place (see J. Langan-Fox et al., 2004, p. 334). Hence, differences in individual mental models – no matter if they are content based or structure based – could lead to different decisions or misunderstandings within a team (see chapter 4.1.1).

The objective of this thesis was therefore the development of a comparative approach for the content of mental models, which also allows their structure to be interpreted. Such a comparative approach allows the aggregation of similar *highly idiosyncratic concepts*. Similar idiosyncratic concepts are concepts which do not necessarily have identical verbal tags, but the meaning of which are shared. As C. Eden and F. Ackermann (1998, p. 195) stated, main problem is to identify synonymous elements in the maps (see also C. Eden et al., 1981, pp. 41-42; P. E. Jones & P. H. M. P. Roelofsma, 2000, p. 1142). Hence, this thesis is driven by the research question of how the similarity of different highly idiosyncratic mental models can be identified and presented (aggregative approach).

5.1.2. Why two Methodological Approaches?

Methodologically, it took two attempts to develop the approach. Hence, the empirical part of this thesis (see chapter 4) is divided into two Approaches, A and B. Approach A (studies I and II) focussed on the elicitation of different idiosyncratic mental models and their comparability, in terms of content and structure. Approach B (studies III, IV, and V) focussed on the elicitation of different idiosyncratic mental models, and the comparability of the idiosyncratic concepts.

In Approach A, study I, based on the two-step approach of Structure-Formation-Technique (see e.g. B. Scheele & N. Groeben, 1888), the idiosyncratic mental models were elicited, and a rule system was developed to build cause-and-effect relationships between idiosyncratic concepts. Study II was used to compare the idiosyncratic concepts of different idiosyncratic mental models in terms of their similarities. For this evaluation process, the Delphi-Method was adapted, and experts who came from the same company as the participants in study I (see C. Eden & F. Ackermann, 1998, p. 196; chapter 3.7.3) were asked to evaluate the mental models. The focus was on the views of the experts, uninfluenced by group dynamics or by the effects of hierarchy. Additionally, there was plenty of time for the experts to solve their task (see N. C. Dalkey & O. Helmer, 1963; P. C. Howze & C. Dalrymple, 2004; see chapter 4.2.2.1). The objective was to replace participants' concepts within different idiosyncratic mental models by the same experts' category. Hence, there was an evaluation of different idiosyncratic mental models with similarities and differences based on the new expert categories. However, this aggregation approach led to ambiguous results. The experts did not always agree on the same category for the participants' concepts within the Delphi process. In addition, by looking at the connection between the idiosyncratic concepts of the participants, various expert categories were seen to match the meaning of the participants' concepts within the participants' mental model. Hence, the participants' concepts could not be replaced by one expert category. Additionally, the validation of the experts' categories by participant 3 to test the credibility of the expert results (see chapter 3.4; S. Lamnek, 2010) showed also discrepancies. I assumed that the information in the mental models of the participants as well as the fact that the experts came from the same organization as the participants (see C. Eden & F. Ackermann, 1998, p.198) are not enough context information for comparing seemingly similar concepts in the idiosyncratic mental models. The conclusion was therefore that the content validity of Approach A is low (see chapter 4.2.4) and the aggregation approach should be adapted (see chapter 4.3).

Maybe the results in Approach A would have been clearer if a face-to-face expert group discussion had taken place, especially with the task in stage 2 of study II (see chapter 4.2.2.2.2). Here, the experts considered the mental model of participant 4, which was framed by expert categories (see Figure 18, p. 103). The experts were asked to reflect on the value of the connection between the participants' concepts when allocating them to experts' categories. This task was perhaps too difficult for the experts. If there had been a group discussion, the experts would have been able to discuss the participants' concepts, their connections, and their perceptions about the company. Then, the participants' concepts and their structures would have been seen from different points of view. The result would have been much clearer. Consequently, the study could be repeated using an expert group discussion. However, a repetition with this procedure would not affect the content validity (see J. Bortz & N. Döring, 2006; M. Amelang & W. Zielinsky, 2002; chapter 3.4). The lack of information about the context, hence why participants chose these concepts and their relationships, would not have been much clearer for the experts (see chapter 4.2.4).

In addition, in study 4, Approach B, it was noticed that one participant changed some concepts from a positive point of view in stage 1 to a negative point of view in stage 2. Presumably, this reflected his thinking style (see chapter 4.5.5). The thinking style is characterized by different attributes (L. Fleck 1980, Org. 1935, p. 130), and it determines what will be perceived in a specific context during a specific time (M. C. Waibel, 2002, p. 16). The experts in study II, Approach A, also had a thinking style during the interviews. It is not clear whether and to what extent, the thinking style of the experts influenced their evaluation of concepts and categories. It is possible that the thinking style influenced the decision about their own preferred categories (see Table 12, p. 106, stage S 3, column 5). This could be one reason why the experts could not always agree on the same category (see chapter 4.2.3). In study 2, the focus was on the further evaluation of categories and concepts about which the experts could agree. Consequently, it is possible that there are many more similarities in the idiosyncratic mental models, which the Delphi-Method did not detect. In this case, the Delphi-Method would not be sensitive enough, and the results would not be trustworthy (see Y. Lincoln & F. Guba, 1985). Therefore, another evaluation could be worthwhile, of dissimilarities, detecting differences in basic perception.

One tool, which is able to detect thinking styles, is the meaning relation tool. It was developed as a method for judging similar meanings during Approach B. The meaning relation tool is a rule system for semantic relations including the rules 'synonym', 'antonym', 'hyponym', 'incompatibility' and 'duplicated' (to the first four relations see e.g. J. Lyons, 1995; A. C. Schalley, 2004; chapter 4.5.1.4). From these rules, especially the rule 'antonym', it is possible to detect thinking styles, because the antonym describes opposites (see chapter 4.5.5).

However, it is not possible to use the meaning relation tool within an expert interview, when focussing on tasks, such as in study 2. There are two reasons for this: firstly, because of its theoretical assumptions (see chapter 4.5.1) and secondly, because of the lack of context information (see chapter 4.2.4). This is because the meaning relation tool draws on the history of the participants' group in determining the meaning of concepts (for the importance of the history of the group in detecting similarities see C. Eden & F. Ackermann, 1998). Hence, when using expert interviews, as it was done in study II, another approach must be developed for similarity evaluations, or expert interviews avoided. This was done in Approach B, where the participants evaluated the similarities between different idiosyncratic mental models by themselves (see chapter 4.3 Conclusion of Approach A and Consequences for Approach B).

Two more aspects changed in Approach B. The first was the eliciting approach, which combined a holistic and a collective approach. In Approach A only a collective approach was used (for the approaches see S. C. Schneider & R. Angelmar, 1993; N. J. Cooke et al., 2000; chapter 3.6). The second aspect was the method to compare idiosyncratic concepts. The meaning relation tool was developed. It was developed during studies III and IV, and it evaluated in study V in an experimental design. The rules of the meaning relation tool were combined with the vertical and horizontal dimension of categorization on a theoretical basis (see L. Wittgenstein, 1953/2001; E. Rosch, 1976a, 1978; G. Lakoff, 1987; G. Kleiber, 1998; see chapter 4.5.1 Theoretical Assumptions). The combination of both, the eliciting approach and the method to compare idiosyncratic concepts, allows the aggregation of idiosyncratic knowledge structures to conclude to shared knowledge, taking into account content and structure of knowledge.

Now it remains to ask:

> *Was it successful to develop a methodological approach for aggregating idiosyncratic mental models to team mental models, in order to determine the similarity in idiosyncratic mental models?*

The answer is that there is a methodological approach to evaluate idiosyncratic concepts about their similarity, using the meaning relation tool and team concepts. Still, this approach should be evaluated again, because the rules for evaluating the similar meaning were incomplete (see the discussion in chapter 4.6.5).

5.1.3. How to Classify the Developed Approach within the Existing Research and How Effective is the Approach?

The aggregation approach developed in this thesis is based upon highly idiosyncratic mental models. Therefore, two aspects should be highlighted here:

- The way of identifying similarities and
- The way of analysing similarities.

The way of **identifying similarities** in idiosyncratic mental models differs to the approach reflected by C. Eden and F. Ackermann (1998). C. Eden and F. Ackermann (1998) discussed the conditions and prerequisites of working with idiographic data for the researcher, when he constructs a compared model. Additionally, they suggest some ways to cope with the main problem of identifying similar verbal tags in the models. One way is to give back the compared model to the participants for an evaluation (see chapter 3.7.2). Something similar was done in Approach A. One participant got the results, which experts had generated. However, because of the results in Approach A, the approach changed (see chapters 4.2.3.5, 4.2.3.6 and 4.2.4). In Approach B, the participants whose mental models were to compare evaluated the meaning of the idiosyncratic concepts by themselves. Hence, instead of using a researcher view of identifying similarities and constructing of an aggregated model, as discussed by C. Eden and F. Ackermann (1998), a participant's view is used to identify similarities. Based on this identification, an aggregated model can be constructed. This could be done because of the combination of a holistic and collective approach. Additionally, this approach also considered the importance of the history of the group in determining the meaning of concepts as described by C. Eden and F. Ackermann (1998).

The way of **analysing similarities** differs from the methods usually employed in most team mental models studies. In most empirical team mental model studies, aggregation methods are numerically based (see N. J. Cooke et al., 2000; chapter 3.6). These would include similarity ratings using self or expert evaluation (S. Mohammed et al., 2010, p. 885). Participants' data are more orientated in a nomothetic and / or quantitative direction, when using these methods to infer shared knowledge (see for instance D. L. Medin et al., 1993; S. S. Webber et al., 2000; chapter 3.7.2). However, in this thesis, participants had a high degree of freedom in generating and constructing mental models, just as they did in the study by K. Daniels et al. (2002; chapter 1.1), and in contrast to those in the study by L. Markóczy and J. Goldberg (1995; chapter 1.1). Hence, the elicited mental models were highly idiosyncratic, and focussed on qualitative data. In contrast to the study by K. Daniels et al. (2002), the similarity analysis in this thesis was based on the assignment of idiosyncratic concepts to team concepts, based on the combination of collective and holistic approach. K. Daniels et al. (2002)

used a similarity rating, which was based on comparing the maps of other participants to the participants own mental model--as it is done in most empirical team mental model studies (S. Mohammed et al., 2010, p. 885). This procedure of similarity rating is criticised by G. P. Hodgkinson (2002), because it will introduce bias into the rating. In addition, social interaction and communication processes, which are thought to emerge team mental models, are ignored (S. Mohammed et al., 2010, p. 885).

This thesis analysed which idiosyncratic concepts were part of the team mental models. The assignment of idiosyncratic concepts from different participants to the same team concept is the basis for inferring shared knowledge. With the procedure to compare the results of the holistic approach and the collective approach, Approach B embodies the basic features of S. C. Schneider and R. Angelmar (1993, p. 360) notion how to test the proposition 'the whole is more than the sum of its parts'. Additionally, with Figure 42, p. 207, an example showed how content and structure of the mental models changed – or did not change – during the different stages. This figure shows a particular section of the individual mental models of stages 1 and 3 and the team mental model of stage 2 of one team of the mixed group. It reveals the result of how social interaction and communication processes have influenced the team mental model building and idiosyncratic mental model building compared to the base line in stage 1 (idiosyncratic mental model). Both, social interaction and communication are processes through which team mental models are assumed to appear (S. Mohammed et al., 2010, p. 885).

However, the aggregation approach developed in this thesis is an indirect consideration of the similarity of the idiosyncratic concepts. A quantitative index, such as A. A. Eckerts (2002) correspondence coefficient (see chapter 3.7.2), which provides information about the similarity of idiosyncratic concepts and beyond idiosyncratic mental models or about the degree of sharedness (see S. Mohammed et al., 2010, pp. 903-904), has not yet been developed.

Anyway, considering the results of study II, discussed in chapter 4.2.4 (see Table 20: Study II – Comparison of Statements by Participant 3 and Participant 4 and Their Fit in Different Meanings, p. 118), the trustworthiness of the results using the meaning relation tool, and consequently the trustworthiness of this approach, has yet to be shown. As outlined in chapter 3.4, it is important that a methodological approach satisfy standards to the quality of the approach. These standards serve to generate trustworthiness for the approach (Y. Lincoln & E. Guba, 1995, p. 290). In this thesis, the following standards were emphasized:

- Credibility of the results through communicative validation,
- Transparency of research,
- Validity through triangulation,

- Credibility of the results through content validation,
- Credibility of the results through consensus and
- Research economics.

Credibility of the results through communicative validation is a standard, which was used predominantly in Approach A. This was because the interviewer picked up the concepts from the taped interview in study I. Therefore, this procedure could have an important influence on the pattern of results. By asking participants in study I to verify the chosen concepts, the validity and consistency of the results could be ensured (S. Lamnek, 2010, p. 139). There was **transparency of research** at all times, by outlining and justifying the specific methods used in the different studies.

Triangulation is the combination of qualitative and quantitative stances in specific ways (see for instance J. C. Greene et al., 1989; A. Tashakkori & C. Teddlie, 1998; R. B. Johnson et al., 2007; see chapter 3.4). In this thesis, nomothetic-qualitative and nomothetic-quantitative as well as idiographic-qualitative and idiographic-quantitative methods were combined to interpret the results for their trustworthiness (see chapter 3.4). Although the objective of this thesis is methodologically based (see chapter 1.2), method development in the context of qualitative dominant research paradigm cannot work without content specific problems (see for instance chapter 3.3). One reason for this is the definition of the mental model construct. Mental models have to serve special purposes (W. B. Rouse & N. M. Morris, 1986, chapter 2.2.3.1). Hence, **content validation** is useful as an indicator for the quality of the aggregation approach (see chapter 3.4). Related to the research objective 'idiosyncratic mental models', the validation question is "How clear are the aggregated results?" Using this content specific question in study II (see chapter 4.2), it was apparent that Approach A for aggregating idiosyncratic concepts had to change. The challenge is that participants evaluated their concepts by comparing them to concepts from other participants. The advantage is that they did this by using their own idiosyncratic knowledge structures and the consensus found in team mental model building. **Consensus** is regarded as evidence of validity, when several people can agree on the credibility and meaning of data (J. Bortz & N. Döring, 2006, p. 328). In this thesis, the evidence shows the validity of the meaning of the team concepts. However, content validation as in Approach A (see chapter 4.2.4) still has to be done for the aggregated results of Approach B. The reason why content validation has yet to take place is that the meaning relation tool is not complete (see chapter 4.6.5). As outlined in chapter 4.6.5, study V should be repeated with a completed meaning relation tool, including the rules 'synonym', 'hyponym', 'antonym', incompatibility' and 'duplication'.

Several aspects turned out to be important when referring to **research economics** (see A. Lienert & U. Raatz, 1998, p. 12). The first is the time needed for eliciting idiosyncratic mental models and team mental models. The second is the cognitive demands made on the participants during the aggregation stage. The third is the way of storing and analysing the results of participants. In both approaches, at least two stages are needed to elicit the idiosyncratic mental models and team mental models. However, Approach B turned out to be much more economic in research terms than Approach A. The interview part was omitted in Approach B. Participants started to write down concepts by themselves and constructed their mental model immediately. Therefore, the elicitation process was simplified. Stage 2 in Approach B was needed to construct the team mental model for evaluating similarity, when comparing idiosyncratic concepts and team concepts. This approach reflects the aggregation process of the idiosyncratic mental models. In Approach A, the aggregation process took many more stages, and it was much more cognitive demanding for the expert-participants. It took so much time, that one expert in study II refused to participate further for reasons of time. In addition, it was found that the results of Approach A are inconclusive, and thus are not trustworthy (see Y. Lincoln & E. Guba, 1995). Approach B is much more economic in eliciting and aggregating idiosyncratic concepts. However, the trustworthiness of the results of Approach B has yet to be shown using content validation (see above).

Additional problems refer to the elicitation and analysis approach of the idiosyncratic mental models and team mental models (see chapter 3.5.1, in addition Figure 8). As outlined in chapter 3.4, methods are economic if they are easy to use as well as quick and easy to evaluate and not time consuming (A. Lienert & U. Raatz, 1998, p. 12). The elicitation method was optimized during the different studies. Mental models and team mental models were elicited using a rather complex Structure-Formation-Technique in Approach A and using a simpler form of concept mapping in Approach B (see chapter 3.5.2). Additionally, tasks changed during the studies, from strategic management and management accounting to marketing. This change happened because it turned out that participants without a business administration background had problems in solving business administration tasks. Therefore, during study V, the validation of the meaning relation tool, I decided to change the task in this way, so that every participant would be able to solve the task, regardless of educational background. This would allow group differences resulting from their composition to be detected. The differences in the participants' specialism have been avoided by using a marketing task.

However, such changes are less than perfect for the evaluation of elicitation techniques. For the purposes of quantitative research, the influence of a variable factor is only apparent when everything else remains constant. This applies both to long-term studies (several studies in succession) and to cross-sectional studies (comparison of groups). The variable factors, such as a change in a group, or the comparison of a variable between groups, will be investigated. If more than one variable has changed, no clear statement about this influence can be made (see introduction literature in statistics and evaluation such as J. Bortz & G. A. Lienert, 2008; J. Bortz & N. Döring, 2006).

In this thesis, at least two variables changed during the investigation. One was the change in the composition of groups (for instance, homogeneous and heterogeneous teams). Another variable was the change in tasks, where the focus shifted between controlling, strategy and marketing. Nevertheless, these changes were made because results from previous studies formed the basis for the following studies into the development of the aggregation approach (see chapter 1.2). The focus was on the sample interviewed during the different studies. Some difficulties were caused by the incomparability of groups (see study IV). Other difficulties arose from a combination of the task and sample (see study III). However, this thesis is in context of discovery (see R. Brühl & S. Buch, 2006; chapter 3.3). It focuses on the development of a comparison approach, which allows the aggregation of idiosyncratic mental models. This approach was evaluated in study V, keeping everything constant except the variable 'type of group' (cross-sectional studies). The assumption behind this was that if there are differences in groups (e.g. individual groups vs. team groups), a valid method should be able to detect these differences (see chapter 3.8). Moreover, a valid method must be applicable to substantive issues from different research areas, and therefore to different problems. Hence, it should not be a problem to apply a valid method to different research areas, such as controlling, strategic management, or marketing. However, it could be a problem during the development process to find out whether the method is valid or not. The problem relates to the interpretation of results (see above). Consequently, the meaning relation tool should be evaluated in different research areas to test its applicability, and thus its validity.

The economic criteria must also be applied to the analysis process, both with the idiosyncratic mental models and team mental models. This applied to the method by which data was recorded and later transferred. In both the paper and pencil method and the Interactive Whiteboard method for constructing models, all data were transferred into VISIO for presentation or further processing. None of this was time efficient, and there was always a possibility of transmission errors. However, it is less time consuming to use the meaning relation tool. It is easy to use, and once the storage and equipment problem is solved, it is quick and the data are easy to evaluate.

5.1.4. What Can be Said about the Shared Knowledge Construct, Using the Meaning Relation Tool?

The nature of idiosyncratic mental models was outlined in chapter 1, and discussed in chapter 4.1.5. It was concluded, that from the findings of study I, and in line with the results achieved by G. P. Hodgkinson and G. Johnson (1994), and R. K. Reger and A. S. Huff (1993), mental models have similarities, but they are also highly idiosyncratic. Subsequent studies in this thesis have attempted to filter out and to present these similarities. The result is an approach to compare and aggregate idiosyncratic mental models. This approach allows an exploration of points in common and differences between idiosyncratic mental models, yielding precise results about the analysis of their contents. Thus, the method can be applied to different research questions, especially about the nature and degree of sharing (see S. Mohammed et al., 2010, pp. 903-904) such as

- Who shares knowledge? – Who should share knowledge?
- What knowledge is shared? – What knowledge should be shared?
- How much knowledge is shared (degree of overlapping)? – How much is optimal?

Such empirical research could determine team dysfunction such as groupthink, false consensus or bad decision making (see for instance P. E. Jones & P. H. M. P. Roelofsma, 2000; P. Badke-Schaub, A. Neumann, K. Lauche, & S. Mohammed, 2007, pp. 14-15; S. Mohammed et al., 2010, p. 90; see also chapter 3.6). For instance, G. Davison and D. Blackman (2005, p. 409) demonstrated in their case study how type and strength of the mental models held by a team contribute to its success.

Moreover, the approach developed in this thesis offers an analysis of the effect on performance by teams or by an individual. The performance here is the output in an input-process-output framework (see e.g. R. Rico et al., 2008, p. 163). Hence, performance is the result (see J. E. Mathieu et al. 2000; see chapter 4.6.2). However, the team performance construct developed in this thesis differs to other indices for instance used by P. Banks and L. J. Millward (2007), B. C. Lim and K. J. Klein (2006) or N. J. Cooke et al. (2003; see chapter 3.9). The team performance index (%) in this thesis is based on qualitative concept mapping technique and reflects cognitive outcomes based on concepts. Hence, the index in this thesis could be used to evaluate teams on a cognitive level (e.g. differences in creativity), which could be important for e.g. innovation or design teams. P. Badke-Schaub, A. Neumann, K. Lauche, and S. Mohammed (2007, p. 17) mention for instance that "in the last decades research on creativity has focussed on the effects of the group and organizational context on individual creativity ... rather than on teams producing creative outcomes".

Two more advantages of the team performance index are its independence from the skills of raters as well as the possibility of identifying of cognitive changes (see chapter 3.9). Thus, the method can also be applied to research questions, such as

- What factors are influenced by teamwork?
- What factors are influenced by the individual?
- What factors influence the stability of the knowledge structures?
- Is there an optimal size and composition of a team to provide the most effective outcome?
- Which indicators determine the best team performance?
- How to impart, develop and change knowledge structures to expand the repertoires for dealing with uncertainties?

(for the last question see G. P. Hodgkinson & M. P. Healey, 2008, p. 394).

The chief disadvantage is that the index is only of relative value. This means that at least, two measurement sessions are needed to get the index. Furthermore, the index is most informative, if changes happen such as changes in work situation or if at least two groups will be compared.

What are the similarities and differences in these idiosyncratic mental models? This still needs to be analysed. A first screening took place of the stability of idiosyncratic mental models in study V (see chapter 4.6.5), and a repetition of concepts was already noticed in study III (see Table 27). Cannon-Bowers et al. (1993) differentiated between four types of mental models: equipment model, task model, team interaction model and team model (see chapter 2.2.3.3). They made different assumptions about the robustness of these different models. However, not all of these models were validated empirically (see K. A. Smith-Jentsch et al., 2005, p. 524). In this thesis, the task model was elicited during the different studies. Cannon-Bowers et al. (1993) assumed that task models are moderately stable (see chapter 2.2.3.3). However, W. B. Rouse and N. M. Morris (1986) stated that mental models serve a special purpose. Consequently, if the purpose of constructing mental models does not change, neither should the mental models. In this thesis, several observations were made during study V, which support the stability of the idiosyncratic mental models. However, this should be analysed systematically. The meaning relation tool could be used as a comparison and aggregation instrument to explore the robustness of different models, which are suggested by Cannon-Bowers et al. (1993).

The thinking style also should be considered when investigating the stability of the idiosyncratic mental models (see to thinking style L. Fleck 1980, Org. 1935). However, the meaning relation tool is able to detect such styles. Hence, mental models can be adjusted by thinking style, and be compared with precision. This is an advantage of this approach. The original data still exist next to the aggregated data. Additionally, the advantage of relying upon qualitative data to verify the robustness is that substantive changes can be verified. Whereas, focussing on quantitative data, individual changes will probably not be detected.

The similarities and differences of idiosyncratic mental models could also be analysed, for example, in combination with the examination of the applicability of the method in other research fields (see above), or in combination with another important question "What causes these similarities and differences?" Different assumptions were made about the reasons for this, and many studies were conducted (see for instance G. P. Hodgkinson & P. R. Sparrow, 2002; G. P. Hodgkinson & G. Johnson, 1994; R. K. Reger, 1990; R. Calori et al., 1992; K. Daniels et al., 2002). The knowledge about, for instance, the causes of competitive advantage is especially important in the context of strategic management and management accounting. It enables a targeted and cost effective approach to support employees, and to produce a common knowledge base. Common knowledge is important for implementing strategies, and is the basis for gaining competitive advantage (I. Bamberger & T. Wrona, 2004). Together with its applicability and validity, the meaning relation tool could be tested also in this context.

5.1.5. Further Limitations Concerning the Interpretation of the Results

In addition to the discussion above, there are limitations concerning the interpretation of the results. The most important limitations concern the sample – such as the small sample size, the extent to which they represent a larger population, as well as the comparability of the sample groups. The sample is important if valid statements are going to be extrapolated to a wider population. Hence, the sample should represent the population, which is being investigated (see for instance J. Bortz & N. Döring, 2006). In all studies, the sample size varied between 3 and 24 participants. These sizes are too small for a representative approach. The difficulties, which arose in testing differences based on the small sample of 2 groups, each with three teams, were outlined in chapter 4.5.5, study IV. Additionally, this chapter also addressed the incompatibility of these groups, one including 'Natural Project Teams', and one including randomized teams. Study III (chapter 4.4) was conducted with three students majoring in fields other than business economics, but working on management tasks. In chapter

4.4.3.2 it was thought that participants with such different backgrounds would not normally be asked to solve such problems in the real world. Study V (chapter 4.6) investigated 24 Participants, which is too small a sample to use parametric tests, but which is big enough for non-parametric tests.

What does this mean for the development of the aggregation method? In chapter 3.1, I described this thesis as being in the tradition of the 'method perspective', which combines quantitative and qualitative methods in a mixed-method design (see J. C. Greene et al., 1996). This was done in the context of qualitative dominant research paradigm (see R. B. Johnson et al., 2007) investigating the similarity of concepts and their relationships. Quantitative aspects of strategies for eliciting, aggregating, and analysing concepts were used to gain deeper insights into the development process of the aggregation approach. They were used, for instance, in study I to find out if the participants differed in the number of cause-and-effect rules, which they used. The participants did not differ substantially. On average, nine out of eleven rules were used (see chapter 4.1.4.2). Therefore, it was concluded that the rule system reflects adequately the cause-and-effect relationships. These are a part of the qualitative data. Another example is the teamwork questionnaire, used in study III (see chapter 4.4). The results of this questionnaire were taken to reflect the difficulties, which arose with participant 2 (see chapter 4.4.3). Additionally, frequency-based analysis was used to reflect the number of generated and assigned concepts, in order to explore a method to make idiosyncratic concepts comparable, as well as to evaluate the task used in this study (see Table 26). So far, quantitative aspects were used to support the development of this approach. Also, studies I, II, III, and IV are inductive (see chapter 3.3). Study V is different, because it is abductive (see chapter 3.3). The results of the other studies were used to develop hypotheses, which were tested in study V. Because this was the objective, the sample had to be bigger. The size of the sample chosen was 24 participants. This was big enough when using non-parametric tests. However, it should be noted that in two studies some participants did not finish their work naturally. This affected the results and weakened their significance. To what extent, it was not possible to evaluate.

The last point, which should be discussed, is the possible influence of cultural factors. As outlined in chapters 1.1 and 4.5.1.2, idiosyncratic mental models, as well as categorising could be influenced by culture. Therefore, it could be possible, that especially in studies IV and V results are influenced by the cultural viewpoint of the participants. In both studies, they came from different countries in Europe, Asia, and Africa. Additionally, during the teamwork stage in study IV, participants were not separated, when they were judging similarity. This was done differently in study V. Here, teams were separated. However, the question which arises is "Could these cultural factors have had an influence on the results, when the meaning relation tool was used?" Participants used the meaning relation tool for similarity judgement, comparing their idiosyncratic concepts with their team concepts. They solved the tasks within a team and discussed solutions. Hence, they knew the meaning of the team mental model concepts, and could compare this with their individual result. The rules of the meaning relation tool reflect these meaning relationships, which could include cultural differences. It is an instrument for the aggregation of different idiosyncratic mental models. The significance of cultural differences requires further analysis and research. The analysis in study V focussed mainly on the number of team concepts. Word based analysis was done for an interpretation of the results using the meaning relation tool. For that reason, I believe that cultural differences probably did not influence the results when the meaning relation tool was used.

5.2. Conclusions drawn and Possible Further Research

Conclusion 1:

The aggregation method developed in this thesis shows that similarities and differences can be discovered and evaluated between not only individual idiosyncratic mental models, but also team mental models (see, for instance, Figure 42).This has major implications within the workplace, for instance:

- Gaps in knowledge and experience can be detected, so education and training can be developed, targeted, and evaluated with greater precision. This will lead to greater accuracy with the development of training programmes and greater control of training costs.

- The reasons for conflicting decisions can often be detected. Similarly, evidence of groupthink will often be identifiable.

- Communication between different groups within a workforce can be improved. This is particularly important for strategy meetings with interdisciplinary teams. The communication between a manager and his staff and between managers of different disciplines will also be improved. This is especially important in high risk or time critical environments.

- It follows there are serious implications for team building, cost effectiveness and competitiveness for a company.

Further Research Suggestions for Conclusion 1:

It could be worth developing a shared knowledge index, based on qualitative data. A quantitative shared knowledge index is a basis for quick evaluation of similarities and differences. The approach developed in thesis could be a first step for this. A difficulty, which would have to be overcome, is the difference in number between the idiosyncratic concepts and idiosyncratic mental models of individuals, as well as the large number of concepts themselves. In other words, the parameters for the research should be well defined and limited.

A further difficulty, which could be researched, could be the practicality of keeping a shared knowledge index up to date.

Conclusion 2:

The meaning relation tool can investigate the stability of idiosyncratic mental models. Although this was not analysed statistically, the trends and patterns were apparent (see, for instance, Table 27, Figure 42, Figure 43). This stability has implications within the workplace, for instance:

- The identification of the stability of a mental model will greatly assist with the development of strategies. Unstable mental models will cause changes, which will affect strategies adversely, because the definition of the strategy will be challenged.
- With both long-term and short-term strategies, there is a need to monitor their progress. This is done by measuring the difference between the intended destination of the strategy and the present position. Although mental models need to be flexible to adapt to changing environmental conditions, their overall stability is necessary for the strategy to succeed. The meaning relation tool can detect this stability.

Further Research Suggestions for Conclusion 2:

A systematic analysis could be undertaken to validate the different types of models, which were suggested by Cannon-Bowers et al. (1993). It would also determine the stability of the idiosyncratic mental models. The meaning relation tool would allow a qualitative analysis. From my point of view, this is necessary to measure similarities, differences, and stability.

Additionally, it could be interesting to see which new aspects of the environmental information will be included in the mental model, and why. This would indicate a method to develop shared knowledge, and determine the strength of information included in the mental model.

Conclusion 3:

The meaning relation tool can detect thinking styles. It showed to be more effective than the Delphi-Method with its use of experts, to decide upon differences and similarities with idiosyncratic mental models (see chapters 4.5.5 and 5.1). This could have implications within the world of employment, for instance:

- A thinking style may affect the formulation of a strategy. For example, a 'negative' thinking style to lower costs may conflict with a 'positive' one to maximise profits. If, for instance, a management group is unable to formulate a strategy because of conflicting thinking styles, the meaning relation tool could assist by detecting these styles. As a result of this diagnosis, further progress could be made in a more appropriate direction.

- A thinking style may affect the nature of leadership, and hence the motivation of teams. If managers have a negative thinking style, it could be harder for them to motivate their team in a positive way. Additionally, a manager's negative thinking style could affect the mood of his team. The meaning relation tool can assist by detecting these styles. As a result of this diagnosis, further progress can be made in a more appropriate direction, for instance through team-building programmes.

- The meaning relation tool could also be used within a team-building programme. It might be used as a basis for understanding team members and their communication styles, which are influenced by their thinking styles. This would allow the effect upon other team members to be appreciated.

Further Research Suggestions for Conclusion 3:

It could be showed whether, and to what extent, the thinking style of experts influence evaluation processes when they giving advice. This would bring into question the role of the expert.

Conclusion 4:

The team produced a greater number of concepts than the number produced by a similar number of individuals when working alone. The thoughts and ideas of an individual were influenced both during the time when working in a team, and afterwards (see Figure 40 and Figure 41). They also stated a preference for working in teams (see the results of the teamwork in chapter 4.6.4.1). This could have major implications within the world of employment, for instance:

- It could be beneficial for employees with different disciplines, or backgrounds, to gain experience of working together in teams. The effect of this on their thoughts and ideas could be to enhance creativity and innovation for the organisation. The meaning relation tool could measure increases in knowledge (see W. Scholl, 2004; see Figure 33).

- By changing the composition of teams from time to time, new ideas could emerge. This could enhance innovation, especially in knowledge-based companies.
- Task-orientated workshops, comprising groups from units which do not normally work together, but whose work has a mutual impact, could lead to an increase in understanding and knowledge of each other's functions. An example of this would be a team comprising mechanical engineers and accountants.
- Employees who spent some time in task-orientated teamwork could be better motivated. Their job satisfaction would be improved, as a result.

Conclusion 5:

Participants identify differences and similarities in idiosyncratic mental models, using concept mapping, more effectively than experts do. Ambiguous results can arise because experts are unaware of the reasons why individuals choose particular concepts, and make judgements about the relationship between them. This has implications:

- The outcome of the work of experts will have limitations. These limitations must be understood.
- The expert's brief must be defined very clearly and precisely.
- The work of experts is beneficial in certain, but not all situations.

Further Thoughts about Further Research

Further research should be done as to whether an abstract allocation of concepts to categories may be an indicator for situational awareness in companies. In study II, it was observed that experts and participants unanimously linked 'coordination processes' with 'danger'. This is an allocation far removed from the original concept 'coordination processes'.

It could be interesting to ask participants to reflect on their abilities to further the competitive advantage of their organisation in their mental model (see the discussion of study II). These observations could influence the development of company strategies, and identify possibilities for career growth and the expansion of personal responsibilities.

The process to elicit and store idiosyncratic mental models needs to be more effective. This is especially important in order to reduce the probability of transmission errors, and to reduce the workload for participants. For example, further research needs to be done to discover ways of transmitting data in a way, which minimises errors.

This thesis focussed on the elicitation of signs and symbols. No behavioural analysis was made about shared knowledge in terms of activities. This could be included in further research.

Lastly, the meaning relation tool could be developed to include different kinds of synonyms and antonyms (see D. A. Cruse, 1986; J. A. Lyons, 1995). This could be a useful and more sensitive additional tool in the selection of recruits.

6. Appendix

Appendix 1:	Construction Rules for Cause-and-Effect Relationships	232
Appendix 2:	Study I – Mental Model of Participant 3	233
Appendix 3:	Study II – Example 'School'	234
Appendix 4:	Study II – Category List for Phase 2	235
Appendix 5:	Study II – Categories and Frequencies of Expert 1	236
Appendix 6:	Study II – Categories and Frequencies of Expert 2	237
Appendix 7:	Study II – Categories and Frequencies of Expert 3	237
Appendix 8:	Study III – Information about Balanced Scorecard	238
Appendix 9:	Study III – Additional Scenario, Stage 2	240
Appendix 10:	Study III – Task, Stage 1	241
Appendix 11:	Study III – Library Example	242
Appendix 12:	Study III – Team Work Questionnaire	243
Appendix 13:	Study III – Concepts Shared between Participants	245
Appendix 14:	Study III – Result Participant 3, Stage 1	248
Appendix 15:	Study III – Result Participant 1, Stage 1	249
Appendix 16:	Study III – Result Participant 2, Stage 1	250
Appendix 17:	Study IV – Task for Semantic Relationships	251
Appendix 18:	Study IV – Outline of Semantic Relations Used – with Examples	253
Appendix 19:	Study IV – Mann-Whitney Test – Team Basis	255
Appendix 20:	Study IV – Median Test – Team Basis	256
Appendix 21:	Study V – Questionnaire about World Class User Experience	257
Appendix 22:	Study V – Logic Rules (Rule System 1)	261
Appendix 23:	Study V – Risk-Chance Rule System (Rule System 2)	261
Appendix 24:	Study V – Task for Practicing the Rule System	262
Appendix 25:	Study V – Introduction to the Study	264
Appendix 26:	Study V – Task Added for Similarity Mapping – Sense Relation Rule System	265
Appendix 27:	Study V – Demographic Questionnaire	267
Appendix 28:	Study V – JE11 – Stage 1	270
Appendix 29:	Study V – JE11 – Stage 2	270
Appendix 30:	Study V – JE11 – Semantic, Stage 1	271
Appendix 31:	Study V – JE11 – Stage 3	271
Appendix 32:	Study V – JE11 – Semantic, Stage 2	272
Appendix 33:	Study V – Concept Numbers of Mixed Group over all three stages	272
Appendix 34:	Study V – Concept Numbers of Control Group 1 (Individual Group)	273
Appendix 35:	Study V – Mean Total Concept Numbers of Different Groups in stage 2	273
Appendix 36:	Study V – Differences in Performance	274

Appendix 1: Construction Rules for Cause-and-Effect Relationships

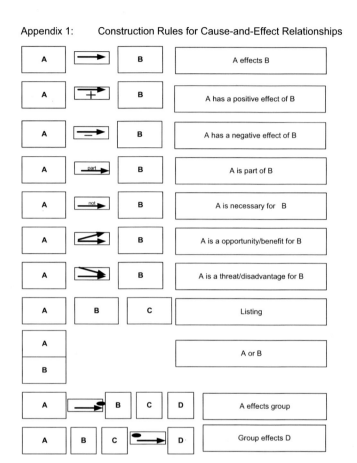

Appendix 2:   Study I – Mental Model of Participant 3

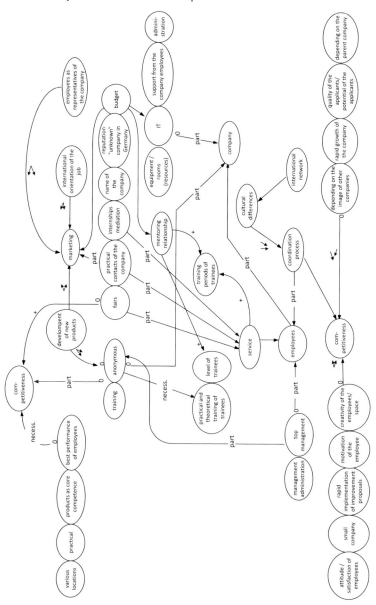

Appendix 3: Study II – Example 'School'

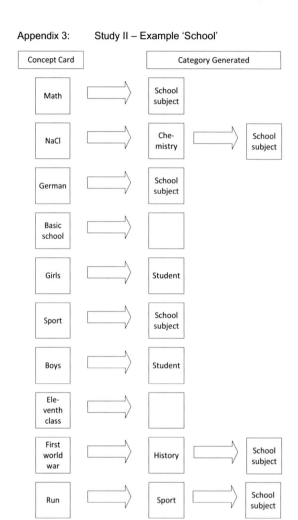

Appendix 4: Study II – Category List for Phase 2

Anonymous	Companies brand name	Employee	Offer	Resources
Abilities	Company	Field	Portfolio	Risk
Adaption	Competence	Finance	PR	Strategy of the company
Administration	Competitor	Graduates	Practical	Trainee certificate
Alignment	Competition	Identification with the company	Practical contact	Trainees
Alignment of the products	Contacts	Infrastructure	Problems	Traineeship
Applicant	Culture	Innovation	Products	USP
Authority	Danger	Internationality	Quality management	
Business	Department	Level	Quality of products	
CI	Development	Network	Research department	

Appendix 5: Study II – Categories and Frequencies of Expert 1

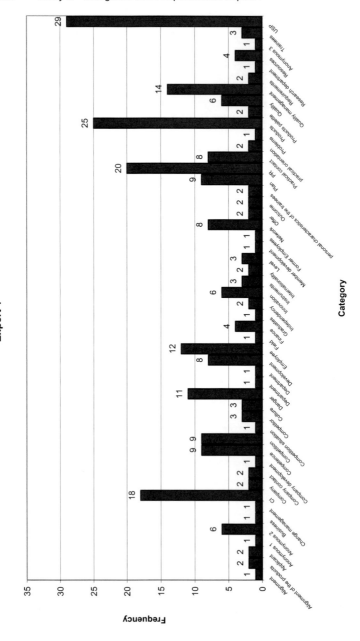

Appendix 6:   Study II – Categories and Frequencies of Expert 2

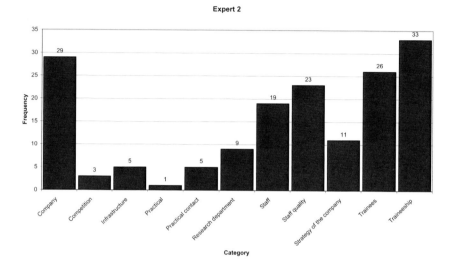

Appendix 7:   Study II – Categories and Frequencies of Expert 3

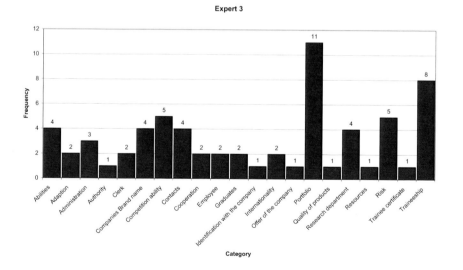

Appendix 8: Study III – Information about Balanced Scorecard

Slide 1: Brief History of the Balanced Scorecard

- Die BSC stellt ein Instrument für das Controlling sowie für das Strategische Management dar
- „Erfunden" 1992 durch Robert S. Kaplan (Professor in Harvard) und David P. Norton (Unternehmensberater)
- Europaweite Verbreitung seit ca. 1997

Slide 2: The Structure of the Balanced Scorecard (next slides following Figure 1-1, R. S. Kaplan & D. P. Norton, 1996a, p. 9)

Grundstruktur der Balanced Scorecard

- Die Balanced Scorecard ist ein System mit vier Perspektiven und folgendem Aufbau:
  - Ziele
  - Messgrößen
  - Zielwerte
  - Maßnahmen zur Erreichung der Zielwerte
- Welche grundlegenden Vorteile lassen sich zunächst ablesen?
  - Ausgewogenes Denken in mehreren Perspektiven
  - Fokussierung auf das Wesentliche
  - Systematische und partizipative Vorgehensweise
  - Transparenz der Zielerreichung - Verfolgbarkeit der Umsetzung

Slide 3: Explanation of the Identification of the Objectives

Strategische Ziele werden aus mehreren Perspektiven bestimmt und helfen bei der Strategieumsetzung

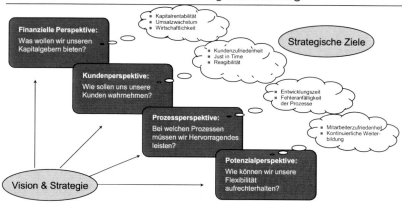

- Die BSC bildet die Unternehmensstrategie mittels 4 Perspektiven
- Bildung strategischer Ziele pro Perspektive → Ableitung aus der Vision und damit der Strategie
- Mission → Vision → Strategie → Strategische Ziel

Slide 4: Explanation of the Identification of the Objectives

Klare Unterscheidung von Zielen und Maßnahmen!

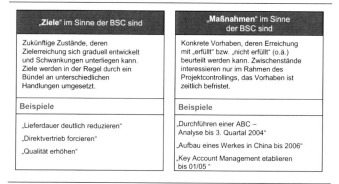

Es ist wichtig, dass eine Trennung zwischen Zielen und Maßnahmen stattfindet... Maßnahmen dienen zur Konkretisierung der Ziele und zur Umsetzung der Zielvorgaben

Appendix 9: Study III – Additional Scenario, Stage 2

Eine tiefer gehende Unternehmensanalyse deckte zusätzliche Problemfelder auf:

Die international ausgerichtete Universität mit einem Ausländeranteil von 30 % spiegelt sich überproportional in der Mensakundschaft wider. Hier beträgt der Ausländeranteil der Kunden ca. 60 %. Diese setzen sich hauptsächlich zusammen aus indischen, chinesischen, russischen, mexikanischen, türkischen und kenianischen Studenten. Diese Gruppe der Studenten bemängelte folgende „Tatsachen":

→ die Menükarte sei nicht immer verständlich

→ keine internationale Ausrichtung des Essens (nur deutsche Küche)

→ schlechte Qualität des Essens.

Des Weiteren muss sich die Universität darauf einrichten, eventuell die Essensversorgung der Schule sowie des Altersheims aus der näheren Umgebung zu übernehmen. Umgestaltungsprozesse können jedoch nur einmal finanziert werden.

Durch das dadurch erhöhte Essensaufkommen könnte es zu Lieferengpässen bei den Zulieferern kommen.

Die geldarme Stadt überlegt zurzeit die Essensversorgung von Ämtern umzustellen auf eine günstigere Fremdversorgung. Sie kam daher mit einem konkreten Wunsch an die Mensa, ein Angebot für diese Serviceleistung zu erstellen. Dies hätte ein Imagegewinn zur Folge, andererseits auch einen erhöhten Koordinationsbedarf für die internen Prozesse.

Darüber hinaus hat die Stadt angekündigt, die Zuschüsse für die einzelnen Mahlzeiten zu kürzen.

Appendix 10:   Study III – Task, Stage 1

Aufgabe:

1. *Identifiziere für die Mensa Möglichkeiten und Ziele, um zukünftig wieder Erfolg zu haben. Orientiere Dich dabei an den vier Perspektiven der BSC. Bilde bitte für alle Perspektiven Ziele, die Zahl sollte für die gesamte BSC 12 nicht unter- und 20 nicht überschreiten.*

Hierbei geht es sowohl um Ziele im eigentlichen betriebswirtschaftlichen Sinn als auch um Ziele, die Du für Dich selbst als wichtig und erfolgsversprechend hältst. Bitte schreibe alle Ziele und Verbesserungsvorschläge auf, die Dir in den Sinn kommen. **Es geht nicht um eine Wertung, ob es gute oder schlechte Ziele sind!**

2. *Stelle Ursache-Wirkungs-Beziehung zwischen den einzelnen Zielen her und verknüpfe die Ziele miteinander.*

Dafür stehen Dir eine Reihe von Relationsregeln auf einem gesonderten Blatt zur Verfügung, die Du einsetzen kannst. Bitte gebe auch immer die Wirkungsrichtung an.

3. *Generiere für jedes Ziel Maßnahmenpakete, d.h. Möglichkeiten, wie dieses Ziel erreicht werden kann, und versuche Möglichkeiten zu finden, die Zielerreichung auch zu überprüfen.*

Du kannst jederzeit weitere Ziele, Maßnahmen, Verbesserungsvorschläge etc. hinzufügen.

Appendix 11:   Study III – Library Example

Ein verkürztes Beispiel aus der Universitätsbibliothek soll Dir die Aufgabe verdeutlichen. Der Anfangspunkt wurde willkürlich gewählt:

Ziele:

Finanzperspektiven	→	Senkung der Kosten für Buchbestellung
Interne Abläufe	→	mehrere Bücher auf einmal bestellen

Ursache-Wirkungs-Beziehung:

Mehrere Bücher auf einmal bestellen —+→ Senkung der Kosten

hat einen positiven Einfluss

Maßnahmenpakete:

Ziel:	Maßnahme:
Senkung der Kosten für Buchbestellung	Einführung eines Kostensenkungsprogramms, …
mehrere Bücher auf einmal bestellen	Sammelbestellformular einführen, Sonderkonditionen der Post in Anspruch nehmen …

Möglichkeiten der Überprüfung der Zielerreichung

Ziel:	Leistungsindikator:
Senkung der Kosten für Buchbestellung	Vergleich der Kosten vorher und nachher, …
mehrere Bücher auf einmal bestellen	Anzahl der Sammelbestellungen zählen, …

Appendix 12:   Study III – Team Work Questionnaire

Vielen Dank, dass Du an meiner Untersuchung teilgenommen hast!

Bitte beantworte noch nun noch kurz die nachfolgenden Fragen. Deine Antworten sind und bleiben selbstverständlich anonym.

Die nun folgenden Fragen sollst Du beantworten im Vergleich zu einer Skala mit den Eckpunkten „Schwarz" = „sehr unsicher/schlecht/wenige" und „Weiß" = „sehr sicher/gut/viele"? Setze ein Kreuz auf die dargestellten Linien.

Wie sicher hast Du Dich bei der Lösung der Aufgabe gefühlt?

Bei der ersten Befragung:

sehr unsicher   sehr sicher

Bei der Teamarbeit:

sehr unsicher   sehr sicher

Bei der letzten Befragung:

sehr unsicher   sehr sicher

Wie empfandst Du die Gruppenarbeit?

sehr schlecht   sehr gut

Wie konntest Du Deine eigenen Ideen einbringen?

sehr schlecht   sehr gut

Wie viele von Deinen eigenen Ideen konntest Du einbringen?

sehr wenige   sehr viele

In % ausgedrückt: Was glaubst Du, in wieweit sich Dein eigenes Mentales Modell der BSC mit der BSC Deines Teams überschneidet?

erste Befragung:_____%

dritte Befragung:_____%

Ich bin   männlich

              weiblich

Ich bin _____ Jahre alt.

Ich studiere (Studienfach):_____

im Semester:_____

Ich habe eine abgeschlossene Berufsausbildung: JA   NEIN

Ich habe berufliche Erfahrungen: JA   NEIN

Ich habe Erfahrungen mit Teamarbeit: JA   NEIN

Ich habe schon bei ca. _____ verschiedenen Firmen als Praktikant/ Aushilfe/Angestellter etc. gearbeitet.

VIELEN DANK!

Appendix 13: Study III – Concepts Shared between Participants

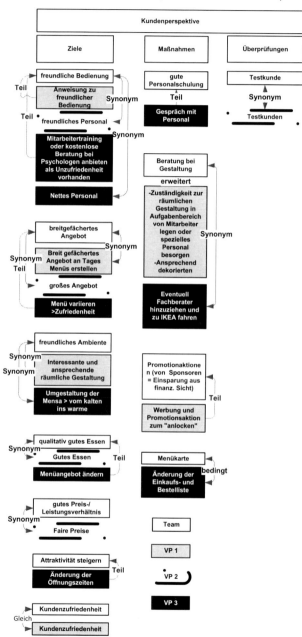

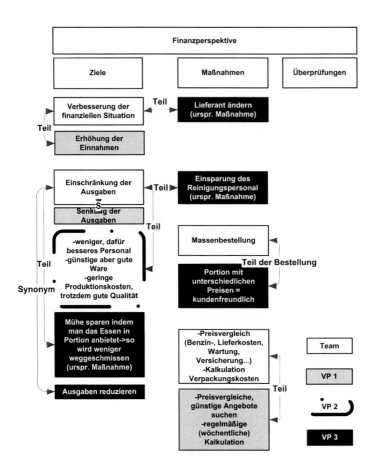

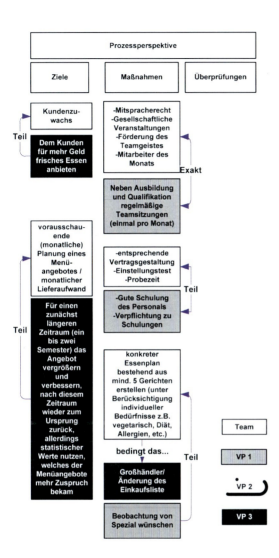

Appendix 14: Study III – Result Participant 3, Stage 1

Note xix: Green = objectives, brown = means, black arrows = cause-and-effect relationships

Appendix 15: Study III – Result Participant 1, Stage 1

Note xx: Red arrows = cause-and-effect relationships

Appendix 16: Study III – Result Participant 2, Stage 1

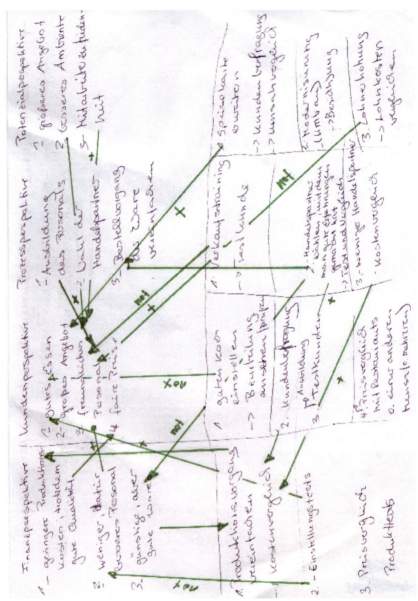

Note xxi: First numbers = objectives, second numbers = means, blue arrows = measurement, green arrows = cause-and-effect relationships

Appendix 17: Study IV – Task for Semantic Relationships

Bitte lesen Sie die nachfolgenden Ausführungen aufmerksam durch. Dabei handelt es sich um kurze Erklärungen zu Relationen. Wenn Sie Fragen haben, wenden Sie sich bitte an den Projektleiter!

Synonym:

Zwei oder mehr Elemente sind dann synonym, wenn die Sätze/Wortgruppen/Wörter dieselbe Bedeutung haben. Bsp. Person A sagt „Brot im Geschäft kaufen" und Person B „kauft Brot und steht gleichzeitig im Geschäft"

Beide Elemente können als synonym bezeichnet werden. Daraus ergibt sich:

Regel:  or

Hyponomie:

Ein spezifischer/konkreter Ausdruck ist in einem allgemeineren/abstrakten Ausdruck vorhanden. Bsp.: Bedeutung von „Tulpe" ist in „Blume" enthalten. Daraus ergibt sich die Regel:

Bsp. „Tulpe" Teil von „Blume"

Regel: 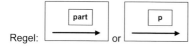 or

Inkompatibilität:

Inkompatibilität ist eine Kontradiktion zwischen Sätze/Wortgruppen/Wörter. Ein Satz negiert hierbei einen anderen Satz, sei es implizit oder explizit. So schließen sich Farben gegenseitig aus (Kontradiktion).

Bsp. Das Buch ist blau. Das Buch ist rot.

Rule: 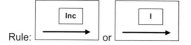 or

Antonymie:

Antonymie bezeichnet einen Gegensatz par excellence.

Beispiele kaufen vs. verkaufen, Ehegatte vs. Ehefrau

Rule: 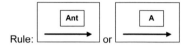 or

Aufgabe:

Benutzen Sie die nachfolgenden Relationen und ordnen Sie die Karteikarten Ihres Mentalen Modells aus der ersten Messung dem nun erstellten Mentalen Modell des Teams zu! Sollten Sie Fragen haben, wenden Sie sich bitte an den Versuchsleiter.

Appendix 18: Study IV – Outline of Semantic Relations Used – with Examples

P**		Synonym				Antonym				Hyponymy				Incompatibility		
	F*	Example		F*		Example		F*		Example		F*		Example		
		Team Concepts	Idiosyncratic Concept			Team Concepts	Idiosyncratic Concept			Team Concepts	Idiosyncratic Concept			Team Concepts	Idiosyncratic Concept	
3	4	erhöhte Gefahr im Straßenverkehr	erhöhtes Verkehrsaufkommen	0				9		Luftverschmutzung	ökologische Probleme	0				
4	6		Risiken durch hohes Verkehrsaufkommen	0				3			Umweltverschmutzung	0				
8	3	Vermarktung des rechtlichen Teils des Infonets	bessere Mitteilung Infonet	4		Nutzung des rechtlichen Teils des Infonets erhöhen	Infonet wird nicht häufig verwendet	7		Struktur zu kompliziert	schlechter Aufbau d. Infonets	1		Verbesserung Struktur & Aufbau d. rechtl. Teils d. Infonets	schlechter Aufbau Infonet	
9	6		Bekanntheitsgrad durch Werbekampagne erhöhen	0				6			schlechte Nutzerfreundlichkeit d. Infonets	0				
10	4	Umweltanalyse	Makro- und Mikroanalyse	0				3		Kenntnis über rechtliche Rahmenbedingungen (Studie)	indische Besonderheiten kennen	0				
11	0			0				0				0				
14	10	alternative Routen: Schiff, Flugzeug	Entlastung des Verkehrs durch alternative Transportwege	0				5		Versorgungsengpässe	kein Gütermangel	0				
15	8		Ermittlung des	1		Ab-	Sicherung der	0				0				

253

P**	F*	Synonym			Antonym			Hyponymy			Incompatibility		
		Example		F*	Example		F*	Example		F*	Example		
		Team Concepts	Idiosyncratic Concept		Team Concepts	Idiosyncratic Concept		Team Concepts	Idiosyncratic Concept		Team Concepts	Idiosyncratic Concept	
16	5		optimalen Anfahrtwegs		wanderung der Kunden zur Konkurrenz	Auftragslage							
			andere Verkehrswege nutzen	1	Versorgungs-engpass	Versorgungs-sicherheit	4	Starke Belastung d. Infrastruktur	Probleme im Straßenverkehr	0			
17	8	Diver-sifikation d. Verkehrs-wege	Aufteilung d. Transporte über mehrere Wege (Schiene/ Straße/ Schifffahrt)	0			4	Lager-haltung	Auflösung v. Engpässen durch intelligente Steuerung d. Supply Chain	0			
18	4	zu wenig Kapazitäten	Infrastruktur-knappheit	0			4	besseres Verkehrs-leitsystem	Verkehrs-beruhigung	1	Nutzung anderer Verkehrswege	Ver-sorgung aus allen Rich-tungen	
19	8	besseres Verkehrsleit-system	Installation eines elektrischen Verkehrsleit-systems	1	generelle Maut für alle Verkehrs-wege	Umgehen der LKW-Mautpflicht	2	gesetzliche Be-stimmungen	Länderüber-greifende Kooperation d. Verkehrsbehörden BB	0			

Note xxii: F*=Frequency of this Rule used, P = Participant No., **

Appendix 19: Study IV – Mann-Whitney Test – Team Basis

Rank

	Team	Sample Size	Median Rank	Rank Sum
Number of Common Used Team Concepts by both Team Members	Homogenous	3	3,50	10,50
	Heterogeneous	3	3,50	10,50
	Total	6		
Common Used Concepts in %	Homogenous	3	3,33	10,00
	Heterogeneous	3	3,67	11,00
	Total	6		
Number of Different Used Team Concepts by both Participants	Homogenous	3	4,00	12,00
	Heterogeneous	3	3,00	9,00
	Total	6		
Distributed Used Concepts in %	Homogenous	3	4,00	12,00
	Heterogeneous	3	3,00	9,00
	Total	6		
Team Performance: Concept Numbers	Homogenous	3	3,50	10,50
	Heterogeneous	3	3,50	10,50
	Total	6		
Team Performance in %	Homogenous	3	3,00	9,00
	Heterogeneous	3	4,00	12,00
	Total	6		

Statistics

Homogeneous vs. Heterogeneous Teams	Number of Common Used Team Concepts by both Team Members	Common Used Concepts in %	Number of Different Used Team Concepts by both Participants	Distributed Used Concepts in %	Team Performance: Concept Numbers	Team Performance in %
Mann-Whitney test	4,500	4,000	3,000	3,000	4,500	3,000
Z	,000	-,218	-,696	-,655	,000	-,655
Asymptotic Significant (2-tailed)	1,000	,827	,487	,513	1,000	,513
Exact Significant (1-tailed)	,500	,500	,350	,350	,500	,350

a Not corrected for linked ranks.

Appendix 20:   Study IV – Median Test – Team Basis

Frequency

		Team	
		Homogenous	Heterogeneous
Number of Team Concepts Shared by both Team Members	> Median	1	1
	<= Median	2	2
Shared Concepts in %	> Median	1	2
	<= Median	2	1
Number of Distributed Team Concepts Used by both Participants	> Median	1	0
	<= Median	2	3
Distributed Concepts Used in %	> Median	2	1
	<= Median	1	2
Team Performance: Concept Numbers	> Median	1	2
	<= Median	2	1
Team Performance in %	> Median	1	2
	<= Median	2	1

Statistics

Homogeneous vs. Heterogeneous Teams	Number of Team Concepts Shared by both Team Members	Shared Concepts in %	Number of Distributed Team Concepts Used by both Participants	Distributed Concepts Used in %	Team Performance: Concept Numbers	Team Performance in %
N	6	6	6	6	6	6
Median	4.00	23.9000	7.0000	34.0000	10.5000	47.7000
Exact Significant	1.000	1.000	1.000	1.000	1.000	1.000

Appendix 21:   Study V – Questionnaire about World Class User Experience

Questionnaire

Task 1

Please write your user number in the left corner on the whiteboard.

Please provide answers for all following tasks, and write your answers with the black pen on the whiteboard (until you want to change the colour of your pen). Write down everything that you think. Please note that there are no right or wrong answers.

Task 2 Question

Have you bought a technical product which was really expensive and that you had to deliberate over, for example, a car, a special computer, or a high-priced TV? Please think about this article when answering this task.

Please list the aspects on the whiteboard which were (or are) important to you when buying this product. You can write as many aspects as you want.

Task 3

Save your answer under your user number and add "-T2".

e.g.: AD19-T2

Task 4 Question

Which consumer electronic product do you have at home which you feel gives you the best usability (i.e., ease of use). Please think about this when answering this task.

Please list the aspects on the whiteboard that relate to why you find this product so usable.

Task 5

Save your answer under your user number and add "-T4".

e.g.: AD19-T4

Task 6 Question

Have you bought a brand (in terms of task 2 and 4)? Please think on this brand when answering this task.

Please list the aspects on the whiteboard that relate to why you chose this brand.

Task 7

Save your answer under your user number and add "-T6".

e.g.: AD19-T6

Task 8 Question

When you bought the consumer electronic product that you described previously did you take a look at any advertising material before you bought it? Please think about such material when answering this task.

Please list the information on the whiteboard that you looked for in the advertising material.

OR

Imagine that your favourite product at home has broken and you have to buy a new one. Would you look for any information in advertising material? If so:

Please list the information on the whiteboard that you would look for in the advertising material.

Task 9

Save your answer under your user number and add "-T8".

e.g.: AD19-T8

Task 10

If you go into a sales point and you want to buy a new product what do you expect there

- When it is a very expensive product, and

- When it is a normal everyday product.

Please list everything you expect in the sales point on the whiteboard.

Task 11

Save your answer under your user number and add "-T10".

e.g.: AD19-T10

Task 12

Imagine you want to buy a new mobile phone. We are interested in what you feel about the usability of the phone and your experience of buying it. Please choose from (or modify) the concepts that you generated before what your new mobile phone needs to have in terms of usability and purchasing experience (underline with a red pen) and the concepts which would be nice to have in terms of usability and purchasing experience (underline with a blue pen). If you feel you need to add some more concepts at this stage then you are welcome doing this.

Task 13

Save your answer under your user number and add "-T12".

e.g.: AD19-T12

Task 14

Imagine that the new phone that you were intending to buy is a 'smart' mobile phone. This is a device that can act as a Personal Data Assistant (PDA), that is, it has all of the functionality of a modern mobile phone, but it can also share files, check emails, browse the internet, and handle your contacts and diary appointments. Are there any concepts of usability, purchasing experience or owner experience that you would like to add to those concepts already generated that relate to what your smart mobile phone needs to have (underline with a red pen) and what it would be nice for it to have (underline with a blue pen). You are free to add to or modify any concepts that you generated previously.

Task 15

Save your answer under your user number and add "-T14".

e.g.: AD19-T14

Task 16

Bring these concepts into a hierarchy and write a "1" on the most important concept, a "2" on the 2nd most important, a "3" on the 3rd most important concept, and so on. There can be no joint most important concept, so each number should only be used once. Please think carefully but don't forget: there are no right or wrong answers! Please group the numbers to the concepts. The project leader will show you how to do this.

Task 17

Save your answer under your user number and add "-T16".

e.g.: AD19-T16

Task 18

For this task, use the rule system 1.

Now take the concept cards and construct your mental model as you have done it with the "tree" example. Start with the most important concept. To make a connection between two concepts draw a line (using a pen); the type of line to draw depends on the connection you intend to use (please see the rules and examples). If you think a logical rule is missing please add your own.

Task 19

Save your answer under your user number and add "-T18".

e.g.: AD19-T18

Task 20

Please erase now only the lines in this mental model and save it again under your user number and add "-T20".

e.g.: AD19-T20

Task 21

For this task, use the rule system 2.

Now we would like to know if there are any positive or negative influences or risks/opportunities you see between the concepts. Please take another colour pen (**please remember to return the first pen to its bay**) and use the 2nd rule system. Again: There are no right or wrong answers!

Task 22

Save your answer.

Appendix 22:   Study V – Logic Rules (Rule System 1)

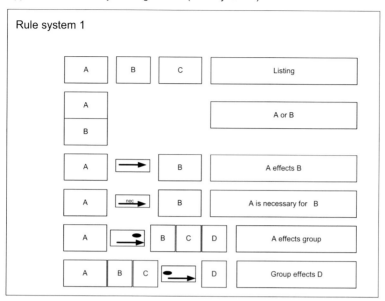

Appendix 23:   Study V – Risk-Chance Rule System (Rule System 2)

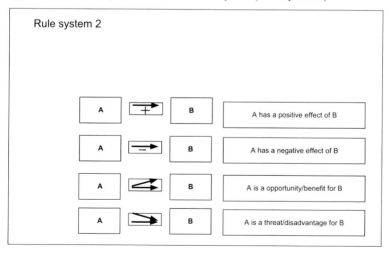

Appendix 24:   Study V – Task for Practicing the Rule System

Description

This task enables you to familiarise yourself with the rule system you will be using. Therefore please construct your mental model about the basic life resources of a tree. There are no right or wrong answers. If you have any questions please ask!

Task 1

For this task use the whiteboard. Write one concept per line and leave some space between concepts.
What does a tree need to live and to grow up?
Please write down as many basic life resources a tree need as come into your mind!

Task 2

Save your answer under your user number and add "-T1-V1".

e.g.: AD19-T1-V1

Task 3

Bring these concepts in a hierarchy and write a "1" on the most important concept, a "2" of the 2nd most important, a "3" of the 3rd most important card and so on. There can be no joint most important so each number should only be used once, please think carefully but don't forget: there are no right or wrong answers!

Task 4

Save your answer under your user number and add "-T1-V1".

e.g.: AD19-T1-V3

Task 5

For this task use the rule system 1!

Now take the concept cards and construct your mental model about basic life resources of a tree on the blackboard. Start with the most important concept and put it on the blackboard first. To make a connection between two concepts draw a line (using a pen); the type of line to draw depends on the connection you intend to use (please see the rules and examples). If you think a logical rule is missing, please add your own!

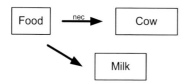

Task 6

Save your answer under your user number and add "-T1-V1".

e.g.: AD19-T1-V5

Task 7

For this task use the rule system 2!

Now would like to know if there are any positive or negative influences or risks/opportunities you see between the concepts. Please take another colour and use the 2nd rule system. You can write down over existing connections or you can make new connections like the following example shows! Again: There are no right or wrong answers!

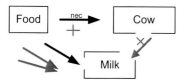

Task 8

Save your answer under your user number and add "-T1-V1".

e.g.: AD19-T1-V7

Appendix 25:   Study V – Introduction to the Study

Dear participant,

Thank you very much for taking part in this research project!

The research project is a collaborative project between Lancaster University and European School of Management, based in Berlin, Germany, and deals with Mental Models and Usability Understanding. Our ultimate goal is to derive a clearer view of how technical products can provide a 'World Class User Experience' for people like you. This means that in the tasks that follow we would like you to think about consumer electronics in a very general way in terms of why you feel they may engender a positive user experience. There will be no right or wrong answers!

The project leader will direct you through the whole testing. There will be 3 stages at 3 different times. Each stage will require 2 hours; although first stage has an additional part to learn the technique and takes 30 minutes longer. Your payment will be 40 Pounds in total and you will only get the money after the 3rd stage. It is therefore <u>absolute necessary</u> to take part in all 3 stages. If you have any questions just ask the project leader.

Due to the nature of the research, it is necessary that you have a "user number". It is essential only you know this number as this keeps your results anonymous. The user number is composed as follows:

- the first letter of your mother's first name
- the last letter of your father's first name
- your birthday

E.g.: If your mother's name is **A**NNE, your father's name is DAVI**D**, and your birthday is **19**.05.1980.

Your personal user number would be: **AD 19.**

Please keep your personal user number in your mind!

Thank you very much!

Appendix 26:   Study V – Task Added for Similarity Mapping – Sense Relation Rule System

Task 23

Please read this instruction carefully. It is a description about semantic relations. If you have any questions please ask the project leader! After reading the description the project leader will explain the task.

Synonym/interchangeably:

Two or more elements are synonymous if sentences/complex phrases/words have the same meaning. E.g. person A <u>says</u> "buying bread in a shop" and person B is buying bread and is to the same time in a shop.

→ Both elements are synonymous. Therefore, use the rule

Rule: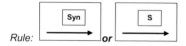

Hyponymy:

A more specific/concrete expression is part of a more common expression. E.g. the meaning of "tulip" is part of the meaning of "flower". Therefore, use the rule

Rule:

Incompatibility:

Incompatibility is a contradiction/discrepancy/antithesis between sentences/complex phrases/words. One sentence negates another sentence, be it implicit or explicit. E.g. colours are alternatives. A book which is blue coloured cannot be red coloured. Therefore, use the rule

Rule:

Antonymy:

An antonym is a word, which is the opposite of another word, e.g. buying vs. selling; healthy vs. ill, light vs. dark. Therefore, use the rule

Rule:

Task

Use this relation to match the concepts of your mental model from the first stage to the concepts of your mental model from this stage. If you have any questions please ask the project leader.

Appendix 27:   Study V – Demographic Questionnaire

Questions to the Person

My user Number is:_____. I am _____years old.   I am   M / F

My highest Level of Qualification is (please circle)

A levels   Bachelor's Degree   Master's Degree   Doctorate Degree

Are you currently working to achieve a degree, if so which (please circle)?

A levels   Bachelor's Degree   Master's Degree   Doctorate Degree

In which field _____

My native language is _____

What are your Research Interests (if any)?: *Example: I am currently looking into the Usability of Windows Vista and also have a general interest in reasoning behind interface design…*

Please write down your degree specialisations (please write down the degree level and next to it its name and what it covered): *Example: B.Sc. Computer Science: General Computer Science including Usability and Software Engineering…*

Do you have any Usability / User Interface Design experience? Please explain briefly:

Questions World Class User Experience

During tasks 18 and 20 we asked you to construct your 'mental model and to include the concept WCUE (Word Class User Experience) if it was part of your mental model. Please think about that concept now and answer the following questions in a short way: What is WCUE for you?

Questions to the Different Tasks

In task 2 we asked you 'Have you brought a technical product which was really expensive and that you had to deliberate over…'. What kind of product did you think about during

    The first stage:_____

    If you worked as a Team: We chose (please circle)

    →my product   →the product of my teammate   →everybody chose their own products

    The second stage:_____

    If you worked as a Team: We chose (please circle)

    →my product   →the product of my teammate   →everybody chose their own products

    The third stage:_____

    If you worked as a Team: We chose (please circle)

    →my product   →the product of my teammate   →everybody chose their own products

In task 4 we asked you 'Which consumer electronic product do you have at home which you feel gives you the best usability …'. What kind of product did you think about during

The first stage:_____

If you worked as a Team: We chose (please circle)

→my product →the product of my teammate   →everybody chose their own products

The second stage:_____

If you worked as a Team: We chose (please circle)

→my product →the product of my teammate   →everybody chose their own products

The third stage:_____

If you worked as a Team: We chose (please circle)

→my product →the product of my teammate   →everybody chose their own products

Questions to the Team Work

Approximately how many of your own ideas entered into the process of constructing the mental models in comparison to the whole team's construction process (0%=none, 100%= all my ideas):

The first stage:_____%   The second stage:_____%   The third stage:_____%

Did you like the teamwork part (please circle)? Yes / No

Why (Please try to give an answer!)? _____

Questions to the Interactive Whiteboard

Did you like working with the interactive whiteboard? Yes / No

What did you like most (pleas choose on and circle)?

→writing on it   →moving of the concepts cards   →grouping of concepts   →nothing

Questions to the Rule Systems

Do you like the RULE SYSTEM 1 (with the logic connection)? Yes / No

Why (Please try to give an answer!)? _____

Do you like the RULE SYSTEM 2 (with the advantages and threats)? Yes / No

Why (Please try to give an answer!)? _____

Do you like the RULE SYSTEM 3 (with the synonyms, antonyms, hyponyms)? Yes / No

Why (Please try to give an answer!)? _____

How easy were these rules? Please rank order the rule systems in terms of ease of use (1=easiest, 3=hardest)!

___Rule system 1   ___Rule system 2   ___Rule system 3

What is the difference between 'positive effect' and 'opportunity/benefit'?_____

Questions to the Purchase Intention or Acquired Purchase

Have you recently bought a mobile phone or a smart phone (within the last 3 month)?

Yes / No

Have you had any other contact with the topic 'mobile phone' or 'smart phone' apart from during the study (e.g. at work or during a seminar)?   Yes / No

Appendix 28: Study V – JE11 – Stage 1

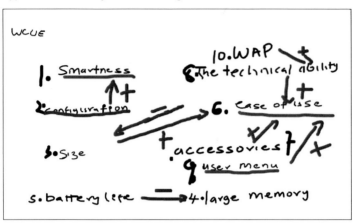

Appendix 29: Study V – JE11 – Stage 2

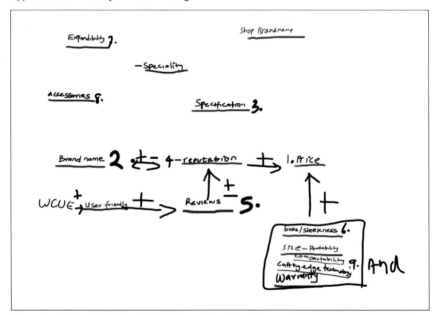

Appendix 30: Study V – JE11 – Semantic, Stage 1

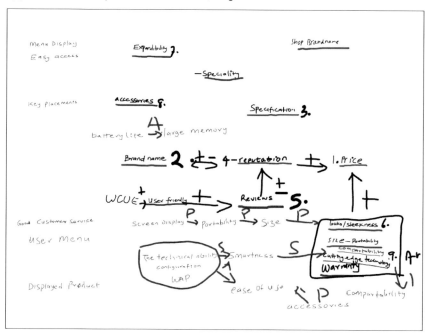

Appendix 31: Study V – JE11 – Stage 3

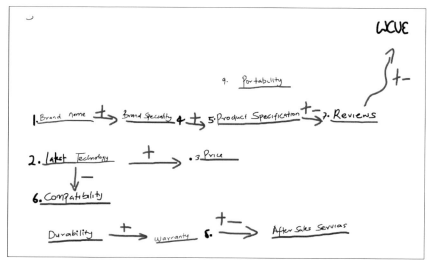

Appendix 32:   Study V – JE11 – Semantic, Stage 2

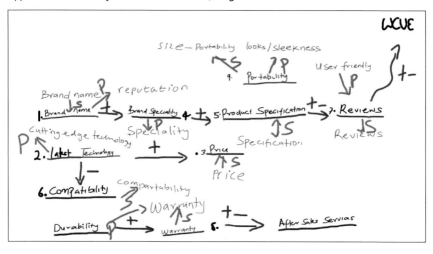

Appendix 33:   Study V – Concept Numbers of Mixed Group over all three stages

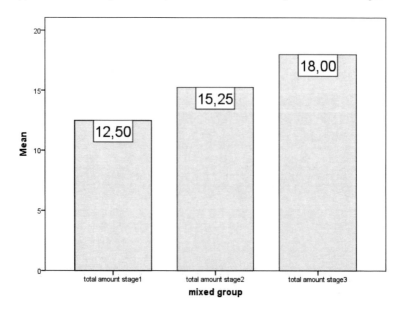

Appendix 34:   Study V – Concept Numbers of Control Group 1 (Individual Group)

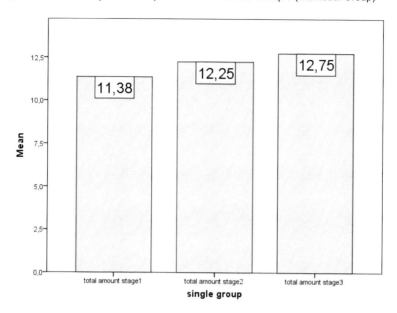

Appendix 35:   Study V – Mean Total Concept Numbers of Different Groups in stage 2

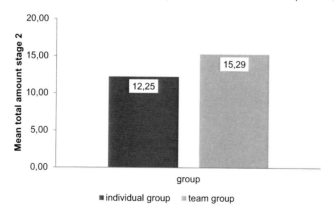

Appendix 36: Study V – Differences in Performance

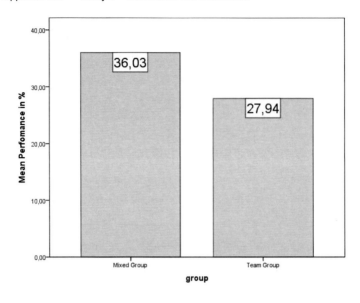

7. References

Abele, S. (2002). Soziale Kognition. In G. Wenniger (Ed.): *Lexikon der Psychologie [CD]*. Heidelberg: Spektrum Akademischer Verlag.

Abernethy, M. A., Horne, M., Lillis, A. M., Malina, M. A., & Selto, F. H. (2005). A Multi-Method Approach to Building Causal Performance Maps from Exert Knowledge. *Management Accounting Research, 16*, pp. 135-155.

Acar, W. & Druckenmiller, D. (2006). Endowing Cognitive Mapping with Computational Properties for Strategic Analysis. *Futures, 38*, pp. 993-1009.

Åhlberg, M. (2004). *Varieties of Concept Mapping*. Paper presented at the First Int. Conference on Concept Mapping, Pamplona, Spain.

Al-Laham, A. (2003). *Organisationales Wissensmanagement*. Eine strategische Perspektive. München: Verlag Franz Vahlen GmbH.

Ambrosini, V. & Bowman, C. (2001). Tacit knowledge: Some Suggestions for Operationalization. *Journal of Management Studies, 38*(6), pp. 811-829.

Ambrosini, V. & Bowman, C. (2005). Reducing Causal Ambiguity to Facilitate Strategic Learning. *Management Learning, 36*(4), pp. 493-512.

Amelang, M. & Zielinski, W. (2002). *Psychologische Diagnostik und Intervention* (3 ed). Berlin: Springer.

Amit, R. & Schoemaker, P. J. H. (1993). Strategic Assets and Organizational Rent. *Strategic Management Journal, 14*(1), pp. 33-46.

Anderson, J. R. (2001). *Kognitive Psychologie* (3 ed.). Heidelberg: Spektrum Akademischer Verlag.

Badke-Schaub, P., Neumann, A., Lauche, K., & Mohammed, S. (2007). Mental Models in Design Teams: A Valid Approach to Performance in Design Collaboration? *CoDesign, 3*(1), pp. 5-20.

Ballstaedt, S.-P., Mandl, H., Schnotz, W., & Tergan, S.-O. (1981). *Texte verstehen, Texte gestalten*. München: Urban und Schwarzberg.

Bamberger, I. & Wrona, T. (2004). *Strategische Unternehmensführung. Strategien, Systeme, Prozesse*. München: Verlag Franz Vahlen GmbH.

Banks, A. P. & Millward, L. J. (2007). Differentiating Knowledge in Teams: The Effect of Shared Declarative and Procedural Knowledge on Team Performance. *Group Dynamics: Theory, Research, and Practice, 11*(2), pp. 95-106.

Barney, J. (1991). Firm Resources and Sustained Competitive Advantage. *Journal of Management, 17*(1), pp. 99-120.

Berry, D. C. & Broadbent, D. E. (1988). Interactive Tasks and The Implicit-Explicit Distinction. *British Journal of Psychology, 79*, pp. 251-271.

Bick, M. (2004). *Knowledge Management Support System – Nachhaltige Einführung organisationsspezifischen Wissensmanagements.* Universität Duisburg-Essen. [available: http://duepublico.uni-duisburg-essen.de/servlets/DerivateServlet/Derivate-12675/DIS S_PUB.PDF, 01.05.2008]

Bell, P. B., Greene, T. C., Fisher, J. D., & Baum, A. (2001). *Environmental Psychology* (5 ed.). Fort Worth, TX: Harcourt.

Blaikie, N. W. H. (2000). *Designing Social Research: The Logic of Anticipation.* Cambridge, UK: Polity Press.

Blasius, J. (2001). *Korrespondenzanalyse.* München: Oldenburg.

Bollen, K. A. & Lennox, R. (1991). Conventional Wisdom on Measurement: A Structural Equation Perspective. *Psychological Bulletin, 110*(2), pp. 305-314.

Bolstad, C. A. & Endsley, M. R. (1999). *Shared Mental Models and Shared Displays: An Empirical Evaluation of Team Performance.* Paper presented at the 43rd Meeting of the Human Factors & Ergonomics Society.

Bonato, M. (1990). *Wissensstrukturierung mittels Struktur-Lege-Techniken. Eine graphentheoretische Analyse von Wissensnetzen.* Frankfurt am Main: Verlag Peter Lang GmbH.

Bortz, J. & Schuster, J. (2010). *Statistik für Human- und Sozialwissenschaftler* (7 ed.). Berlin: Springer Verlag.

Bortz, J. & Döring, N. (2006). *Forschungsmethoden und Evaluation für Human- und Sozialwissenschaftler* (4. ed.). Heidelberg: Springer Medizin Verlag.

Bortz, J. & Lienert, G. A. (2008). *Kurzgefaßte Statistik für die klinische Forschung. Leitfaden für die verteilungsfreie Analyse kleiner Stichproben* (3 ed.). Berlin: Springer Medizin Verlag.

Brannen, J. (2005). Mixing Methods: The Entry of Qualitative and Quantitative Approaches into the Research Process. *International Journal of Social Research Methodology, 8*(3), pp. 173-184.

Brannick, M. T. & Prince, C. (1997). An Overview of Team Performance Measurement. In M. T. Brannick, E. Salas, & C. Prince (Eds.): *Team Performance Assessment and Measurement: Theory, Methods, and Applications* (pp. 3-16). Hillsdale, N.J.: Lawrence Erlbaum and Associates.

Bromme, R. & Rambow, R. (2001). Experten-Laien-Kommunikation als Gegenstand der Expertiseforschung: Für eine Erweiterung des psychologischen Bildes vom Experten. In: R.K. Silbereisen & M. Reitzle (Eds.): *Psychologie 2000. Bericht über den 42. Kongress der Deutschen Gesellschaft für Psychologie in Jena 2000* (pp. 541-550). Lengerich: Pabst Science Publishers. [available: http://wwwpsy.uni-muenster.de/inst3/AE bromme/web/veroef/2000/93Bro-Ram01Exp-Lai.pdf, 06.07.2010]

Bromme, R., Jucks, R., & Rambow, R. (2004). Experten-Laien-Kommunikation im Wissensmanagement. In G. Reinmann & H. Mandl (Eds.): *Psychologie des Wissensmanagements. Perspektiven, Theorien und Methoden* (pp. 176-188). Göttingen: Hogrefe.

Brühl, R. (2006). Abduktion und Induktion in wissenschaftlichen Untersuchungen. *Wirtschaftswissenschaftliches Studium, 35*(4), pp. 182-186.

Brühl, R. (2009). *Controlling. Grundlagen des Erfolgscontrollings* (2 ed.). München: Oldenbourg Wissenschaftsverlag GmbH.

Brühl, R. & Buch, S. (2005). *The Construction of Mental Models in Management Accounting: How to Discribe Mental Models of Causal Inferences* (3. ed.). Working Paper No 15. Berlin: ESCP-EAP Europäische Wirtschaftshochschule Berlin.

Brühl, R. & Buch, S. (2006). *Einheitliche Gütekriterien in der empirischen Forschung? Objektivität, Reliabilität und Validität in der Diskussion.* Working Paper No 20. Berlin: ESCP-EAP Europäische Wirtschaftshochschule Berlin.

Buch, S. (2007). *Strukturgleichungsmodelle – Ein einführender Überblick.* Working Paper No 29. Berlin: ESCP-EAP Europäische Wirtschaftshochschule Berlin.

Buckley, C. (1995). Delphi: A Methodology for Preferences More than Predictions. *Library Management, 16*(7), pp. 16-19.

Bukh, P. N. & Malmi, T. (2005). *Re-Examining the Cause-and-Effect Principles of the Balanced Scorecard.* Malmö: Liber and Copenhagen Business School Press. [available: http://www.pnbukh.com/files/nyheder/BSC_NL_-_February_25_-_final.pdf, 03.09.2010]

Büssing, A., Herbig, B., & Latzel, A. (2002). *Das Zusammenspiel zwischen Erfahrung, impliziten und expliziten Wissen beim Handeln in kritischen Situationen.* Bericht Nr. 66. München: Berichte aus dem Lehrstuhl für Psychologie der TU München.

Buzan, T. & Buzan, B. (2005). *Das Mind-Map-Buch. Die beste Methode zur Steigerung ihres geistigen Potenzials* (Vol. 5). Heidelberg: MVG.

Cabrera A. & Cabrera E. F. (2002). Knowledge-Sharing Dilemmas. *Organization Studies, 23*(5), pp. 687-710.

Calori, R., Johnson, G., & Sarnin, P. (1992). French and British Top Managers' Understanding of the Structure and the Dynamics of their Industries: A Cognitive Analysis and Comparison. *British Journal of Management, 3*(2), pp. 61-78.

Calori, R., Johnson, G., & Sarnin, P. (1994). CEO's Cognitive Maps and the Scope of the Organization. *Strategic Management Journal, 15*, pp. 437-457.

Cannon-Bowers, J. A. & Salas, E. (1997). Teamwork Competencies: The Interaction of Team Member Knowledge, Skills, and Attitudes. In O. F. O'Neil (Ed.): *Workforce Readiness: Competencies and Assessment* (pp. 151-174). Hillsdale, NJ: Erlbaum.

Cannon-Bowers, J. A. & Salas, E. (1998). Individual and Team Decision Making Under Stress: Theoretical Underpinnings. In J. A. Cannon-Bowers & E. Salas (Eds.): *Making Decisions Under Stress. Implications for Individual and Team Training* (pp. 17-38). Washington, DC: American Psychological Association.

Cannon-Bowers, J. A. & Salas, E. (2001). Reflections on Shared Cognition. *Journal of Organizational Behavior, 22*, pp. 195-202.

Cannon-Bowers, J. A., Salas, E., & Converse, S. A. (1993). Shared Mental Models in Expert Decision Teams. In N. J. Castellan (Ed.): *Individual and Group Decision Making* (pp. 221-246). Hillsdale, NJ: Lawrence Erlbaum Associates Inc, US.

Cassidy, M. F. & Buede, D. (2009). Does the Accuracy of Expert Judgment Comply with Common Sense: caveat emptor. *Management Decision, 47*(3), pp. 454-469.

Chavan, M. (2009). The Balanced Scorecard: A New Challenge. *Journal of Management Development, 28*(5), pp. 393-406.

Chi, M. T. H. (2006). Two Approaches to the Study of Experts' Characteristics. In K. A. Ericsson, N. Charness, R. R. Hoffman, & P. J. Feltovich (Eds.): *The Cambridge Handbook of Expertise and Expert Performance* (pp. 21-30). Cambridge: Cambridge University Press.

Choy, A. K. & King, R. R. (2005). An Experimental Investigation of Approaches to Audit Decision Making: An Evaluation Using Systems-Mediated Mental Models. *Contemporary Accounting Research, 22*(2), pp. 311-350.

Cobbold, I. M. & Lawrie, G. J. G. (2002, 17-19 July 2002). *The Development of the Balanced Scorecard as a Strategic Management Tool.* Paper presented at the Performance Measurement and Management, Research and Action, Boston, MA, USA.

Cohen, J. (1992). A Power Primer. *Psychological Bulletin, 112,* pp. 155-159.

Cohen, S. G. & Bailey, D. E. (1997). What Makes Teams Work: Group Effectiveness Research from the Shop Floor to the Executive Suite. *Journal of Management, 23*(3), pp. 239-290.

Cooke, N. J. & Gorman, J. C. (2006). Assesment of Team Cognition. In W. Karwowski (Ed.): *International Encyclopedia of Ergonomics and Human Factors* (2 ed., pp. 270-275). London: Taylor & Francis.

Cooke, N. J., Gorman, J. C., Duran, J. L., & Taylor, A. R. (2007a). Team Cognition in Expierenced Command-and-Control Teams. *Journal of Experimental Psychology: Applied, 13*(3), pp. 146-157.

Cooke, N. J., Gorman, J. C., & Winner, J. L. (2007b). Team Cognition. In F. T. Durso, R. S. Nickerson, S. T. Dumais, S. Lewandowsky, & T. J. Perfect (Eds.): *Handbook of Applied Cogntion* (2 ed., pp. 239-268). Hoboken, NJ: John Wiley.

Cooke, N. J., Kiekel, P. A., & Helm, E. E. (2001). Measuring Team Knowledge During Skill Acquisition of a Complex Task. *International Journal of Cognitive Ergonomics, 5*(3), pp. 297-315.

Cooke, N. J., Kiekel, P. A., Salas, E., Stout, R., Bowers, C., & Cannon-Bowers, J. A. (2003). Measuring Team Knowledge: A Window to the Cognitive Underpinnings of Team Performance. *Group Dynamics: Theory, Research, and Practise, 7*(3), pp. 179-199.

Cooke, N. J., Salas, E., Cannon-Bowers, J. A., & Stout, R. e. (2000). Measuring Team Knowledge. *Human Factors, 42*(1), pp. 151-173.

Cossette, P. & Audet, M. (1992). Mapping of an Idiosyncratic Schema. *Journal of Management Studies, 29*(3), pp. 325-347.

Creswell, J. W. & Plano Clark, V. L. (2007). *Designing and Conducting Mixed Methods Research*. Thousand Oaks, CA: Sage.

Creswell, J. W., Shope, R., Plano Clark, V. L., & Green, D. O. (2006). How Interpretive Qualitative Research Extends Mixed Methods Research. *Research in the Schools, 13*(1), pp. 1-11.

Creswell, J. W. & Tashakkori, A. (2007). Editorial: Differing Perspectives on Mixed Methods Research. *Journal of Mixed Methods Research, 1,* pp. 303-308.

Cruse, D. A. (1986). *Lexical Semantics*. Cambridge: University Press.

Cruse, A. (2011). *Meaning in Language: An Introduction to Semantics and Pragmatics* (Oxford Textbooks in Linguistics, 3 ed.). Oxford: Oxford University Press.

Dalkey, N. C. & Helmer, O. (1963). An Experimental Application of the Delphi Method to the Use of Experts. *Management Science, 9*(3), pp. 458-467.

Daniels, K., Johnson, G., & Chernatony, L. d. (1994). Differences in Managerial Cognitions of Competition. *British Journal of Management, 5*(Special Issue), S21-S29.

Daniels, K., Johnson, G., & Chernatony, L. d. (2002). Task and Institutional Influences on Managers' Mental Models of Competition. *Organization Studies, 23*(1), pp. 31-62.

Dann, H.-D. (1992). Variation von Lege-Strukturen zur Wissensrepräsentation. In B. Scheele (Ed.): *Struktur-Lege-Verfahren als Dialog-Konsens-Methodik* (pp. 2-41). Münster: Aschendorffsche Verlagsbuchhandlung.

Davison, G. & Blackman, D. (2005). The Role of Mental Models in Innovative Teams. *European Journal of Innovation Management, 8*(4), pp. 409-423.

DeChurch, L. A. & Mesmer-Magnus, J. R. (2010a). Measuring Shared Team Mental Models: A Meta-Analysis. *Group Dynamics: Theory, Research, and Practice, 14*(1), pp. 1-14.

DeChurch, L. A. & Mesmer-Magnus, J. R. (2010b). The Cognitive Underpinnings of Effective Teamwork: A Meta-Analysis. *Journal of Applied Psychology, 95*(1), pp. 32-53.

de Kleer, J. & Seely Brown, J. (1983). Assumptions and Ambiguities in Mechanistic Mental Models. In D. Gentner & A. L. Stevens (Eds.): *Mental Models* (pp. 99-129). Hillsdale, NJ: Lawrence Erlbaum.

De Vega, M., Marschark, M., Intons-Peterson, M. J., Johnson-Laird, P. N., & Denis, M. (1996). Representations of Visuospatial Cognition: A Discussion. In M. De Vega, M. Intons-Peterson, M. Marschark, P. N. Johnson-Laird, & M. Denis (Eds.): *Models of Visuospatial Cognition* (pp. 198-226). Oxford: Oxford University Press.

Denison, D. R., Hart, S. L., & Kahn, J. A. (1996). From Chimney to Cross-Functional Teams: Developing and Validating a Diagnostic Model. *Academy of Management Journal, 39*(4), pp. 1005-1023.

Domeinski, J., Wagner, R., Schöbel, M., & Manzey, D. (2007). Human Redundancy in Automation Monitoring. Effects of Social Loafing and Social Compensation. *Proceedings of the Human Factors and Ergonomics Society 51st Annual Meeting*. Baltimore, USA.

Dörschner, N. (1996). *Lexikalische Strukturen. Wortfeldkonzeption und Theorie der Prototypen im Vergleich* (Vol. 26). Münster: Nodus Publikationen.

Downward, P. & Mearman, A. (2007). Retroduction as Mixed-Methods Triangulation in Business Administration Research: Reorienting Business Administrations into Social Science. *Cambridge Journal of Business Administrations, 31*, pp. 77-99.

Doyle, J. K., Radzicki, M. J., & Trees, W. S. (2008). Measuring Change in Mental Models of Complex Dynamic Systems. In H. Qudrat-Ullah, M. J. Spector, & P. I. Davidsen (Eds.): *Complex Decision Making: Theory and Practice* (pp. 269–294). Berlin: Springer-Verlag.

Eckert, A. (2000). Die Netzwerk-Elaborierungs-Technik (NET) - Ein computerunterstütztes Verfahren zur Diagnose komplexer Wissensstrukturen. In H. Mandl & F. Fischer (Eds.): *Wissen sichtbar machen. Wissensmanagement mit Mapping-Techniken* (pp. 137-157). Göttingen: Hogrefe.

Eden, C. (2004). Analyzing Cognitive Maps to Help Structure Issues or Problems. *European Journal of Operational Research, 159*, pp. 673-686.

Eden, C. & Ackermann, F. (1998). Analysing and Comparing Idiographic Causal Maps. In C. Eden & J.-C. Spender (Eds.): *Managerial and Organizational Cognition* (pp. 192-209). London: Sage.

Eden, C. & Ackermann, F. (2002). A Mapping Framework for Strategy Making. In A. S. Huff & M. Jenkins (Eds.): *Mapping Strategic Knowledge* (pp. 173-195). London: Sage.

Eden, C., Ackermann, F., & Cropper, S. (1992). The Analysis of Cause Maps. *Journal of Management Studies, 29*(3), pp. 309-324.

Eden, C., Jones, S., Sims, D., & Smithin, T. (1981). The Intersubjectivity of Issues and Issues of Intersubjectivity. *Journal of Management Studies, 18*(1), pp. 37-47.

Edwards, B. D., Day, E. A., Arthur, W., & Bell, S. T. (2006). Relationships among Team Ability Composition, Team Mental Models, and Team Performance. *Journal of Applied Psychology, 91*(3), pp. 727-736.

Edwards, D. (1991). Categories are for Talking. On the Cognitive and Discursive Bases of Categorization. *Theory & Psychology, 1*(4), pp. 515-452.

Eisenhardt, K. M. & Martin, J. A. (2000). Dynamic Capabilities: What are They? *Strategic Management Journal, 21*(10/11), pp. 1105-1121.

Ellis, A. P. J. (2006). System Breakdown: The Role of Mental Models and Transactive Memory in the Relationship between Acute Stress and Team Performance. *Academy of Management Journal, 49*(3), pp. 576–589.

Endsley, M. R. (2000). Theoretical Underpinnings of Situation Awareness: A Critical Review. In M. R. Endsley & D. J. Garland (Eds.): *Situation Awareness Analysis and Measurement* (pp. 1-24). Mahwah, NJ: Lawrence Erlbaum.

Ericsson, K. A. & Smith, J. (1991). Prospects and Limits of the Empirical Study of Expertise: an Introduction. In K. A. Ericcson & J. Smith (Eds.): *Toward a General Theory of Expertise. Prospects and Limits* (pp. 1-38). Cambridge: University Press.

Erzberger, C. & Kelle, U. (2003). Making Inferences in Mixed Methods: The Rules of Integration. In A. Tashakkori & C. Teddlie (Eds.): *Handbook of Mixed Methods in Social & Behavioral Research* (pp. 457-488). Thousand Oaks: Sage Publications.

Espevik, R., Johnsen, B. H., Eid, J., & Thayer, J. F. (2006). Shared Mental Models and Operational Effectiveness: Effects on Performance and Team Processes in Submarine Attack Teams. *Military Psychology, 18*(Suppl.), pp. S23–S36.

Espinosa, J. A., Kraut, R. E., Slaughter, S. A., Lerch, J. F., Herbsleb, J. D., & Mockus, A. (2002). *Shared Mental Models, Familiarity, and Coordination: A Multi-Method Study of Distributed Software Teams*. Paper presented at the Twenty-Third International Conference on Information Systems.

Everitt, B. S. & Skrondal, A. (2010). *The Cambridge Dictionary of Statistics* (4. ed.). Cambridge: Cambridge University Press.

Field, A. (2009). *Discovering Statistics Using SPSS* (3 ed.). London: Sage.

Figge, F., Hahn, T., Schaltegger S., & Wagner, M. (2002). The Sustainability Balanced Scorecard – Linking Sustainability Management to Business Strategy. *Business Strategy and the Environment, 11*, pp. 269–284.

Fiol, C. M. & Huff, A. S. (1992). Maps for Managers: Where are We? Where Do We Go from Here? *Journal of Management Studies, 29*(3), pp. 267-285.

Fisseni, H.-J. (1997). *Lehrbuch der psychologischen Diagnostik* (Vol. 2., überarbeitete und erweiterte Auflage). Göttingen: Hogrefe, Verlag für Psychologie.

Fleck, L. (1980, Orig. 1935). *Entstehung und Entwicklung einer wissenschaftlichen Tatsache: Einführung in die Lehre vom Denkstil und Denkkollektiv*. Frankfurt am Main: Suhrkamp.

Fokkinga, B., Bleijenberg, I., & Vennix, J. A. M. (2009). *Group Model Building Evaluation in Single Cases: A Method to Assess Changes in Mental Models*. In Paper presented at the 27th International Conference of the System Dynamics Society, New Mexico, USA. [cit. after M. Schaffernicht & S. N. Groesser, 2011; paper available: http://www.systemdynamics.org/conferences/2009/proceed/papers/P1261.pdf, 17.05.2011]

Forsyth, D. R. (2009). *Group Dynamics* (5 ed.). Belmond, CA: Cengage Learning.

Geeraerts, D. (2010). *Theories of Lexical Semantics* (Oxford Linguistics). Oxford: Oxford University Press.

Gentner, D. (2002). Psychology of Mental Models. In N. J. Smelser & P. B. Bates (Eds.): *International Encyclopaedia of the Social and Behavioral Sciences* (pp. 9683-9687). Amsterdam: Elsevier.

Gentner, D. & Gentner, D. R. (1983). Flowing Waters or Teeming Crowds: Mental Models of Electricity. In D. Gentner & A. L. Stevens (Eds.): *Mental Models* (pp. 99-129). Hillsdale, NJ: Lawrence Erlbaum.

Gentner, D. & Stevens, A. L. (1983). *Mental Models*. Hillsdale, NJ: Lawrence Erlbaum.

Gibson, C. B. (2001). From Knowledge Accumulation to Accommodation: Cycles of Collective Cognition in Work Groups. *Journal of Organizational Behavior, 22*(2), pp. 121-134.

Ginsberg, A. (1994). Minding the Competition: From Mapping to Mastery. *Strategic Management Journal, 15*, pp. 153-174.

Goldsmith, T. E., Johnson, P. J., & Acton, W. H. (1991). Assessing Structural Knowledge. *Journal of Educational Psychology, 83*(1), pp. 88-96.

Goodhew, G. W., Cammock, P. A., & Hamilton, R. T. (2005). Managers' Cognitive Maps and Intra-Organisational Performance Differences. *Journal of Managerial Psychology, 20*(2), pp. 124-136.

Greene, J. C., Caracelli, V. J., & Graham, W. F. (1989). Toward a Conceptual Framework for Mixed Method Evaluation Designs. *Educational Evaluation and Policy Analysis, 11*(3), pp. 255-274.

Greeno, J. G., Collins, A. M., & Resnick, L. B. (1996). Cognition and Learning. In D. C. Berliner & R. C. Calfee (Eds.): *Handbook of Educational Psychology* (pp. 15-46). New York: Macmillan.

Griepentrog, B. K. & Fleming, P. J. (2003). *Shared Mental Models and Team Performance: Are You Thinking What We're Thinking?* Paper presented at the 18th Annual conference of the society of industrial and organizational psychology, Orlando, Florida.

Groeben, N. & Scheele, B. (2000, Juni). Dialog-Konsens-Methodik im Forschungsprogramm Subjektive Theorien [9 Absätze]. *Forum Qualitative Sozialforschung.* Forum Qualitative Sozialforschung / Forum: Qualitative Social Research [Online Journal], 1(2). Revised 7/2008: Groeben, Norbert & Scheele, Brigitte (2001). Dialogue-Hermeneutic Method and the "Research Program Subjective Theories" [9 paragraphs]. Forum Qualitative Sozialforschung / Forum: Qualitative Social Research, 2(1), Art. 10, http://nbn-resolving.de/urn:nbn:de:0114-fqs0002105. [19.07.2010].

Groeben, N., Wahl, D., Schlee, J., & Scheele, B. (1988). *Das Forschungsprogramm Subjektive Theorien: Eine Einführung in die Psychologie des reflexiven Subjekts.* Heidelberg: A. Francke.

Guzzo, R. A. & Dickson, M. W. (1996). Teams in Organizations: Recent Research on Performance and Effectiveness. *Annual Review of Psychology, 47*(1), pp. 307-338.

Häder, M. (2009). *Delphi-Befragungen: Ein Arbeitsbuch* (2 ed.). Wiesbaden: VS Verlag für Sozialwissenschaften.

Harrison, D. A., Mohammed, S., McGrath, J. E., Florey, A. T., & Vanderstoep, S. W. (2003). Time Matters in Team Performance: Effects of Member Familiarity, Entertainment, and Task Discontinuity on Speed and Quality. *Personnel Psychology, 56*(3), pp. 633-669.

Harvey, S., Millett, B., & Smith, D. (1998). Developing Successful Teams in Organisations. *Australian Journal of Management & Organisational Behaviour, 1*(1), pp. 1-8.

Hays, W. L. (1988). *Statistics* (4 ed.). New York: Holt, Rinehart and Winston, Inc.

Higgs, M. (2006a). How do Top Teams Succeed? Factors that Contribute to Successful Senior Management Team Performance. *Journal of General Management, 32*(2), pp. 77-99.

Higgs, M. (2006b). What Makes for Top Team Success? A Study to Identify Factors Associated with Successful Performance of Senior Management Teams. *Irish Journal of Management, 27*(2), pp. 161-188.

Hodgkinson, G. P. (1997). The Cognitive Analysis of Competitive Structures: A Review and Critique. *Human Relations, 50*(6), pp. 625-654.

Hodgkinson, G. P. (2002). Comparing Manager's Mental Models of Competition: Why Self-Report Measures of Belief Similarity Won't Do. *Organization Studies, 23*(1), pp. 63-72.

Hodgkinson, G. P. & Healey, M. P. (2008). Cognition in Organizations. *Annual Review of Psychology , 59*, pp. 387-417.

Hodgkinson, G. P. & Johnson, G. (1994). Exploring the Mental Models of Competitive Strategists: The Case for a Processual Approach. *Journal of Management Studies, 31*(4), pp. 525-551.

Hodgkinson, G. P. & Sparrow, P. R. (2002). *The Competent Organization*. Buckingham: Open University Press.

Howze, P. C. & Dalrymple, C. (2004). Consensus Without All the Meetings: Using the Delphi Method to Determine Course Content for Library Instruction. *Reference Services Review, 32*(2), pp.174-184.

Huff, A. S. (1990). Mapping Strategic Thought. In A. S. Huff (Ed.): *Mapping Strategic Thought* (pp. 11-49). Chichester, UK: John Wiley.

Hsu, C.-C. & Sandford, B. A. (2007). The Delphi Technique: Making Sense of Consensus. *Practical Assessment, Research & Evaluation, 12*(10), pp. 1-8.

Iederan, O. C., Curşeu, P. L., Vermeulen P. A. M., & Geurts, J. L. A. (2011). Cognitive - Representations of Institutional Change. Similarities and Dissimilarities in the - Cognitive Schema of Entrepreneurs. *Journal of Organizational Change Management, 24*(1), pp. 9-28.

Ilgen, D. R., Hollenbeck, J. R., Johnson, M., & Jundt, D. (2005). Teams in Organizations: From Input-Process-Output Models to IMOI Models. *Annual Review of Psychology, 56*, pp. 517-543.

Ittner, C. D. & Larcker, D. F. (2001). Assessing Empirical Research in Managerial Accounting: A Value-Based Management Perspective. *Journal of Accounting & Business Administrations, 32*(1-3), pp. 349-410.

Ittner, C. D. & Larcker, D. F. (2003). Coming Up Short on Nonfinancial Performance Measurement. *Harvard Business Review, 81*, pp. 88-95.

Jackendoff, R. (1996). Semantics and Cognition. In S. Lappin (Ed.): *The Handbook of Contemporary Semantic Theory* (pp. 539-559). Cambridge, MA: Blackwell.

Janis, I. L. (1972). *Victims of Groupthink: A Psychological Study of Foreign Policy Decisions and Fiascoes*. Boston: Houghton Mifflin.

Janis, I. L. (1983). *Groupthink: Psychological Studies of Policy Decisions and Fiascoes*. Boston: Houghton Mifflin.

Janssen, J. & Laatz, W. (2006). *Statistische Datenanalyse mit SPSS für Windows: Eine Anwendungsorientierte Einführung in das Basissystem und das Modul Exakte Tests* (5 ed.). Berlin: Springer-Verlag.

Ji, Y. G. (2001). A Framework for Improving Organizational Learning Through A User-Adaptive Intranet Portal Organizational Memory Information. *International Journal of Aviation Psychology, 11*(2), pp. 123-148.

Johnson-Laird, P. N. (1983). *Mental Models. Towards a Cognitive Science of Language, Inferences, and Consciousness.* Cambridge: Cambridge University Press.

Johnson-Laird, P. N. (1989). Mental Models. In M. I. Posner (Ed.): *Foundations of Cognitive Science* (pp. 469-499). Cambridge, MA: MIT Press.

Johnson, B. R. & Onwuegbuzie, A. J. (2004). Mixed Methods Research: A Research Paradigm Whose Time Has Come. *Educational Researcher, 33*(7), pp. 14-26.

Johnson, R. B., Onwuegbuzie, A. J., & Turner, L. A. (2007). Toward a Definition of Mixed Methods Research. *Journal of Mixed Methods Research, 1*(2), pp. 112-133.

Jones, P. E. & Roelofsma, P. H. M. P. (2000). The Potential for Social Contextual and Group Biases in Team Decision-Making: Biases, Conditions and Psychological Mechanisms. *Ergonomics, 43*(8), pp. 1129-1152.

Kaplan, R. S. (2000). *The Strategy-focused Organization: How Balanced Scorecard Companies thrive in the New Business Environment: How Balanced Scorecard Companies Thrive in the New Business Environment.* Boston, Mass.: HBS Press.

Kaplan, R. S. & Norton, D. P. (1996a). *The Balanced Scorecard. Translating Strategy into Action.* Boston, MA: Harvard Business School Press.

Kaplan, R. S. & Norton, D. P. (1996b). Using the Balanced Scorecard as a Strategic Management System. *Harvard Business Review* (January-February), pp. 75-85. [available: https://noppa.tkk.fi/noppa/kurssi/tu-22.1500/luennot/TU-22_1500_pre-reading__1__kaplan___norton__1996_.pdf, 13.05.2011]

Kaplan, R. S. & Norton, D. P. (2004). *Strategy Maps: Converting Intangible Assets into Tangible Outcomes.* Boston, MA: Harvard Business School Press.

Katz, J. J. (1972). *Semantic Theory.* New York: Harper & Row, Publishers.

Katzenbach, J. R. & Smith, D. K. (1993). The Discipline of Teams. *Harvard Business Review, 71*(2), pp. 111-120.

Kelle, U. & Erzberger, C. (2005). Qualitative und quantitative Methoden: kein Gegensatz. In U. Flick, E. von Kardorff, & I. Steinke (Eds.): *Qualitative Forschung: Ein Handbuch* (4 ed., pp. 299-309). Reinbek bei Hamburg: Rowohlt.

Kellermanns, F. W., Floyd, S. W., Pearson A. W., & Spencer. B. (2008). The Contingent Effect of Constructive Confrontation on the Relationship between Shared Mental Models and Decision Quality. *Journal of Organizational Behavior, 29*, pp. 119–137.

Kerlen, C. (2003). *„Problemlos beraten? Die Problemdefinition als Startpunkt organisationalen Lernens.* Berlin: edition sigma.

Kirk, J . & Miller, M. (1986). *Reliability and Validity in Qualitative Research.* Beverly HIlls, CA: Sage.

Kirkman, B. L., Tesluk, P. E., & Rosen, B. (2001). Assessing the Incremental Validity of Team Consensus Ratings Over Aggregation of Individual-Level Data in Predicting Team Effectiveness. *Personnel Psychology, 54*, pp. 645-667.

Kleiber, G. (1998). *Prototypensemantik. Eine Einführung* (Vol. 2. überarbeitete). Tübingen: Gunter Narr Verlag.

Klimoski, R. & Mohammed, S. (1994). Team Mental Model: Construct or Metaphor? *Journal of Management, 20*(2), pp. 403-437.

Klocke, U. (2004). *Folgen von Machtausübung und Einflussnahme für Wissenszuwachs und Effektivität in Kleingruppen.* Unveröffentlichte Doktorarbeit, Humboldt-Universität zu Berlin, Berlin.

Kluwe, R. H. (2002). Kognition. In G. Wenniger (Ed.): *Lexikon der Psychologie* [CD]. Heidelberg: Spektrum Akademischer Verlag.

Kozlowski, S. W. J. & Ilgen, D. R. (2006). Enhancing the Effectiveness of Work Groups and Teams. *Psychological Science in the Public Interest, 7*(3), pp. 77-124.

Kutschker, M. & Schmid, S. (2008). *Internationales Management* (6 ed.). München: Oldenbourg.

Krauth, J. (1995). *Testkonstruktion und Testtheorie.* Weinheim: Psychologie Verlags Union.

Lachiche, N. (2000). Abduction and Induction. From a Non-Monotonic Reasoning Perspective. In P. A. Flach & A. C. Kakas (Eds.): *Abduction and Induction* (pp. 107-116). Dordrecht: Kluwer.

Lakoff, G. (1987). *Women, Fire, and Dangerous Things. What Categories Reveal about the Mind.* Chicago: The University of Chicago Press.

Lakoff, G. & Johnson, M. (1999). *Philosophy in the Flesh. The Embodied Mind and its Challenge to Western Thought.* New York, N.Y.: Basic Books.

Lamnek, S. (2010). *Qualitative Sozialforschung* (5 ed.). Weinheim: Beltz.

Langan-Fox, J., Anglim, J., & Wilson, J. R. (2004). Mental Models, Team Mental Models, and Performance: Process, Development and Future Directions. *Human Factors and Ergonomics in Manufacturing, 14*(4), pp. 331-352.

Langan-Fox, J., Code, S., & Langfield-Smith, K. (2000). Team Mental Models: Techniques, Methods, and Analytic Approaches. *Human Factors, 42*(2), pp. 242-271.

Langan-Fox, J., Wirth, A., Code, S., Langfield-Smith, K., & Wirth, A. (2001). Analyzing Shared and Team Mental Models. *International Journal of Industrial Ergonomics, 28*(2), pp. 99-112.

Laukkanen, M. (1990). Describing Management Cognition: The Cause Mapping Approach. *Scandinavian Journal of Management, 6*(3), pp. 197-216.

Laukkanen, M. (1994). Comparative Cause Mapping of Organizational Cognitions. *Organization Science, 5*(3), pp. 322-343.

Levesque, L. L., Wilson, J. M., & Wholey, D. R. (2001). Cognitive Divergence and Shared Mental Models in Software Development Project Teams. *Journal of Organizational Behavior, 22*, pp. 135-144.

Lewin, K. (1947). Frontiers in Group Dynamics. *Human Relations, 1*(1), pp. 143-153.

Lewis, K. (2003). Measuring Transactive Memory Systems in the Field: Scale Development and Validation. *Journal of Applied Psychology, 88*(4), pp. 587-604.

Lienert, G. A. & Raatz, U. (1998). *Testaufbau und Testanalyse* (6 ed.). Weinheim: Psychologie Verlags Union.

Lim, B.-C. & Klein, K. J. (2006). Team Mental Models and Team Performance: A Field Study of the Effects of Team Mental Model Similarity and Accuracy. *Journal of Organizational Behavior, 27*(4), pp. 403-418.

Lincoln, Y. S. & Guba, E. G. (1985). *Naturalistic Inquiry*. Beverly Hills, CA: Sage.

Linstone, H. A. & Turoff, M. (1975/2002a). Introduction. In H. A. Linstone & M. Turoff (Eds.): *The Delphi Method: Techniques and Applications* (pp. 3-12). Reading, MA: Addison-Wesley. [available: http://www.is.njit.edu/pubs/delphibook/, 2009-10-13]

Linstone, H. A. & Turoff, M. (Eds.) (1975/2002b). *The Delphi Method: Techniques and Applications*. Reading, MA: Addison-Wesley. [available: http://www.is.njit.edu/pubs/ delphibook/, 2009-10-13]

Löbel, J., Schröger, H.-A., & Closhen, H. (2005). *Nachhaltige Managementsysteme: Sustainable Development durch ganzheitliche Führungs- und Organisationssysteme - Vorgehensmodell und Prüflisten* (2 ed.). Berlin: Schmidt (Erich).

Lyons, J. (1995). *Einführung in die moderne Linguistik* (Vol. 8). München: Verlag C. H. Beck.

Mandl, T. (2000). *Einsatz neuronaler Netze als Transferkomponenten beim Retrieval in heterogenen Dokumentbeständen* (No. 20). Bonn: IZ Informationszentrum Sozialwissenschaften.

Mangasser-Wahl, M. (2000a). *Von der Prototypentheorie zur empirischen Semantik*. Frankfurt am Main: Peter Lang Europäischer Verlag der Wissenschaften.

Mangasser-Wahl, M. (Ed.) (2000b). *Prototypentheorie in der Linguistik. Anwendungsbeispiele - Methodenreflexion – Perspektiven*. Tübingen: Stauffenburg Verlag Brigitte Narr GmbH.

Markman, A. B. & Gentner, D. (2001). Thinking. *Annual Review of Psychology, 52*, pp. 223-247.

Markoczy, L. & Goldberg, J. (1995). A Method for Eliciting and Comparing Causal Maps. *Journal of Management, 21*(2), pp. 305-333.

Marks, M. A., Mathieu, J. E., & Zaccaro, S. J. (2001). A Temporally based Framework and Taxonomy of Team Processes. *Academy of Management Review, 26*(3), pp. 356-376.

Marks, M. A., Sabella, M. J., Burke, C. S., & Zaccaro, S. J. (2002). The Impact of Cross-Training on Team Effectiveness. *Journal of Applied Psychology, 87*(1), pp. 3-13.

Marks, M. A., Zaccaro, S. J., & Mathieu, J. E. (2000). Performance Implication of Leader Briefings and Team-Interaction Training for Team Adaption of Novel Environments. *Journal of Applied Psychology, 85*(6), pp. 971-986.

Mathieu, J. E., Heffner, T. S., Goodwin, G. F., Cannon-Bowers, J. A., & Salas, E. (2005). Scaling the Quality of Teammates' Mental Models: Equifinalitly and Normative Comparisons. *Journal of Organizational Behavior, 26*, pp. 37-56.

Mathieu, J. E., Heffner, T. S., Goodwin, G. F., Salas, E., & Cannon-Bowers, J. A. (2000). The Influence of Shared Mental Models on Team Process and Performance. *Journal of Applied Psychology, 85*(2), pp. 273-283.

Maxcy, S. J. (2003). Pragmatic Threads in Mixed Methods Research in the Social Sciences: The Search for Multiple Modes of Inquiry and the End of the Philosophy of Formalism. In A. Tashakkori & C. Teddlie (Eds.): *Handbook of Mixed Methods in Social & Behavioral Research* (pp. 51-89). Thousand Oaks, CA: Sage.

Mayring, P. (2002). *Einführung in die qualitative Sozialforschung* (5 ed.). Weinheim: Beltz.

Mayring, P. (2010). *Qualitative Inhaltsanalyse. Grundlagen und Techniken* (11 ed.). Weinheim: Beltz.

McGaghie, W. C., McCrimmon, D. R., Mitchell, G., & Thompson, J. A. (2004). Concept Mapping in Pulmonary Physiology Using Pathfinder Scaling. *Advances in Health Education, 9*, pp. 225-240.

McGrath, J. E. (1984). *Groups: Interaction and Performance*. Englewood Cliffs, N.J.: Prentice-Hall, Inc.

McGrath, J. E. (1991). Time, Interaction, and Performance (TIP). A Theory of Groups. *Small Group Research, 22*(2), pp. 147-174.

McGrath, J. E., Arrow, H., & Berdahl, J. L. (2000). The Study of Groups: Past, Present, and Future. *Personality & Social Psychology Review (Lawrence Erlbaum Associates), 4*(1), pp. 95-105.

Medin, D. L., Goldstone, R. L., & Gentner, D. (1993). Respect for Similarity. *Psychological Review, 100*(2), pp. 254-278.

Meffert, H. (1998). *Marketing. Grundlagen marktorientierter Unternehmensführung. Konzepte – Instrumente – Praxisbeispiele* (8 ed.). Wiesbaden: Verlag Dr. Th. Gabler GmbH.

Mertens, D. M. (2003). Mixed Methods and the Politics of Human Research: The Transformative-Emancipatory Perspective. In A. Tashakkori & C. Teddlie (Eds.): *Handbook of Mixed Methods in Social & Behavioral Research* (pp. 135-164). Thousand Oaks, CA: Sage.

Merton, R. K. (1968). *Social Theory and Social Structure*. New York: Free Press.

Mesmer-Magnus, J. R. & DeChurch, L. A. (2009). Information Sharing and Team Performance: A Meta-Analysis. *Journal of Applied Psychology, 94*(2), pp. 535-546.

Mieg, H. A. (2001). *The Social Psychology of Expertise. Case Studies in Research, Professional Domains and Expert Roles*. Mahwah, NJ: Lawrence Erlbaum Associates.

Mohammed, S. & Dumville, B. C. (2001). Team Mental Models in a Team Knowledge Framework: Expanding Theory and Measurement across Disciplinary Boundaries. *Journal of Organizational Behavior, 22*, pp. 89-106.

Mohammed, S., Ferzandi, L., & Hamilton, K. (2010). Metaphor No More: A 15-Year Review of the Team Mental Model Construct. *Journal of Management, 36*(4), pp. 876-910.

Mohammed, S., Klimoski, R., & Rentsch, J. R. (2000). The Measurement of Team Mental Models: We Have no Shared Schema. *Organizational Research Methods, 3*(2), pp. 123-165.

Moray, N. (1999). Mental Models in Theory and Practice. In D. Gopher & A. Koriat (Eds.): *Attention and Performance XVII: Cognitive Regulation of Performance: Interaction of Theory and Application* (pp. 223-258). London: MIT Press.

Morgan, D. L. (2007). Paradigms Lost and Pragmatism Regained: Methodological Implications of Combining Qualitative and Quantitative Methods. *Journal of Mixed Methods Research, 1*(1), pp. 48-76.

Mullen, P. M. (2003). Delphi: Myths and Reality. *Journal of Health Organization and Management, 17*(1), pp. 37-52.

Müller-Stewens, G. & Lechner, C. (2005). *Strategisches Management. Wie strategische Initiativen zum Wandel führen* (Vol. 3). Stuttgart: Schäffer-Poeschel Verlag.

Newman, I., Ridenour, C. S., Newman, C., & DeMarco, G. M. P., Jr. (2003). A Typology of Research Purposes and its Relationship to Mixed Methods. In A. Tashakkori & C. Teddlie (Eds.): *Handbook of Mixed Methods in Social & Behavioral Research* (pp. 167-188). Thousand Oaks, CA: Sage.

Niiniluoto, I. (1999). Defending Abduction. *Philosophy of Science, 66 (Proceedings)*, S436-S451.

Nonaka, I. (1991). The Knowledge-Creating Company. *Harvard Business Review, 69*(6), pp. 96-104.

Nonaka, I. & Konno N. (1998). The Concept of "Ba": Building a Foundation for Knowledge Creation. *California Management Review, 40*(3), pp. 40-54.

Nonaka, I., von Krogh, G., & Voelpel, S. (2006). Organizational Knowledge Creation Theory: Evolutionary Paths and Future Advances. *Organization Studies, 27*(8), pp. 1179-1208.

Norman, D. A. (1983). Some Observations On Mental Models. In D. Gentner & A. L. Stevens (Eds.): *Mental Models* (pp. 7-14). Hillsdale, NJ: Lawrence Erlbaum.

Novak, J. D. & Gowin, D. B. (1984). *Learning How To Learn.* New York: Cambridge University Press.

O'Connor, D. L., Johnson, T. E., & Khalil, M. K. (2004). *Measuring Team Cognition: Concept Mapping Elicitation as a Means of Constructing Team Shared Mental Models in an Applied Setting.* Paper presented at the First International Conference in Concept Mapping, Pamplona, Spain.

Oakhill, J. & Garnham, A. (Eds.) (1996). *Mental Models in Cognitive Science.* Hove, East Sussex: Psychology Press.

Onwuegbuzie, A. J. & Johnson, R. B. (2006). The Validity Issue in Mixed Research. *Research in the Schools, 13*(1), pp. 48-63.

Onwuegbuzie, A. J. & Leech, N. L. (2004). Enhancing the Interpretation of Significant Findings: The Role of Mixed Methods Research. *The Qualitative Report, 9*(4), pp. 770-792.

Orasanu, J. M. (1990). Shared Mental Models and Crew Decision Making. *Twelfth Annual Conference at the Cognitive Science Society* MIT, Cambridge.

Paris, C. R., Salas, E., & Cannon-Bowers, J. A. (2000). Teamwork in Multi-Person Systems: A Review and Analysis. *Ergonomics, 43*(8), pp. 1052-1075.

Payne, S. J. (2003). Users´ Mental Models: The Very Ideas. In J. M. Carroll (Ed.): *HCI Models, Theories, and Frameworks: Toward a Multidisciplinary Science* (pp. 135-156). Oxford: Elsevier LTD.

Pearsall, M. J., Ellis, A. P. J., & Bell, B. S. (2010). Building the Infrastructure: The Effects of Role Identification Behaviors on Team Cognition Development and Performance. *Journal of Applied Psychology, 95*(1), pp. 192–200.

Porac, J. F. & Thomas, H. (1990). Taxonomic Mental Models in Competitor Definition. *Academy of Management Review, 15*(2), pp. 224-240.

Porac, J. F. & Thomas, H. (1994). Cognitive Categorization and Subjective Rivalry Among Retailers in a Small City. *Journal of Applied Psychology, 79*(1), pp. 54-66.

Porter, M. E. (1985). *Competitive Advantage.* New York, NY: The Free Press.

Portoraro, F. (2007). Automated Reasoning. *The Stanford Encyclopaedia of Philosophy*, Spring Edition. [available: http://plato.stanford.edu/archives/spr2007/entries/reasoning-automated/, 04.07.2008]

Probst, G., Raub, S., & Romhardt, K. (2006). *Wissen managen: Wie Unternehmen ihre wertvollste Ressource optimal nutzen (5 ed).* Wiesbaden: Verlag Dr. Th Gabler GmbH.

Psillos, S. (2000). Abduction: Between Conceptual Richness and Computational Complexity. In P. A. Flach & A. C. Kakas (Eds.): *Abduction and Induction* (pp. 59-74). Dordrecht: Kluwer.

Randsley de Moura, G., Leader, T., Pelletier, J., & Abrams, D. (2008). Prospects for Group Processes and Intergroup Relations Research: A Review of 70 Years' Progress. Group Processes and Intergroup Relations, 11(4), pp. 575-596.

Rasch, B., Friese, M., Hofmann, W. J., & Naumann, E. (2009). *Quantitative Methoden, Band 2*. Heidelberg: Springer-Verlag GmbH.

Rasker, P. C. & Post, W. M. (2000). Effects of Two Types of Intra-Team Feedback on Developing a Shared Mental Model in Command and Control Teams. *Ergonomics, 43*(8), pp. 1167-1189.

Rasmussen, J. (1986). *Information Processing and Human-Machine Interaction: An Approach to Cognitive Engineering*. Amsterdam: North-Holland.

Reger, R. K. (1990). Managerial Thought Structures and Competitive Positioning. In A. S. Huff (Ed.): *Mapping Strategic Thought* (pp. 71-88). Chichester, England: John Wiley.

Reger, R. K. & Huff, A. S. (1993). Strategic Groups: A Cognitive Perspective. *Strategic Management Journal, 14*, pp. 103-124.

Reichenbach, H. (1938). *Experience and Prediction*. Chicago: University of Chicago Press.

Reichertz, J. (2004). Abduktion, Deduktion und Induktion in der qualitativen Forschung. In U. Flick, E. v. Kardorff, & I. Steinke (Eds.): *Qualitative Forschung* (3 ed., pp. 276-286). Reinbek bei Hamburg: Rowohlt.

Reinmann-Rothmeier, G. (2003). Alles klar? Neue Herausforderungen für Wissensmanagement aus pädagogisch-psychologischer Sicht. In U. Reimer, A. Abecker, S. Staab, & G. Stumme (Eds.): *WM 2003: Professionelles Wissensmanagement – Erfahrungen und Visionen* (pp. 507-510). Bonn: Köllen.

Reinmann, G. (2005). *Individuelles Wissensmanagement - ein Rahmenkonzept für den Umgang mit personalem und öffentlichem Wissen*. Augsburg: Universität Augsburg Philosophisch-Sozialwissenschaftliche Fakultät.

Rentsch, J. R. & Klimoski, R. (2001). Why Do 'Great Minds' Think Alike?: Antecedents of Team Member Schema Agreement. *Journal of Organizational Behavior, 22*, pp. 107-120.

Rentsch, J. R., Small, E. E., & Hanges, P. J. (2008). Cognitions in Organizations and Teams. What Is the Meaning of Cognitive Similarity? In D. B. Smith (Ed.): *The People make the place. Dynamic Linkages between Individuals and Organizations* (pp. 127-156). New York, N. Y.: Lawrence Erlbaum Assoc Inc.

Rescher, N. (1978). *Peirce's Philosophy of Science*. London: University of Notre Dame Press.

Resick, C. J., Dickson, M. W., Mitchelson, J. K., Allison, L. K., & Clark, M. A. (2010). Team Composition, Cognition, and Effectiveness: Examining Mental Model Similarity and Accuracy. *Group Dynamics: Theory, Research, and Practice, 14*(2), pp. 174–191.

Richardson, M. & Ball, L. (2009). Internal Representations, External Representations, and Ergonomics: Toward a Theoretical Integration. *Theoretical Issues in Ergonomics Science, 10*(4), pp. 335–376.

Rico, R., Sánchez-Manzanares, M., Gil, F., & Gibson, C. (2008). Team Implicit Coordination Process: A Team Knowledge-Based Approach. *Academy of Management Review, 33*(1), pp. 163-184.

Rogers, Y., Rutherford, A., & Bibby, P. A. (Eds.) (1992). *Models in the Mind*. London: Academic Press.

Roos, L. L. & Hall, R. I. (1980). Influence Diagrams and Organizational Power. *Administrative Science Quarterly, 25*(1), pp. 57-71.

Rosch, E. (1973). On the Internal Structure of Perceptual and Semantic Categories. In T. E. Moore (Ed.): *Cognitive Development and the Acquisition of Language* (pp. 111-144). New York: Academic Press.

Rosch, E. (1978). *Principles of Categorization*. Hillsdale, NJ: Lawrence Erlbaum Associates, Publishers.

Rosch, E., Carol, S., & Miller, S. R. (1976b). Structural Bases of Typicality Effects. *Experimental Psychology: Human Perception and Performance, 2*(4), pp. 491-502.

Rosch, E. & Lloyd, B. B. (1978). Introduction. In E. Rosch & B. B. Lloyd (Eds.): *Cognition and Categorization* (pp. 1-3). Hillsdale, N.J.: Lawrence Erlbaum Associates, Publishers.

Rosch, E., Mervis, C. B., Gray, W. D., Johnson, D. M., & Boyes-Braem, P. (1976a). Basic Objects in Natural Categories. *Cognitive Psychology, 8*, pp. 382-439.

Rost, J. (2004). *Lehrbuch Testtheorie – Testkonstruktion*. Bern: Verlag Hans Huber.

Rouse, W. B. & Morris, N. M. (1986). On Looking Into the Black Box: Prospects and Limits in the Search for Mental Models. *Psychological Bulletin, 100*(3), pp. 349-363.

Ruiz-Primo, M. A. & Shavelson, R. J. (1996). Problems and Issues in the Use of Concept Maps in Science Assessment. *Journal of Research in Science Teaching, 33*(6), pp. 569-600.

Salas, E., Sims, D. E., & Burke, C. S. (2005). Is there a "Big Five" in Teamwork?. *Small Group Research, 36*(5), pp. 555-599.

Salas, E., Stagl, K. C., Burke, C. S., & Goodwin, G. F. (2007). Fostering Team Effectiveness in Organizations: Toward an Integrative Theoretical Framework of Team Performance. In R. A. Dienstbier, J. W. Shuart, W. Spaulding, & J. Poland (Eds.): *Modeling Complex Systems: Motivation, Cognition and Social Processes. Nebraska Symposium on Motivation* (Vol. 51, pp. 185-243). Lincoln, NE: University of Nebraska Press.

Sasse, M.-A. (1992). User's Models of Computer Systems. In Y. Rogers, A. Rutherford, & P. A. Bibby (Eds.): *Models in the Mind* (pp. 225-239). London: Academic Press.

Sauer, J., Felsing, T., Franke, H., & Rüttinger, B. (2006). Cognitive Diversity and Team Performance in a Complex Multiple Task Environment. *Ergonomics, 49*(10), pp. 934-954.

Schaffernicht, M. & Groesser, S. N. (2011). A Comprehensive Method for Comparing Mental Models of Dynamic Systems. *European Journal of Operational Research, 210*(1), pp. 57-67.

Schalley, A. C. (2004). *Cognitive Modeling and Verbal Semantics: A Representational Framework Based an UML* (Vol. 154). Berlin: Walter de Gruyter GmbH & Co. KG.

Scheele, B. & Groeben, N. (1986). Methodological Aspects of Illustrating the Cognitive-Reflective Function of Aesthetic Communication. *Poetics, 15*, pp. 527-554.

Scheele, B. & Groeben, N. (1988). *Dialog-Konsens-Methoden zur Rekonstruktion Subjektiver Theorien*. Heidelberg: A. Francke.

Schein, E. H. (2010). *Organizational Culture and Leadership* (4 ed.). San Fransisco, CA: John Wiley & Sons.

Schneider, S. C. & Angelmar, R. (1993). Cognition in Organizational Analysis: Who's Minding the Store? *Organization Studies, 14*(3), pp. 347-374.

Schnell, R., Hill, P. B., & Esser, E. (2008). *Methoden der empirischen Sozialforschung* (8 ed.). München: R. Oldenbourg.

Scholl, W. (2004). *Innovation und Information. Wie in Unternehmen neues Wissen produziert wird*. Gottingen: Hogrefe-Verlag.

Seale, C. (1999). *The Quality of Qualitative Research*. London: Sage.

Seel, N. M. (1991). *Weltwissen und mentale Modelle*. Göttingen: Hogrefe.

Seiler, T. B. (2001a). *Begreifen und Verstehen. Ein Buch über Begriffe und Bedeutungen*. Mühltal: Verlag Allgemeine Wissenschaft - HRW e.K.

Seiler, T. B. (2001b). Entwicklung als Strukturgenese. In S. Hoppe-Graff & A. Rümmele (Eds.): *Entwicklung als Strukturgenese* (pp. 15-122). Hamburg: Kovac.

Seiler, T. B. (2003). Thesen zum Wissensbegriff - Die phänomenale und personale Natur des menschlichen Wissens. *Wirtschaftspsychologie, 5*(3), pp. 41-49.

Seiler, T. B. (2004). Wissen und Wissensverarbeitung aus humanwissenschaftlicher Perspektive. In G. Jüttemann (Ed.): *Psychologie als Humanwissenschaft. Ein Handbuch* (pp. 302-317). Göttingen: Vandenhoek & Ruprecht.

Seiler, T. B. & Reinmann, G. (2004). Der Wissensbegriff im Wissensmanagement: Eine strukturgenetische Sicht. In G. Reinmann & H. Mandl (Eds.): *Psychologie des Wissensmanagements. Perspektiven, Theorien und Methoden* (pp. 11-23). Göttingen: Hogrefe Verlag GmbH & Co. KG.

Selten, R. (2002). What is Bounded Rationality? In G. Gigerenzer & R. Selten (Eds.): *Bounded Rationality: The Adaptive Toolbox* (pp. 13-36). Cambridge, Massachusetts: The MIT Press.

Shanteau, J. (1992a). Competence in Experts: The Role of Task Characteristics. *Organizational Behavior and Human Decision Processes, 53*, pp. 252-266. [available: http://www.clovia.org/psych/ cws/pdf/obhdp_paper 91.PDF, pp. 1-24, 02.07.2010]

Shanteau, J. (1992b). The Psychology of Experts: An Alternative View. In G. Wright & F. Bolger (Eds.): *Expertise and Decision Support* (pp. 11-23). New York, NY: Plenum Press. [available https://kats.ksu.edu/psych/cws/pdf/wb_chapter92.PDF, pp. 1-13, 02.07.2010]

Shaw, D., Ackermann, F., & Eden, C. (2003). Approaches to Sharing Knowledge in Group Problem Structuring. *Journal of the Operational Research Society, 54*, pp. 936-948.

Silverman, D. (1993). *Interpreting Qualitative Data*. London: Sage.

Simon, H. A. (1992). What is an 'Explanation' of Behavior? *Psychological Science, 3*(3), pp. 150-161.

Simons, R. (2000). *Performance Measurement & Control Systems for Implementing Strategy*. Upper Saddle River, NJ: Prentice-Hall.

Smith-Jentsch, K. A., Campbell, G. E., Milanovich, D. M., & Reynolds, A. M. (2001). Measuring Teamwork Mental Models to Support Training Needs Assessment, Development, and Evaluation: Two Empirical Studies. *Journal of Organizational Behavior, 22*, pp. 179-194.

Smith-Jentsch, K. A., Mathieu, J. E., & Kraiger, K. (2005). Investigating Linear and Interactive Effects of Shared Mental Models on Safety and Efficiency in a Field Setting. *Journal of Applied Psychology, 90*(3), pp. 523-535.

Speckbacher, G., Bischof, J., & Pfeiffer, T. (2003). A Descriptive Analysis on the Implementation of Balanced Scorecards in German-speaking Countries. *Management Accounting Research, 14*(4), pp. 361-387.

Spender, J.-C. & Eden, C. (1998). Introduction. In C. Eden & J.-C. Spender (Eds.): *Managerial and Organizational Cognition* (pp. 1-12). London: Sage.

Spicer, D. P. (1998). Linking Mental Models and Cognitive Maps as an Aid to Organisational Learning. *Career Development International, 3*(3), pp. 125-132.

Stout, R. J., Cannon-Bowers, J. A., Salas, E., & Milanovich, D. M. (1999). Planning, Shared Mental Models, and Coordinated Performance: An Empirical Link Is Established. *Human Factors, 41*(1), pp. 61-71.

Story, V., Hurdley, L., Smith, G., & Saker, J. (2001). Methodological and Practical Implications of the Delphi Technique in Marketing Decision-Making: A Re-Assessment. *The Marketing Review, 1*, pp. 487-504.

Strauss, A. L. & Corbin, J. (1994). Grounded Theory Methodology. An Overview. In N. K. Denzin & Y. S. Lincoln (Eds.): *Handbook of Qualitative Research* (pp. 273-285). Thousand Oaks, California: Sage.

Strauss, A. L. & Corbin, J. (1998). *Basics of Qualitative Research. Techniques and Procedures for Developing Grounded Theory* (2 ed.). Thousand Oaks, California: Sage.

Stubbart, C. I. (1989). Managerial Cognition: A Missing Link in Strategic Management Research. *Journal of Management Studies, 26*(4), pp. 325-347.

Tannenbaum, S. I., Salas, E., & Cannon-Bowers, J. A. (1996). Promoting Team Effectiveness. In M. A. West (Ed.): *Handbook of Work Group Psychology* (pp. 503-529). Chichester: John Wiley and Sons Ltd.

Tashakkori, A. & Creswell, J. W. (2007). Editorial: The New Era of Mixed Methods. *Journal of Mixed Methods Research, 1*(1), pp. 3-7.

Tashakkori, A. & Teddlie, C. (1998). *Mixed Methodology. Combining Qualitative and Quantitative Approaches*. Thousand Oaks, CA: Sage.

Tashakkori, A. & Teddlie, C. (2003a). Issues and Dilemmas in Teaching Research Methods Courses in Social and Behavioural Sciences: US Perspective. *International Journal of Social Research Methodology, 6*(1), pp. 61-77.

Tashakkori, A. & Teddlie, C. (2003b). The Past and Future of Mixed Method Research: From Data Triangulation to Mixed Model Designs. In A. Tashakkori & C. Teddlie (Eds.): *Handbook of Mixed Methods in Social & Behavioral Research* (pp. 671-701). Thousand Oaks, CA: Sage.

Tashakkori, A. & Teddlie, C. (2003c). Glossary. In A. Tashakkory & C. Teddlie (Eds.): *Handbook of Mixed Methods in Social & Behavioral Research* (pp. 703-718). Thousand Oaks, CA: Sage.

Teddlie, C. & Tashakkori, A. (2003). Major Issues and Controversies in the Use of Mixed Methods in the Social and Behavioral Sciences. In A. Tashakkori & C. Teddlie (Eds.): *Handbook of Mixed Methods in Social & Behavioral Research* (pp. 3-50). Thousand Oaks, CA: Sage.

Teece, D. J., Pisano, G., & Shuen, A. (1997). Dynamic Capabilities and Strategic Management. *Strategic Management Journal, 18*(7), pp. 509-533.

Tegarden, D. P. & Sheetz, S. D. (2003). Group Cognitive Mapping: A Methodology and System for Capturing and Evaluating Managerial and Organizational Cognition. *Omega, 31*, pp. 113-125.

Thalemann, S. (2003). Die Rolle geteilten Wissens beim netzbasierten kollaborativen Problemlösen. In W.-u. V. Fakultät (Ed.): Freiburg i. Brsg.: Albert-Ludwigs-Universität. [available: http://www.freidok.uni-freiburg.de/volltexte/1327/pdf/Dissertation_Thalemann.pdf, Zugriff: 07.06.2010]

Thompson, H. L. (2010): *The Stress Effect: Why Smart Leaders Make Dumb Decisions--And What to Do About It*. San Francisco, CA: John Wiley & Sons.

Thompson, L., Peterson, E., & Kray, L. (1995). Social Context in Negotiation: An Information Processing Perspective. In R. Kramer & D. Messick (Eds.): *Negotiation as Social Process* (pp. 5-36). Beverly Hills, CA: Sage.

Timmerman, T. A. (2005). Missing Persons in the Study of Groups. *Journal of Organizational Behavior, 26*(1), pp. 21-36.

Tylor, B. B. & Gnyawali, D. R. (2009). Managerial Collective Cognitions: An Examination of Similarities and Differences of Cultural Orientations. *Journal of Management Studies, 46*(1), pp. 93-126.

Unterreitmeier, A. (2004). *Unternehmenskultur bei Mergers & Acquisitions. Ansätze zu Konzeptualisierung und Operationalisierung*. Wiesbaden: Deutscher Universitätsverlag / GWV Fachverlage GmbH.

Vandenbosch, B. & Higgins, C. A. (1995). Executive Support Systems and Learning: A Model and Empirical Test. *Journal of Management Information Systems, 12*(2), pp. 99-130.

Vandenbosch, B. & Higgins, C. A. (1996). Information Acquisition and Mental Models: An Investigation into the Relationship between Behaviour and Learning. *Information Systems Research, 7*(2), pp. 198-214.

Vandenbosch, B. & Huff, S. L. (1997). Searching and Scanning: How Executives Obtain Information From Executive Support Systems. *MIS Quarterly, 21*(1), pp. 81-107.

Vennix, J. A. M. (1999). Group Model-Building: Tackling Messy Problems. *System Dynamics Review, 15*(4), pp. 379-401.

Wahl, D. (1991). *Handeln unter Druck. Der weite Weg vom Wissen zum Handeln bei Lehrern, Hochschullehrern und Erwachsenenbildern*. Weinheim: Deutscher Studien Verlag.

Waibel, M. C. (2002). *Lokales Wissen in der betrieblichen Lebenswelt. Theoretische und empirische Studien zur Wissensentwicklung in Praxisgemeinschaften der industriellen Fertigung*. Hamburg: Technische Universität Hamburg-Harburg.

Waller, M. J., Gupta, N., & Giambatista, R. C. (2004). Effects of Adaptive Behaviors and Shared Mental Models on Control Crew Performance. *Management Science, 50*(11), pp. 1534–1544.

Walsh, J. P. (1995). Managerial and Organizational Cognition: Notes From a Trip Down Memory Lane. *Organization Science, 6*(3), pp. 280-321.

Ward, J. C. & Reingen, P. H. (1990). Sociocognitive Analysis of Group Decision Making among Consumers. *The Journal of Consumer Research, 17*(3), pp. 245-262.

Webber, S. S., Chen, G., Payne, S. C., Marsh, S. M., & Zaccaro, S. J. (2000). Enhancing Team Mental Model Measurement with Performance Appraisal Practices. *Organizational Research Methods, 3*(4), pp. 307-322.

Weick, K. E. & Bougon, M. G. (2001). Organizations as Cognitive Maps: Charting Ways to Success and Failure. In K. E. Weick (Ed.): *Making Sense of the Organization* (pp. 308-329). Oxford: Blackwell.

Welge, M. K. & Al-Laham, A. (2003). *Strategisches Management. Grundlagen - Prozesse - Implementierung* (4 ed.). Wiesbaden: Gabler Verlag.

Wernerfelt, B. (1984). A Resource-Based View of the Firm. *Strategic Management Journal, 5*(2), pp. 171-180.

Wilson, J. R. & Rutherford, A. (1989). Mental Models: Theory and Application in Human Factors. *Human Factors, 31*(6), pp. 614-634.

Witt, Harald (2001, Januar). Forschungsstrategien bei quantitativer und qualitativer Sozialforschung [36 Absätze]. Forum Qualitative Sozialforschung / Forum: Qualitative Social Research [Online Journal], 2(1). Verfügbar über: http://qualitativeresearch.net/fqs/ fqs.htm [Datum des Zugriffs: 19.07.2010].

Wittenbaum, G. M. & Moreland, R. L. (2008). Small-Group Research in Social Psychology: Topics and Trends over Time. *Social and Personality Psychology Compass 2*(1), pp. 187-203.

Wittgenstein, L. (1953/2001). *Philosophical Investigations*: Blackwell Publishing.

Wittgenstein, L. (2002). *Philosophical Investigations. The German Text, with a Revised English Translation. 50th Anniversary Commemorative Edition* (G. E. M. Anscombe, Trans. Corr. 2nd ed. Vol. 50th Anniversary Commemorative Edition): Blackwell Publishers Ltd.

Wright, R. P. (2006). Rigor and Relevance Using Repertory Grid Technique in Strategy Research. *Research Methodology in Strategy and Management, 3*, pp. 289-341.

Zaichkowsky, J. L. (1985). Measuring the Involvement Construct. *Journal of Consumer Research, 12*(3), pp. 341-352.

Zhou, Y. & Wang, E. (2010). Shared Mental Models as Moderators of Team Process-Performance Relationships. *Social Behavior and Personality, 38*(4), pp. 433-444.

Ziegler, M. & Bühner, M. (2009). *Statistik für Psychologen und Sozialwissenschaftler*. München: Pearson Studium.

CONTROLLING

Herausgegeben von Prof. Dr. Volker Lingnau, Kaiserslautern, Prof. Dr. Albrecht Becker, Innsbruck, und Prof. Dr. Rolf Brühl, Berlin

Band 13
Anna Bassler
Die Visualisierung von Daten im Controlling
Lohmar – Köln 2010 ♦ 244 S. ♦ € 56,- (D) ♦ ISBN 978-3-89936-939-7

Band 14
Tatiana Villalobos Baum
Organisationales Lernen und Anreizsysteme nach dem Börsengang – Ein verhaltensorientierter Ansatz
Lohmar – Köln 2010 ♦ 248 S. ♦ € 56,- (D) ♦ ISBN 978-3-89936-971-7

Band 15
Jürgen Kantowski
Einsatz von Realoptionen im Investitionscontrolling am Beispiel Biotechnologie
Lohmar – Köln 2011 ♦ 248 S. ♦ € 56,- (D) ♦ ISBN 978-3-8441-0022-8

Band 16
Michael Rademacher
Prozess- und wertorientiertes Controlling von M&A-Projekten
Lohmar – Köln 2011 ♦ 368 S. ♦ € 64,- (D) ♦ ISBN 978-3-8441-0110-2

Band 17
Carmen Kühn
Psychopathen in Nadelstreifen
Lohmar – Köln 2012 ♦ 244 S. ♦ € 56,- (D) ♦ ISBN 978-3-8441-0138-6

Band 18
Jörn Sebastian Basel
Heuristic Reasoning in Management Accounting – A Mixed Methods Analysis
Lohmar – Köln 2012 ♦ 268 S. ♦ € 57,- (D) ♦ ISBN 978-3-8441-0160-7

Band 19
Sabrina Buch
Shared Knowledge – The Comparability of Idiosyncratic Mental Models
Lohmar – Köln 2012 ♦ 320 S. ♦ € 62,- (D) ♦ ISBN 978-3-8441-0186-7

JOSEF EUL VERLAG